Population Aging, Intergenerational Transfers and the Macroeconomy

Population Aging, Intergenerational Transfers and the Macroeconomy

Edited by

Robert Clark

Professor of Economics and Professor of Management, Innovation and Entrepreneurship, North Carolina State University, USA

Naohiro Ogawa

Deputy Director, Nihon University Population Research Institute and Professor, Advanced Research Institute for the Sciences and Humanities, Nihon University, Japan

Andrew Mason

Professor of Economics, University of Hawaii at Manoa and Senior Fellow, Population and Health Studies, East–West Center, Hawaii, USA

Edward Elgar

Cheltenham, UK • Northampton, MA, USA

Published by
Edward Elgar Publishing Limited
Glensanda House
Montpellier Parade
Cheltenham
Glos GL50 1UA
UK

Edward Elgar Publishing, Inc.
William Pratt House
9 Dewey Court
Northampton
Massachusetts 01060
USA

A catalogue record for this book
is available from the British Library

Library of Congress Cataloguing in Publication Data
Population aging, intergenerational transfers and the macroeconomy /
edited by Robert Clark, Naohiro Ogawa, Andrew Mason.
p. cm.
Includes bibliographical references and index.
1. Age distribution (Demography)—Economic aspects. 2. Aging—Economic aspects. 3. Economic forecasting I. Clark, Robert, 1949– II. Ogawa, Naohiro, 1944– III. Mason, Andrew, 1947–
HD1531.P67 2007
339.01′12—dc22

2007010616

ISBN 978 1 84720 099 0

Printed and bound in Great Britain by MPG Books Ltd, Bodmin, Cornwall

Contents

PART IV POLICY

Contributors

David E. Bloom (dbloom@hsph.harvard.edu) is Professor of Economics and Demography, Harvard School of Public Health, Harvard University, Boston, Massachusetts.

David Canning (dcanning@hsph.harvard.edu) is Professor of Economics and International Health, Harvard School of Public Health, Harvard University, Boston, Massachusetts.

Robert Clark (clark@gw.fis.ncsu.edu) is Professor, College of Management, North Carolina State University, Raleigh.

David de la Croix (delacroix@core.ucl.ac.be) is Professor at the Department of Economics and at the Center for Operational Research and Econometrics, Université catholique de Louvain.

Axel Gosseries (gosseries@etes.ucl.ac.be) is Permanent Research Fellow at the Belgian National Science Foundation (FNRS), based at the Hoover Chair in economic and social ethics, Université catholique de Louvain.

Ross Guest (r.guest@griffith.edu.au) is Professor of Economics, Griffith Business School, Griffith University, Queensland.

Peter S. Heller (heller@petersheller.com), now retired, was until recently Deputy Director, Fiscal Affairs Department, International Monetary Fund, Washington, DC.

Heinrich Hock (hhock@fsu.edu) is Assistant Professor, Department of Economics, and Research Associate, Center for Demography and Population Health, Florida State University, Tallahassee.

Ronald Lee (rlee@demog.berkeley.edu) is Professor of Demography and Economics, University of California, Berkeley.

Thomas Lindh (thomas.lindh@framtidsstudier.se) is Research Director, Institute for Futures Studies, Stockholm.

Bernhard Mahlberg (mahlberg@iwi.ac.at) is Researcher, Institute for Industrial Research, Vienna.

Maliki (maliki@hawaii.edu) is a member of the Planner Staff, National Development and Planning Agency (Bappenas), Jakarta, and Visiting Fellow, Nihon University Population Research Institute, Tokyo.

Bo Malmberg (bo.malmberg@framtidsstudier.se) is Research Director, Institute for Futures Studies, Stockholm, and Professor, Department of Human Geography, Stockholm University.

Andrew Mason (amason@hawaii.edu) is Professor of Economics and Chair of the Population Studies Program, University of Hawaii at Manoa, and Senior Fellow, Population and Health Studies, East–West Center, Honolulu.

Rikiya Matsukura (matsukura@eco.nihon-u.ac.jp) is Staff Researcher, Nihon University Population Research Institute, and Research Assistant, Advanced Research Institute for the Sciences and Humanities, Nihon University, Tokyo.

Michael Moore (m.moore@qub.ac.uk) is Professor of Finance, Queen's University of Belfast.

Kazuro Nemoto (knemoto@stat.go.jp) is Researcher, Statistical Research & Training Institute, Ministry of Internal Affairs and Communications, Tokyo.

Naohiro Ogawa (ogawa@eco.nihon-u.ac.jp) is Deputy Director, Nihon University Population Research Institute, and Professor, Advanced Research Institute for the Sciences and Humanities, Nihon University, Tokyo.

Alexia Prskawetz (Alexia.Fuernkranz-Prskawetz@oeaw.ac.at) is Senior Scholar, Vienna Institute of Demography, Austrian Academy of Sciences, and Research Associate, Institute for Social and Economic Research, University of Essex, Colchester.

Vegard Skirbekk (skirbekk@iiasa.ac.at) is Research Scholar, International Institute of Applied Systems Analysis (IIASA), Laxenburg.

Younghwan Song (songy@union.edu) is Assistant Professor of Economics, Union College, Schenectady, New York.

David N. Weil (david_weil@brown.edu) is Professor of Economics, Brown University, Providence, Rhode Island, and Research Associate, National Bureau of Economic Research, Cambridge, Massachusetts.

Preface

With the populations of many countries around the world growing old, the twenty-first century is likely to become the century of population aging. The macroeconomic implications of population aging depend in a fundamental way on the intergenerational transfer systems that redirect resources from the working-age population to children and the elderly. These systems vary widely around the world. The public sector dominates in some countries while the private sector – familial support systems, in particular – is more important elsewhere. Many countries rely on transfer programs to support the elderly, whereas others emphasize savings and capital accumulation. These generational transfers are also influenced by the effect of aging on the productivity and quality of the labor force.

These vital socioeconomic issues were addressed at a conference, held in Tokyo from 26 to 28 June 2006, hosted by the Nihon University Population Research Institute (NUPRI). The chapters in this volume arose from papers presented at that conference, the fourth in a series of international conferences organized by a working group on macroeconomic aspects of demographic change. The working group comprises five institutions: Institute for Futures Studies (Stockholm), East–West Center (Honolulu), Vienna Institute of Demography (Vienna), Harvard Center for Population and Development Studies (Cambridge) and NUPRI (Tokyo). Members of the organizing committee for the fourth conference include David Bloom, Thomas Lindh, Wolfgang Lutz, Bo Malmberg, Andrew Mason and Naohiro Ogawa.

The editors are grateful for the financial support under the 'Academic Frontier' Project for Private Universities: matching fund subsidy from MEXT (Ministry of Education, Culture, Sports, Science and Technology), 2006–10, granted to the Nihon University Population Research Institute. We also wish to acknowledge Professor Katsue Kojima, President of Nihon University, and Professor Hirofumi Ando, Director of NUPRI, for their sustained support in relation to the conference and post-conference publication. In addition, we have received outstanding logistical support from NUPRI's staff, including Emmi Okada, Naomi Makabe and

Maki Ogawa. Last but not least, Sandra Ward has effectively helped us edit the manuscript.

Robert Clark
Andrew Mason
Naohiro Ogawa
December 2006

PART I

Introduction

1. Economic and policy implications of population aging

Robert Clark, Andrew Mason and Naohiro Ogawa

All developed countries are experiencing rapid population aging, and in most over 12 percent of the population is now age 65 and older. In Japan the proportion of the elderly population surpassed the 20 percent level in 2005; a number of other developed countries are not far behind. Across the developed world, national population projections indicate continued aging, with some countries facing the prospect of actual population decline and a super aging of the population. In addition to these relatively rich, developed countries, a number of other countries that are in the earlier stages of economic development are now aging rapidly, especially the countries in Asia that have experienced rapid economic growth, such as China and South Korea, but also some countries that have enjoyed much less economic success. Countries that become old before they are rich will face especially great challenges in the coming decades.

Economists, policy analysts, social scientists and government leaders are now debating the macroeconomic implications of population aging, slower population growth and even the decline in the absolute size of national populations. Economic and policy responses to population aging and population decline may hold the key to continued economic growth for many countries. Important questions that must be considered include the following:

- How will economic performance be affected when a population is declining and the workforce is substantially older? Should nations be concerned about the level and growth of their gross domestic product? Or should national policies focus solely on income or consumption per capita?
- How will countries finance national retirement systems? Will taxes be raised? Will benefits be cut? Will retirement ages be increased? Does prefunding of retirement programs make sense at the national level? If so, can governments successfully make the transition from current pay-as-you-go plans to funded plans?

- How will health care systems be influenced by population aging? What policies should be adopted, if any, to curtail rapid growth in health care spending?
- Can we save more now to increase production in the future? Was there a dividend from slowing population growth? If so, what happened to it? Can the first dividend from declines in child dependency be maintained and produce a second 'demographic dividend'?
- Can the size of the labor force be maintained in the face of population aging by increasing the participation rates of women and the elderly or by relaxing immigration standards? Will older workers be as productive as current workers?
- Can pronatalist policies increase national fertility rates? If so, should governments adopt such policies to influence family planning decisions?

Answers to these and other important questions will determine the economic well-being of future generations. While there are no easy answers, the chapters in this volume provide innovative new analyses of the likely macroeconomic and policy responses to population aging. The chapters are written by internationally prominent scholars from Europe, Asia, North America and Oceania. Their methodology, concerns and approaches to these questions reflect their own research backgrounds as well as the cultural differences associated with a diverse set of countries, all of which are confronting rapid population aging.

The remaining chapters are organized into three parts. The first part focuses on the changing age composition of the labor force and the economic implications of an aging labor force. Analyzing data from Japan, Austria and the United States, the authors examine the relationships between population aging and compensation policies, estimate an age-productive profile and how it varies by industry and firm size, and explore how individuals are responding to their increasing longevity.

The second part examines the relationship between population aging and the macroeconomy over the entire demographic transition. The chapters in this section develop theoretical models that refine our understanding of how population growth and changes in age structure, the economic life-cycle and public policy interact to determine economic growth, saving and investment, international trade and investment flows, and important economic sectors, such as the health care sector.

The final part of the volume highlights potential national policy responses to population aging and the challenges that it poses. One author raises interesting questions concerning whether governments should adopt policies to encourage higher fertility and then describes a controversial policy that might lead to a higher birth rate. Another evaluates a new Australian policy to establish a fund that will accumulate sufficient monies to pay for the higher cost of an increasing elderly population. The final chapter describes the attempts of the emerging Asian economies to develop national retirement plans.

In summary, the following chapters provide an interesting mixture of theoretical and empirical analyses of the macroeconomic and policy implications of population aging. The chapters span the globe by examining data from Europe, Asia, the United States and Australia. Together they provide significant new insights into the important linkages between expected demographic changes and the economic health of aging nations. The remainder of this chapter provides a more detailed overview of the volume and serves as a road map for the interested reader.

AGING, PRODUCTIVITY AND RETIREMENT

Low fertility coupled with mortality declines and increasing life expectancy produces an aging of the population and thus an aging of the work force, increases the old-age dependency ratio and has the potential to result in the actual decline in a nation's labor force. Understanding the economic effects of past and future demographic changes is necessary if optimal adjustments are to be made by national governments, firms and individuals. Chapters 2 to 4 examine several of the important aspects of such adjustments by governments, firms and individuals.

Employment and compensation policies are determined by national culture, economic conditions, the age structure of the population and the labor force, social policies and government regulation of the labor market. Companies develop their human resource policies on the basis of current labor market conditions that reflect these factors. Changes in government policies, trends in economic growth and population aging alter optimal employer policies. Because of these differences, we can expect countries to develop different retirement and employment policies when confronted with demographic change. Research and international comparisons offer the opportunity for nations to learn from each other as they age.

Over the past 35 years Japan has been the most rapidly aging country in the world. The resulting trends in the age composition of the labor force have caused employers to reassess their industrial-relations policies. With the aging of the population the Japanese government has also adopted new policies and regulations that have required firms to raise their mandatory retirement ages, reform the national social security system and restructure employer pension policies. Rapid economic growth in the 1970s and 1980s also altered compensation policies, but the bursting of the bubble economy and the lack of economic growth in the last 15 years have produced another round of adjustments in employment and compensation practices.

In Chapter 2, Robert Clark, Naohiro Ogawa and Rikiya Matsukura examine the major changes in the Japanese labor market in the final years of the bubble economy and analyze how employers adjusted their policies to reflect the new conditions of the 'lost decade'. Over the past 20 years the Japanese economy has gone from boom to bust, the population has continued its rapid aging and the government has substantially altered national retirement policies and the regulation of employment policies. The authors describe these fundamental changes in human resource policies and then examine the labor market's responses to the new circumstances. Using a variety of data sources, they first discuss changes in mandatory retirement, social security and employer pensions. Next, they estimate changes in earnings profiles as the economy goes from boom to bust. Finally, they examine the trend among an increasing proportion of young Japanese to opt for a lifestyle that does not include full-time employment. The analysis in Chapter 2 shows that changes in retirement policies have altered the transition from work to retirement in Japan by increasing the labor supply of males aged 55 to 59 and by enhancing their earnings as long as they remain with their career employer. These findings suggest that a further increase in the mandatory retirement age would result in more older persons remaining in the labor force, and this increase could partially offset the expected decline in the size of the labor force.

Austria's demography is similar to Japan's, with low fertility rates and a relatively high life expectancy. Its working-age population will shrink and age during the next few decades. In particular the aging of the baby-boom generation will put a great deal of pressure on firms' human resource management. In Chapter 3, Alexia Prskawetz, Bernhard Mahlberg and Vegard Skirbekk point out that the demographic pressure will be exaggerated by continued disincentives for work at older ages and for hiring old workers; those disincentives are inherent in Austria's public and private retirement systems. Austria's employment rate of older people is among the lowest of the EU countries. According to recent data compiled by EUROSTAT, the labor force participation of persons aged 55 to 64 in 2004 was 29.9 percent in Austria compared with an EU-15 average of 45.3 percent.

The central issue considered by Prskawetz, Mahlberg and Skirbekk is whether older workers can be productive. If the lower proportion of older persons working is the result of lower productivity and hence lower value to firms, efforts to increase the labor force participation of older workers and to raise the effective retirement age will provide less relief from population aging than might otherwise be anticipated. The authors adopt several alternative methods to estimate age-productivity profiles, including age-earnings profiles, supervisors' ratings, work-sample tests and employer–employee matched data sets. Their analysis relies on an innovative approach to measuring how productivity varies with age, based on a newly created matched employer–employee data set for Austria in 2001. These data are used to estimate how a firm's value added is affected by the age of its work force. They confront a number of important and difficult econometric issues that arise in part because the productivity of firms depends on many factors, some of which are unobserved.

Despite these difficulties, the analysis by Prskawetz, Mahlberg and Skirbekk supports broad conclusions that are consistent with the current literature, but also important details not previously addressed. They find that an increase of the share of older workers (50 years and older) depresses firm productivity for small firms regardless of the economic sector in which they operate. The effect of age on labor productivity is different in large firms. For firms in the mining and manufacturing industries the age structure of the work force has no discernible effect on productivity, whereas for firms in the nonmanufacturing industries an increase in the share of younger workers reduces firm productivity. These results suggest that at least in some sectors the older work force can be expanded without reducing firm productivity. In other firms, however, flexibility with respect to pay and other employment practices may be necessary to increase the employment of older workers.

Delaying retirement is a response that will mitigate the effects of increased longevity at both the aggregate and the individual level. Even if average productivity declines with age, many older workers remain highly productive. Moreover, the available evidence suggests that the health of older adults is improving along with their survival chances. Hence the productivity of older workers may be increasing over time. Nonetheless, the global trend has been toward a younger, not an older, age at retirement. The United States stands out as something of an exception to this trend. The downward trend in the percentage of older adults in the work force has leveled off and even increased modestly in recent years. An important policy question is why workers are not extending their years in the work force as their life expectancy rises. Is this a matter of choice? Or are there institutional barriers that are driving older adults from the work force prematurely?

In Chapter 4, David Bloom, David Canning, Michael Moore and Younghwan Song explore how workers' perceptions about their own longevity influence the retirement decision and the decision to accumulate wealth. Is it possible that older adults are so myopic that they are not responding at all to increased longevity? Or is it that they do not understand that life expectancy is increasing or perhaps are unaware of the economic consequences of a longer retirement period? Using microdata drawn from the Health and Retirement Study for the United States, Bloom, Canning, Moore and Song investigate the proposition that expected longevity affects retirement decisions and accumulated wealth. They use data on a person's subjective probability of survival to age 75 as a proxy for the person's prospective lifespan. To control for the presence of measurement error and focal points in responses, as well as reverse-causality, they instrument subjective survival probabilities using information on current age, or age at death, of the respondent's parents.

Bloom and his colleagues conclude that increased subjective probabilities of survival result in increased household wealth among couples but do not affect the length of the working life. These findings are consistent with the view that retirement decisions are driven by institutional constraints and incentives and the view that a longer expected lifespan leads to increased wealth accumulation. Policies that increase labor force flexibility and reduce the incentives for early retirement may well lead to a later age at retirement and lower rates of saving among workers.

POPULATION AGING AND THE MACROECONOMY

Changes in population age structure influence national economies through a variety of channels, which are explored in Chapters 5 through 8. The analyses are not limited to population aging but encompass changes in age structure over the entire demographic transition. The chapters emphasize different channels through which the effects of age structure influence the economy: changes in the share of the population in the highly productive ages; responses in saving and wealth to age composition, fertility decline and rising longevity; changes in saving, investment and the current account; and the influence of age structure on health care spending.

In Chapter 5, Heinrich Hoch and David Weil focus on changes in share of the population in the working ages. With the consumption rate and output per worker held constant, an increase in the share of the population in the highly productive working ages will lead to any increase in per capita consumption. Hock and Weil introduce a new theoretical model that allows them to analyze the relationship between fertility, mortality, the length of working life, and economic dependency in steady states and along transition paths. Using a detailed and realistic model and relying on age profiles of consumption from Japan and the United States, they estimate the consumption-maximizing fertility rate and the gains in consumption that would be realized by moving from the current rate to the consumption-maximizing fertility rate. They conclude that, in both Japan and the United States, higher consumption could be realized by increasing the fertility rate.

Are there economic forces at play that are likely to lead to this outcome? The authors are quite pessimistic on this score. Their view is that population aging is likely to lead to ever lower fertility because the increase in old-age dependency will reduce consumption. This may lead adults of childbearing age to reduce their fertility further in an effort to maintain their living standards and may undermine the willingness of all adults to devote public resources toward pronatalist goals. Although higher fertility would lead to higher consumption, the gains would accrue in the future with no benefit to many current decision-makers.

In Chapter 6, Andrew Mason and Ronald Lee also explore how changes in age structure over the demographic transition influence living standards as measured by per capita consumption. The authors rely on a detailed simulation model to consider two effects of age structure. One effect, called the *first dividend*, measures the gains in consumption from an increase in the portion of the population in the highly productive ages. This is the same effect explored by Hoch and Weil. However, Mason and Lee also quantify the *second dividend*: gains related to an increase in wealth that occur because of changes in age structure and behavioral change related to the demographic transition.

In the Mason and Lee model the decline in the number of children reared, increases in adult survival, and changes in adult age structure combine to increase saving rates and wealth. The size of the second dividend depends on an important policy feature: the extent to which a country relies on public and familial transfers to meet the retirement needs of its population. If transfers play a relatively small role, the demographic transition leads to a substantial, permanent increase in assets, income and consumption. This is not a free lunch, however. Consumption must not rise as rapidly as the first dividend would allow if the second dividend is to be realized.

Changes in age structure and the rate of growth of the population influence both the demand for capital by firms and the supply of savings by households. In closed economies the result would be swings in asset prices and rates of return to capital. In a world with globalized and well-integrated financial markets, however, the swings in age structure in economies in one phase of the demographic transition may result primarily in capital flows to and from economies in a different phase of the demographic transition. This would tend to dampen the swings in rates of return and asset prices that would otherwise be generated from the demographic transition, but all countries would be subject to the same global changes: that is, slower economic growth and population aging.

The extent to which demographic change differentially affects saving and investment is an important and largely unresolved empirical issue that is addressed by Thomas Lindh and Bo Malmberg in Chapter 7. Using a panel of annual OECD data, they find that the effects of population age structure on gross investment differ from the effects on national saving. Their results differ in an important respect from earlier work in that they find that investment rises with an increase in the share of the population at older ages. By disaggregating investment they conclude that populations with large young cohorts invest more in housing whereas populations with larger concentrations at older working age have higher fixed business investment. Investment in inventories is positively correlated with the concentration of the population in the young retirement ages. Lindh and Malmberg conclude that changes in age structure have independent and distinct effects on saving and investment, with potentially important implications for future external balances. Their analysis implies that changes in population age structure will lead initially to an increase and then to a decline in OECD current-account balances over the next few decades.

The authors point out that changes in the current account also reflect the balance between exports and imports. They find that the share of the population in the 30 to 49-year-old age group is positively correlated to exports and that the share of the population at the young retirement ages is positively correlated to imports. They conclude that the effect of changes in age structure on capital flows may be muted to some extent by the effect on trade flows, but that the overall response of the macroeconomics of OECD countries to population aging is likely to be very pronounced.

Although population aging has broad implications for all economic sectors, the implications of aging for the health sector are critical. The elderly consume health services at a much higher rate than any other demographic group in the industrialized countries and perhaps in developing countries as well. Technological change is creating new opportunities to improve the quality of health care and extend life, but new technologies often involve much higher costs. Moreover, health care in many countries is provided in a complex partnership between the private and public sectors. In many cases the government is heavily involved in deciding what services will be available and at what price.

The health sector and health policy in Japan is of great interest for several reasons, as pointed out by Naohiro Ogawa, Andrew Mason, Maliki, Rikiya Matsukura and Kazuro Nemoto in Chapter 8. Japan's population is the oldest in the world and rapidly aging. Life expectancy in Japan is very high, the highest in the world for women and among the highest for men. Hence, by this measure, Japan's health sector is very successful. One might well expect high and rapidly increasing health care costs, but this has not been the case. Japan spends a much smaller share of GDP on health care than does the United States, for example. Two aspects of public policy in Japan have been particularly important in controlling costs. The first is that the health sector is heavily managed in Japan. Prices are administered, the services made available are heavily controlled, and the number of hospitals and health personnel trained is determined by the government. The second factor is that reforms during the last 15 years have shifted more of the costs to users by increasing the required co-payment. In particular, policy changes have reduced the extent to which the elderly are subsidized relative to the non-elderly.

By no means does this imply that continued aging in Japan will not lead to an increase in health care costs. Ogawa and his collaborators show that health care costs rise rapidly with age in Japan and that the public share is still very high for the oldest old. As these age groups increase in size, total health care costs will increase substantially. Given current patterns, the rising costs will be borne primarily by prime-age adults – taxpayers in the case of public costs and adult children in the case of private costs. The strains will be substantial because the number of prime-age adults is already in decline in Japan and will continue to decline for the foreseeable future.

CHANGING POLICIES IN AN AGING WORLD

Part IV of the volume focuses on possible national policy responses to population aging. One possibility is to pursue population policies to offset the aging of the population by encouraging higher rates of childbearing or immigration by younger workers. Higher fertility and greater immigration would reduce the pace of population aging. A second possibility is to design policies that minimize the potentially disruptive effects of rapid population aging, especially the increased cost of providing retirement income and health care to the growing aged population.

In Chapter 9, David de la Croix and Alex Gosseries offer an interesting and provocative approach to population policy in the form of tradable quotas. Tradable quotas are increasingly used in pollution control and natural-resource management, but recently their use has been proposed, but not implemented, in additional settings – inflation control, reduction of unemployment rates and tradable deficits for European Union members, for example. The use of tradable quotas as an approach to population policy was first suggested by Kenneth Boulding in 1964. De la Croix and Gosseries review his proposal and a few others that have followed. They describe how tradable quotas can be used to pursue either antinatalist or pronatalist objectives, thus generalizing earlier work. They then look more specifically at three effects of their proposal on income inequalities: a differential productivity effect, a differential fertility effect and a tradability effect.

In the second section they turn their attention to migration and discuss two possible schemes. First, they consider a domestic scheme of tradable emigration quotas among skilled people, serving as a possible alternative to a Bhagwati tax.[1] The second policy examined is a regional or global scheme of tradable immigration quotas of unskilled workers in rich countries, serving as a 'burden sharing' mechanism. Special attention is given to several conjectures about the effects of emigration on education levels and average income in (poor) sending countries.

The extent to which governments will turn to demographic policies and whether those policies will prove to be successful is unknown. There is certainly nothing to suggest, however, that there will be major reversals in population aging any time soon. Hence, the inevitable question is how best to accommodate population aging that is likely to come. The final two chapters consider this question.

In Chapter 10, Ross Guest evaluates Australia's Future Fund from a social welfare perspective. Australia's Future Fund is a vehicle for tax smoothing whereby the federal government plans to run budget surpluses that will be deposited into a fund to be managed by an independent board of directors. The accumulation phase of the Fund will continue until at least 2020, after which funds can be withdrawn to meet the fiscal costs of population aging, primarily the federal government's superannuation liabilities. Creation of the Fund was motivated by the desire to smooth out the fiscal costs of population aging. The rationale for this, although not clearly stated by the government, appears to be twofold: an efficiency argument based on minimizing the deadweight losses from taxation, and an intergenerational equity argument, by which it is considered equitable to reduce the tax burden on younger generations that would otherwise be associated with the fiscal costs of funding the retirement incomes and health expenditures of an older population.

Guest discusses the anticipated operation of the Future Fund and the way in which it shifts the tax burden of population aging between generations. He then reports simulations of the efficiency and equity effects of the Future Fund based on an overlapping-generations Computable General Equilibrium (CGE) model. Although the simulations are stylized, they serve to illustrate how tax smoothing brings unambiguous efficiency gains but has implications for intergenerational equity that are less clear-cut because it tends to create generations of winners and losers. These efficiency and intergenerational-equity effects are weighed here by means of a social welfare function. Guest concludes that tax smoothing of the order implied by the Future Fund yields net gains in social welfare that range from 0.15 to 0.55 percent in equivalent annual increases in GDP, which implies gains of between $60 and $220 per year per person, given a population of 20 million and a GDP of $800 billion. Positive net gains such as these provide support for tax smoothing. However, there are other considerations that the simulations do not capture and that make the policy of tax smoothing via the Future Fund more controversial than these simulation results suggest.

In the final chapter, Peter Heller considers whether the countries of Asia are prepared for the significant fiscal liabilities arising from the demands of future elderly populations for retirement income, medical care and long-term care. Heller reviews the situation in China, Singapore, South Korea, Hong Kong SAR, Thailand, Malaysia, Indonesia, India and the Philippines. He takes stock of the present status of social insurance provision in terms of medical care and pensions. He then assesses the state of preparedness of these countries using twin strategies, macroeconomic and microeconomic, which he argues must underlie any society's effort at 'preparing' for the aging of its population.

Heller's report card on Asia's preparedness for an aging population is decidedly mixed. Most countries are pursuing policies supportive of rapid economic growth that will enlarge the income available to finance higher living standards when their populations become aged. Most have been fiscally prudent, reducing public debts and providing flexibility to absorb greater burdens of future public spending in connection with an aged population. Moreover, with the exception of China and perhaps South Korea, most now have only limited implicit debt from existing social insurance obligations. It is in the area of social insurance and labor market policies, however, where much effort is still needed to lay down a policy framework that can accommodate the challenges of an aging population.

Incentives for later retirement should soon begin to be put in place. Most of the social insurance systems that have emerged in Asia to date have not been designed to cope with aging populations, and that fact introduces difficult issues of intergenerational burden sharing and complex ethical issues associated with medical care for the elderly. As more comprehensive social insurance systems are in put in place, they must be designed to ensure that their key policy provisions are consistent with fiscal sustainability. This will also require reform of already introduced systems. Reform will have to grapple particularly with the design of a zero-pillar safety-net scheme to address the needs of the large number of elderly residing in the urban informal and rural sectors, outside the coverage of formal social insurance schemes. Long-term care will also be a serious burden. With increasing longevity, a significant share of the elderly may be subject to long periods of disability or living in 'single' elderly households. The burden of these groups will need to be addressed.

THE IMPORTANCE OF UNDERSTANDING THE ECONOMIC AND POLICY IMPLICATIONS OF POPULATION AGING

To summarize, national populations around the globe are aging and many are aging very rapidly. Some countries face the prospect of absolute declines in their population and labor force. How governments and economies respond to these demographic changes will determine in large measure the living standards of future generations. This volume is composed of 11 chapters that examine a broad range of economic responses to population aging. Their findings and conclusions show that economic effects of demographic change will be large and could significantly alter the course of economic growth. The studies also illustrate that countries, governments, firms, and individuals have choices concerning how they will respond to slower population growth, population aging, and increasing life expectancy. Policy decisions and individual choices will determine the macroeconomic impact of population aging. The research presented in this volume provides new information on possible responses and the findings should be influential in charting the optimal course of public policy in the future.

NOTE

1. A Bhagwati tax is a tax by a developing country on the income of emigrants residing in developed countries. This idea was proposed by economist Jagdish Bhagwati as a method for a developing country to recover its investment in the human capital of its citizens who after receiving educational subsidies migrate to developed countries in order to earn higher incomes.

PART II

Population aging and labor markets

2. Population aging, changing retirement policies and lifetime earnings profiles in Japan

Robert Clark, Naohiro Ogawa and Rikiya Matsukura

Employment and compensation policies are determined by national culture, economic conditions, the age structure of the population and the labor force, social policies, and government regulation of the labor market. Companies develop their human resource policies on the basis of current labor market conditions that reflect these factors. Changes in government policies, trends in economic growth and population aging alter optimal employer policies. Since the 1970s, Japan has had the most rapidly aging population in the world. The resulting trends in the age composition of the labor force have caused employers to reassess their industrial-relations policies. With the aging of the population the Japanese government too has adopted new policies and regulations reforming the national Social Security system and requiring firms to raise their mandatory retirement ages and restructure their pension policies. Rapid economic growth in the 1970s and 1980s also altered compensation policies, but the bursting of the bubble economy in the early 1990s and the lack of growth since then have produced another round of adjustments in employment and compensation practices.

Previous studies (Clark and Ogawa, 1992a, 1992b, 1996, 1997) have examined changes in employment and compensation policies associated with the aging of the labor force during the boom years of the Japanese economy. In this chapter the focus is on the major changes that took place in the Japanese labor market during the final years of the bubble economy and how employers, after the bubble burst, adjusted their policies to reflect the new conditions of the 'lost decade'.[1] We describe fundamental changes in human resource policies and then examine the labor market's responses to the new circumstances. Using a variety of data sources, we first discuss changes in mandatory retirement, social security and employer pensions. Next we estimate changes in earnings profiles as the economy went from boom to bust. Finally we examine the trend among an increasing proportion of young

Japanese to opt for a lifestyle that does not include lifetime employment. Together these changes indicate how Japan has adjusted to the demographic and economic realities of the lost decade.

CHANGING LABOR MARKET CONDITIONS

The primary objective of this analysis is to examine changes in the earnings profiles of full-time male workers in Japan as the economy moved from boom to bust. The bursting of the economic bubble in Japan in the early 1990s occurred in conjunction with the continued rapid aging of the labor force. The twin forces of economic and demographic change have altered the basic human resource policies that have characterized Japan in the post-World War II period. The Japanese industrial-relations system is often described as including lifetime employment of high school and college graduates, low turnover rates, seniority-based increases in annual earnings, mandatory retirement and widespread coverage by employer-provided pension and severance plans. This section briefly describes the key changes in those practices while the next section presents estimates of how those determinants have altered employer-compensation policies.

Economic growth

Between 1962 and 1972, Japan's average annual rate of growth in GDP was almost 10 percent. During the next 20 years the average annual rate of GDP growth was lower but still high by international standards at slightly over 4.0 percent (see Figure 2.1). The rapid economic growth between 1962 and 1991 encouraged companies to adopt employment and compensation policies that enabled them to attract and retain quality workers. It also resulted in a relatively low unemployment rate and, in general, an excellent job market for Japanese workers. Between 1960 and 1991, the national unemployment rate ranged between 1.1 and 2.8 percent. Because the population was also growing during that period, employers were able to hire the desired number of new high school and college graduates. In such a labor market, many employers developed human resource systems that rewarded continued service but also encouraged early retirement so that more costly older workers could be replaced by new graduates who were paid much lower salaries.

Beginning in 1992, the rate of economic growth slowed considerably and the average annual growth rate in GDP fell to 1.0 percent. Slower economic growth reduced the demand for labor, and companies responded by changing their employment and compensation policies. Layoffs became more

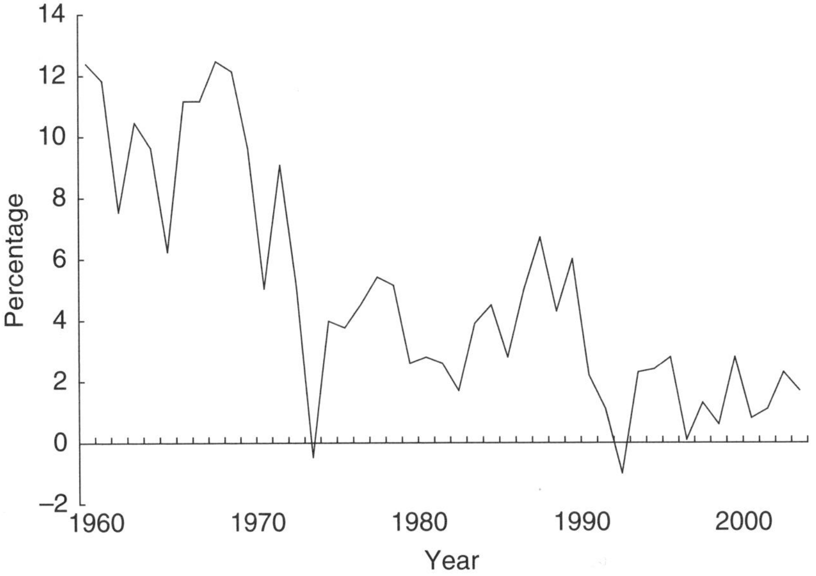

Source: Economic and Social Research Institute (various years).

Figure 2.1 Growth rate of gross domestic product: Japan, 1960–2004

common and fewer younger workers were employed. The unemployment rate rose steadily from 2.1 percent in 1991 to 5.0 percent in 2002. One of our primary objectives in this chapter is to estimate how earnings profiles changed during that period and how an increase in earnings with an additional year of job tenure changed between the boom and bust periods.

Population and Labor Force Aging

Since the end of World War II, Japan has gone from having a very young population to having one of the oldest in the world. Fertility rates have fallen steadily, and in 2005 the total fertility rate was below 1.25 children per woman. Life expectancy at birth has surpassed 85 years. As a result, Japan has the most rapidly aging population in the world and currently has the highest proportion of people aged 65 and older. In 1980, only 9.1 percent of its population was aged 65 and older. By 2004, this percentage had increased to 19.5, and current projections indicate that, by 2025, 31.0 percent of the Japanese population will be aged 65 and older (Ogawa, 2003).

In response to these demographic trends, the Japanese labor force has also aged rapidly. Figure 2.2 shows the dramatic increase in the proportion of the

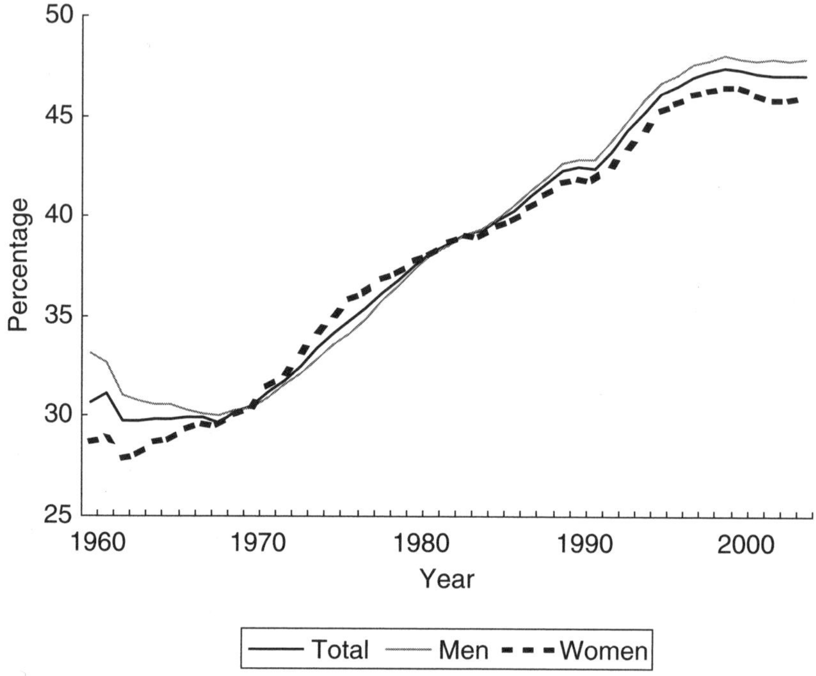

Source: Statistics Bureau, *Annual Report on the Labour Force Survey* (various years).

Figure 2.2 Proportion of labor force aged 45 and older: Japan, 1960–2004

labor force aged 45 and older. Between 1960 and 1970, older workers represented approximately 30 percent of the Japanese labor force. Since 1970, the percentage of the labor force aged 45 and older has risen virtually every year. By 2004, older workers accounted for almost 50 percent of the labor force (not shown in Figure 2.2). During the boom years the aging of the labor force required firms to reassess their compensation and employment policies. Clark and Ogawa (1992b) showed that, between 1971 and 1986, the age-earnings profiles of full-time male workers were altered so that earnings grew more slowly and peaked later in the working life. One of the questions examined below is how the continued aging of the labor force has affected compensation policies during the slow and no-growth period since 1992.

Mandatory Retirement Policies

In the postwar period most Japanese firms adopted mandatory retirement policies and set the age for compulsory retirement at 55. A relatively young

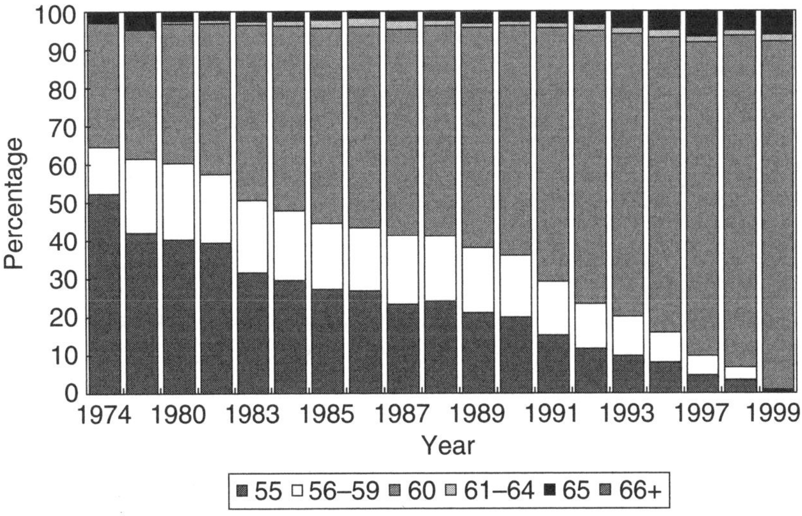

Source: Ministry of Health, Labour and Welfare, *Report on Employment Management Survey* (various years).

Figure 2.3 Percentage of firms with 5000 or more employees requiring mandatory retirement at various ages: Japan, selected years

population created a large pool of potential employees that allowed firms to retire older, more expensive workers and replace them with well-trained younger workers who were much less expensive to employ. As the population aged, and under pressure from the government, most companies increased the age for mandatory retirement to 60 in the 1980s. This upward trend in the age of mandatory retirement was completed in the early 1990s. Figure 2.3 shows that, by 1995, virtually all firms with 5000 or more employees had a mandatory retirement age of 60.[2] With the absolute size of the labor force declining, the government is now encouraging firms to increase the age of mandatory retirement to 65 to provide employment opportunities for the aging labor force.[3] It is expected that a higher age of mandatory retirement will result in a greater proportion of older workers remaining on the job, thus retarding the decline in the labor force.

Clark and Ogawa (1992a) have shown that increases in the age of mandatory retirement during the boom years were associated with a further flattening of the tenure–earnings profile. Thus the rate of growth of earnings was slowed and annual earnings peaked at older ages. Ogawa et al. (2006) have shown that, as mandatory retirement ages rose from 55 to 60, the employment rates and the earnings of persons aged 55 to 59 increased.

In fact these older workers now behave more like people aged 50 to 54 and are less likely to have employment and earnings patterns of persons aged 60 to 64. Given population aging and the actual decline in the total population, older workers must stay in the labor force if the Japanese work force is to remain stable at its current level.[4]

Employer Pension Plans

Virtually all Japanese companies provide their employees with some type of retirement program. Employers traditionally offered lump-sum severance-pay plans, but beginning in the 1960s many employers established pension plans that provided annuities to retiring workers (Clark, 1991; Clark and Mitchell, 2002). The system of employer pensions included both tax-qualified pension plans (TQPPs) and employees' pension funds (EPFs). Both types of retirement plans are defined-benefit plans and were used to provide retirement income to workers who were required to retire at relatively young ages. The EPF plans allowed employers to contract out a component of the national Social Security benefit provided that the benefit was supplemented by an additional retirement benefit. The plan sponsor was responsible for the funding of both the contracted-out component and the supplemental benefit. Clark (1991) provides a detailed discussion of the development of the two pension systems.

During the 1970s and 1980s, EPFs were adopted by many large employers while many smaller firms tended to establish TQPPs. With the ending of the bubble economy in the early 1990s, the asset values in Japanese pension plans were sharply reduced and many retirement plans became dramatically underfunded. The reduced economic status of pension plans and the implied obligations of the companies that sponsored them resulted in the passage, in 2001, of the Defined Benefit Corporate Pension Plans Law and the Defined Contribution Pension Plans Law. These laws enabled firms to terminate the EPFs under favorable conditions, required the termination of TQPPs, and provided for the establishment of defined-contribution plans.

The sponsors of EPFs were allowed to return to the government the liabilities associated with the substituted portion of the Social Security benefit. Companies were required to return plan assets that were being held to pay those benefits, but favorable calculations were used to determine the funds that should be returned to the government. EPF plan sponsors were also allowed to transfer any remaining assets to either a new defined-benefit plan or a newly established defined-contribution plan. The new laws required companies to terminate their TQPPs within ten years. Thus, by 2010, employers with TQPPs must decide whether their plans will be converted to defined-benefit plans or to defined-contribution plans. In general these changes in employer pensions have tended to lower costs for firms, reduce compensation to workers, and result in lower retirement benefits. As a result, workers can be expected to want to retire at later ages.

Social Security

National pay-as-you-go retirement programs in nearly all developed countries are facing the same basic problem: population aging reduces the worker-to-retiree ratio and raises the tax rate needed to provide any given level of retirement benefits. The rapid population aging in Japan has resulted in significant increases in the payroll tax. Between 1985 and 2004, the government adopted a series of reforms that have reduced future benefits, raised the normal retirement age, and scheduled further increases in taxes.[5] A higher normal retirement age for receiving Social Security benefits and lower benefits tend to reduce retirement rates and encourage older men to remain in the labor force. Higher payroll tax rates to finance Social Security also influence companies' human resource policies.

In Japan, all employees are covered by mandatory, national retirement plans that consist of two separate systems: the National Pension and the Employees Pension Insurance. Employees are covered by both systems whereas self-employed individuals are covered only by the National Pension. Currently a benefit for both an employee with average earnings and his spouse represents approximately 60 percent of the worker's career earnings (Clark and Mitchell, 2002; Sakamoto, 2005). Because of the reforms adopted in 2004, however, the replacement rate is expected to decline over the next 25 years to 50 percent for the average wage earner. During this period the normal retirement age will gradually increase to 65 (Sakamoto, 2005). Lower benefits and a higher normal retirement age for Social Security provide incentives for workers to remain in the labor force until older ages either in their career job or in a transitional job. These changes can be expected to influence retirement decisions of workers and employment decisions of firms in the coming years. One of the reasons why the new law increases the age of mandatory retirement to 65 is to align the retirement age with the age of eligibility for Social Security benefits.

EARNINGS PROFILES IN A SLOW-GROWTH BUT AGING ECONOMY

The use of seniority-based pay systems by Japanese employers has been widely examined. Most studies conclude that across-the-board wage increases with each additional year of job tenure are common, especially among large employers. Hashimoto and Raisian (1985) found that the gain in annual earnings from increased tenure was much greater for full-time male workers in Japan than for similar employees in the United States. Clark and Ogawa (1992a, 1992b) showed that the importance of tenure for Japanese workers declined and earnings profiles flattened during the boom years from 1971 to 1986 as the population aged and firms raised mandatory retirement ages. These results, however, were for a period of rapid economic growth and before the bursting of the bubble economy. Our own analysis extends this line of research and seeks to determine how compensation profiles have changed during the low-growth years since 1992.

Data

The data used to examine trends in earnings profiles is from the Basic Survey on Wage Structure, an annual government survey. We analyze Basic Survey data for the period from 1982 to 2002, using observations for every fifth survey. The sample observations are cell means of earnings for full-time male employees stratified by firm size, educational level, age group and industry. Firms are divided into companies with fewer than 100 workers, those with between 100 and 999 employees, and those with more than 1000 workers. The data on employees are sorted by level of educational attainment: junior high school, high school, junior college, and university. The cell means are for five-year age ranges between 20 and 24 and 60 and 64 plus a 65+ category.

Table 2.1 shows the ratio of average earnings for male full-time employees at various ages as a percentage of the average earnings of men aged 20 to 24.

Table 2.1 *Age–earnings profiles of full-time male employees: Japan, selected years (percentages)*

Ages	1982	1987	1992	1997	2002
20–24	100	100	100	100	100
25–29	134	130	131	130	129
30–34	167	160	158	160	159
35–39	195	187	181	183	188
40–44	211	209	203	200	206
45–49	215	221	220	215	216
50–54	209	214	220	224	219
55–59	174	182	190	204	206
60–64	131	137	134	140	144
65+	117	124	114	118	129

Source: Ministry of Health, Labour and Welfare, *Basic Survey on Wage Structure* (various years).

These age–earnings profiles show that annual earnings peaked earlier in the years of the bubble economy and later in the slow-growth years. Peak earnings are recorded for men aged 45 to 49 in 1982, 1987 and 1992. After the ending of the bubble economy, earnings peaked at ages 50 to 54 in the 1997 and 2002 surveys. Figure 2.4 depicts the flattening of the age–earnings profile by comparing the earnings profile for 1982 with the profiles for 1992 and 2002.

The data also show the effects of increases in the age of mandatory retirement and the ability of workers to remain in their career jobs until older ages. For example, over time the earnings and labor market behavior of men aged 55 to 59 has come to more closely resemble that of men of 50 to 54 and less like the earnings and labor market behavior of men of 60 to 64. In 1982, the average earnings of men of 55 to 59 represented only 83 percent of the average earnings of men of 50 to 54 and 132 percent of the earnings of men

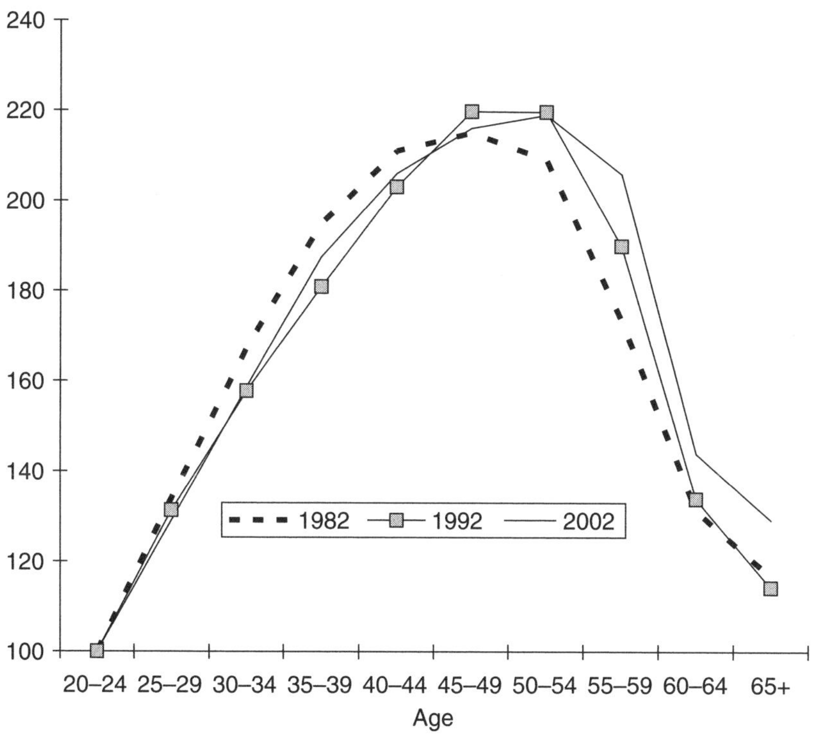

Source: Ministry of Health, Labour and Welfare, *Basic Survey on Wage Structure* (various years).

Figure 2.4 Age–earnings profiles for full-time male employees: Japan, 1982, 1992 and 2002

of 60 to 64. By 2002, however, the earnings of men of 55 to 59 had risen to 94 percent of the average earnings of men aged 50 to 54 and to 143 percent of the earnings of men aged 60 to 64. This finding is consistent with the implicit contracting theory described by Lazear (1979) and Hutchens (1989). Their model suggests that higher ages of mandatory retirement in the context of a long-term contract should result in flatter age–earnings profiles that peak later in workers' careers. Clark and Ogawa (1992a) provide empirical support for this prediction for Japan between 1981 and 1986.

Estimating Earnings Profiles

We estimate earnings using a specification similar to that adopted by most studies of the Japanese labor market. The log of annual earnings, including bonuses, is estimated as a function of general labor market experience (EXP), experience squared, years of service with current employer (TEN), tenure squared, and an interaction term between experience and tenure (EXP times TEN). In addition the specification includes a series of dichotomous variables indicating the level of educational attainment, firm size, and industry.

Table 2.2 presents the estimated coefficients for each of the five years included in the analysis. The estimated coefficients for the education and firm-size variables are consistent with economic expectations and are similar in size to those reported by Clark and Ogawa (1992b) for the two surveys from the 1980s. Men with a senior high school diploma had annual earnings between 10.6 and 12.2 percent higher than men with only a junior high school diploma. In 1982, a junior college degree added a further 13 percent to annual earnings over a high school diploma; by 2002, however, the added value of that degree had declined to only 7.5 percent. In 1982, men with a university degree earned 37.7 percent more than those with only a junior high school diploma. Their advantage in earnings declined by two to three percentage points in the slow-growth period between 1992 and 2002. In contrast, the difference in earnings between those with a junior college degree and a university degree widened during the same period, from 12 to 17 percent.

As in most countries, in Japan employees of large companies are paid more than those employed by small companies. Table 2.2 shows that workers in firms with between 100 and 999 employees earned 4 to 8 percent more than employees in firms with fewer than 100 employees. Employees in firms with more than 1000 employees had earnings of 12 to 18 percent more than employees in small firms. The advantage of working in larger firms declined between 1987 and 1992 but then increased during the next decade as the economy slowed.

Table 2.2 Estimated coefficients for male full-time employees: Japan, selected years

All	1982	1987	1992	1997	2002
Intercept	7.1780***	7.3165***	7.5780***	7.6277***	7.5345***
exp	0.0467***	0.0401***	0.0442***	0.0447***	0.0435***
exp 2	−0.0009***	−0.0008***	−0.0009***	−0.0009***	−0.0008***
Tenure	0.0378***	0.0425***	0.0294***	0.0276***	0.0323***
tenure2	−0.0006***	−0.0007***	−0.0003***	−0.0002**	−0.0001
extenure	0.0002**	0.0002	0.0002**	0.0001	−0.0001
srhi	0.1221***	0.1092***	0.1119***	0.1055***	0.1140***
Jrc	0.2557***	0.2363***	0.2187***	0.1958***	0.1886***
UNIV	0.3766***	0.3765***	0.3785***	0.3406***	0.3552***
mfirm	0.0641***	0.0807***	0.0356***	0.0443***	0.0666***
lfirm	0.1346***	0.1663***	0.1184***	0.1261***	0.1841***
Adj R^2	0.8862	0.8493	0.881	0.8851	0.8518
N	1124	1118	1116	1098	1093

Notes: *** coefficient differs significantly from zero at the 1 percent level; ** coefficient differs significantly from zero at the 5 percent level.

Table 2.3 Estimated earnings profiles of full-time male employees by years on the job: Japan, selected years

Years of tenure and experience	Relative earnings by year (%)				
	1982	1987	1992	1997	2002
0	100	100	100	100	100
5	148	146	141	140	142
10	204	200	188	187	191
15	263	254	239	239	243
20	318	303	289	290	293
25	359	337	332	336	335
30	379	351	362	372	362
35	375	340	375	392	370
40	347	309	369	393	358
45	300	262	345	377	328

The effects of an extra year of job tenure and of another year of general work experience are shown by the five coefficients for these variables in Table 2.2. Across the years, all the coefficients for experience, experience squared, tenure, and tenure squared are highly significant, with the exception of tenure squared in 2002. The estimated coefficient on the interaction term is small and insignificant in three of the years.

To determine the shape of the earnings profiles, it is necessary to consider these coefficients together. Table 2.3 illustrates the effect of tenure and experience together for a worker beginning with zero years of work and continuing over the next 45 years for each of the five survey years. Figure 2.5 compares the earnings profiles for 1982, 1992 and 2002. The table and figure show the effect of the ending of the bubble economy and the effect of the growth of earnings for male employees. The values for each point in the work life represent earnings as a percentage of the annual earnings for a man with zero years of tenure and experience. For example, in 1982, a man with 20 years of tenure and 20 years of work experience had earnings that were 318 percent of the earnings of a man just entering the labor market with zero years of tenure and experience.

Our analysis, which is consistent with the findings of Clark and Ogawa (1992b), indicates that the earnings of workers in 1992 grew more slowly and peaked later than in 1982. After the ending of the bubble economy the profile for 2002 is very similar to that for 1992, with the exception of the lower values after 35 years of work. These results are consistent with our expectations based on changes in the Japanese labor market described

Source: Estimated coefficients as shown in Table 2.2.

Figure 2.5 Estimated earnings profiles for full-time male employees by number of years on the job: Japan, 1982, 1992 and 2002

earlier. Continued population aging over the 20-year period, along with the increase in the age of mandatory retirement and shifts in pension and Social Security policies, has altered the shape of lifetime earnings profiles.

A remaining question concerns the relative importance of tenure and experience on earnings growth in the bubble economy compared with the lost decade. To disentangle these effects, we calculate separately the respective roles of tenure and general work experience on earnings growth. The results are presented in Tables 2.4 and 2.5 and Figures 2.6 and 2.7. In the lost decade the effects of tenure became more important, whereas general work experience declined in value. These changes reflect the state of the labor market and show both that workers who remained with their employers continued to receive wage increases and that the size of the increases did not decline with greater years of tenure. This result is indicated by the much smaller negative effects of the tenure-squared coefficients in 1997 and 2002 (the tenure-squared coefficient for 2002 is also insignificantly different from zero).

Over the two decades covered by our analysis there have been some interesting changes in the average tenure of male Japanese employees. For all male employees, average tenure increased slightly, from 11.4 years in 1982 to 12.9 years in 2002. This small change masks substantial differences,

Table 2.4 Estimated effect of tenure on earnings for full-time male employees: Japan, selected years

Years of tenure	Relative earnings by year (%)				
	1982	1987	1992	1997	2002
0	100	100	100	100	100
5	119	121	115	114	117
10	137	142	130	130	136
15	153	160	144	146	157
20	165	174	157	163	180
25	172	182	168	180	204
30	175	183	177	197	230
35	171	178	183	215	258
40	163	167	186	232	287
45	150	150	186	248	316

Table 2.5 Estimated effect of an additional year of work experience: full-time male employees

Years of experience	Relative earnings by year (%)				
	1982	1987	1992	1997	2002
0	100	100	100	100	100
5	124	120	122	122	122
10	146	138	143	143	143
15	165	154	160	161	160
20	179	164	172	173	173
25	186	169	177	177	179
30	185	167	174	175	178
35	175	159	165	165	170
40	160	146	149	149	156
45	139	128	129	128	137

however, in changes in age-specific tenure. Average tenure for employees younger than 45 years of age held constant or even declined slightly between 1982 and 2002. In contrast, average tenure for older workers increased. For example the average tenure for men aged 55 to 59 rose from 16.1 years in 1982 to 22.6 years in 2002. The rather large increases in tenure for older workers reflect the changes in mandatory retirement policies as well as the fluctuations in the economic climate.

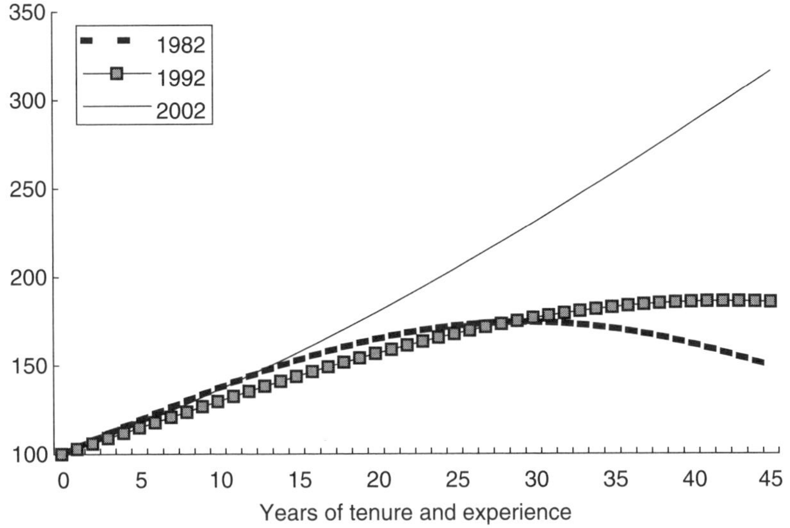

Source: Estimated coefficients as shown in Table 2.2.

Figure 2.6 Estimated effect of tenure on earnings of full-time male employees: Japan, 1982, 1992 and 2002

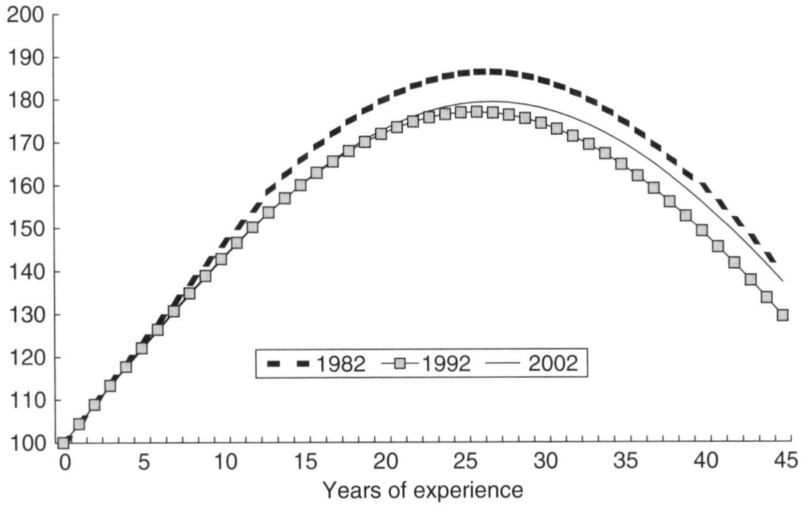

Source: Estimated coefficients as shown in Table 2.2.

Figure 2.7 Estimated effect of an additional year of work experience for full-time male employees: Japan, 1982, 1992 and 2002

DROPPING OUT OF THE FORMAL LABOR MARKET

Another change that could be affecting employment and compensation profiles in Japan is the growing proportion of young Japanese who are deciding to remain outside the formal labor force. Although this may be due in part to a decline in employment opportunities, the new lifestyle has reduced the supply of young workers and forced firms to adjust their human resource policies (Japan Institute for Labour Policy and Training, 2000; Kosugi and Hori, 2004). The decline in the proportion of young Japanese who are full-time workers may have influenced the changes in the earnings profiles shown in Figure 2.6.

National surveys show that an increasing proportion of Japanese youths aged 15 to 34 are choosing alternative lifestyles that do not include finding and keeping full-time, career jobs in the formal sector of the economy (Cabinet Office, 2003).[6] The increasing proportion of young people who are choosing not to seek permanent full-time jobs after graduation or who decide to quit their first jobs is causing considerable concern among policy-makers in Japan. A country with a declining population must strive to have a very high proportion of its potential labor force actually working.

Two terms that are frequently used to describe young persons who remain outside the formal labor force are 'freeter' and 'NEET' (Kosugi, 2005).[7] 'Freeter' is the term given to a young person who chooses to seek part-time and casual employment instead of a full-time job, and 'NEET' is the term for an individual who has dropped out of the labor force altogether and is not seeking any type of employment.[8]

There is no single, agreed-upon method of classifying youths into freeters and NEETs, and so estimates of the number of these individuals vary somewhat among studies.[9] The Japanese government defines freeters as individuals between the ages of 15 and 34 who are part-time employees or persons who are unemployed and seeking only part-time employment. It defines NEETs as individuals of ages 15 to 34 who do not have a job of any kind and do not want any type of employment. Between 1982 and 2002, the proportion of Japanese in that age group who were freeters rose from 1.9 percent to 7.4 percent. In contrast, the proportion of Japanese in that age group who were NEETs remained virtually unchanged at 1.6 percent. This means that, in 2002, there were 2.5 million freeters and 0.5 million NEETs among younger Japanese. Thus 9.0 percent of Japanese aged 15 to 34, or more than three million individuals, were outside the formal labor force and did not want to join it.[10]

To examine the rise in the nonworking population, we divided our sample from the Basic Survey on Wage Structure into four five-year age groups: 15–19, 20–24, 25–29 and 30–34. The proportion of the population

Table 2.6 Percentage of freeters and NEETs by sex: Japan, selected years

Both sexes	1982	1987	1992	1997	2002
15–19	3.5	4.2	4.6	5.2	5.9
20–24	4.9	6.0	6.9	10.4	14.6
25–29	3.3	3.9	4.7	6.6	9.7
30–34	2.0	2.3	2.6	3.9	6.1
Men	1982	1987	1992	1997	2002
15–19	4.1	2.6	2.9	3.7	4.1
20–24	3.7	5.0	6.0	8.4	12.7
25–29	2.3	2.8	3.4	5.0	8.1
30–34	1.7	2.0	2.0	3.0	4.8
Women	1982	1987	1992	1997	2002
15–19	2.9	2.0	2.2	3.1	4.5
20–24	6.1	6.0	7.4	11.8	15.6
25–29	4.3	4.5	5.9	8.0	10.8
30–34	2.3	2.4	3.3	4.9	7.2

Note: The Japanese government defines 'freeters' as persons of ages 15–34 who choose to seek part-time and casual employment instead of a full-time job. 'NEETs' are individuals of ages 15–34 who have no job of any kind and do not want any type of employment.

Source: Statistics Bureau, *Employment Status Survey* (various years).

choosing the freeter or NEET lifestyle in each of these age groups has grown over time (Table 2.6). The data indicate that the incidence of the two new lifestyles has risen in each of the four age groups, with the percentages among persons over the age of 20 tripling. For example, the proportion of persons aged 20 to 24 who were either freeters or NEETs was only 4.9 percent in 1982 but had risen to 14.6 percent by 2002, while the incidence among youths of 25 to 29 years of age had risen from 3.3 percent to 9.7 percent.

By following the diagonal entries in Table 2.6, we can compare the experiences of the various birth cohorts over the period between 1982 and 2002. For example, among persons born between 1963 and 1967, only 3.5 percent were freeters or NEETs in 1982, when they were 15 to 19 years old. As they aged over the 20-year period, the incidence of being freeter or NEET among this birth cohort rose to 6.0 percent when they were 20 to 24 in 1987 and then fell over the next ten years to 3.9 percent in 1997. The 1968–72 birth cohort had a similar experience: in 1987, when its members were 15 to 19 years of age, the incidence of their being freeters or NEETs was 4.2 percent. It then rose to 6.9 percent when they were 20 to 24, before falling over the next ten years to 6.1 percent in 2002. Thus the pattern for these two cohorts was an initial incidence of about 4.0 percent when they were 15 to 19, a modest increase of about 2.5 percentage points over the next five years, and then a decline in the incidence as they continued to age. The main difference was in the bigger decline in freeter or NEET incidence for the 1963–67 birth cohort between age groups 20 to 24 and 30 to 34.

The story appears to be different for the subsequent two cohorts, although they have not yet attained the ages of 30 to 34. The 1973–77 and 1978–82 birth cohorts entered the sample ages with only a slightly higher freeter or NEET percentage at ages 15 to 19 than the earlier two birth cohorts. Each of the younger cohorts, however, had sharp increases in the incidence of being freeters or NEETs at ages 20 to 24. The incidence for the 1973–77 cohort jumped from 4.6 percent at age group 15 to 19 to 10.4 percent at age group 20 to 24. The incidence for the 1978–82 cohort was 5.2 percent at ages 15 to 19 and then surged to 14.6 percent at ages 20 to 24. Of further concern is the observation that the incidence of being a freeter or NEET fell only slightly as the 1973–77 cohort reached ages 25 to 29.

The finding that the incidence of being a freeter or NEET remains very high for the latest birth cohort as its members enter their 30s raises the possibility that a significant proportion of this generation of Japanese youths may never find full-time career jobs in the formal sector of the economy. That possibility has important implications for the growth rate of the economy, national tax revenues and funding the national Social Security system. Therefore a better understanding of the reasons why individuals choose this life style is essential for developing policies to facilitate the transition of freeters and NEETs into the regular labor force as they age.

CONCLUSIONS

Japan is adjusting to the demographic reality of rapid population aging, rising life expectancy and the absolute decline in the size of its population. The government has made fundamental reforms in Social Security in an effort to limit taxes and contributions needed to finance retirement benefits. Nevertheless, significant tax increases will occur in the next 25 years, and they will affect firms' labor costs and consumers' income. Consequently, they will influence economic activity. Reductions in future retirement benefits and increases in the normal retirement age for retirement benefits will tend to delay the retirement of older Japanese.

In conjunction with these reforms in Social Security, the government has made fundamental changes in regulations of employer pension plans. In response to those changes and to government pressure to increase the age of mandatory retirement, companies are terminating many existing pension plans, establishing new plans and in general altering their retirement policies. Since 1990, these changes have occurred in a slow or no-growth economy. Our analysis has attempted to estimate changes that have occurred in the employment and compensation policies of Japanese companies. The results indicate that increases in earnings among workers with seniority have slowed and that earnings peak later in work life. Lifetime employment seems less likely for many Japanese as unemployment has risen and a larger proportion of younger Japanese seek alternative lifestyles.

A key question facing the government is how to maintain economic growth while the size of the labor force is declining. An important component of future policy will be to retain older Japanese in the labor force by delaying retirement. Many of the policy changes instituted during the lost decade should provide incentives to firms and workers to postpone retirement.

NOTES

1. The 'lost decade' refers to the 1990s, when the bubble economy collapsed, economic growth stalled, unemployment rose and the value of most assets sharply declined. With the dramatic change in the economy, 'the people were shocked and confused as a wave of anxiety and pessimism rapidly pervaded Japanese society' (Yoshikawa, 2001). This change represented a severe reversal of fortune and attitudes of the population from the view of 'Japan as No. 1' that prevailed only a few years earlier (Vogel, 1979).
2. Smaller firms also tended to increase their mandatory retirement ages during that period. For example, by 1995, 97 percent of all firms with 1000–4999 employees had established a mandatory retirement age of 60, whereas the percentages of firms with 300–999 employees and with 100–299 employees that had set the age of mandatory retirement at 60 were only slightly lower, at 92 and 87, respectively.
3. In response to population aging and the decline in the size of the labor force, in June 2004 the Diet passed the Law to Partially Amend the Law Concerning Stabilization of Employment of Older Persons. The objective was to allow older persons to continue in their career jobs until they were eligible to receive Social Security benefits. The law states that employers should adopt new policies to gradually extend the retirement age to 65 by 2013. See Matsumoto, Kitagawa and Hirai (2006) for a discussion of the law.
4. Given current attitudes and national policies, it seems unlikely that Japan will seek to increase its labor force through immigration. Another alternative would be to increase the participation rates of women. Ogawa et al. (2006) explore this option in some detail.
5. Sakamoto (2005) provides a detailed assessment of the 2004 reforms and how they will affect future costs and benefits. See also Clark (1991).
6. This phenomenon has also been observed in certain Western European countries.
7. 'Freeter' is a Japanese term formed from the English word 'free' and the German word for worker, 'arbeiter', and literally means a free worker or one who has a lifestyle free from full-time and permanent employment (Yoshitaka, 2005). 'NEET' is a term coined in Britain and is an acronym for Not in Employment, Education, or Training. It indicates that the person to whom it applies is not currently working, in school, or in a training program and is also not currently interested in finding a job (UK Social Exclusion Unit, 1999).

8. Women who are married and who fit these categories are not classified as either freeters or NEETs.
9. The Japanese government is sufficiently concerned about the rising incidence of freeters and NEETs that it has commissioned studies to examine this trend and offer policy recommendations.
10. The proportion of women who are freeters and NEETs has consistently been higher than the incidence for men. In 2002, the incidence of being either a freeter or a NEET among men was 7.9 percent, compared with 10.3 percent among young, single women.

REFERENCES

Cabinet Office (2003), *Annual Report on the National Lifestyle*, Tokyo: Gyosei.

Clark, Robert (1991), *Japanese Retirement Systems*, Homewood, IL: Dow Jones-Irwin.

Clark, Robert and Olivia Mitchell (2002), 'Strengthening employment-based pensions in Japan', *Benefits Quarterly*, 2nd quarter, 22–43.

Clark, Robert and Naohiro Ogawa (1992a), 'The effects of mandatory retirement on earnings profiles in Japan', *Industrial and Labor Relations Review*, **45**(2), 258–66.

Clark, Robert and Naohiro Ogawa (1992b), 'Employment tenure and earnings profiles in Japan and the United States: Comments', *American Economic Review*, **82**(1), 336–45.

Clark, Robert and Naohiro Ogawa (1996), 'Human resource policies and older workers in Japan', *The Gerontologist*, **36**(5), 627–36.

Clark, Robert and Naohiro Ogawa (1997), 'Transition from career jobs to retirement in Japan', *Industrial Relations*, **36**(2), 255–70.

Economic and Social Research Institute (various years), *Annual Report on National Accounts*, Tokyo: Printing Bureau, Ministry of Finance.

Hashimoto, Masanori and John Raisian (1985), 'Employment tenure and earnings profiles in Japan and the United States', *American Economic Review*, **75**(4), 721–35.

Hutchens, Robert (1989), 'Seniority, wages and productivity: a turbulent decade', *Journal of Economic Perspectives*, **3**(4), 49–64.

Japan Institute for Labour Policy and Training (2000), 'Freeter no Ishiki to Jittai' (Attitudes and lives of Freeters), Research Report 136, Tokyo.

Kosugi, Reiko (2005), *Freeter to NEET (Freeter and NEET)*, Tokyo: Keiso Shobou.

Kosugi, Reiko and Yukie Hori (2004), 'Jakunen Mugyou / Shuhenteki Freeter Souno Genjo Mondai' (Jobless youth and periphery Freeters in Japan), *Shakai Kagaku Kenkyu* (*Journal of Social Science*), **55**(2), 5–28.

Lazear, Edward (1979), 'Why is there mandatory retirement?', *Journal of Political Economy*, **87**(6), 1261–84.

Matsumoto, Atsuko, Ikuko Kitagawa and Hiroshi Hirai (2006), 'Older workers valued, but no jobs for some', *Daily Yomiuri Online*, www.yomiuri.co.jp/dy/features/0004/08.htm, accessed 3 March 2006.

Ministry of Health, Labour and Welfare (various years), *Basic Survey on Wage Structure*, Tokyo: Rodohoreikyokai.

Ministry of Health, Labour and Welfare (various years), *Report on Employment Management Survey*, Tokyo: Romugyosei (in Japanese).

Ogawa, Naohiro (2003), 'Population aging and its impact on the socioeconomic system in Japan', *Aging in Japan 2003*, Tokyo: Japan Aging Research Center, pp. 123–50.

Ogawa, Naohiro, Robert Clark, Rikiya Matsukura, Kazuo Nemoto and Katsuya Akasaka (2006), *Japan's Changing Demographic Structure and Its Employment Status, Patterns*, Tokyo: Nihon University Population Research Institute (in Japanese).

Sakamoto, Junichi (2005), *Japan's Pension Reform*, Special Protection Discussion Paper 541, Washington: World Bank.

Statistics Bureau (various years), *Annual Report on the Labour Force Survey*, Tokyo: Japan Statistical Association.

Statistics Bureau (various years), *Employment Status Survey*, Tokyo: Japan Statistical Association.

UK [United Kingdom] Social Exclusion Unit (1999), *Bridging the Gap: New Opportunities for 16–18 Year Olds Not in Education, Employment or Training*, London: Cabinet Office of Britain.

Vogel, Ezra (1979), *Japan As Number One: Lessons for America*, Cambridge, MA: Harvard University Press.

Yoshikawa, Hiroshi (2001), *Japan's Lost Decade*, Tokyo: International House of Japan.

Yoshitaka, Mori (2005), 'Culture-politics: the emergence of new cultural forms of protest in the age of freeter', *Inter-Asia Cultural Studies*, **6**(1), 17–29.

3. Firm productivity, work-force age and educational structure in Austrian industries in 2001

Alexia Prskawetz, Bernhard Mahlberg and Vegard Skirbekk[1]

As in other industrialized countries, in Austria the working-age population will shrink and age during the next decades (OECD, 2005). In particular the aging of the baby-boom generation will put great pressure on the human resource management of firms. As argued in Grund and Westergård-Nielsen (2005, 14), 'A lack of young specialists and executive staff in the near future is easily foreseeable. Therefore, firms should elaborate a proper strategy to react to this challenge already today.' The demographic pressure will be exaggerated by continued disincentives for work at older ages. Austria's employment rate of older people is among the lowest of European Union countries. According to recent data from Eurostat New Chronos (2006), in Austria 31.8 percent of persons aged 55 to 64 participated in the labor force in 2005, compared with an EU-15 average of 44.1 percent.[2] The effective retirement age in 2001 was 58.7 years for males and 57.3 years for women. Though life expectancy has increased, the retirement age has dropped. 'The expected retirement duration has, therefore, increased rapidly: it more than doubled from 9.6 years in 1950 to 20.9 years in 2000 for men, and from 12.3 to 27.6 years over the same period for women' (OECD, 2005, 52). If the lower employability of older workers is associated with lower productivity, efforts to increase the labor force participation of older workers and to increase the effective retirement age have to be reconsidered.

Though an aging work force is often thought to be associated with lower productivity, there are no clear-cut empirical findings to support the relationship. It may be argued, on the one hand, that the greater experience and higher average firm-specific human capital of older workers and their lower turnover may be advantageous for firms since they indicate that such workers have been optimally matched to the job. On the other hand, the labor market may become less flexible when the share of the older labor force is higher, because older people are less mobile than younger people. As a consequence the process of structural change slows down, and that in turn makes matching people and jobs less efficient. Moreover, since productivity at the individual level depends not only on experience but also on skills acquired before entering the labor market, an older work force implies a more outdated human capital level of formal and general education, which may hinder productivity, in particular in times of rapid technological change. Of course the demand for various types of skills will not be uniform, either across industries or over time. Higher education may lead to more specialized skills with more limited markets and higher requirements for mobility. Thus the aggregate effects of aging in combination with rising education levels among younger workers are highly uncertain and may be quite sensitive to the rate of innovation and structural conditions in particular industries.

These differences between younger and older workers suggest synergies and therefore imperfect substitution between younger and older workers. As discussed in Prskawetz, Fent and Guest (2006), imperfect substitutability of workers at different ages implies that the age mix of a given work force affects output, and thus gives rise to the notion of an optimal age mix that maximizes output.

In recent years several approaches have been followed to estimate age–productivity profiles. It is well known that workers of different ages may have different levels of productivity (as well as different capacities for learning), although the exact shape of the age–productivity curve is still highly disputed and strongly dependent on the occupation, technological progress and possible cohort effects that work through schooling levels (see Skirbekk, 2004, for a review). Alternative methods to estimate those profiles have been suggested in the literature and include age–earnings profiles, supervisors' ratings, work-sample tests and employer–employee matched data sets. Understanding the age–productivity profiles is central to understanding retirement incentives at the individual and firm level. Strategies for encouraging older workers to remain longer in the work force need to be evaluated in tandem with the productivity profile of older workers.

In this chapter we follow the approach of measuring age–productivity profiles using a newly created matched employer–employee data set for Austria in 2001.[3] This approach is likely to be less subjective than other ways of measuring productivity by age, such as those based on supervisors' ratings; and there are fewer problems of sample selection than in studies based on piece rates (which measure the quantity and quality of individuals' output). In our approach the main challenge is to isolate the effect of the employees' age from the other influences on the company's value added, and it therefore requires strong identifying assumptions. Such an approach also requires high-quality longitudinal data on both the company's and individuals' characteristics.

We present an overview of how employer–employee studies relate to age in the Appendix. Most of the employer–employee studies report an inverted U-shaped work-performance profile (Andersson, Holmlund and Lindh, 2002; Crépon, Deniau and Perez-Duarte, 2002; Haltiwanger, Lane and Spletzer, 1999; Hægeland and Klette, 1999; Ilmakunnas, Maliranta and Vainiomaki, 2004). In those studies individuals in their 30s and 40s were found to have the highest productivity levels. Employees above the age of 50 were found to have lower productivity than younger individuals, despite their higher wage levels.

In a study of American companies, Hellerstein, Neumark and Troske (1999) estimated productivity to increase with age, with employees above age 55 contributing the most to output levels. The authors found, however, that peak productivity shifted to 35 to 54-year-olds when they used the companies' value added instead of output levels as an indicator of productivity. Moreover, an earlier analysis based on the same data set (Hellerstein, Neumark and Troske, 1996) concluded that workers' productivity decreased with age even when the companies' output was used as an indicator of productivity. Using more recent data, Hellerstein and Neumark (2004) have found a decrease in productivity from the mid-50s onward. Another recent study using French data (Aubert and Crépon, 2003) reports that productivity increases to ages 40 to 44 but the development at subsequent ages is uncertain.

A problem with the fact that most studies on age–productivity differences are based on cross-sectional evidence is that seniority leads to occupational shifts. Good workers tend to be promoted, whereas inefficient workers lose their jobs or are demoted. This can cause estimation bias, since selectivity increases with age. Employer–employee data sets also have a problem: a company's success can increase the number of new employees and thus lead to a younger work force, and this possibility may erroneously affect estimates because a young work force could be the consequence rather than the cause of a company's success. On the other hand, some workers may stay in the labor force simply because they cannot afford to retire.

Older individuals may be given less training than younger ones for lack of incentives, as both older workers and firms are likely to have a shorter period in which to benefit from investments in training. Wages could also have incentive effects. High wages could lead to somewhat higher productivity because well-paid individuals may be afraid of losing their jobs. Using a lagged measure of a company's age composition to estimate current productivity can overcome this problem, as worker influx to or outflow from the company will then have less effect on workers' productivity. Andersson, Holmlund and Lindh (2002) use such lagged measures of workers' ages in their analysis of employer–employee data, and their findings support the idea that older workers tend to be less productive than younger ones. But they also find that tertiary nontechnical workers tend to affect productivity positively until higher ages.

As the above discussion suggests, there is possibly a correlation between the share of older workers and the unobserved level of firm productivity. Unfortunately, our data are restricted to a cross-section in 2001 and allow us to control for observed heterogeneity across firms only. We capture firms' heterogeneity by including firm-specific characteristics in our regressions. Moreover, since labor is heterogeneous not only with regard to age, we also control for the educational, occupational and gender-specific structure of the work force. Our data do not include information on hours worked and allow us to control only for the share of part-time and full-time employees at the firm level. Despite these restrictions, our results are in line with the findings summarized in the Appendix. We find that productivity is lower for firms with a higher share of older workers and that this age–productivity pattern is caused mainly by the characteristics of small firms (those with fewer than 50 employees). For large firms the age–productivity profile becomes flat in the case of mining and manufacturing industries, whereas for the nonmanufacturing industries it is the share of younger workers, not the share of older ones, that decreases productivity.

The remainder of the chapter is structured as follows. First we present our data and describe the methodology used to estimate the age–productivity profile. Next we present our results for different subsamples of our data classified by industry and size of firms. In presenting the results we first estimate simple models in which we do not account for interaction effects between age and education. Then we examine the interaction between age and education of the work force. In the final section we summarize our conclusions.

DATA AND METHODOLOGY

Data

We use a cross-section of employer–employee matched data from Statistics Austria for the year 2001.[4] The data set emerged from matching individual data of structural business statistics[5] with the population census of Austria. It covers NACE (Nomenclature générale des activités économiques dans les Communautés européennes) sections C (mining and quarrying) to K (real estate, renting and business activities) and contains selected economic indicators of 34 375 enterprises as well as selected socio-demographic indicators of 1 563 873 employees. The economic indicators include, for example, information about branch affiliation, number of white-collar and blue-collar employees at the end of 2001, and the value added in 2001 from structural business statistics. Socio-demographic indicators taken from the population census provide information on age, education and occupation of individuals employed in establishments on 15 May 2001. Currently the construction of a panel is not possible because information on the plant-level classification number for each person interviewed in the census was available only in the 2001 census. Structural business statistics and census data can be merged only by using this indicator. Since value added is available only at the firm level,[6] our analysis is restricted to the firm level and not extended to the plant level.

Like Crépon, Deniau and Perez-Duarte (2002), we divide our sample into firm-level data from mining and manufacturing sectors (NACE sections C and D) and nonmanufacturing sectors (NACE sections E through K). We have measures of the age, education and occupation compositions of the work force of about 9000 firms in the mining and manufacturing sectors and of about 24 800 firms in the nonmanufacturing sectors. The data are somewhat 'noisy' for at least two reasons. First, in the population census the affiliation of individuals employed may be somewhat imprecise (owing to such factors as ascertainment error), so that matching is imperfect or somewhat uncertain in a minor number of cases. Put differently, according to the population census data, we have too many or too few employees for some firms. Second, economic data about enterprises refer to the status at the end of 2001, whereas data about the age and education of employees, as well as data on occupational affiliation, refer to the employment status in mid-May 2001 (the date of the population census). Consequently, not every employee in the population census could be assigned to a firm, nor could every enterprise be assigned to employees. For our analysis we assume that the matching process did not cause any systematic bias and that the sample is representative of Austrian industries.

The advantage of the data set is the combination of economic data (for example, value added) of enterprises, on the one hand, and socio-demographic data (such as age, gender, education and occupation) of employees for each firm, on the other. Socio-demographic data are not otherwise covered by structural business statistics. Similarly, the population census contains information on the characteristics of employees but no economic information on the firms the employees work for. The employer–employee matched data allow us not only to compare the productivity levels of enterprises with different age and educational structures of their employees, but also to control for possible firm-specific effects such as size and age of the firm or type of organization (for example, multi-plant versus single-plant firms).

Table 3.1 Employment and value added: all sectors of the Austrian economy, 2001

Code	Sector	Employment		Value added	
		In figures	Share (%)	In 1000 EUR	Share (%)
A/B	Agriculture and forestry/fishing	544 651	13.14	4 148 894	2.14
C	Mining and quarrying	7 322	0.18	830 871	0.43
D	Manufacturing	661 351	15.95	39 256 633	20.21
E	Electricity, gas and water supply	33 216	0.80	4 256 171	2.19
F	Construction	273 673	6.60	14 528 342	7.48
G	Wholesale and retail trade	613 215	14.79	25 623 723	13.19
H	Hotels and restaurants	224 066	5.40	8 283 104	4.26
I	Transport, storage and communication	258 826	6.24	13 926 884	7.17
J	Financial intermediation	117 355	2.83	10 376 919	5.34
K	Real estate, renting and business activities	418 493	10.09	32 720 192	16.84
L	Public administration, national defense and social security	250 443	6.04	11 821 248	6.08
M	Education system	206 628	4.98	10 392 142	5.35
N	Health and social work	345 283	8.33	10 464 595	5.39
O	Other community, social and personal service activities	182 112	4.39	7 176 125	3.69
P	Activities of households	9 892	0.24	471 759	0.24
	All sectors	4 146 526	100.00	194 277 602	100.00

Source: Statistics Austria (2005).

Table 3.1 summarizes the structure of employment and value added in all sectors of the Austrian economy in 2001 according to the National Accounts. Regarding employment and value added, the share of the mining and manufacturing sectors taken together is 16.13 percent and 20.64 percent, respectively. Sectors E through K comprise 46.75 percent of the employment and 56.11 percent of value added.

In Table 3.2 we report the number of employees and amount of value added for NACE classifications C through K as they resulted in our matched employer–employee data set. In the column denoted by 'Share(%)' we record the share of employees and respective value added that is captured

Table 3.2 Employment (yearly averages) and value added in sectors C through K: Austrian economy, 2001

Code	Sector	Employment		Value added	
		In figures	Share (%)	In 1000 EUR	Share (%)
C	Mining and quarrying	4612	84.04	502521	89.76
D	Manufacturing	543573	86.48	32521209	90.83
E	Electricity, gas and water supply	32765	96.64	4395017	97.74
F	Construction	157038	66.94	7584685	71.25
G	Wholesale and retail trade	355022	63.33	15429764	69.33
H	Hotels and restaurants	53795	25.41	1508133	29.18
I	Transport, storage and communication	199038	80.55	11256630	87.20
J	Financial intermediation	91746	78.29	11212241	84.92
K	Real estate, renting and business activities	165839	56.66	10023321	64.88
	All sectors	1603428	61.49	86848836	63.04

Source: Matched employer–employee data set, own calculations.

for each sector in the matched employer–employee data set as compared with the values from the Structural Business Statistics (see Statistics Austria, 2003). For instance, in sector C our created data set that resulted from matching the structural business statistics with the population census captures about 84 percent of the employees and about 90 percent of the value added as compared with the values reported in the Structural Business Statistics (Statistics Austria, 2003). The reasons why we capture only some of the firms reported in the Structural Business Statistics in our data set are twofold. First, small firms (with fewer than 20 employees) are underrepresented in the sample in the Structural Business Survey. Second, the Structural Business Survey is the fundamental basis for an extrapolation to the main part of the Austrian economy. Consequently the data we use represent a subset of business activities in Austria.

Descriptive statistics of the variables that we include in our econometric setup are given in Table 3.3. Log value added per worker in mining and manufacturing (sample 1) is about 3574 EUR and 3411 EUR in non-manufacturing sectors (sample 2). In the first sample the average firm has about 60 employees and is 18 years old. In the second subsample the average firm is smaller, with 42 employees, and also younger, at 15 years.

Table 3.3 Descriptive statistics: selected variables

Variables	Mining and manufacturing (C&D)		Nonmanufacturing (E through K)	
	Mean	Std. dev.	Mean	Std. dev.
Firm characteristics				
Ln (value added per worker)	3574	0.714	3411	0.974
Size of firm (in no. of persons employed)	60.40	204.87	41.71	441.58
Age of firm (in years)	17.68	16.22	15.15	15.55
Multiplant (0,1)	0.22	0.41	0.20	0.40
Employee characteristics				
Proportion by age				
under 30	0.28	0.19	0.26	0.23
30–49	0.55	0.20	0.56	0.27
over 49	0.16	0.17	0.18	0.24
Proportion by education				
basic	0.25	0.19	0.22	0.23
lower-secondary	0.63	0.21	0.56	0.30
upper-secondary	0.09	0.13	0.15	0.22
tertiary	0.03	0.08	0.07	0.18
Proportion by sex				
males	0.68	0.25	0.59	0.33
females	0.32	0.25	0.41	0.32
Proportion by occupation				
self-employed	0.12	0.24	0.24	0.34
white-collar	0.28	0.24	0.41	0.37
blue-collar	0.53	0.26	0.31	0.33
apprenticeship	0.07	0.10	0.04	0.09
home worker	0.003	0.03	0.002	0.05
Proportion by time worked				
part-time	0.10	0.16	0.14	0.22
full-time	0.90	0.16	0.86	0.22

Source: Matched employer–employee data set, own calculations.

On average, about 20 percent of all firms are multiplant firms in both sectors. The share of part-time employees is slightly more significant in the nonmanufacturing industries than in the manufacturing industries (14 percent versus 10 percent).

We group the employees into three age groups: young employees (below age 30), prime-age employees (ages 30–49) and older employees (above age 49).[7] The distribution of these age shares is similar in both subsamples, though the standard deviation indicates a higher variance in the nonmanufacturing industries. The share of prime-age workers dominates in both subsamples, accounting for more than 50 percent of all employees on average.

Educational levels are grouped by attainment into (a) basic education (up to nine years); (b) lower-secondary education, which includes apprenticeships and normally between 10 and 12 years of schooling; (c) upper-secondary education, which encompasses the Austrian gymnasium and its equivalents, such as corresponding nonacademic vocational training at a similar level (secondary colleges); and (d) tertiary education, including postgraduate studies, the training of teachers for primary school and for the gymnasium, training in art academics, and so on. The lower-secondary educational level is the most prevalent category in the industries considered, and its share is highest in the mining and manufacturing industries, accounting for 63 percent of employees. Tertiary education accounts respectively for only 3 percent (first subsample) and 7 percent (second subsample) of the employees. As with the age categories, the standard deviations of educational characteristics are higher in the nonmanufacturing than in the manufacturing sector.

The share of female workers is higher in the nonmanufacturing industries, accounting for 41 percent of the employees on average. In the mining and manufacturing industries the share of females among all employees is only 32 percent.

We group occupational affiliations into five categories: self-employed, white-collar, blue-collar, apprenticeship and home worker. The distribution on this variable varies across the two groups of industries. In the nonmanufacturing sector, white-collar employees account on average for 41 percent, blue-collar employees for 31 percent and the self-employed for 24 percent. Apprenticeship employees and home workers are rather small groups. In the mining and manufacturing industries blue-collar workers constitute the biggest group, representing 53 percent of all employees on average. White-collar workers and the self-employed are less common there than in the nonmanufacturing sector. Again, the standard deviation across these categories is lower in the mining and manufacturing industries.

Methodology

As do Crépon, Deniau and Perez-Duarte (2002), we assume perfect substitutability of workers of different types $k = 0,\ldots,K$.[8] The total amount of human capital, L^*, can be written as:

$$L^* = \sum_0^K \lambda_k L_k = \lambda_0 L + \sum_1^K (\lambda_k - \lambda_0) L_k = L\lambda_0 \left(1 + \sum_1^K \left(\frac{\lambda_k}{\lambda_0} - 1\right) \frac{L_k}{L}\right)$$
$$= L\lambda_0 \left(1 + \sum_1^K \gamma_k W_k\right), \tag{3.1}$$

where L is the sum of the labor input, λ_0 is the productivity of the workers taken as the reference category, $(L_k/L) = W_k$ denotes the share of workers of type k and γ_k is equal to $(\lambda_k/\lambda_0 - 1)$. Applying the approximation $\log(1+x) \sim x$ we can write (3.1) as: [9]

$$\log(L^*) = \log(L) + \log(\lambda_0) + \log\left(1 + \sum_1^K \gamma_k W_k\right)$$
$$= \log(L) + \log(\lambda_0) + \sum_1^K \gamma_k W_k. \tag{3.2}$$

As discussed in Crépon, Deniau and Perez-Duarte (2002,7ff), 'by crossing the different types of variables (gender, qualification, age), we can classify the work force in a great number of categories: young unskilled males, young unskilled females, and so on'. To reduce the number of categories, they introduce an approach that they term the 'simple model'. In principle their approach assumes either that relative coefficients across a group are equal along all other characteristics or that the categories are overlapping and not disjoint. For instance, if we assume the existence of three age groups and four occupational groups, the simple model would exclude one age group and one occupational group as the reference category and include the remaining two age groups and three occupational groups as the variables that characterize the labor force. By following this approach we assume that the relative coefficients on the age categories are the same across all occupational groups and similarly that the relative coefficients on the occupational categories are the same across the age categories. A model that would account for the interaction of age and occupational groups would include 11 age–occupational categories, leaving out one of the groups as the reference category. This model is termed an 'extended model' in Crépon, Deniau and Perez-Duarte (2002).

Owing to the lack of appropriate data on the capital stock[10] at the firm level, we restrict our analysis to labor productivity defined as value added per employee at the firm level and denoted by v_i where i indicates the firm. We then estimate a multivariate linear model in which we regress log value added per employee on the log level of human capital as defined in equation (3.2) and additional firm-specific characteristics X_i to account for firm heterogeneity. Our final model is

$$\log(v_i) = const. + \sum_{1}^{K} \gamma_{ki} W_{ki} + X_i + \varepsilon_i, \tag{3.3}$$

where the subscript *i* denotes the firm level. The inclusion of additional firm-specific characteristics is aimed at capturing the heterogeneity across firms.

In the empirical analysis we shall differentiate labor by age, gender, educational attainment, occupational classification and number of hours worked (cf. Table 3.3). Unfortunately we can apply only a rough classification for hours worked into part-time versus full-time employment. For firm characteristics we include the size and age of the firm and whether or not it is a multiplant firm.

STATISTICAL ESTIMATES FOR THE RELATION BETWEEN PRODUCTIVITY, AGE AND EDUCATIONAL STRUCTURE

Simple Model Estimates

We perform the following regressions at the enterprise level. The dependent variable is the logarithm of value added per worker. The denominator is the average number of workers in 2001 as contained in the structural business statistics. Whenever possible, the independent variables are taken from the structural business statistics. However, several socio-demographic variables, such as age and educational level (both measured as shares), have to be taken from the set of workers that was matched with the 2001 census. Since we could not match all workers, this implies that some of the independent variables are based on a sample that is smaller than the number of workers in the structural business statistics. We assume that the matching procedure did not produce any selectivity and have checked this assumption for variables that are available in both the structural business statistics and the census (for example, employee's gender). The results of the estimates are shown in Table 3.4 for the mining and manufacturing industries (subsample 1) and in Table 3.5 for the nonmanufacturing industries (subsample 2).

At this point a clarification is in order. The regression coefficients presented in the subsequent tables indicate the marginal effect of an increase in the respective share, assuming that the omitted share adjusts.

In the first model (1) value added per worker is regressed on three age-share variables, four educational-share variables and the share of gender. As reference category we choose prime age, basic education and male

Table 3.4 Basic regressions for mining and manufacturing (C&D) on enterprise level (all size classes)

Variable	(1)	(2)	(3)	VIF for (3)
Young	−0.05	−0.18**	−0.07*	1.53
Older	−0.27**	−0.15**	−0.15**	1.20
Tertiary education	0.30**	0.35**	−0.07	1.24
Upper-secondary education	0.46**	0.55**	0.18**	1.50
Lower-secondary education	−0.13**	0.08*	0.06	1.56
Female	−0.65**	−0.57**	−0.57**	1.26
Ln Size of firm		0.16**	0.03**	2.07
Ln Age of firm		0.02**	0.02**	1.05
Multiplant		−0.04*	−0.04**	1.16
Self-employed			−1.51**	2.24
Blue-collar			−0.53**	1.82
Apprenticeship			−1.50**	1.51
Home worker			−1.28**	1.04
Part-time			−0.50**	1.21
Constant	3.87**	3.23**	4.25**	
R square	0.07	0.20	0.30	
F-test	110.39**	197.09**	267.47**	
No. of observations	9012	8882	8882	

Notes: * significant at 5 percent; ** significant at 1 percent; reference category: prime age, basic education, male, white-collar, full-time.

employees. These estimates indicate a hump-shaped pattern for the age variable for our first subsample (Table 3.4); that is, firms where the share of young or old workers increases by 1 percent (and the share of prime-age workers adjusts) exhibit on average only 95 percent and 73 percent, respectively, of the productivity. To calculate the effect of an increase in the share of old workers, assuming that the share of young workers adjusts, one can take the difference between the two coefficients: $-0.27+0.05$. Note, however, that the negative effect on the young age share is not significant.

The results are different for our second subsample (Table 3.5), where the pattern of the age variable is declining. Firms where the share of young workers or old workers increases have respectively a higher and a lower productivity. These results could partly reflect the endogeneity of worker flows; that is, more productive firms may hire more employees and these are mainly in the younger age groups. As it will turn out, by controlling for firm characteristics, part of the heterogeneity at the firm level can be captured and the coefficient on the young age share loses significance for the second subsample.

Table 3.5 Basic regressions for nonmanufacturing (E–K) on enterprise level (all size classes)

Variable	(1)	(2)	(3)	VIF for (3)
Young	0.28**	0.04	−0.06	1.36
Older	−0.19**	−0.17**	−0.13**	1.18
Tertiary education	0.57**	0.72**	0.38**	1.50
Upper-secondary education	0.55**	0.63**	0.26**	1.74
Lower-secondary education	0.19**	0.24**	0.10**	1.94
Female	−0.41**	−0.37**	−0.45**	1.23
Ln Size of firm		0.16**	−0.004	2.37
Ln Age of firm		0.09**	0.07**	1.14
Multiplant		−0.09**	−0.04*	1.27
Self-employed			−1.41**	2.21
Blue-collar			−0.53**	1.57
Apprenticeship			−1.04**	1.28
Home worker			−0.65**	1.02
Part-time			−0.78**	
Constant	3.32**	2.76**	4.01**	
R square	0.04	0.12	0.23	
F-test	190.36**	347.92**	527.01**	
No. of observations	24798	23964	23964	

Notes: * significant at 5 percent; ** significant at 1 percent; reference category: prime age, basic education, male, white-collar, full-time.

For education we find that an increase in the share of tertiary and upper-secondary education positively affects productivity in Tables 3.4 and 3.5, model (1). For lower-secondary education the results are different across the two subsamples. Whereas a higher share of lower-secondary education increases productivity in Table 3.5, it decreases productivity in Table 3.4. It may well be that employees with lower-secondary education are more likely matched to low-productivity firms. Again, by including firm characteristics, part of the heterogeneity can be captured and lower-secondary education becomes insignificant in our first subsample.

The coefficient of the gender shares has to be interpreted with caution. Although in both subsamples (Tables 3.4 and 3.5) a higher share of females exerts a negative effect on productivity (the effect is stronger in the first subsample), this does not necessarily mean that females work less productively. One reason for our findings could be that proportionately more female workers work in branches with low labor productivity. Since we are working only with cross-sectional data we cannot control for such endogenous selection of employees by firms. Another reason could be that, on average, females do not have high levels of education and may be more likely to work part-time. Although we have controlled for education and the share of part-time work (compare model 3), the latter covariate is unsatisfactory since we cannot control for the number of hours worked. It is reasonable to assume that part-time work may be based on fewer hours worked for industries with high female shares. As a consequence the variable for part-time share may not capture the whole story and the remaining effect of fewer hours worked on productivity is captured by the female share.

In model 2, we extend the econometric setup by adding firm-specific variables such as the logarithm of the size of the firm (in terms of the number of employees and measured by a continuous variable), the logarithm of the firm's age (measured by a continuous variable) and whether or not it is a multiplant firm (coded as a dummy variable). Our argument is that the employee's age variable may be correlated to firm characteristics, most obviously a firm's age, and hence employee's age may be correlated to the error term if we do not control for the age of the firm. Failure to control for firm characteristics would therefore imply the classical omitted-variable bias.

When firm-specific characteristics are added, the coefficients of the other variables – and in particular those on age shares – remain rather stable. The hump-shaped pattern of the age profile in Table 3.4 is robust and not caused by firm-specific effects, at least not by those we have taken into account. For the subsample of nonmanufacturing industries, however, the positive effect of the share of young workers becomes insignificant, indicating that the share of younger workers may be correlated to the age of the firm. The coefficients on the educational shares are robust, with the exception that, by including firm-specific characteristics, lower-secondary education no longer negatively affects productivity in the mining and manufacturing sectors. It is interesting to see that the size of the firm increases productivity by about 16 percent in both subsamples. This could be an indicator of slight economies of scale, and the effect is the same for both subsamples (Tables 3.4 and 3.5). The age of the firm has a positive effect, indicating that older firms are slightly more productive than younger ones. Likewise, multiplant firms have lower productivity than single-plant firms. Various arguments can be suggested to explain these findings. Firm-specific economies of scale could be present and are more likely in single-plant firms. Informal social communication among employees could be better in single-plant firms. Multiplant firms need administrative departments for each plant, which could increase their fixed costs. The fact that multiplant firms are more prevalent in specific industries, however, could indicate that lower productivity is not a feature of multiplant firms as such, but rather characteristic of those industries in which they are prevalent.

In model 3 we add a further set of variables, which measures the share of workers in various occupations and the share of part-time workers. We take white-collar workers and full-time workers as the reference category. Once we include the occupational structure and the part-time share of workers in firms as additional variables, the negative marginal effect of the young workers declines to only 7 percent in the first subsample (Table 3.4) and becomes insignificant in the second subsample. From the coefficients for the occupational structure we may conclude that productivity is lower in firms with a higher share of self-employed workers, blue-collar workers, apprentices and home workers relative to the share of white-collar workers. In addition, the share of part-time workers is negatively related to productivity, and this effect is stronger for the nonmanufacturing sector. Again, these results need to be interpreted with caution since we cannot control for the endogeneity of the regressors. Less productive firms may be forced to increase their share of part-time workers or may attract employees who opt for a lower number of working hours. The fact that the hump-shaped pattern of age – in particular the negative coefficient on older workers – is slightly reduced across models 1 to 3 indicates that part of the age-structure effect is indeed due to the endogeneity of the employees' age structure.

With respect to the educational structure of the work force we may conclude that for mining and manufacturing industries only the positive effect of upper-secondary education is robust, and this effect decreases across the three models. Once we take age and occupational characteristics of the work force as well as firm characteristics into account, we find that firms with a higher share of employees with upper-secondary education are more productive by about 18 percent (Table 3.4). For the second subsample (Table 3.5) we find a robust positive educational gradient, though it decreases over the three models. A higher share of employees with lower-secondary education is related to a 10 percent increase in productivity, whereas an increase in the share of employees with tertiary education is related to a 38 percent increase.

Aubert and Crépon (2003), who estimated the age effect on productivity in a panel data design for France (cf. Table A3.1), showed that the age profile might be sensitive to the control of heterogeneity and simultaneity bias. Their findings indicated a rising and concave age profile of productivity at least up to ages 40–44 when they controlled for all types of biases. When they did not control for the heterogeneity bias or simultaneity, they found a negative bias for older workers, which is consistent with the fact that older workers are more often matched to lower-productivity firms (heterogeneity bias) and that older workers show a slower adjustment to exogenous productivity shocks; that is, they are less mobile than younger workers (simultaneity bias).

With reference to the findings of Aubert and Crépon (2003), part of our negative age effect could be caused by heterogeneity and simultaneity bias. The fact that the negative age effect declined over models 1 through 3 indeed suggests that this may be the case. Since our data are restricted to a cross-section, however, we are not able to apply the required panel-data methods to correct for those biases.

The lack of robustness for some covariates when we move from model 1 to model 3 could also indicate a problem of multicollinearity.[11] To assess the multicollinearity in our set of independent variables we have calculated the Variance Inflation Factor (VIF) that measures the inflation in the variances of the parameter estimates due to collinearities that exist among the regressors. As indicated in the fourth column of Tables 3.4 and 3.5, these factors are rather small (well below the threshold level of 4 commonly suggested in empirical analysis to qualify as multicollinearity).

In a next step we again divided each subsample into one subsample of small firms with a maximum work force of 49 employees and another subsample of large firms with a work force of 50 or more employees. Thus we investigated the influence of firm size in more detail (Tables 3.6 and 3.7). The numbers of observations are very unequal. The sample of small firms contains more than three times as many observations as the sample of large firms in the mining and manufacturing sector, and this ratio increases to 6 to 1 for the nonmanufacturing sectors. The large number of small firms reflects the dominance of small and medium-sized enterprises in the Austrian economy. In our sample the share of large firms is larger than the figures stated by Statistics Austria (2003) because large firms are overrepresented in the structural business statistics sample of Statistics Austria.

We estimate model 3, which includes firm characteristics, occupational categories and part-time shares in addition to the age and educational structure of the work force for each subsample; that is, small versus large firms and the two subsamples of mining and manufacturing versus nonmanufacturing industries. The results for small firms differ from those for large firms. For small firms we find similar results, in particular for the age and educational profile, as we found in Tables 3.4 and 3.5, where we did not distinguish by firm size. There are some noteworthy differences, however. A higher share of younger workers in the mining and manufacturing industries is no longer related to a lower level of productivity. The coefficient of the dummy for multiplant firms is insignificant in the mining and manufacturing industries. A plausible explanation is that small enterprises are hardly ever organized as multiplant firms. For the nonmanufacturing small-sized industries the results are again similar to those obtained for the whole sample.

In the analysis of large firms, observations having log value added below 2 and above 6 were classified as outliers and removed from the sample. The

Table 3.6 Basic regressions for mining and manufacturing (C&D) on enterprise level, small firms (fewer than 50 employees) versus large firms (more than 50 employees)

Variable	Small firms	Large firms
Young	−0.02	−0.15
Older	−0.17**	0.23
Tertiary education	−0.16	1.16**
Upper-secondary education	0.19**	−0.03
Lower-secondary education	0.04	0.27*
Female	−0.56**	−0.57**
Ln Size of firm	−0.04**	0.11**
Ln Age of firm	0.02**	0.01
Multiplant	−0.03	−0.09**
Self-employed	−1.66**	−4.61**
Blue-collar	−0.49**	−0.38**
Apprenticeship	−1.45**	−1.83**
Home worker	−1.26**	−0.32
Part-time	−0.53**	−0.21
Constant	4.39**	3.60**
R square	0.28	0.18
F-test	195.33**	29.71**
No. of observations	6948	1934

Notes: * significant at 5 percent; ** significant at 1 percent; reference category: prime age, basic education, male, white-collar, full-time.

sample size was reduced by only a few firms. The results of the regressions are shown in Tables 3.6 and 3.7, second column, and they differ from those on the whole sample. Most interestingly, for both subsamples of industries a higher share of older workers is no longer related to a lower level of productivity. For the mining and manufacturing sector no clear pattern of the effect of the age structure on productivity can be observed in large firms. A plausible explanation could be that generous social programs cause the layoff of the older workers in larger firms. Hence larger firms may be more able to optimize their age structure. In smaller firms less productive older workers are still occupied. Another plausible argument may be that, for larger firms, we observe a dominance of physical capital over human capital and hence we cannot discern any significant pattern for the age structure.[12] For the nonmanufacturing industries it is now the share of young workers that is negatively correlated to productivity. The latter result may be explained by the fact that younger employees are predominantly in

Table 3.7 Basic regressions for nonmanufacturing (E through K) on enterprise level, small firms (fewer than 50 employees) versus large firms (more than 50 employees)

Variable	Small firms	Large firms
Young	−0.01	−1.00**
Older	−0.14**	0.02
Tertiary education	0.34**	1.37**
Upper-secondary education	0.21**	1.90**
Lower-secondary education	0.09	0.69**
Female	−0.45**	−0.27**
Ln Size of firm	−0.02**	0.02
Ln Age of firm	0.07**	0.07**
Multiplant	−0.04*	−0.03
Self-employed	−1.44**	0.12
Blue-collar	−0.54**	−0.10
Apprenticeship	−0.97**	−0.13
Home worker	0.82**	0.40
Part-time	−0.78**	−0.88**
Constant	4.07**	3.29**
R square	0.22	0.29
F-test	427.16**	89.90**
No. of observations	20 825	3139

Notes: * significant at 5 percent; ** significant at 1 percent; reference category: prime age, basic education, male, white-collar, full-time.

apprenticeship and hence do not yet fully contribute to productivity. Apprenticeship is also more prevalent in larger firms, as verified by a significant correlation coefficient of 0.21 in the nonmanufacturing industries. (The corresponding correlation coefficient in the manufacturing industries is not significant.)

A further interesting result indicated in Tables 3.6 and 3.7 is that, for larger firms, but not smaller ones, increasing shares of higher education are positively correlated with higher productivity. For the nonmanufacturing industries an increase in the share of tertiary education among employees is correlated to an increase in firm-level productivity that is more than twice as high as that in firms without such a share of tertiary education. For the mining and manufacturing industries a similar result can be observed. In contrast to small firms, in large ones it is the shares of the tertiary and lower-secondary education that are correlated to an increase in productivity for the mining and manufacturing sector. Our findings therefore indicate that formal qualification seems to be of greater importance in larger than in smaller firms.

Two other interesting results are observed for large firms, in contrast to small ones. For the mining and manufacturing industries the share of part-time workers loses significance, whereas for the nonmanufacturing industries the share of female workers is less negatively correlated to productivity.

Extended Model Estimates

So far our estimates indicate that an increase in the share of older workers reduces productivity at the firm level (model 3 in Tables 3.4 and 3.5). The results on the educational share are mixed. We find a positive effect on productivity for firms in mining and manufacturing industries if the share of upper-secondary education increases. For firms in the nonmanufacturing sectors the effect coefficient on the educational share variable is positive; that is, productivity increases with increasing shares of higher education.

Distinguishing the sample by the size of firms, we find that the effect coefficients on the age and educational share variables are not robust. While the share of older workers is negatively related to productivity in the sample of small firms, we find no significant age share effects for large firms in the sample of mining and manufacturing industries and a negative effect of the share of young employees in the sample of nonmanufacturing industries. The results on the educational share variable are rather mixed. For the mining and manufacturing sector we find that for small firms the share of upper-secondary education and for large firms the share of tertiary and lower-secondary education is positively correlated to productivity. For firms in the nonmanufacturing sector the effect coefficients on the educational share variables are consistent over all subsamples, although for large firms the highest productivity effects are obtained if the share of upper-secondary and not, as in case of small firms, the share of tertiary education, increases.

It is puzzling that the share of upper-secondary education seems to have a more positive effect than the share of tertiary education for the overall sample and for the small-firm sample in the mining and manufacturing sector as well as for the large-firm sample of the nonmanufacturing industries. As already noted, these effects may be caused by the low share of tertiary education, the correlation between age and educational share variables, or both. That the effects may be due to the correlation between age and educational share variables reflects the fact that educational attainment as well as educational quality may be higher in younger than in older cohorts.

For a more detailed view of the way labor composition and productivity of the plant are connected, we can subdivide the work force into finer categories that do not overlap. In this way we differentiate between the education of different age groups and thus compensate for the changes that have taken place both in the overall supply of education among different cohorts and in its content and hence its relevance for current technology.

To control for these possible interaction effects, we introduce a new variable that divides the work force into finer categories that do not overlap. Within each age group we differentiate several educational groups. This yields 12 nonoverlapping categories, and we choose young workers of primary education as the reference category.

The coefficients on the age-educational variable are depicted in Figure 3.1 for firms in the mining and manufacturing sectors (subsample 1) and in Figure 3.2 for firms in the nonmanufacturing sectors (subsample 2). Within each subsample we present three figures: (a) all firms, (b) small firms and (c) large firms, and plot only those coefficients that turned out to be significant.

In Figure 3.1, panels a and b imply that there is a clear difference in the level of educational attainment independent of age structure for the whole sample and the small-firm sample. Upper-secondary education indeed yields the highest productivity irrespective of the age group. We ignore the shape of the tertiary educational level since none of the age effects within this group is significant. This could be partly explained by the fact that the share of tertiary education is rather low in all age groups. It will be low in the young age group because at young ages individuals with tertiary education have not yet entered the labor force. For the prime-age and old-age groups we may expect low numbers caused by the cohort effect: not many in those groups have had the opportunity of tertiary education. Most interestingly, once we include the interaction of age and educational structure the coefficient on the old-age share loses significance. The lower productivity for firms with a higher share of young workers in Table 3.4, model 3, seems to be caused by the young workers with basic education only and does not hold for the other educational categories. The fact that the share of young workers loses significance if we restrict our sample to small firms seems to be caused only by the cancellation of two effects (Figure 3.1, panel b). Within upper-secondary education the share of younger workers has the highest positive effect on productivity while the share of younger workers has the lowest positive effect on productivity within basic schooling. In Figure 3.1, panel c, we plot the results, restricting our sample to large firms. Note, however, that except for the old-age share among workers with lower-secondary education, and the young-age share among those with tertiary education, none of the other coefficients is significant.

In Figure 3.2 we plot the age-educational share coefficients for firms in the nonmanufacturing industries. The results are straightforward. Irrespective of age we find a positive educational gradient for the whole sample (panel a) and the sample of small firms (panel b), but not for the sample of large firms. Except for basic schooling we find a hump-shaped

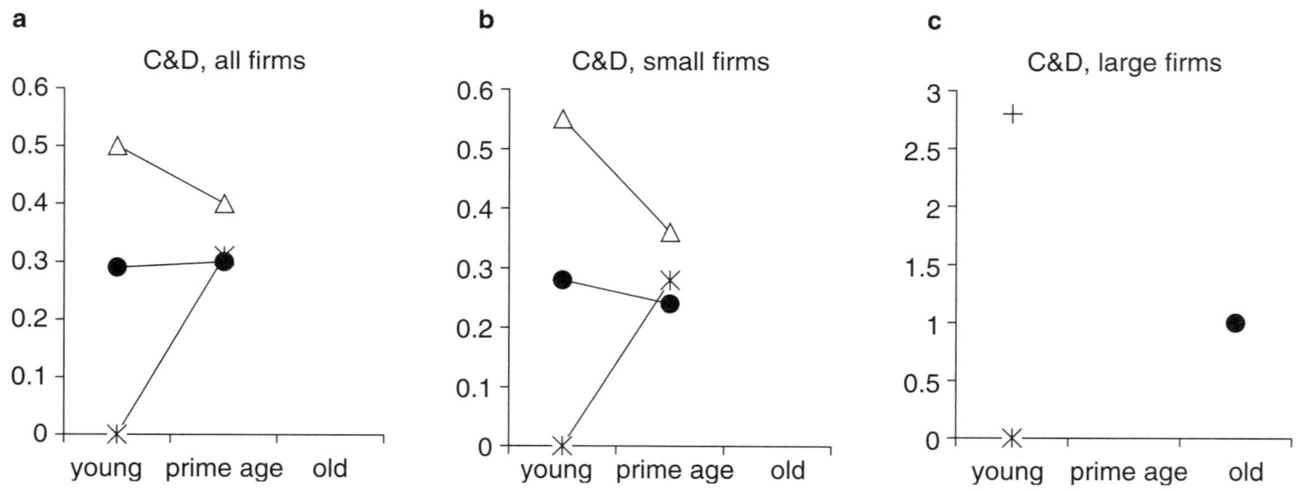

Notes: * = basic education, • = lower secondary education, Δ = upper secondary education, + = tertiary education. Reference category: young, basic education. We plot only significant marginal effects.

Figure 3.1 Estimated coefficient values with disjunctive age–education shares (model 3)

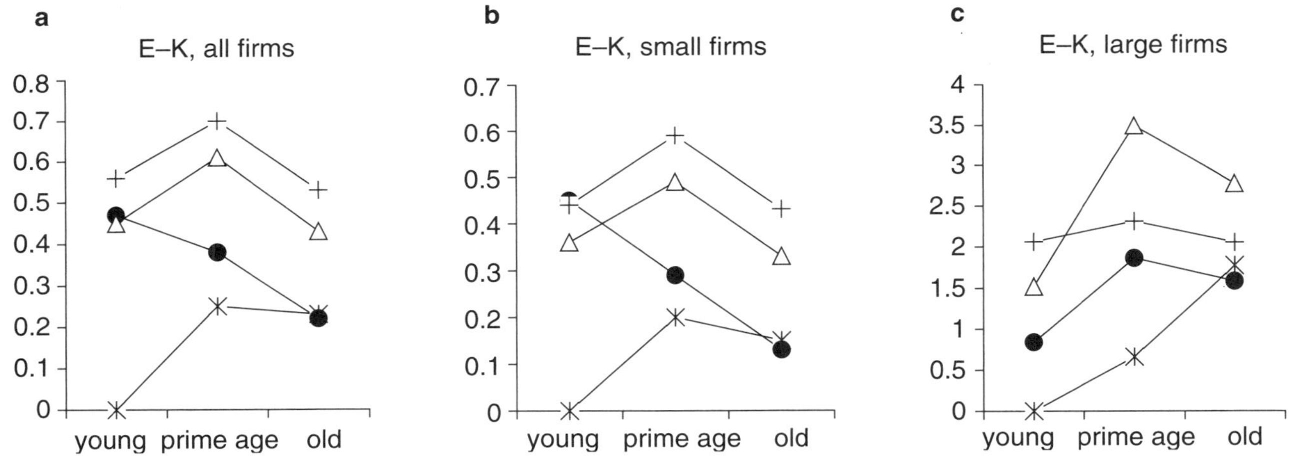

Notes: * = basic education, • = lower secondary education, Δ = upper secondary education, + = tertiary education; reference category: young, basic education. We only plot significant marginal effects.

Figure 3.2 Estimated coefficient values with disjunctive age–education shares (model 3)

and respectively decreasing (in case of upper-secondary schooling) age–productivity profile. For large firms (panel c) we observe that the productivity gains are highest if the share of upper-secondary education increases, and this pattern is rather consistent across age groups (except for young employees). Note that the specific age–productivity profiles for basic education and upper-secondary education may drive the results we obtained in Table 3.7, where we found that the share of younger workers was negatively related to productivity whereas the share of older workers had an insignificant effect. A plausible explanation may be that in large firms there are enough workers in these specific age and educational groups for these effects to be revealed. The lower values on the younger age groups in the upper-secondary educational group compared with the prime-age and old-age groups could be explained intuitively by a negative tenure effect. On the one hand, those employees, though having attained a higher level of education, have not yet obtained the experience necessary for the production process. On the other hand, the explanation for the increasing levels of productivity when age increases within the group with basic education could be that these are positively selected employees and that, for those with basic education, the negative vintage effect of human capital accumulation is compensated by the positive tenure effect.

Summing up, though the interpretation of the interaction effects is necessarily of a speculative nature (since we cannot control for selectivity or unobserved heterogeneity, nor are we able to disentangle cohort, age and period effects), the results in Figures 3.1 and 3.2 support our previous findings. Our assumption that relative coefficients across age groups are equal among the educational groups (as we assumed in Tables 3.4 through 3.7 by applying a model without interaction) seems to hold for most of the results.

CONCLUSIONS

Summing up the microevidence for Austrian industries, we find a negative productivity effect of the share of older workers (50 years and older) for the whole sample and for small firms (irrespective of the economic sector we consider), which is similar to the finding of most employer–employee studies analyzed in Table A3.1. If we restrict our sample to large firms, the age-productivity profile changes. For firms in the mining and manufacturing industries the age structure of the work force cannot be related to productivity whereas for firms in the nonmanufacturing sectors only the share of younger workers can be related to productivity, namely negatively. Our results are similar to the findings of Crépon, Deniau and Perez-Duarte (2002) for large firms; they also found a concave age-productivity profile.

Though the sample size decreases when we move to large firms, we are more confident in our results for this subsample since in larger firms we may expect that all age and educational shares are represented.

For educational shares we found mixed results. In the mining and manufacturing sector it is the share of upper-secondary education that increases productivity. For firms in the nonmanufacturing industries we find a positive educational gradient: the higher the education, the greater the increase in productivity.

Results for a more detailed work force composition that includes the interaction of age and educational shares do not yield new insights. We may therefore conclude that the age and educational share coefficients are rather stable across educational and, respectively, large age categories.

Our results for the other control variables (size and age of firm, occupational structure, gender decomposition of the work force) are similar to findings in the literature so far. For instance, Crépon, Deniau and Perez-Duarte (2002) also found that an increase in the female share of employees decreases productivity, though to a smaller extent (about 11 percent in manufacturing and 7 percent in nonmanufacturing) than in our results.

As we have indicated throughout the text, our results need to be interpreted with caution since we cannot control for endogeneity of the regressors within our cross-sectional data set. A clear result of our study is the differing age–productivity profile in small versus large firms. We find that the share of older workers is negatively related to productivity only for small firms. As we argued, this result may indicate that larger firms are more able to optimize their age structure or alternatively that within larger firms the age structure of the employees is of less importance than other factors of production. A third alternative hypothesis, more related to the mode of production, could be that the substitutability of workers at different ages is different in small versus large firms. In our econometric setup of the model we assumed perfect substitutability of workers at different ages. Future research needs to verify this assumption.

Our study cannot offer definite policy advice regarding the productivity of older workers and their employability as it concerns the increase in retirement age. Our study does indicate, however, that part of the negative effect of the share of older workers on productivity we find may be firm-specific rather than individual-specific given that the effect disappears for large firms.

NOTES

1. The project has been funded by EU tender VT/2004/056 and the Austrian National Bank under contract number ÖNB11621.A preliminary draft of the paper was presented at the

workshop on 'Population Aging, Intergenerational Transfers, and the Macroeconomy' in Tokyo, June 2006. We thank the participants of the workshop and in particular the discussant for helpful comments and suggestions.
2. The EU-15 countries include Austria, Belgium, Denmark, Finland, France, Germany, Greece, Ireland, Italy, Luxembourg, Netherlands, Portugal, Spain, Sweden and United Kingdom.
3. A survey of analyses based on matched employer–employee data can be found in Abowd and Kramarz (1999).
4. For a more detailed description of the data and variables, see Prskawetz and Lindh (2006).
5. Our data are collected from the Structural Business Survey (year 2001) of Statistics Austria. The Structural Business Statistics are produced by extrapolating the results of the survey to the main part of the Austrian economy. For details of sample selection and the focus of the survey as well as the extrapolation mechanism, see Statistics Austria (2003).
6. We use the term 'firm' or 'enterprise' interchangeably to denote the unit of analysis.
7. We have tried a finer age structure, but our results are robust. For ease of comparability with other studies we have opted for three age groups.
8. Marginal productivities may differ among the different types of employees.
9. This approximation will be valid as long as x is rather small. In our case the approximation may be rather crude (since x represents the sum of share variables). We follow the convention in the literature and apply the approximation that facilitates the application of a linear regression.
10. Ilmakunnas and Maliranta (2002) use a step-by-step procedure in which they start off by including a comprehensive set of independent variables in their productivity estimates and show that, by applying a more and more limited data set (which also excludes capital), they obtain fairly consistent results.
11. We thank one of the referees for suggesting this point to us.
12. We thank the discussant for pointing out this argument to us.

REFERENCES

Abowd, John M. and Francis Kramarz (1999), 'The analysis of labour markets using matched employer–employee data', in Orley Ashenfelter and David Card (eds), *Handbook of Labour Economics*, vol. 3, Amsterdam: Elsevier Science, pp. 2630–72.

Andersson, B., B. Holmlund and T. Lindh (2002), 'Labor productivity, age and education in Swedish mining and manufacturing, 1985–96', mimeo, Department of Economics, University of Uppsala, Sweden.

Aubert, P. and B. Crépon (2003), 'La productivité des salariés âgés: une tentative d'estimation', *Economie et Statistique*, **368**, 95–119.

Crépon, B., N. Deniau and S. Perez-Duarte (2002), 'Wages, productivity and worker characteristics: a French perspective', mimeo, Institut National de la Statistique et d'Études Économiques (INSEE), Paris, France.

Dostie, Benoit (2006), 'Wages, productivity and aging', mimeo, 20 January; available at client.norc.org/jole/SOLEweb/Dostie.pdf.

Eurostat New Cronos (2006), Source Eurostat delivered 13 July by ESDS International (MIMAS) University of Manchester.

Grund, C. and N. Westergård-Nielsen (2005), 'Age structure of the workforce and firm performance', IZA Discussion Paper no. 1816, Institute for the Study of Labor, Bonn, Germany.

Hægeland, Torbjørn and Tor Jakob Klette (1999), 'Do higher wages reflect higher productivity? Education, gender and experience premiums in a matched plant-worker data set', in J.L. Haltiwanger, J.R. Spletzer, J. Theeuwes and K. Troske (eds), *The Creation and Analysis of Employer–Employee Matched Data*, Amsterdam: Elsevier Science.

Haltiwanger, J.C., J.I. Lane and J.R. Spletzer (1999), 'Productivity differences across employers: the roles of employer size, age and human capital', *American Economic Review*, **89**(2), 94–8.

Hellerstein, J.K. and D. Neumark (1995), 'Are earnings profiles steeper than productivity profiles? Evidence from Israeli firm-level data', *Journal of Human Resources*, **30**(1), 89–112.

Hellerstein, J.K. and D. Neumark (2004), 'Production function and wage equation estimation with heterogeneous labor: evidence from a new matched employer–employee data set', NBER Working Paper no. 10325, National Bureau of Economic Research, Cambridge, Massachusetts.

Hellerstein, J.K., D. Neumark and K.R. Troske (1996), 'Wages, productivity and worker characteristics: evidence from plant level production function and wage equations', NBER Working Paper Series. no. 5626, National Bureau of Economic Research, Cambridge, Massachusetts.

Hellerstein, J.K., D. Neumark and K.R. Troske (1999), 'Wages, productivity and worker characteristics: evidence from plant level production function and wage equations', *Journal of Labor Economics*, **17**, 409–46.

Ilmakunnas, P. and M. Maliranta (2002), 'Labor characteristics and wage–productivity gaps', paper presented at the DILEED (Database Integration and Linked Employer-Employee Data) Conference, Wellington, New Zealand, 21–22 March.

Ilmakunnas, P., M. Maliranta and J. Vainiomaki (2004), 'The roles of employer and employee characteristics for plant productivity', *Journal of Productivity Analysis*, **21**, 249–76.

OECD (Organisation for Economic Co-operation and Development) (2005), *Ageing and Employment Policies. Austria*, Paris.

Prskawetz, Alexia and Thomas Lindh (eds) (2006), *The Impact of Ageing on Innovation and Productivity Growth in Europe*, Research Report no. 28, Vienna Institute of Demography, Austrian Academy of Sciences.

Prskawetz, Alexia, Thomas Fent and Ross Guest (2006), 'Workforce ageing and labor productivity: the role of supply and demand for labor in the G7', in Alexia Prskawetz, David Bloom and Wolfgang Lutz (eds) (2007), *Population Aging, Human Capital Accumulation, and Productivity Growth*, supplement to *Population and Development Review*.

Skirbekk, Vegard (2004), 'Age and individual productivity: a literature survey', in G. Gustav Feichtinger (ed.), *Vienna Yearbook of Population Research*, Vienna: Verlag der Österreichischen Akademie der Wissenschaften, pp. 133–54.

Statistics Austria (2003), *Leistungs und Strukturerhebung 2002* (Structural Business Statistics Manufacturing and Services 2002), Vienna.

Statistics Austria (2005), Aufkommens- und Verwendungstabelle 2001 (Supply and Use Table 2001), Vienna.

Table A3.1 Overview of employer–employee data sets

Authors	Region/ country	Sample size	Individual variables	Age categories	Control variables	Productivity measurement	Age–productivity profile	Remarks
Aubert and Crépon (2003)	France	70 680 companies, >3 000 000 employees	Unknown	<25, 25–29, 30–34, 35–39, 40–44, 45–49, 50–54, 55–59	Industry type	Firm's value added	Productivity peaks at ages 40–44, stable or uncertain thereafter	Corrects for the fact that older workers are located in low-productivity firms, assumes they would otherwise be more productive
Andersson et al. (2002)	Sweden	2874 companies	Education	16–29, 30–39, 40–49, 50–59, 60–64, 64+	Period, plant and industry effects	Firm's value added	Workers aged 50+ with primary and secondary education have lower productivity, tertiary educated aged 50+ have higher productivity	Manufacturing and mining industries; longitudinal analysis confirms findings
Crépon et al. (2002)	France	77 868 companies, >3 000 000 employees	Gender, occupation, no. of hours worked	<25, 25–34, 35–49, 49+	Company's age and size, industry type, capital	Firm's output	Productivity peaks for 25–34 age group; lowest for those aged 50+	Manufacturing and non-manufacturing

Dostie (2006)	Canada	5499 workplaces, >20 000 employees	Gender, union, education	<35, 35–55, 55+	Capital, company size, age	Firm's value added	Productivity peaks for 35–55 age group; lowest for those aged 55+	Manufacturing and non-manufacturing
Haltiwanger et al. (1999)	Maryland/US	Unknown (all companies in Maryland 1984–97)	Gender, education, immigrant status	<30, 30–54, 54+	Company's age and size, industry type, period effects	Sales per employee	Workers aged 55+ have lowest productivity	All industries
Hellerstein and Neumark (1995)	Israel	933 companies	Occupation	<35, 35–54, 54+	Industry type, no. of employees, companies' capital and input factors, R&D spending	Firm's output	Productivity peaks at 55+	Poor quality of data and high inflow of young immigrants; lower validity of the study
Hellerstein et al. (1999)	US	3102 companies, 128 460 employees	Gender, race, occupation, marital status, education	<35, 35–54, 54+	No. of employees, region, type of establishment, industry type	Firm's output or value added	Productivity peaks at 55+ if output is used as estimate; productivity lowest for 55+ if value added is used	Manufacturing
Grund and Westergård-Nielsen (2005)	Denmark	29 863 companies, >3 000 000 employees	Education, gender, experience, blue-collar	Average employee age at each company examined	Firm age, firm size, period, industry	Firm's value added	Productivity peak age 37	

Table A3.1 (continued)

Authors	Region/ country	Sample size	Individual variables	Age categories	Control variables	Productivity measurement	Age–productivity profile	Remarks
Ilmakunnas et al. (2004)	Finland	>3882 companies, >279 181 employees	Education, experience, no. of hours worked	Average employee age at each company examined	Company's age, capital	Firm's value added	Productivity peak around age 40	Manufacturing
Hellerstein and Neumark (2004)	US	<3101 companies, <265 412 individuals	Occupation, race, education, marital status	<35, 35–54, 54+	Capital, materials, region, no. of employees	Firm's output	Productivity highest for ages 35–54	Manufacturing
Hægeland and Klette (1999)	Norway	7122 companies, 270 636 employees	Education, experience, no. of hours worked	Dependent on length of education and length of experience	Companies' age, industry type, region, public ownership, foreign ownership	Firm's value added	Productivity peaks in the 30s, declines in the late 30s	Manufacturing

4. The effect of subjective survival probabilities on retirement and wealth in the United States

David E. Bloom, David Canning, Michael Moore and Younghwan Song[1]

The lifecycle model of savings is among the best-established constructs in the field of economics. According to this model, people save during their prime working years to finance their consumption during retirement. Although the main predictions of this theory are well-supported empirically, pure lifecycle models are not naturally suited to explaining sharp increases in savings rates at all ages, such as those observed in East Asia between 1950 and 1990 (see Deaton, 1992, for Thailand; Deaton and Paxson, 1994, 1997, 2000, for Taiwan).[2]

Lee, Mason and Miller (1998, 2000) hypothesize that the need to finance a longer period of retirement can account for an upward shift in the age–savings profile. They simulate for Taiwan a lifecycle model with a fixed retirement age to demonstrate that rapidly improving life expectancy can account for a rise in savings at all ages and a concomitant surge in the rate of national savings. Tsai, Chu and Chung (2000) show that the timing of the rise in household savings in Taiwan coincides closely with the increases in life expectancy of the population.

Bloom, Canning and Graham (2003) construct a model of aggregate savings that includes life expectancy as an argument and estimate the parameters of the model using cross-country panel data. Their findings suggest that increases in life expectancy play a large role in savings behavior and can account for the observed savings boom in East Asia. Although such an effect is plausible given strong disincentives for the delay of retirement, Deaton and Paxson (2000) argue that, in a flexible economy, without mandatory retirement, a rise in longevity will primarily affect the span of the working life, not the rate of savings. Bloom, Canning and Moore (2004) formalize this argument to show that under reasonable assumptions the optimal response to an improvement in health and a rise in life expectancy is to increase the length of working life, though less than proportionately, with no need to raise savings rates at all (owing to the gains derived from compound interest over a longer life span).[3] This result implies that the institutional features of retirement systems, such as mandatory retirement that prevents workers from lengthening their working lives, drive the positive effect of longevity on savings found in cross-country studies.[4] To examine this issue, Bloom et al. (2007) construct a model in which retirement and savings decisions are jointly determined and in which variations in health status, expected longevity, and features of the Social Security system are allowed to influence retirement and savings behavior. Their empirical results indicate that longer life expectancy increases savings in countries with mandatory retirement, but has little effect on savings in countries where incentives for retirement are close to age-neutral.[5]

This chapter further examines these ideas using microdata drawn from the Health and Retirement Study (HRS) for the United States. The HRS provides data on labor supply and household wealth and a rich set of controls for a large representative sample of individuals aged 51 to 61 in 1992 who were followed through 2004. The HRS is ideally suited to our study because it includes information on respondents' subjective probabilities of survival. We analyze the validity of this variable as a proxy for life expectancy and use information on the current ages or the ages at death of respondents' parents as instruments to correct for the presence of classical measurement error, focal points in responses and possible reverse causality.

In the following section we describe the nature and configuration of the HRS data and summarize previous studies of the information content of key HRS variables. Next we motivate our instrumental-variables estimators by focusing on the validity of the subjective survival probabilities. Then we report and discuss our IV probit estimates of the determinants of retirement and our IV estimates of the determinants of wealth, with the subjective survival probability being the main determinant of interest. In the final section we summarize our results and discuss their policy implications.

DATA

To investigate the effects of expected longevity on retirement and wealth, we use data drawn from the Health and Retirement Study (HRS). The HRS is a nationally representative panel survey of noninstitutionalized individuals aged 51 to 61 in 1992 and their spouses or partners, whose ages can fall outside this range. The first wave of the HRS consists of 12 652 individuals. The HRS collects extensive information about the retirement, health and economic well-being of the respondents. After the initial wave of interviews in 1992, subsequent waves of interviews were fielded biennially. We use the RAND HRS data file, which is a cleaned and streamlined version of the HRS that includes some additional derived variables.

As a proxy for expected longevity, we use the subjective survival probability available in the HRS.[6] In the first wave of interviews in 1992, 12 questions in the HRS asked for subjective probabilities about future events. They include the following two questions about surviving to the target ages of 75 and 85: 'Using any number from zero to ten where 0 equals absolutely no chance and 10 equals absolutely certain, what do you think are the chances you will live to be 75 or more?' '85 or more?'[7] At the aggregate level, the answers to these questions about subjective survival probabilities have been found to measure mortality risk fairly reasonably: they aggregate well to averages that are close to corresponding figures based on age-specific survival probabilities calculated from cross-sectional life tables, and they vary plausibly with income, wealth, schooling, and risk factors such as smoking (Hurd and McGarry, 1995). In panel analysis the subjective survival probabilities to age 75 at wave 1, independent of self-assessed health status, are reasonably predictive of actual mortality during the two years between waves 1 and 2 (Hurd and McGarry, 2002). If one controls for self-assessed health status, however, subjective survival probabilities to age 75 from the HRS are poor predictors of mortality during the three years after wave 1 (Siegel, Bradley and Kasl, 2003).

At the individual level the quality of subjective survival probabilities as predictors of respondents' life expectancy seems to suffer from the presence of classical measurement error and focal points in responses (Hurd and McGarry, 1995; Hurd, McFadden and Gan, 1998; Bassett and Lumsdaine, 2001). Hurd and McGarry (1995) present clear evidence of response error by showing that 2.5 percent of the respondents reported larger values for the survival probability to age 85 than for the survival probability to age 75. Hurd, McFadden and Gan (1998) show that, owing to cognition and response error, many respondents systematically provided focal-point answers (0, 0.5 or 1) to the questions on subjective survival probabilities in the sample of older individuals (aged 70 and over in 1993) in the Study of Assets and Health Dynamics among the Oldest Old (AHEAD). Unlike the younger generation of respondents in the HRS, however, the older respondents in the AHEAD study reported average subjective survival probabilities that were substantially higher than those from life tables. Thus the problem of focal points in responses may be a less severe one in the HRS than in the AHEAD study. Bassett and Lumsdaine (2001) demonstrate the possibility of systematic response error, showing that respondents who gave probabilistically inconsistent answers to the two questions regarding Social Security in the HRS also reported higher values for subjective survival probabilities.[8]

To improve the information content of responses to the subjective survival probabilities in the AHEAD study, Hurd, McFadden and Gan (1998) transform the error-ridden survival probabilities with focal points into continuous probabilities. They show that savings is positively associated with their new survival probabilities among couples, though not among singles.[9] But they do not validate their new survival probabilities, for instance, by using actual mortality information from panel data. Bassett and Lumsdaine (2001) try to validate their measures for other subjective probabilities in the HRS. Their analysis of patterns in the minimum, maximum, mean and range of the entire set of responses to the subjective probability questions in the first wave of the HRS suggests the presence of unobserved individual heterogeneity. To adjust for this individual fixed effect, they create five benchmark measures by renormalizing the location or scale of reported subjective probabilities. The result is inconclusive. In predicting the actual outcomes observed by the third wave of the HRS, their benchmark measures for the subjective probability of working full-time past age 62 and for the subjective probability of making a gift to family members perform poorly relative to the reported responses.

We control for these measurement errors in the HRS by instrumenting the subjective survival probabilities of respondents using information on the mortality experience of their parents. The instrumental-variables estimator also addresses the potential endogeneity of subjective survival probabilities, a problem that would arise if the subjective survival probabilities were affected by wealth and retirement decisions.

Hurd and McGarry (1995) show that parents' ages or ages at death are substantially correlated with the subjective survival probabilities of respondents, and the relationships between parents' ages at death and the subjective survival probabilities are nonmonotonic: the subjective survival probabilities of respondents are higher if the parents are alive than if the parents have died; but if the parents died before age 51, the subjective survival probabilities of respondents are higher than if the parents died between ages 51 and 65, presumably because accidental deaths are more likely among deaths that occur at younger ages; and if the parents died at an age greater than 65, the subjective survival probabilities of respondents increase with the parents' ages at death.[10] In their analysis of HRS panel data, Hurd and McGarry (2002) report that respondents modify their subjective survival probabilities in response to the death of a parent.

VALIDATION

Using the sample of respondents whose actual mortality is known by wave 6 of the HRS, completed in 2002, we test how well the instrumented survival probability to age 75 predicts actual mortality in the subsequent waves, relative to the reported survival probability from the first wave. Our validation process is similar to that in Hurd and McGarry (2002). Details of the validation results are reported in the Appendix. We find that the instrumented survival probability, which corrects for measurement error, performs substantially better than the reported survival probability as a predictor of long-term mortality. In the next two sections we employ this instrumented subjective survival probability to investigate the effects of subjective survival probabilities on retirement and wealth.

EMPIRICAL RESULTS

In this section we estimate the effect of subjective survival probabilities on wealth accumulation and retirement. We find that higher subjective survival probabilities lead to greater household wealth among couples, but not among singles, and no significant differences in the probability of retirement for individuals in either demographic group.

Retirement Analysis

Using the summary labor force status variable in the RAND HRS data, we define individuals as in the labor force if they are working full-time, working part-time, or are unemployed. Respondents who are not in the labor force – retired, partially retired, disabled, or not in the labor force in the summary labor force status variable – are defined as retired in our analysis.[11]

The sample we use in our cross-sectional analysis of retirement consists of individuals aged 50 to 70 in 1992 who were not represented by a proxy respondent. We exclude those with missing data on subjective survival probabilities and on parental mortality (3 percent of the initial sample). Our sample includes respondents outside the 51 to 61 age range because we include spouses of the age-eligible respondents. Of the 9388 observations in the final sample used for our cross-sectional analyses, 8235 (88 percent) were born between 1931 and 1941 and 1153 (12 percent) were born either before 1931 or after 1941. We present the results using the subjective survival probabilities to age 75 as our measure of subjective survival probabilities.[12]

Figure 4.1 reports the retirement rate by age for the whole sample. The proportion of respondents retired rises with age, with sharp jumps between

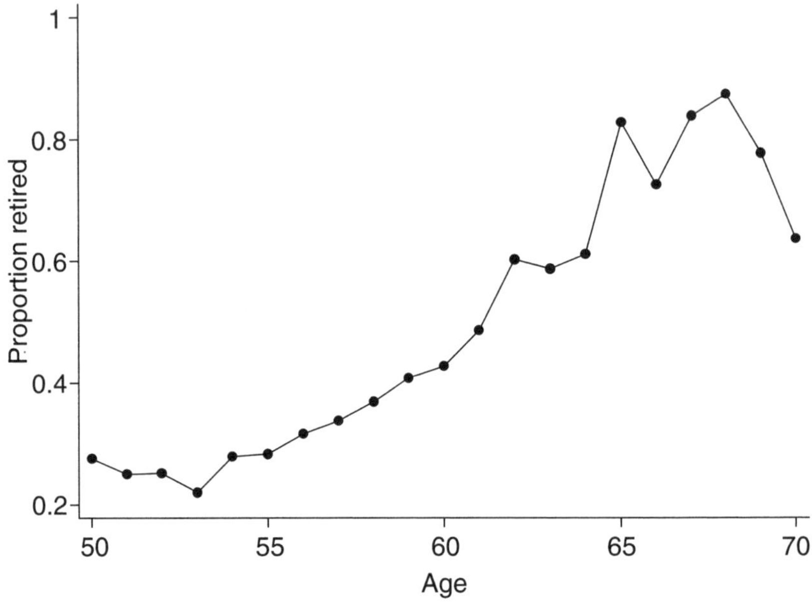

Figure 4.1 Proportion retired by age, whole sample

61 and 62 and again between 64 and 65. These jumps correspond to the ages of eligibility for rising levels of Social Security benefits.[13]

We conduct separate analyses by household living arrangements (that is, single or couple) and by sex. In addition to the subjective survival probability to age 75 and a standard set of demographic variables – age, three race/ethnicity dummies (the reference group is white), years of education, and number of children – we also generate, as regressors, five dummy variables based on the financial planning horizon (the reference group is the planning horizon of a few months),[14] four dummy variables for self-reported health status (the reference group is 'poor health'), a dummy variable for the presence of a health problem that limits the kind or amount of paid work of the respondent, and the amount of lump-sum payments received from inheritance, insurance, and pension during 1991.[15] For couples our specification includes these explanatory variables as well as the survival probability for each spouse in order to control for joint decision-making. Accordingly our instrumental-variables estimates instrument the survival probabilities of both spouses with the parental mortality experience of both spouses.

Table 4.1 reports the results of the retirement probit and the IV retirement probit for singles.[16] Among singles, there is no evidence that higher subjective survival probabilities decrease the probability of retirement, regardless of sex and estimation method. Other significant variables are consistent with the findings in the literature. Older individuals are more likely to have retired in our sample.[17] More-educated women are less likely to have retired than less-educated women. Those in poor health and having health problems are more likely to have retired than those in better health with no health problems. Women with the longest planning horizon are more likely to have retired than those with the shortest planning horizon (a few months).

The conclusions from Table 4.1 on the effect of subjective survival probabilities on retirement behavior do not change in Table 4.2, where we report probit and IV probit results for couples. The coefficients on the subjective survival probabilities are statistically insignificant for both spouses, except for males in column 1, which is significant at the 10 percent level. The coefficients on the age-dummy variables among men clearly demonstrate sharp jumps at ages 62 and 65. Having an older spouse increases the likelihood of retirement, as does receiving more lump-sum income in 1991.

Overall, there is no evidence that higher subjective survival probabilities decrease the probability of retirement regardless of couple status, sex, control variables, and estimation method.

Wealth Analysis

We define wealth as the sum of all household wealth components less all debt, exclusive of Social Security and pension wealth. We use imputed values in the RAND HRS when any of the wealth components is missing. The unit of analysis is the household because wealth is measured at the household level. We conduct separate analyses by couple status. Figure 4.2 presents the distribution of wealth by couple status. Because some households have zero or negative wealth, we do not use a logarithmic specification. The mean wealth and median wealth for singles are \$95 711 and \$27 990, respectively, and the mean wealth and median wealth for couples are \$239 109 and \$118 500 respectively.

Table 4.3 reports the results of the OLS and IV estimation of the wealth equation for singles. We use the same set of explanatory variables as we use in the retirement equations.[18] Among singles there is no evidence that higher subjective survival probabilities increase the wealth of the respondent, regardless of estimation method. The result of the Durbin–Wu–Hausman test cannot reject the null hypothesis that the OLS estimate in column 1 of Table 4.3 is consistent. Other explanatory variables in Table 4.3 show expected signs. Women have less wealth than men. Blacks have less wealth than whites. Consistent with the literature, better-educated people

Table 4.1 Retirement probit estimation, singles

Predictor variable	Men		Women	
	(1) Probit	(2) IV Probit	(3) Probit	(4) IV Probit
SURVIVAL PROBABILITY TO 75	0.100 (0.214)	1.239 (1.405)	−0.021 (0.141)	0.572 (0.849)
Age 51	0.816* (0.440)	0.830* (0.450)	0.218 (0.254)	0.261 (0.264)
Age 52	0.558 (0.436)	0.624 (0.455)	0.017 (0.262)	0.057 (0.272)
Age 53	0.519 (0.435)	0.572 (0.449)	0.091 (0.262)	0.125 (0.269)
Age 54	0.571 (0.448)	0.521 (0.463)	0.098 (0.256)	0.146 (0.268)
Age 55	0.286 (0.458)	0.337 (0.470)	−0.030 (0.268)	−0.017 (0.271)
Age 56	0.589 (0.448)	0.579 (0.458)	0.302 (0.252)	0.356 (0.267)
Age 57	0.708 (0.436)	0.694 (0.446)	0.195 (0.255)	0.231 (0.261)
Age 58	1.263** (0.441)	1.231** (0.450)	0.235 (0.254)	0.295 (0.272)
Age 59	0.995** (0.439)	0.942** (0.452)	0.525** (0.252)	0.551** (0.258)
Age 60	0.762* (0.445)	0.710 (0.459)	0.795** (0.247)	0.836** (0.259)
Age 61	1.399** (0.457)	1.476** (0.483)	0.871** (0.259)	0.895** (0.265)
Age 70			0.822 (0.1.217)	0.817 (0.1.137)
Black	0.312** (0.150)	0.145 (0.245)	0.283** (0.094)	0.250** (0.105)
Hispanic	0.398* (0.238)	0.347 (0.253)	0.240* (0.142)	0.276* (0.154)
Other	0.195 (0.593)	0.096 (0.636)	0.474* (0.254)	0.490* (0.260)
Years of education	0.026 (0.021)	0.022 (0.022)	−0.060** (0.015)	−0.064** (0.016)

HEALTH				
Excellent	−1.057** (0.300)	−1.552** (0.710)	−0.851** (0.191)	−1.049** (0.345)
Very good	−0.838** (0.273)	−1.219** (0.568)	−0.613** (0.171)	−0.752** (0.265)
Good	−0.858** (0.252)	−1.170** (0.492)	−0.778** (0.160)	−0.889** (0.229)
Fair	−0.445* (0.240)	−0.605* (0.334)	−0.519** (0.150)	−0.572** (0.170)
Health limits work	1.618** (0.163)	1.538** (0.179)	1.452** (0.108)	1.457** (0.111)
PLANNING HORIZON				
Next year	0.162 (0.226)	0.200 (0.242)	0.003 (0.151)	−0.0003 (0.152)
Next few years	0.024 (0.180)	−0.019 (0.196)	−0.202* (0.108)	−0.198* (0.109)
Next 5–10 years	0.049 (0.186)	−0.010 (0.206)	−0.226* (0.121)	−0.247* (0.127)
Longer than 10 years	0.235 (0.261)	0.091 (0.331)	0.427** (0.160)	0.398** (0.166)
Planning horizon missing	0.340 (0.335)	0.361 (0.346)	0.210 (0.240)	0.215 (0.245)
HOUSEHOLD CHARACTERISTICS				
Number of children	−0.021 (0.029)	−0.027 (0.032)	0.019 (0.019)	0.013 (0.021)
Lump sum income (in $1000s)	0.005 (0.005)	0.004 (0.006)	0.008** (0.002)	0.008** (0.002)
P-value of Wald test of exogeneity	0.4374		0.4862	
Proportion retired	0.326		0.337	
No. of observations	681		1515	

Notes: Standard errors in parentheses. Three observations in the male equation and one observation in the female equation are dropped because age dummies perfectly predict outcomes. * Statistically significant at the 0.10 level; ** statistically significant at the 0.05 level.

Table 4.2 Retirement probit estimation, couples

Predictor variable	Men		Women	
	(1) Probit	(2) IV Probit	(3) Probit	(4) IV Probit
Self survival probability to 75	−0.176* (0.094)	−0.431 (0.537)	0.111 (0.095)	−0.598 (0.437)
Spouse survival probability to 75	0.035 (0.100)	−0.393 (0.464)	0.058 (0.090)	−0.309 (0.516)
SELF CHARACTERISTICS				
Age 51	−0.009 (0.216)	−0.006 (0.219)	0.151 (0.116)	0.150 (0.119)
Age 52	0.215 (0.214)	0.193 (0.214)	0.135 (0.118)	0.134 (0.121)
Age 53	0.053 (0.217)	0.040 (0.221)	−0.123 (0.122)	−0.118 (0.124)
Age 54	0.438** (0.212)	0.414* (0.216)	−0.037 (0.120)	−0.033 (0.122)
Age 55	0.479** (0.208)	0.460** (0.212)	−0.017 (0.119)	−0.025 (0.122)
Age 56	0.493** (0.208)	0.459** (0.213)	0.196 (0.122)	0.189 (0.124)
Age 57	0.485** (0.208)	0.468** (0.213)	0.178 (0.126)	0.165 (0.129)
Age 58	0.491** (0.212)	0.464** (0.216)	0.209 (0.127)	0.246* (0.131)
Age 59	0.705** (0.210)	0.647** (0.218)	0.266** (0.128)	0.258** (0.131)
Age 60	0.769** (0.208)	0.708** (0.217)	0.334** (0.131)	0.324** (0.135)
Age 61	0.962** (0.212)	0.921** (0.217)	0.513** (0.139)	0.499** (0.142)
Age 62	1.571** (0.217)	1.487** (0.226)	0.909** (0.265)	0.991** (0.277)
Age 63	1.493** (0.225)	1.418** (0.234)	1.575** (0.411)	1.614** (0.409)
Age 64	1.464** (0.230)	1.410** (0.238)	1.066** (0.368)	1.140** (0.378)
Age 65	2.374** (0.256)	2.275** (0.271)	0.961** (0.399)	0.965** (0.402)
Age 66	1.907** (0.259)	1.784** (0.279)	a	a
Age 67	2.626** (0.303)	2.556** (0.313)	0.434 (0.565)	0.679 (0.591)
Age 68	2.431** (0.334)	2.329** (0.347)	a	a
Age 69	1.923** (0.340)	1.812** (0.352)	0.635 (0.909)	0.701 (0.932)

Age 70	1.819** (0.377)	1.721** (0.392)	a	a
Black	0.151 (0.255)	0.122 (0.260)	−0.109 (0.283)	−0.080 (0.289)
Hispanic	−0.056 (0.201)	−0.071 (0.204)	−0.158 (0.209)	−0.182 (0.215)
Other	−0.416* (0.245)	−0.427* (0.248)	−0.115 (0.224)	−0.144 (0.228)
Years of education	0.008 (0.010)	0.007 (0.010)	−0.076** (0.012)	−0.069** (0.013)
HEALTH				
Excellent	−0.655** (0.129)	−0.837** (0.227)	−0.635** (0.150)	−0.382* (0.214)
Very good	−0.735** (0.123)	−0.874** (0.193)	−0.639** (0.145)	−0.435** (0.191)
Good	−0.697** (0.115)	−0.798** (0.162)	−0.561** (0.141)	−0.403** (0.171)
Fair	−0.646** (0.117)	−0.680** (0.130)	−0.322** (0.144)	−0.217 (0.159)
Health limits work	1.184** (0.070)	1.214** (0.075)	0.753** (0.072)	0.746** (0.074)
PLANNING HORIZON				
Next year	−0.132 (0.101)	−0.125 (0.103)	−0.177* (0.083)	−0.198** (0.095)
Next few years	−0.226** (0.079)	−0.223** (0.080)	−0.261** (0.073)	−0.273** (0.075)
Next 5–10 years	−0.172** (0.082)	−0.174** (0.083)	−0.244** (0.078)	−0.238** (0.080)
Longer than 10 years	0.118 (0.104)	0.077 (0.117)	0.086 (0.105)	0.106 (0.109)
Planning horizon missing	−0.033 (0.187)	−0.021 (0.191)	0.241 (0.205)	0.159 (0.213)
SPOUSE CHARACTERISTICS				
Age	0.013** (0.005)	0.015** (0.006)	0.018** (0.005)	0.021** (0.008)
Black	0.070 (0.261)	0.063 (0.265)	0.147 (0.282)	−0.111 (0.288)
Hispanic	−0.071 (0.189)	−0.110 (0.194)	−0.013 (0.203)	0.014 (0.208)
Other	0.177 (0.199)	0.187 (0.201)	0.274 (0.200)	−0.213 (0.206)
Years of education	−0.000 (0.012)	−0.002 (0.013)	−0.010 (0.009)	0.012 (0.010)
SPOUSE HEALTH				
Excellent	−0.126 (0.149)	0.018 (0.217)	−0.087 (0.129)	0.091 (0.230)
Very good	−0.092 (0.142)	0.038 (0.191)	−0.055 (0.123)	0.096 (0.196)
Good	−0.134 (0.137)	−0.039 (0.172)	−0.133 (0.117)	−0.007 (0.167)

Table 4.2 (continued)

Predictor variable	Men		Women	
	(1) Probit	(2) IV Probit	(3) Probit	(4) IV Probit
Fair	−0.026 (0.138)	0.039 (0.153)	−0.148 (0.118)	−0.071 (0.134)
Health limits work	−0.074 (0.077)	−0.090 (0.078)	−0.044 (0.070)	−0.052 (0.074)
SPOUSE PLANNING HORIZON				
Next year	−0.092 (0.095)	−0.099 (0.097)	0.040 (0.099)	0.039 (0.101)
Next few years	−0.086 (0.077)	−0.081 (0.078)	0.030 (0.078)	0.034 (0.079)
Next 5–10 years	−0.116 (0.082)	−0.112 (0.083)	−0.019 (0.081)	0.005 (0.084)
Longer than 10 years	0.081 (0.107)	0.113 (0.110)	0.195 (0.102)	0.259** (0.115)
Planning horizon missing	0.042 (0.201)	0.029 (0.208)	0.089 (0.175)	0.109 (0.178)
HOUSEHOLD CHARACTERISTICS				
Number of children	−0.016 (0.013)	−0.018 (0.013)	0.001 (0.012)	0.004 (0.013)
Lump sum income (in $1000)	0.005** (0.002)	0.005** (0.002)	0.004** (0.002)	0.005** (0.002)
P-value of Wald test of exogeneity	0.3491		0.1950	
Proportion retired	0.2932		0.4411	
No. of observations	3858		3108	

Notes: Standard errors in parentheses.
[a] Nine observations in the female equation are dropped because age dummies perfectly predict outcomes. * Statistically significant at the 0.10 level; ** statistically significant at the 0.05 level.

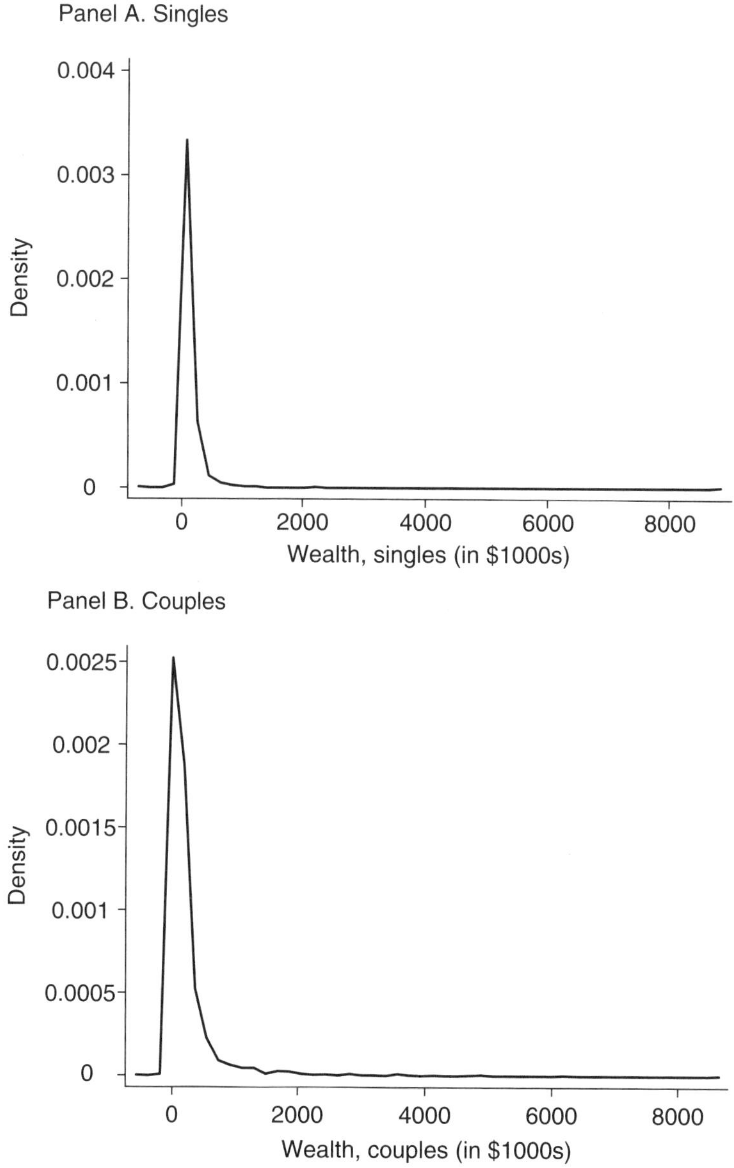

Figure 4.2 Kernel density graph of wealth

Table 4.3 *Wealth regression results, single households: dependent variable: household wealth (in $1000s)*

Predictor variable	(1) OLS	(2) IV
Survival probability to 75	4.01 (20.27)	216.16 (142.81)
Age	9.71 (57.85)	19.91 (59.67)
Age squared	−0.06 (0.52)	−0.15 (0.53)
Female	−49.32** (12.90)	−59.80** (14.94)
Black	−61.39** (13.89)	−78.52** (18.24)
Hispanic	−23.81 (21.52)	−16.55 (22.58)
Other	−21.71 (38.99)	−19.66 (39.98)
Years of education	14.18** (2.06)	12.97** (2.26)
Health		
Excellent	24.95 (27.80)	−54.98 (60.38)
Very good	33.20 (25.92)	−25.15 (47.07)
Good	−9.66 (24.12)	−57.72 (40.44)
Fair	10.73 (22.10)	−12.40 (27.39)
Health limits work	−22.90 (17.25)	−22.54 (17.68)
Planning horizon		
Next year	7.75 (21.81)	10.26 (22.41)
Next few years	27.94* (16.00)	25.61 (16.47)
Next 5–10 years	58.28** (17.26)	49.82** (18.56)
Longer than 10 years	82.07** (24.77)	67.06** (27.28)
Planning horizon missing	31.08 (33.00)	35.89 (33.97)
Number of children	−2.84 (2.83)	−4.90 (3.21)
Lump sum income	0.74* (0.41)	0.84* (0.43)
Constant	4.01 (20.27)	−748.72 (1667.38)
R^2	0.0906	0.0448
P-value of Durbin–Wu–Hausman test	0.1221	
P-value of Sargan test	0.0061	
Craig–Donald statistic	3.90	
No. of observations	2200	

Notes: Standard errors in parentheses. * Statistically significant at the 0.10 level; ** Statistically significant at the 0.05 level.

have more wealth than less-educated people. Individuals with planning horizons of longer than five years have more wealth than those with shorter planning horizons.

Table 4.4 reports the results of the OLS and IV estimation of the parameters of the wealth equation for couples. Column 2 of Table 4.4 shows that, among couples, higher subjective survival probabilities of both spouses

Table 4.4 Wealth regression results, couple households: dependent variable: household wealth (in $1000s)

Predictor variable	(1) OLS	(2) IV
Husband's survival probability to 75	18.70 (25.95)	276.32* (152.73)
Wife's survival probability to 75	11.23 (27.46)	326.89** (132.13)
HUSBAND'S CHARACTERISTICS		
Age	58.88* (34.09)	55.69 (35.23)
Age squared	−0.47 (0.29)	−0.46 (0.30)
Black	−109.30 (73.43)	−128.56* (76.36)
Hispanic	−117.63** (54.78)	−109.59* (56.70)
Other	58.46 (60.19)	−83.79 (62.83)
Years of education	11.99** (2.72)	10.80** (2.85)
HUSBAND'S HEALTH		
Excellent	100.14** (37.07)	−11.69 (65.69)
Very good	33.93 (35.41)	−57.48 (56.01)
Good	5.14 (33.71)	−66.52 (47.38)
Fair	8.30 (34.14)	−30.62 (38.33)
Health limits work	−31.71 (20.82)	−25.44 (22.51)
HUSBAND'S PLANNING HORIZON		
Next year	−14.53 (29.12)	−3.11 (30.38)
Next few years	0.15 (22.48)	−0.61 (23.24)
Next 5–10 years	12.79 (22.98)	5.89 (23.86)
Longer than 10 years	55.78* (30.16)	22.79 (33.97)
Planning horizon missing	63.73 (53.13)	60.10 (54.96)
WIFE'S CHARACTERISTICS		
Age	11.32 (12.41)	17.28 (12.98)
Age squared	−0.06 (0.12)	−0.12 (0.13)
Black	13.23 (75.24)	−5.80 (78.00)
Hispanic	130.59** (51.52)	121.80** (53.88)
Other	16.52 (53.76)	15.12 (55.58)
Years of education	15.38** (3.38)	11.96** (3.69)
WIFE'S HEALTH		
Excellent	78.52* (51.22)	−32.25 (61.87)
Very good	72.50* (39.58)	−15.29 (54.77)
Good	11.96 (38.06)	−58.95 (48.88)
Fair	13.38 (38.64)	−27.71 (43.76)
Health limits work	−25.70 (21.31)	−27.00 (22.24)
WIFE'S PLANNING HORIZON		
Next year	−21.15 (27.18)	−8.05 (28.44)
Next few years	20.69 (21.58)	26.71 (22.41)
Next 5–10 years	10.91 (22.67)	9.91 (23.43)
Longer than 10 years	146.75** (30.25)	146.85** (31.84)
Planning horizon missing	68.48 (58.26)	109.06* (61.66)

Table 4.4 (continued)

Predictor variable	(1) OLS	(2) IV
HOUSEHOLD CHARACTERISTICS		
Number of children	−6.98* (3.57)	−7.89** (3.76)
Lump sum income (in $1000)	2.41** (0.35)	2.47** (0.37)
Constant	−2436.85** (1046.37)	−2585.43** (1082.35)
R^2	0.1191	0.0597
P-value of Durbin–Wu–Hausman test	0.0065	
P-value of Sargan test	0.7122	
Craig–Donald statistic	4.97	
No. of observations	3858	

Notes: Standard errors in parentheses. * Statistically significant at the 0.10 level; ** statistically significant at the 0.05 level.

significantly increase the wealth of the household in the IV estimation. The coefficients on the subjective survival probabilities in column 2 of Table 4.4 indicate that a 10 percentage point increase in the husband's subjective survival probability results in roughly a $27 600 increase in household wealth, while a 10 percentage point increase in the wife's subjective survival probability results in roughly a $32 700 increase in household wealth. These amounts are more than 10 percent of the mean household wealth for couples.

Table 4.4 also reports the results of three tests for the validity of our approach. The Durbin–Wu–Hausman test indicates that the OLS estimates are inconsistent. The p-value from the Sargan test of overidentification indicates that our instruments are uncorrelated with the error term and also that they are correctly excluded from the wealth equation. Finally the Craig–Donald statistic shows that one cannot regard the instruments as weak.[19]

Overall, the difference in the effect of subjective survival probabilities by couple status reported in Tables 4.3 and 4.4 is consistent with the findings of Hurd, McFadden and Gan (1998).

SUMMARY AND CONCLUSION

We find that increased subjective probabilities of survival result in increased household wealth among couples, with no effect on the length of the working life. This finding is consistent with the view that a longer expected lifespan leads to increased wealth accumulation because institutional incentives effectively constrain retirement decisions. We intend to exploit the panel nature of the HRS in future work by extending the analysis forward through the seventh wave (2004). We also intend to explore the use of answers to other questions on subjective probabilities as instruments for the subjective survival probabilities, and to study lifetime savings directly by analyzing HRS data that are linked to individual records on lifetime Social Security earnings. Future analyses will also encompass individual data from the English Longitudinal Study of Ageing (ELSA) and the Survey of Health, Ageing and Retirement in Europe (SHARE), so that we can test more directly whether institutions influence retirement incentives (see Bloom, Canning, Moore and Song, 2006).

Our results indicate that expected lifetime horizons influence economic decisions of consequence. This suggests that improving the accuracy of people's estimates of those horizons, and of the state of their health during those years, could enhance their lifetime welfare. Further research, along the lines of Bongaarts and Feeney (2003), that aims to extract information about the survival probabilities of true cohorts from data on the survival probabilities of synthetic cohorts (on which life expectancy estimates are typically formed) would be quite worthwhile.

Our results also suggest that eliminating institutional arrangements that impinge on retirement behavior, or making those arrangements responsive to changes in life expectancy, could lead to welfare-enhancing changes in labor supply and savings. The Social Security system in the United States has started down this path by increasing the age at full retirement from 65 for cohorts born before 1937 to 67 for cohorts born after 1960. These changes coincide closely with the 1980–2003 increase in life expectancy at age 65 from 16.4 to 18.4 years. In view of the projection of Li and Lee (2005) that life expectancy at birth in the United States will rise to 84.9 by 2050 (from 77.5 in 2003), further increases in the Social Security retirement age may well be in the offing.

APPENDIX

Our validation sample consists of 10 070 individuals who were 45–65 in 1992, who were not represented by a proxy interview at wave 1, and whose mortality status by wave 6 is known.[20] We exclude those with missing data on subjective survival probabilities and the mortality of parents. The cumulative mortality rate among this sample of 10 070 individuals is reported by each wave in Table A4.1. By wave 6 (2002), almost 12 percent of the sample had died.[21] For each and every wave, men show significantly higher cumulative mortality rates than women.

Figure A4.1 reports the histogram of the distribution of the reported subjective survival probability to age 75 that has been normalized to [0, 1] from [0, 10]. The figure clearly illustrates that there are substantial focal-point responses, regardless of sex: more than 40 percent of the respondents answered that their survival probability to age 75 is either 0.5 or 1. The fact that respondents had to choose a number between 0 and 10 may have aggravated the problem of focal-point responses.

Table A4.2 shows how well this subjective survival probability at wave 1 predicts actual mortality between wave 1 and each subsequent wave by way of probit estimation. The dependent variable is equal to 1 if the individual has died by wave t (t=2, 3, 4, 5, and 6) and 0 if he or she has survived. Overall the reported marginal effects of the survival probability to age 75 in Table A4.2 show that higher values of subjective survival probability to age 75 at wave 1 significantly reduce the probability of dying before subsequent waves. When the question regarding the subjective survival probability to age 75 was asked of respondents who were 45–65 years old in 1992, it was intended to measure the long-term mortality (or survival) probability over the next 10 to 30 years. The fact that the marginal effects of the subjective survival probability to age 75 at wave 1 are both significant and increasing in magnitude over time in

Table A4.1 Cumulative number and proportion of respondents deceased by wave 2 through 6

Wave	All respondents	Females	Males
2	171 (1.70)	71 (1.25)	100 (2.27)
3	379 (3.76)	149 (2.63)	230 (5.22)
4	596 (5.92)	250 (4.42)	346 (7.85)
5	867 (8.61)	358 (6.32)	509 (11.54)
6	1 199 (11.91)	508 (8.97)	691 (15.67)
No. of observations	10 070	5661	4409

Note: Mortality rates are in parentheses.

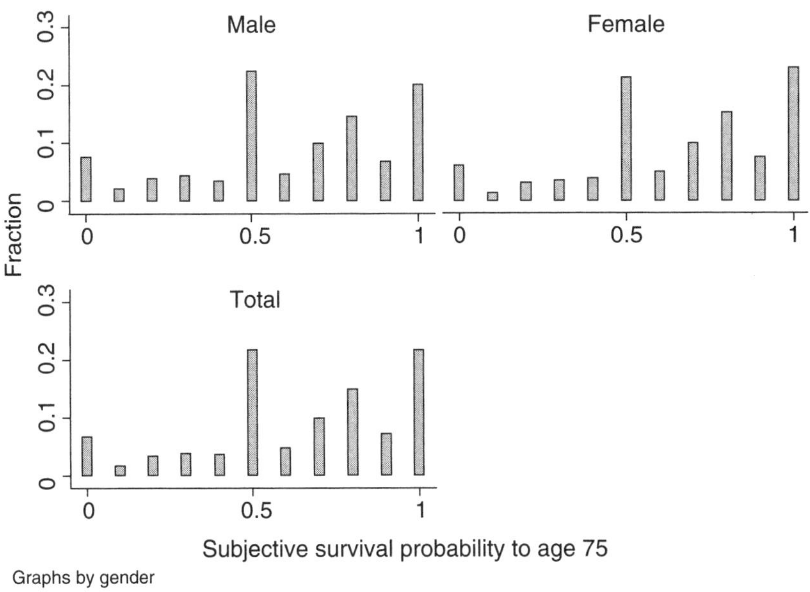

Figure A4.1 *Histogram of the reported survival probability to age 75*

Table A4.2 *Marginal effects of subjective survival probability from probit estimation of the observed mortality, waves 2 through 6*

Wave 1 controls	(1) Wave 2	(2) Wave 3	(3) Wave 4	(4) Wave 5	(5) Wave 6
Survival probability to 75	−0.0279** (0.0037)	−0.0518** (0.0058)	−0.0715** (0.0075)	−0.0927** (0.0092)	−0.1215** (0.0108)
Pseudo R^2	0.0334	0.0255	0.0214	0.0188	0.0190
Log pseudo likelihood	−837.50	−1573.70	−2214.48	−2899.05	−3606.28
No. of observations			10 070		

Note: Robust standard errors in parentheses. * Statistically significant at the 0.10 level; ** statistically significant at the 0.05 level.

Table A4.2 provides some evidence that the subjective survival probability to age 75 at wave 1 does indeed predict people's long-term mortality.

However, it is possible that the marginal effects of the subjective survival probability in Table A4.2 reflect the effects of other factors that would affect mortality, such as age, sex, education, health status, disease conditions, smoking behavior, income and wealth, because these factors have not been controlled for in Table A4.2.[22] We include these factors from wave 1 in Table A4.3 as explanatory variables in addition to the subjective survival probability to age 75.[23]

Consistent with the findings of Hurd and McGarry (2002), higher values of subjective survival probability to age 75 significantly reduce the probability of dying by wave 2, as shown in column 1 of Table A4.3. Significant coefficients on other explanatory variables have the expected signs. Mortality increases with age. Women have lower mortality rates than men. The four dummy variables for subjective health status (poor health is the reference group) are significant with the expected signs. Disease conditions increase mortality rates. Current and past smoking increases mortality rates.

However, columns 2 through 5 of Table A4.3 reveal that, when it comes to predicting long-term mortality by waves 3 through 6, the reported survival probability does not provide additional explanatory power after other risk factors are controlled. The marginal effects of the reported survival probability are insignificant and the magnitude does not increase over time, though the sign is correct. Such an outcome is possible given that the reported subjective survival probability is subject to measurement error.

To correct for measurement error, we instrument the reported subjective survival probability to age 75 by using 12 dummy variables for the mortality experience of the parents. Table A4.4 reports the results of the first-stage linear-probability estimation to predict the subjected survival probability to age 75 in the mortality equation. The table includes other exogenous variables from the main mortality equation, and they show reasonable signs. For the 12 dummy variables for the mortality experience of the parents, the reference group consists of those respondents whose parents died between the ages of 50 and 65. In the first stage of the IV estimation, the coefficients on these instrumental variables are significant with the expected signs and magnitudes, even after we control for smoking behavior and disease conditions. If the parents are alive, the subjective survival probability to age 75 of the respondent is greater by 0.051~0.095 in comparison with those whose parents died between the ages of 50 and 65. The effect of the parents' age at death on the subjective survival probabilities is nonmonotonic: if the parents died before age 50, the subjective survival probability to age 75 of the respondent increases by 0.037~0.040; if the parents died between the ages of 66 and 75, the subjective survival probability to age 75 increases by 0.023~0.027; and if the parents died after age 75, the subjective survival probability to age 75 increases even more.

Figure A4.2 reports the histogram and kernel density graph of the instrumented subjective survival probability based on the results reported

Table A4.3 Marginal effects of subjective survival probability from probit estimation of the observed mortality, by selected variables, waves 2 through 6

Wave 1 controls	(1) Wave 2	(2) Wave 3	(3) Wave 4	(4) Wave 5	(5) Wave 6
Survival probability to 75	−0.0043*	−0.0068	−0.0098	−0.0045	−0.0089
	(0.0024)	(0.0042)	(0.0060)	(0.0077)	(0.0097)
Age	0.0004*	0.0008**	0.0025**	0.0041**	0.0059**
	(0.0002)	(0.0003)	(0.0005)	(0.0006)	(0.0007)
Female	−0.0062**	−0.0164**	−0.0199**	−0.0330**	−0.0477**
	(0.0018)	(0.0032)	(0.0042)	(0.0052)	(0.0065)
Black	0.0045*	0.0121**	0.0179**	0.0137**	0.0142*
	(0.0028)	(0.0046)	(0.0061)	(0.0070)	(0.0084)
Hispanic	0.0002	−0.0040	−0.0039	−0.0161*	−0.0241**
	(0.0031)	(0.0047)	(0.0071)	(0.0078)	(0.0094)
Other	−0.0017	0.0143	0.0116	0.0103	−0.0018
	(0.0046)	(0.0121)	(0.0148)	(0.0169)	(0.0209)
Years of education	−0.0001	−0.0002	0.0004	−0.0004	−0.0011
	(0.0003)	(0.0005)	(0.0007)	(0.0008)	(0.0010)
Married	−0.0032*	−0.0077**	−0.0058	−0.0104*	−0.0205**
	(0.0021)	(0.0035)	(0.0045)	(0.0057)	(0.0072)
HEALTH					
Excellent	−0.0083**	−0.0190**	−0.0331**	−0.0492**	−0.0723**
	(0.0019)	(0.0037)	(0.0053)	(0.0066)	(0.0084)
Very good	−0.0086**	−0.0201**	−0.0230**	−0.0479**	−0.0703**
	(0.0020)	(0.0037)	(0.0055)	(0.0068)	(0.0086)
Good	−0.0088**	−0.0195**	−0.0290**	−0.0396**	−0.0574**
	(0.0018)	(0.0033)	(0.0049)	(0.0063)	(0.0082)
Fair	−0.0046**	−0.0094**	−0.0150**	−0.0184**	−0.0272**
	(0.0015)	(0.0030)	(0.0046)	(0.0062)	(0.0082)

Table A4.3 (continued)

Wave 1 controls	(1) Wave 2	(2) Wave 3	(3) Wave 4	(4) Wave 5	(5) Wave 6
High blood pressure	0.0034*	0.0122**	0.0144**	0.0270**	0.0344**
	(0.0019)	(0.0033)	(0.0043)	(0.0054)	(0.0066)
Diabetes	0.0068**	0.0328**	0.0620**	0.0780**	0.1039**
	(0.0035)	(0.0072)	(0.0099)	(0.0115)	(0.0135)
Cancer	0.0418**	0.0632**	0.0783**	0.1138**	0.1153**
	(0.0092)	(0.0125)	(0.0144)	(0.0173)	(0.0186)
Lung disease	0.0070**	0.0225**	0.0361**	0.0521**	0.0783**
	(0.0042)	(0.0076)	(0.0102)	(0.0125)	(0.0157)
Ever had heart attack	0.0090**	0.0204**	0.0300**	0.0483**	0.0511**
	(0.0034)	(0.0055)	(0.0072)	(0.0090)	(0.0105)
Stroke	0.0113**	0.0182**	0.0270**	0.0546**	0.1019**
	(0.0067)	(0.0101)	(0.0135)	(0.0187)	(0.0246)
Arthritis	−0.0016	0.0011	−0.0015	−0.0077	−0.0138**
	(0.0016)	(0.0028)	(0.0038)	(0.0047)	(0.0059)
BMI	−0.0000	−0.0009**	−0.0011**	−0.0015**	−0.0015**
	(0.0001)	(0.0003)	(0.0004)	(0.0005)	(0.0006)
Smoker	0.0083**	0.0236**	0.0500**	0.0707**	0.1040**
	(0.0030)	(0.0052)	(0.0072)	(0.0087)	(0.0102)
Former smoker	0.0047**	0.0101**	0.0200**	0.0317**	0.0416**
	(0.0022)	(0.0038)	(0.0053)	(0.0064)	(0.0078)
Pseudo R^2	0.1843	0.1805	0.1716	0.1896	0.1882
Log pseudo likelihood	−706.82	−1323.29	−1874.67	−2394.49	−2984.37
No. of observations			10070		

Notes: Robust standard errors in parentheses. The reported regressions also include income and its square, wealth and its square. * Statistically significant at the 0.10 level; ** statistically significant at the 0.05 level

Table A4.4 First-stage regression results in IV probit estimation of observed mortality: linear probability model of survival to age 75

Predictor variable	(1) Coefficient	(2) Standard error
Age	0.004**	0.001
Female	0.036**	0.006
Black	0.069**	0.009
Hispanic	−0.040**	0.012
Other	0.010	0.020
Years of education	0.005**	0.001
Married	−0.0001	0.007
Health: excellent	0.343**	0.016
Health: very good	0.266**	0.015
Health: good	0.213**	0.015
Health: fair	0.114**	0.015
High blood pressure	−0.012*	0.006
Diabetes	−0.013	0.011
Cancer	−0.028**	0.013
Lung disease	−0.032**	0.014
Ever had heart attack	−0.040**	0.010
Stroke	0.014	0.021
Arthritis	0.003	0.006
BMI	−0.0001	0.001
Smoker	−0.027**	0.007
Former smoker	0.007	0.006
Parent alive		
Mother's age < 75	0.088**	0.012
Father's age < 75	0.051**	0.017
Mother's age 75–85	0.075**	0.009
Father's age 75–85	0.072**	0.009
Mother's age > 85	0.095**	0.013
Father's age > 85	0.080**	0.015
Parent deceased		
Mother's age at death < 50	0.040**	0.014
Father's age at death < 50	0.037**	0.011
Mother's age at death 66–75	0.023**	0.011
Father's age at death 66–75	0.027**	0.008
Mother's age at death > 75	0.057**	0.010
Father's age at death > 75	0.077**	0.008
R^2	0.1846	
No. of observations	10070	

Notes: The reported regressions also include income and its square, wealth and its square.
* Statistically significant at the 0.10 level; ** statistically significant at the 0.05 level.

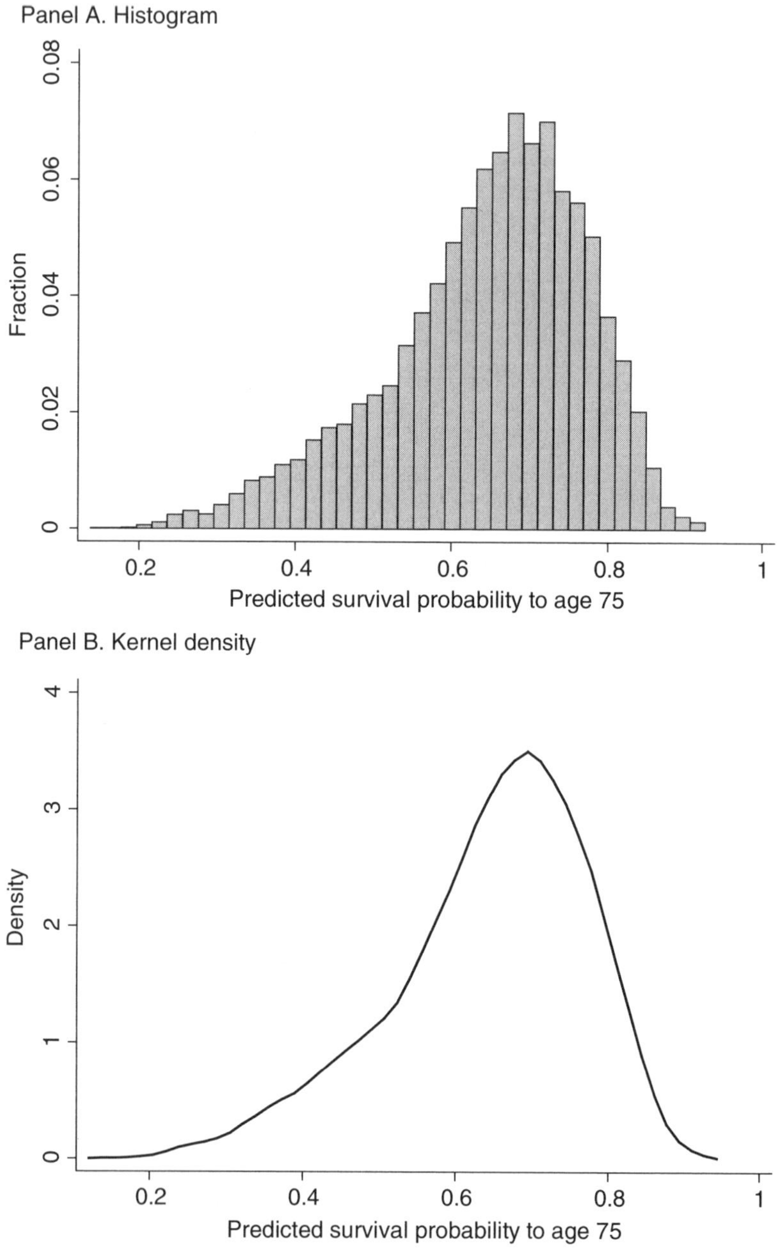

Figure A4.2 Distribution of the instrumented survival probability to age 75 in the estimation of observed mortality

Table A4.5 *Marginal effects of instrumented subjective survival probability from IV probit estimation of the observed mortality, waves 2 through 6*

Wave 1 controls	(1) Wave 2	(2) Wave 3	(3) Wave 4	(4) Wave 5	(5) Wave 6
Survival probability to 75	−0.0584** (0.0304)	−0.1052** (0.0411)	−0.2050** (0.0559)	−0.2997** (0.0636)	−0.4464** (0.0715)
Log pseudo likelihood	−2691.84	−3427.70	−4065.28	−4746.63	−5447.14
No. of observations			10 070		

Notes: Robust standard errors in parentheses. * Statistically significant at the 0.10 level; ** statistically significant at the 0.05 level.

in Table A4.4. In comparison with the histograms of the reported survival probability in Figure A4.1, the distribution of the instrumented subjective survival probability in Figure A4.2 is unimodal and continuous, and it falls well within 0 and 1.[24] In the full sample the correlation coefficient between the reported survival probability and the instrumented survival probability is 0.4297 and statistically significant at the 1 percent level.

Tables A4.5 and A4.6 report the marginal effects of the instrumented subjective survival probability from probit estimation of the mortality equation for each wave. Similar to the results in Table A4.2, the magnitude of the marginal effects of the instrumented subjective survival probability on actual mortality increases over time in Table A4.5, where no control variables have been included other than the instrumented subjective survival probability. Furthermore, one notices that, when the same columns from the two tables are compared, the magnitudes of the marginal effects are substantially larger in Table A4.5 than in Table A4.2, especially in columns 3, 4 and 5. This indicates that the instrumented subjective survival probability is a better predictor of long-term mortality than the reported subjective survival probability.

This conclusion does not change in Table A4.6, where other control variables are included. In predicting long-term mortality between waves 3 through 6, the marginal effect of the instrumented survival probability becomes gradually larger in absolute magnitude, except for wave 3, and significant in predicting long-term mortality by wave 6.[25]

Table A4.6 Marginal effects of instrumented subjective survival probability from IV probit estimation of the observed mortality, by selected variables, waves 2 through 6

Wave 1 controls	(1) Wave 2	(2) Wave 3	(3) Wave 4	(4) Wave 5	(5) Wave 6
Survival probability to 75	−0.0057	0.0037	−0.0257	−0.0436	−0.1271*
	(0.0180)	(0.0311)	(0.0433)	(0.0525)	(0.0681)
Age	0.0004*	0.0008**	0.0026**	0.0042**	0.0065**
	(0.0002)	(0.0004)	(0.0005)	(0.0006)	(0.0008)
Female	−0.0061**	−0.0169**	−0.0194**	−0.0318**	−0.0442**
	(0.0019)	(0.0037)	(0.0044)	(0.0054)	(0.0068)
Black	0.0046	0.0112**	0.0193**	0.0169**	0.0235**
	(0.0033)	(0.0052)	(0.0075)	(0.0085)	(0.0104)
Hispanic	0.0002	−0.0037	−0.0044	−0.0173**	−0.0278**
	(0.0032)	(0.0049)	(0.0072)	(0.0077)	(0.0098)
Other	−0.0016	0.0142	0.0118	0.0108	−0.0010
	(0.0046)	(0.0122)	(0.0149)	(0.0170)	(0.0214)
Years of education	−0.0001	−0.0003	0.0004	−0.0002	−0.0004
	(0.0003)	(0.0005)	(0.0007)	(0.0009)	(0.0011)
Married	−0.0032	−0.0077**	−0.0059	−0.0105*	−0.0210**
	(0.0021)	(0.0035)	(0.0045)	(0.0058)	(0.0074)
Health: Excellent	−0.0080**	−0.0213**	−0.0297**	−0.0409**	−0.0453**
	(0.0039)	(0.0077)	(0.0108)	(0.0136)	(0.0196)
Health: Very good	−0.0084**	−0.0222**	−0.0265**	−0.0405**	−0.0471**
	(0.0037)	(0.0073)	(0.0100)	(0.0119)	(0.0165)
Health: Good	−0.0086**	−0.0211**	−0.0266**	−0.0333**	−0.0380**
	(0.0031)	(0.0062)	(0.0082)	(0.0105)	(0.0145)

Health: Fair	−0.0045**	−0.0103**	−0.0137**	−0.0149*	−0.0164
	(0.0019)	(0.0041)	(0.0059)	(0.0080)	(0.0112)
High blood pressure	0.0034*	0.0124**	0.0142**	0.0265**	0.0331**
	(0.0019)	(0.0035)	(0.0043)	(0.0055)	(0.0067)
Diabetes	0.0068**	0.0332**	0.0616**	0.0771**	0.1014**
	(0.0035)	(0.0074)	(0.0099)	(0.0114)	(0.0134)
Cancer	0.0416**	0.0644**	0.0773**	0.1114**	0.1096**
	(0.0096)	(0.0134)	(0.0145)	(0.0173)	(0.0184)
Lung disease	0.0069	0.0233**	0.0351**	0.0499**	0.0721**
	(0.0043)	(0.0081)	(0.0103)	(0.0126)	(0.0156)
Ever had heart attack	0.0089**	0.0212**	0.0291**	0.0461**	0.0453**
	(0.0036)	(0.0063)	(0.0075)	(0.0094)	(0.0108)
Stroke	0.0113*	0.0181*	0.0273**	0.0554**	0.1044**
	(0.0067)	(0.0102)	(0.0135)	(0.0189)	(0.0249)
Arthritis	−0.0016	0.0010	−0.0014	−0.0076	−0.0136**
	(0.0016)	(0.0028)	(0.0039)	(0.0048)	(0.0061)
BMI	−0.00002	−0.0009**	−0.0011**	−0.0015**	−0.0016**
	(0.0001)	(0.0003)	(0.0004)	(0.0005)	(0.0006)
Smoker	0.0083**	0.0241**	0.0493**	0.0693**	0.1001**
	(0.0031)	(0.0057)	(0.0074)	(0.0088)	(0.0104)
Former smoker	0.0047**	0.0100**	0.0202**	0.0321**	0.0429**
	(0.0022)	(0.0038)	(0.0053)	(0.0065)	(0.0080)
Log pseudo likelihood	−1715.35	−2331.76	−2883.13	−3402.73	−3991.21
No. of observations			10 070		

Notes: Robust standard errors in parentheses. The reported regressions also include income and its square, wealth and its square. * Statistically significant at the 0.10 level; ** statistically significant at the 0.05 level.

NOTES

1. The authors are grateful to David de la Croix and to the organizers of the Conference on Population Aging, Intergenerational Transfers, and the Macroeconomy and its participants for their thoughtful comments and suggestions.
2. For example, the private savings rate in Taiwan rose from around 5 percent in the 1950s to well over 20 percent in the 1980s and 1990s.
3. Kalemli-Ozcan and Weil (2005) develop a model that examines the effect of declining uncertainty about age at death on the number of years spent in retirement at the end of the lifecycle. For an overlapping-generations model that highlights the effect of longevity on retirement and the accumulation of cohort-specific schooling capital, see Boucekkine, de la Croix and Licandro (2002). For a general-equilibrium overlapping-generations model that highlights the effect of longevity on both retirement and savings, see Kulish, Smith and Kent (2006).
4. According to Gruber and Wise (1998) and Blondal and Scarpetta (1997), social security systems in many countries offer individuals strong financial incentives to retire at particular ages. These studies also provide evidence that workers respond by retiring earlier than they would in the absence of these incentives.
5. There is one other potential explanation for an effect of longer life expectancy on wealth accumulation but not age at retirement: if the years of life gained are not healthy ones, age at retirement will tend to be stable and an increase in lifecycle savings will be needed to finance consumption during a longer period of 'physiologically forced' retirement. Recent evidence for the US tends to counter this explanation, supporting the Fries (1980) conjecture of a 'compression of morbidity' whereby the duration of time spent in chronic ill health toward the end of life has declined – in relative, and possibly also absolute terms (see Fries, 1989; Crimmins, Saito and Ingegneri, 1997; Costa, 2002; Crimmins, 2004; Mor, 2005).
6. In an early economic study of the information content of subjective survival probabilities, Hamermesh (1985) reports evidence that individuals' subjective survival probabilities are reasonably consistent with actuarial evidence on those probabilities and strongly correlated with the longevity of their parents and grandparents. Hamermesh derives evidence from two survey data sets: one consisting of 411 male economists ranging in age from 26 to 65, and the other consisting of 363 males between ages 20 and 70 who resided in a medium-sized sample metropolitan statistical area in the Midwestern part of the US. In another analysis of the same data sets, Hamermesh and Hamermesh (1983) report that subjective survival probabilities are reflective of individual-specific information on smoking and obesity, but not exercise.
7. The other questions involving subjective probabilities were as follows: 'What do you think are the chances that housing prices in your neighborhood will go up faster than prices in general over the next 10 years?', 'What do you think are the chances that the U.S. economy will experience a major depression sometime during the next 10 years or so?', 'What do you think are the chances that the U.S. economy will experience double-digit inflation sometime during the next 10 years or so?', 'What do you think are the chances that you [or your (husband/wife/partner)] will have to give major financial help to family members during the next 10 years?', 'Thinking about work generally and not just your present job, what do you think are the chances that you will be working full-time after you reach age 62?', 'And what about the chances that you will be working full-time after you reach age 65?', 'How likely is it that you will lose your job during the next year?', 'What about the chances that your health will limit your work activity during the next 10 years?', 'And what are the chances that Congress will change the Social Security law to make the system more generous than it is now?', and 'How about the chances that Congress will change Social Security so that it becomes less generous than now?'
8. According to Bassett and Lumsdaine (2001) the sum of the probabilities given for each of the two questions about Social Security – Congress will change the Social Security law to make the system more generous or less generous? – should be less than or equal

to 100; but they report that 1492 respondents (about 18 percent of their sample) gave answers that summed to more than 100. The initial assumption is problematic, however, as there is no reason to think that Social Security benefits could not become more generous at some point in the future and less generous at some other point.

9. Hurd, McFadden and Gan (1998) used a simple ordered probit analysis in which the dependent variable was the categorical information on whether each respondent was a net saver, a zero saver, or a net dissaver.
10. Hurd, McFadden and Gan (1998) also use the parental mortality experience to correct for errors in subjective survival probabilities in their sample from the AHEAD study. They too find that greater parental longevity is in general associated with greater subjective probability of survival, but the relationship is statistically significant only for females when the father's longevity is higher. In addition to the differences in data, two other differences make the results by Hurd, McFadden and Gan (1998) not directly comparable to those by Hurd and McGarry (1995). First, according to Hurd and McGarry (1995), the effects of parental longevity on the subjective survival probability of the respondents are not linear. Hurd, McFadden and Gan (1998) employed a linear specification. Second, Hurd and McGarry (1995) create dummy indicators for surviving parents, whereas Hurd, McFadden and Gan (1998) use the expected age at death conditional on the age attained, calculated from life tables.
11. The summary labor force status variable in the RAND HRS data is based on the following information: working for pay, employment status, retired, looking for work, usual hours worked per week, usual weeks worked per year, and information on second job. Hurd, Smith and Zissimopoulos (2004) use the same definition of retirement. According to Gustman and Steinmeier (2000), there are alternative definitions of retirement in the HRS. We plan to conduct further analyses based on these alternative definitions of retirement.
12. The results do not substantially change when the subjective survival probabilities to age 85 are used instead.
13. The drop in the retirement rate observed after age 68 seems to be due to small sample sizes. The numbers of observations for ages 69 and 70 are 36 and 22, respectively. Moreover, t-tests confirm that the retirement rates are not significantly different between ages 68 and 69 or between ages 69 and 70.
14. Respondents were asked about the time period that was important when planning their savings and spending. The results do not substantially change when dummy variables for planning horizon are excluded.
15. The amount of inheritance is not separately available in the RAND HRS files.
16. In the first-stage IV estimation of the retirement and wealth equations, the coefficients on the dummy variables for the mortality experience of the parents, though unreported, show the same signs and significance as those reported in Table A4.1.
17. The reference group is age 50.
18. Instead of the age dummy variables, we have included age and its square in the wealth equation.
19. Critical values for the Craig–Donald statistic for the presence of weak instruments based on two-stage least squares bias are 20.69, 11.05, 6.06 and 4.32 for the 5 percent, 10 percent, 20 percent and 30 percent bias, respectively. If the Craig–Donald statistic is less than the critical value, the instruments are weak. See Stock and Yogo (2002) for details.
20. Outside the age range 51–61, the sample is not representative of the population in 1992. Yet our analysis includes those respondents outside the age range 51–61 who are spouses or partners of age-eligible individuals to have more age variation and more observed deaths than in the age-eligible sample.
21. The individuals whom we exclude because of missing data on subjective survival probabilities and the mortality of parents (502 observations) have significantly higher cumulative mortality rates than those included in the sample. By wave 6, for instance, about 17 percent of the individuals in this excluded group had died.
22. Our income and wealth measures refer to wave 1 and can therefore be regarded as exogenous in the estimation of mortality in subsequent waves.

23. Hurd and McGarry (2002) use almost the same explanatory variables.
24. The minimum and maximum values for the instrumented subjective survival probability are 0.14 and 0.93 respectively.
25. Those who were 45–65 years old in wave 1 were 55–75 years old in wave 6.

REFERENCES

Bassett, William F. and Robin L. Lumsdaine (2001), 'Probability limits: are subjective assessments adequately accurate?', *Journal of Human Resources*, **36**(2), 327–63.

Blondal, Sveinbjorn and Stefano Scarpetta (1997), 'Early retirement in OECD countries: the role of social security systems', *OECD Economic Studies*, **29**(1997/II), 7–54.

Bloom, David E., David Canning and Bryan Graham (2003), 'Longevity and life-cycle savings', *Scandinavian Journal of Economics*, **105**, 319–38.

Bloom, David E., David Canning and Michael Moore (2004), 'Health, longevity, and optimal retirement', NBER Working Paper 10919, National Bureau of Economic Research, Cambridge, Massachusetts, August.

Bloom, David E., David Canning, Rick Mansfield and Michael Moore (2007), 'Demographic change, social security systems, and savings', *Journal of Monetary Economics*, **54**(1), 92–114.

Bloom, David E., David Canning, Michael Moore and Younghwan Song (2006), 'The effect of subjective survival probabilities on retirement and saving', manuscript, Harvard School of Public Health, Boston, Massachusetts, July.

Bongaarts, John and Griffith Feeney (2003), 'Estimating mean lifetimes', *Proceedings of the National Academy of Sciences*, **100**(23), 13127–33.

Boucekkine, Raouf, David de la Croix and Omar Licandro (2002), 'Vintage human capital, demographic trends, and endogenous growth', *Journal of Economic Theory*, **104**, 340–75.

Costa, Dora L. (2002), 'Changing chronic disease rates and long-term declines in functional limitation among older men', *Demography*, **39**, 119–37.

Crimmins, Eileen M. (2004), 'Trends in the health of the elderly', *Annual Review of Public Health*, **25**, 79–98.

Crimmins, Eileen M., Yasuhiko Saito and Dominique Ingegneri (1997), 'Trends in disability-free life expectancy in the United States, 1970–90', *Population Development Review*, **23**, 555–72.

Deaton, A. (1992), *Understanding Consumption*, Oxford: Oxford University Press.

Deaton, Angus and Christina H. Paxson (1994), 'Savings, growth, and aging in Taiwan', in David Wise (ed.), *Studies in the Economics of Aging*, Chicago: National Bureau of Economic Research and University of Chicago Press.

Deaton, Angus and Christina H. Paxson (1997), 'The effects of economic and population growth on national savings and inequality', *Demography*, **34**, 97–114.

Deaton, Angus and Christina H. Paxson (2000), 'Growth, demographic structure, and national savings in Taiwan', *Population and Development Review*, **26**(Supplement), 141–73.

Fries, James F. (1980), 'Aging, natural death, and the compression of morbidity', *New England Journal of Medicine*, **303**, 130–35.

Fries, James F. (1989), 'The compression of morbidity: near or far?', *Milbank Quarterly*, **67**, 208–32.
Gruber, Jonathan and David Wise (1998), 'Social security and retirement: an international comparison', *American Economic Review*, **88**, 158–63.
Gustman, Alan L. and Thomas L. Steinmeier (2000), 'Retirement outcomes in the Health and Retirement Study', *Social Security Bulletin*, **63**(4), 57–71.
Hamermesh, Daniel S. (1985), 'Expectations, life expectancy, and economic behavior', *Quarterly Journal of Economics*, **100**(2), 389–408.
Hamermesh, Daniel S. and Frances W. Hamermesh (1983), 'Does perception of life expectancy reflect health knowledge?', *American Journal of Public Health*, **73**(8), 911–14.
Hurd, Michael D. and Kathleen McGarry (1995), 'Evaluation of the subjective probabilities of survival', *Journal of Human Resources*, **30**(Supplement), S268–92.
Hurd, Michael D. and Kathleen McGarry (2002), 'The predictive validity of subjective probabilities of survival', *Economic Journal*, **112**(October), 966–85.
Hurd, Michael D., Daniel McFadden and Li Gan (1998), 'Subjective survival curves and life cycle behavior', in David Wise (ed.), *Inquiries in the Economics of Aging*, Chicago: University of Chicago Press.
Hurd, Michael D., James P. Smith and Julie M. Zissimopoulos (2004), 'The effects of subjective survival on retirement and Social Security claiming', *Journal of Applied Econometrics*, **19**, 761–75.
Kalemli-Ozcan, Sebnem and David N. Weil (2005), 'Mortality change, the uncertainty effect, and retirement', manuscript, Brown University, Providence, Rhode Island, August.
Kulish, Mariano, Kathryn Smith and Christopher Kent (2006), 'Ageing, retirement, and savings: a general equilibrium analysis', research discussion paper, Economic Research Department, Reserve Bank of Australia, Sydney, June.
Lee, Ronald D., Andrew Mason and Tim Miller (1998), 'Saving, wealth, and population', unpublished manuscript, University of California at Berkeley.
Lee, Ronald D., Andrew Mason and Tim Miller (2000), 'Life cycle saving and the demographic transition: the case of Taiwan', *Population and Development Review*, **26**(Supplement), 194–219.
Li, Nan and Ronald Lee (2005), 'Coherent mortality forecasts for a group of populations: an extension of the Lee–Carter method', *Demography*, **42**(3), 575–94.
Mor, Vincent (2005), 'The compression of morbidity hypothesis: a review of research and prospects for the future', *Journal of the American Geriatric Society*, **53**, S308–9.
Siegel, Michele, Elizabeth H. Bradley and Stanislav V. Kasl (2003), 'Self-rated life expectancy as a predictor of mortality: evidence from the HRS and AHEAD surveys', *Gerontology*, **49**, 265–71.
Stock, James H. and Motohiro Yogo (2002), 'Testing for weak instruments in Linear IV Regression', NBER Technical Working Paper 284, National Bureau of Economic Research, Cambridge, Massachusetts, November.
Tsai I.-J., C.Y.C. Chu and Cyrus F. Chung (2000), 'Demographic transition and household saving in Taiwan', *Population and Development Review*, **26**(supplement), 174–93.

PART III

Saving and wealth

5. Modeling the effects of population aging on consumption in the presence of intergenerational transfers

Heinrich Hock and David N. Weil

Most developed countries are now on the cusp of a dramatic rise in old-age dependency. The implications of this growing dependency for the overall performance of the economy, and especially for the fiscal positions of governments, have been the subject of intense scrutiny. The coming rise in old-age dependency is part of a much broader phenomenon of population aging, which has been going on for decades. Not all of the economic consequences of population are negative. For example, the coming rise in old-age dependency largely mirrors the decline in youth dependency that took place in the middle of the twentieth century as birth rates fell in most developed countries. Many developing countries, by contrast, are only now starting to reap the benefits of the 'demographic dividend' that results from lower fertility. Similarly, the slowdown in population growth that results from declining fertility means that there is less capital dilution, as well as an age structure more favorable toward saving.[1]

In this chapter we consider the effects of population aging and the associated changes in economic dependency in the larger context of adjustment of the population age structure to changing fertility and mortality. To isolate analytically these channels of influence, we use a new dynamic model of population age structure. Our model is a continuous-time, overlapping-generations (OG) model in which individuals proceed through three life stages: dependent youth, working age, and dependent elderly. The model has the advantages that it can be represented in a simple two-dimensional diagram and can be solved explicitly. It represents a useful alternative to existing discrete-time OG models, which either have only a few life stages (allowing for analytic solutions but very difficult to compare with real-world dynamics) or have many life stages but cannot be solved analytically. The model we present has applications well beyond those pursued here, and it represents a new and convenient way of conceptualizing demographic–economic interactions. Here we examine both the steady-state relationship between fertility, youth dependency, and old-age dependency, and also the dynamic evolution of dependency ratios.

We then consider the implications for consumption by turning our attention to a needs-weighted support ratio similar to that of Cutler et al. (1990). Setting aside the effects of the age structure on labor productivity and capital, declines in fertility are always associated with a transient demographic dividend, during which reduced youth dependency raises consumption in an economy. As the age structure shifts toward the elderly, however, the steady-state effect of a fertility decline on consumption may be positive or negative, depending on various demographic and economic fundamentals. Our model allows us to solve for the fertility rate that minimizes the support ratio, which is equivalent to maximizing consumption in our framework. We are also able to examine how the consumption-maximizing fertility rate adjusts to changes in the other fundamentals.

Although our dynamic model of population age structure is useful in establishing general points about the effects of fertility changes, it is too crude for realistic quantitative analysis. Thus we also examine the same issues addressed by the model in a more fully fleshed-out demographic model. Using actual life-table data and measures of relative consumption needs of people of different ages, we are able to solve for the consumption-maximizing fertility rates as a function of mortality profiles and retirement ages. We find that for Japan and the United States the consumption-maximizing fertility rates are substantially higher than actual fertility rates for all plausible scenarios.

The rest of the chapter is structured as follows. In the next section we lay out our model of the population age structure and dependency ratios. Then we use the model to analyze the dynamic response of the economy to changes in fertility and also examine the levels of consumption in steady states and along transition paths. Next we use a more fully fleshed-out demographic model to analyze consumption-maximizing fertility rates resulting from changes in mortality and retirement. In the subsequent section we discuss the possibility that changes in consumption brought about by population aging may in turn feed back to affect fertility, thus causing future aging. We summarize our conclusions in the final section.

A DYNAMIC MODEL OF THE AGE STRUCTURE

People age through economic and demographic stages in a fashion that is largely, though not completely, predictable. They are dependent when young, work in the middle years of life, and, in wealthy countries, spend time out of the labor force between their working years and death. They do most of their investment in education when young, produce children during the first half of their working years, smooth their consumption by saving prior to retirement, and so on. At a given point in time, an economy is composed of individuals at various stages of the economic lifecycle, and the interaction of these individuals determines such aggregate quantities as the interest rate, wages, and the tax rate required to support government transfers. The interest of macroeconomists in population aging is in determining exactly how changes in the relative numbers of people at different stages of their lifecycles will affect these aggregate quantities.

Condensing the variation in the human lifecycle described above into a sparse aggregative framework is a challenge when constructing macroeconomic models that include a demographic component. There is an inherent trade-off between analytic tractability and realism. At one end of the spectrum are OG models in which individuals live for either two periods (work and old age) or three periods (childhood, work and old age). These models possess the virtue that they can be analyzed graphically or analytically. They suffer from two problems, however. First, the structure of the model imposes the constraint that an individual spend an equal amount of time in each of the model's functional categories (that is, working and retired, or child, working and retired). Not only is this constraint unrealistic, but also many of the questions one would like to address with such a model are about what happens when the amount of time spent in one category or another changes. Second, the time periods in such models are inevitably long (either half or a third of a lifetime), and so the dynamic response of the model to a shock is extremely 'lumpy' and hard to compare with real-world data. At the other end of the spectrum are OG models such as those of Auerbach and Kotlikoff (1987) and Kotlikoff, Smetters and Walliser (2001), in which the economic lifecycle is divided into pieces that correspond to individual years of age. These models achieve a much higher degree of realism, at the cost of analytic tractability; they can be solved only by using a computer.

In this chapter we develop an approach that corrects some of the problems described above. Specifically, we extend Blanchard's (1985) continuous-time model of 'perpetual youth' to encompass three economic stages of life. In our model individuals pass through stages of dependent youth, working age, and dependent old age. Unlike a traditional OG model, however, the amount of time spent in each life cycle stage is not fixed. Rather, individuals transfer from one stage to another with constant (stage-specific) hazard rates.[2] Casting the model in continuous time allows us to overcome the lumpiness that is usually present in OG models. This allows a more realistic model-based analysis of the demographic dynamics in which we are interested. Continuous time also allows us to dispense with the problem present in most two- or three-period OG models: that the amount of time spent in each life stage has to be equal. In our model the average time that an individual spends in a life stage is the inverse of the probability of exiting that life stage. By working with only three age groups, we are able to retain analytic tractability. Further, as will be seen below, the model has a graphical representation in which the demographic condition of the economy is summarized by the ratio of children to working-age adults and the ratio of elderly to working-age adults.

The triple (A_Y, A_M, A_O) characterizes the age structure of the population: A_Y is the stock of young people who have never worked, A_M is the stock of people in the economy who are in their working years, and A_O is the stock of people who once worked but are now retired. Individuals progress monotonically through the age structure. Adapting Blanchard's framework to our structure, we assume constant exit probabilities from each group. For the young and the working, λ_Y and λ_M give the hazard of transition to work and retirement. Among the elderly, λ_O is the probability of dying.[3]

These hazards determine all of the flows in the model, except the flow of births into A_Y, which is given by N. These dynamics are summarized in the following system of equations:

$$\dot{A}_Y(t) = N(t) - \lambda_Y A_Y(t), \tag{5.1}$$

$$\dot{A}_M(t) = \lambda_Y A_Y(t) - \lambda_M A_M(t), \tag{5.2}$$

$$\dot{A}_O(t) = \lambda_M A_M(t) - \lambda_O A_O(t). \tag{5.3}$$

Each exit parameter λ_j gives the inverse of the average time spent in age group j, which we will call the width of the age group and denote as T_j. In our empirical work below we will use demographic and economic data to determine the widths of the age groups.

Dynamics of the Dependency Ratios

We focus our analysis on the youth and old-age dependency ratios: $y(t) = A_Y(t)/A_M(t)$ and $o(t) = A_O(t)/A_M(t)$. The equations describing the movement of the dependency ratios represent a reduced version of the dynamical system governing the age structure, that is, equations (5.1)–(5.3). The equation of motion for $o(t)$ reduces cleanly to a function of the dependency ratios:

$$\dot{o}(t) = \lambda_M - (\lambda_O - \lambda_M)o(t) - \lambda_Y y(t)o(t). \tag{5.4}$$

The dynamics of the youth-dependency ratio, however, depend additionally on the aggregate flow of births, $N(t)$, which is a function of both the stock of fecund persons and the rate of fertility among the fecund. We treat individuals as the reproductive unit of analysis. We assume that workers are fecund for an expected length of time $T_F < T_M$, and denote by ϕ the proportion of the workforce that is fecund. In principle we could augment the model to allow the fecund share of the workforce to evolve along with the rest of the age structure. However, this complicates the analysis we present below, while adding little qualitatively. Consequently we assume that ϕ is fixed and equal to T_F/T_M. Denoting by $n(t)$ the average fertility rate among the fecund at time t, under this assumption the dynamic equation for the youth dependency ratio is

$$\dot{y}(t) = \phi n(t) - (\lambda_Y - \lambda_M)y(t) - \lambda_Y[y(t)]^2, \tag{5.5}$$

where $\phi n(t)$ is the flow of births per worker.

Equilibrium with Constant Fertility, Mortality and Retirement

The two equations describing the movement of the dependency ratios, (5.4) and (5.5), characterize a dynamical system that is quite straightforward to analyze graphically. The dynamics of the youth dependency ratio are independent of the old-age dependency ratio and mortality. Consequently, given a fixed fertility rate, we may simply solve for the equilibrium youth dependency ratio, y. This is more conveniently represented as a function of the gross reproduction rate (GRR). Given that individuals are the reproductive unit of analysis in our model, the GRR is the expected number of children born, assuming individuals follow the currently prevailing rate of fertility for the entirety of their childbearing years. Given our assumptions regarding the stock of fecund persons, the gross reproduction rate is $G = T_F n$ and the flow of births per worker is $\phi n = G/T_M$. Substituting this expression for the flow of births per worker into equation (5.5) and setting it equal to zero yields one positive root:

$$\bar{y} = -\frac{1}{2}\left(1 - \frac{T_Y}{T_M}\right) + \sqrt{\left[\frac{1}{2}\left(1 - \frac{T_Y}{T_M}\right)\right]^2 + \frac{T_Y}{T_M}G}, \tag{5.6}$$

where we have used that fact that $\lambda_j = (T_j)^{-1}$. The equation of motion for y implies that this root is stable.

Setting (5.4) equal to zero yields a locus of steady-state values of the old-age dependency ratio that is conditional on the youth dependency ratio and can be written as

$$Z_o(y) = \frac{1}{(T_M/T_O - 1) + (T_M/T_Y)y}.$$

Hence, for a given value of y, there is exactly one equilibrium value of the old-age dependency ratio. Since $d[\dot{o}(t)]/d[o(t)]<0$, these equilibrium values are stable. The graph of $Z_O(y)$ in (y, o)-space is downward-sloping and convex with respect to the origin, as depicted in Figure 5.1. Given constant demographic parameters, $Z_O(y)$ is equivalent to a locus of stable populations, and we call its slope the *marginal rate of demographic substitution*.

The demographic steady state is determined from the widths of the age groups and the fixed fertility rate, which pins down the equilibrium youth dependency ratio, $\bar{y}$. The equilibrium old-age dependency ratio is traced out from $\bar{y}$ using the locus of stable populations. Graphically, Figure 5.1 portrays the global dynamics of the population dependency ratios, which converge monotonically to the equilibrium point $(\bar{y},\bar{o})$. When the GRR is at the replacement rate of 1, the equilibrium dependency ratios simplify to

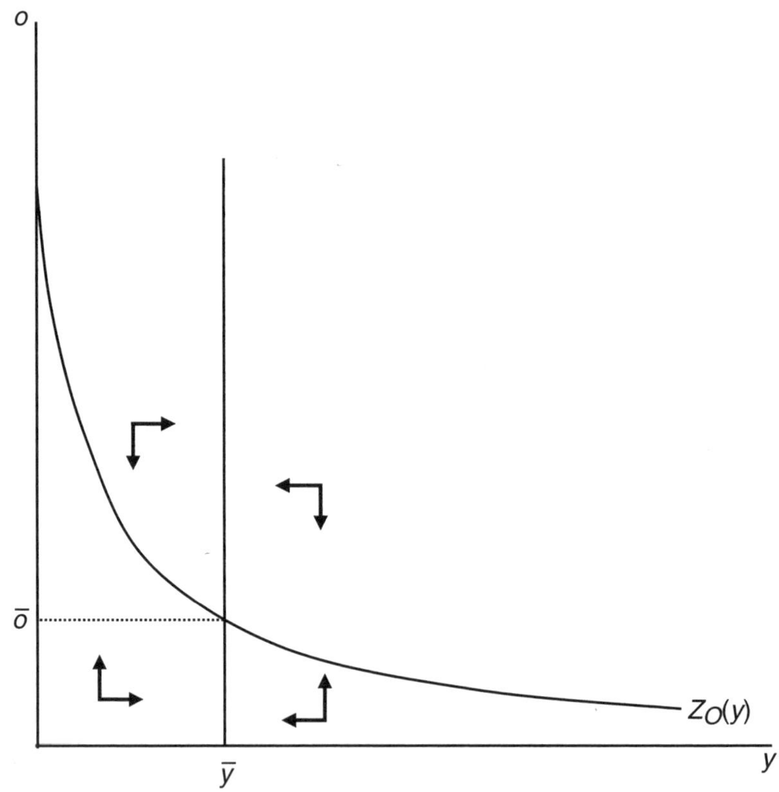

Figure 5.1 Demographic equilibrium with constant fertility, mortality and retirement

$\bar{y}^r = T_Y/T_M$, and $\bar{o}^r = T_O/T_M$. These results are fairly intuitive, and they parallel those in basic demographic theory. In a stable population with replacement fertility, the relative sizes of the age groups in equilibrium should simply be the ratios of their widths.

THE CONSUMPTION SUPPORT RATIO AND CONSUMPTION-MAXIMIZING FERTILITY

The support ratio is defined as the ratio of workers to total population. It provides a very basic measure of the consumption possibilities in an economy, leaving aside considerations of capital accumulation and labor force productivity.[4] However, consumption tends to vary substantially with age (Lee, Lee and Mason, 2006), meaning that changes in youth dependency and elderly dependency will have different implications for per capita resource availability. In our model we assume that the young and old have consumption needs equivalent to χ_Y and χ_O times that of the working. The *consumption support ratio* (CSR) is given by

$$\alpha(t) = \frac{A_M(t)}{\chi_Y A_Y(t) + A_M(t) + \chi_O A_O(t)} = \frac{1}{1 + e(t)},$$

where $e(t) = \chi_Y y(t) + \chi_{\hat{O}} o(t)$ is the degree of economic dependency in the economy. Increases in youth and elderly dependency both reduce potential per capita consumption, but their effects on α are proportional to the relative consumption needs of the young and old. Below we consider the impact of changes in the fertility rate on economic dependency and consumption. We then consider the consequences of population aging due to increased life expectancy among the elderly, and the effects of changes in the retirement age.

Declining Fertility, Dependency and the Consumption Support Ratio

The recent trend toward population aging in the developed world is largely a product of reductions in fertility over the twentieth century. Our model can be used to describe analytically the resulting transitional dynamics. After a fall in G the equilibrium youth dependency ratio falls, according to equation (5.6). As shown in Figure 5.2, a decline in $\bar{y}$ ultimately maps to a higher equilibrium value of the old-age dependency ratio along the $Z_O(y)$ locus. Early in the transition, declines in youth dependency are much larger than the increases in old-age dependency, so that the consumption support ratio naturally falls. Later in the transition there comes a turning point, after which the fall in economic dependency caused by declining youth dependency is more than offset by the increased burden of old-age dependency. As a result the CSR begins to decrease as the economy approaches the new equilibrium.[5] Hence the consumption benefits from the demographic dividend are time-limited. These analytic results essentially parallel the historical and projected movements of the consumption support ratio shown for the United States in Cutler et al. (1990) and for Austria in Prskawetz and Fent (2004).

An important consideration that, to our knowledge, has not been addressed in the literature is that the net effect of a fertility decline on equilibrium economic dependency is, *a priori*, ambiguous. The inset of Figure 5.2 shows a general set of paths for the youth dependency, elderly dependency and consumption support ratios after a decline in the fertility rate in the case where the new equilibrium has a lower value of α and a higher level of economic dependency. As shown in the empirical section below, this

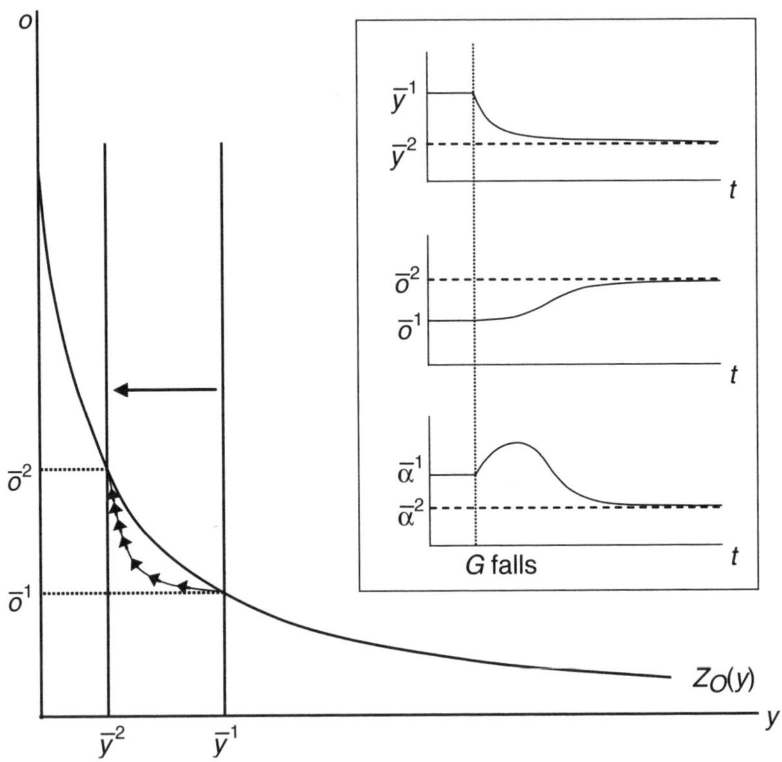

Figure 5.2 The effects of a decline in the fertility rate

likely represents the effects of recent fertility declines in most of the highly developed world.

Consumption-maximizing Fertility

Our model allows us to characterize the fertility rate that maximizes the consumption support ratio or alternatively minimizes economic dependency. Following Weil (1999), we accomplish this graphically using *iso-dependency lines*: combinations of y and o associated with a fixed level of economic dependency, e. These are represented in (y, o) space as $o = I_e(y)$. Iso-dependency lines that are closer to the origin are associated with a lower rate of economic dependency and a higher consumption support ratio.

Overlaying a set of iso-dependency lines across the $Z_O(y)$ locus allows us to compare the level of economic dependency at different equilibrium age structures. Because it is convex with respect to the origin, there is a unique equilibrium pair of dependency ratios $(\bar{y}^m, \bar{o}^m)$, at which an iso-dependency line is tangent to the $Z_O(y)$ locus. (See Figure 5.3.) At this point the

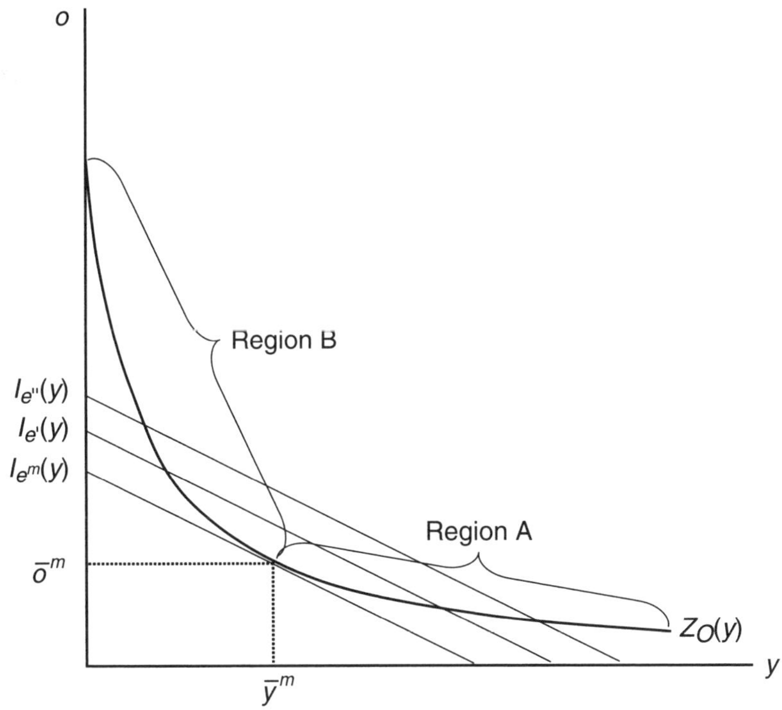

Figure 5.3 Economic dependency and the locus of stable populations

marginal rate of demographic substitution is equated with the ratio of relative consumption needs, which implies that the CSR is maximized.[6] There is a unique fertility rate G^m that generates the equilibrium $(\bar{y}^m,\bar{o}^m)$, given values of the other parameters. For fertility rates above G^m, corresponding to equilibria in Region A of the $Z_O(y)$ locus in Figure 5.3, small declines in G lead to a higher CSR. The opposite occurs in Region B, where further reductions from low fertility rates ultimately lead to a lower consumption support ratio.

The broad pattern of fertility change in the developed world has been that of decline. Reductions in fertility from high levels $G^h > G^m$ are associated with a higher consumption support ratio at all future dates, as is evident in Figure 5.4. Thus, although α follows an inverted-U shaped path along the transition, not all of the gains in consumption are term-limited. If fertility rates in the developed world are still above the consumption-maximizing rate, the coming decline in the consumption support ratio is simply a partial reversal of an earlier demographic golden age.

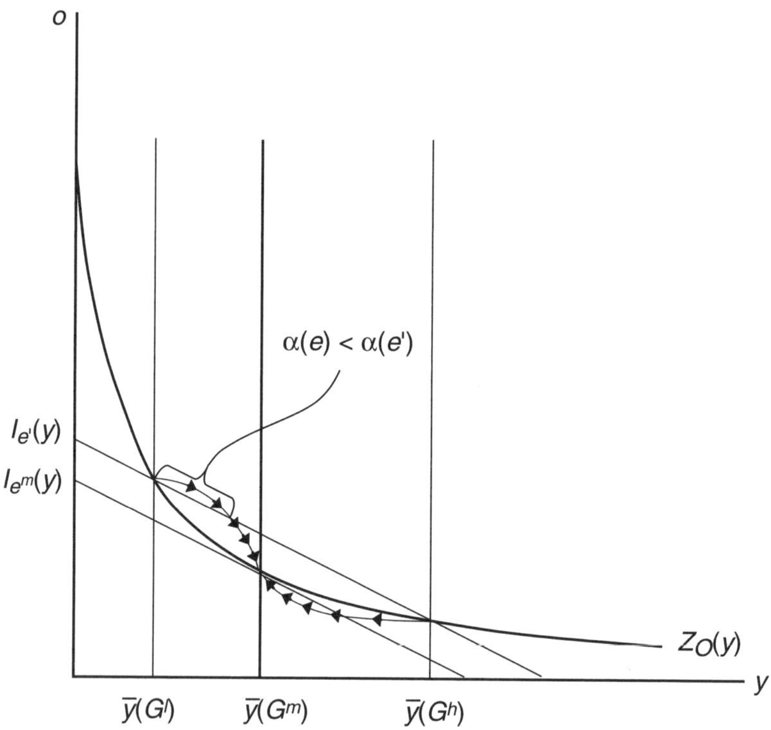

Figure 5.4 Transition to the consumption-maximizing equilibrium

However, as we shall show below, it is likely that fertility rates in many highly developed countries have already fallen below their respective consumption-maximizing rates. In this scenario, further declines in fertility are still associated with a transient demographic dividend, but an eventually higher equilibrium support ratio. Additionally, for such countries an increase in fertility toward the consumption-maximizing rate is associated with a costly transition. As shown in Figure 5.4, in a country with the same initial economic dependency as implied by G^h and a fertility rate of $G^l < G^m$, economic dependency must initially increase. This occurs because of the immediately higher burden of youth dependency and implies an early decline in the consumption support ratio. It is only later in the transition, as the elderly dependency ratio declines, that the consumption benefits from the increase in fertility are realized.

Mortality, Retirement and the Consumption-maximizing Rate of Fertility

While falling fertility has been the dominant factor in recent population aging trends in the developed world, declining mortality also plays a role. Of particular relevance are the gains in elderly life expectancy. In the United States, for example, life expectancy at age 65 has risen by approximately 3.5 years since 1950, and standard forecasts predict a similar, although slightly smaller, rise over the next 50 years.[7] Other highly developed countries have seen comparable or greater reductions in old-age mortality over the past half-century and can be expected to follow a similar trend in the future.[8] Holding the other parameters constant, our model generates relatively straightforward dynamics when elderly life expectancy rises. The old-age dependency ratio increases monotonically toward the new equilibrium, driving up the consumption support ratio along the way, while the youth dependency ratio remains unchanged. Below we discuss the possibility of a feedback from rising elderly dependency to the fertility choices individuals make; here we focus on the implications for the consumption-maximizing rate of fertility.

Our model predicts that, *ceteris paribus*, higher life expectancy after retirement is associated with a higher consumption-maximizing fertility rate, G^m. While an increase in fertility would cause youth dependency to rise in equilibrium, the consumption-maximizing rate is set to balance the marginal effects of old-age and youth dependency on economic dependency. Higher life expectancy after retirement raises the total cost of supporting the elderly, and more importantly it implies a larger *marginal* reduction in old-age dependency for an increase in youth dependency along the locus of stable populations. Thus, whereas a marginal reduction in fertility from the initial consumption-maximizing fertility rate lowers the consumption support ratio through a higher $\bar{y}$, this effect is more than offset by the eventual decrease in elderly dependency. For countries with a fertility rate that is initially higher than G^m, the new consumption-maximizing rate draws closer to their existing fertility rate. Not only does the best-attainable level of consumption fall, so does the steady-state gain from reducing the fertility rate.[9] For countries in which the fertility rate is already below G^m, the consumption-maximizing fertility rate moves further away as old-age mortality rises. Although the best-attainable level of consumption falls, the equilibrium α associated with $G^l < G^m$ falls even more, meaning that there are greater potential equilibrium gains from raising fertility rates. Hence the continued decline in childbearing rates exhibited in many highly developed countries is at odds with the fertility strategy that would maximize the future consumption support ratio. We return to this point when we analyze the feedback from population aging to low fertility.

The retirement age also plays a role in determining the degree of dependency in a population. Although the secular trend over the last 25 years in most developed countries has been toward earlier retirement (OECD, 2004, table SS8.2), at a policy level the movement has been in the other direction. Owing to the rising burden of elderly dependency, some developed countries have raised, or are in the process of raising, the retirement age for state-sponsored retirement programs, and most others are actively discussing it. In our model the effects of a change in the retirement age ($R \equiv T_Y + T_M$), holding life expectancy ($T_Y + T_M + T_O$) constant, will have an ambiguous effect on the consumption-maximizing rate of fertility. The ambiguity arises because of two opposing factors. Increasing the retirement age reduces the marginal demographic cost of o for any value of y on the locus of stable populations. *Ceteris paribus*, moving toward an age structure with less youth dependency would reduce total economic dependency.[10] However, the increase in the retirement age also de facto decreases the equilibrium burden of youth dependency for any fertility rate. Whether the necessary or realized reduction in youth dependency is marginally larger depends on the other parameters and the consumption profiles, and G^m adjusts accordingly. In the next section we assess quantitatively the impact of changes in the retirement age, conditional on various mortality profiles, on the consumption-maximizing fertility rate.

QUANTITATIVE ANALYSIS

Our model provides a useful tool for considering analytically the broad relationship between fertility and the consumption support ratio, but an analogous demographic model with many age groups provides a more accurate framework in which to undertake a quantitative analysis. In this section we use such a disaggregated framework to calculate the consumption-maximizing total fertility rate (TFR) in the United States and Japan.[11] Our strategy for calculating the consumption-maximizing fertility rate based on lifecycle data is as follows. We use age-specific mortality and fertility profiles to produce the associated stable population for each country. We then calculate the consumption support ratio, described below, associated with that stable population. This exercise is repeated for a variety of TFRs, implemented by proportionately scaling current age-specific fertility rates until a maximum CSR is obtained. This consumption-maximizing rate of fertility (F^m) is, of course, specific to the lifecycle profiles used to generate it. Hence, after computing F^m using recent estimates of lifecycle parameters, we explore how it changes on the basis of differing retirement and mortality profiles.

Consumption-maximizing Fertility Based on Recent Lifecycle Data

In addition to the age structure of the population, the consumption ratio will depend on (a) the age of entry into the workforce, T_Y; (b) the retirement age, R; and (c) estimates of relative consumption needs. Since data on the age of entry into the labor force are difficult to come by, we set T_Y equal to 20. Table 5.1 provides values for the average age at retirement in the countries we consider, based on recent OECD data. It also lists calculated values of life expectancy after retirement, corresponding to T_O in our theoretical model, for the sake of comparison.[12] While the average age at retirement is slightly lower in Japan, life expectancy after retirement is higher by a good margin. Using the OECD retirement data, we construct estimates of the potential labor force as

$$L(t) = \sum_{s=1}^{2} \sum_{x=20}^{R^s} A_x^s(t),$$

where s denotes gender, R^s the gender-specific retirement age and A_x^s the population of gender s at exact age x. Where the retirement age is fractional, we split the age group that spans it using linear interpolation.

Lifecycle consumption data used to compute the consumption support ratio come from the National Transfer Accounts Database (2006).[13] These data include estimates of both private consumption and public expenditures per capita at each age. We construct a lifecycle consumption profile vector (c_x), with each element defined as consumption per capita at age x divided by the average across ages 20 through 64. Figure 5.5 plots the lifecycle consumption profiles for Japan and the United States. In the US,

Table 5.1 Age at retirement and life expectancy at retirement: Japan and the United States, recent years

Country	Age at retirement[a]			Life expectancy at retirement[b]		
	Females	Males	Average	Females	Males	Average
Japan	62.8	64.8	63.8	24.3	17.7	21.0
United States	64.0	65.0	64.5	20.0	16.3	18.1

Notes:

[a] The age at retirement we report is the average of the official and 'effective' retirement age in 2002, the latter of which is based on observed changes in labor force participation rates.

[b] Life expectancy data are for the year 2000.

Sources: OECD (2004, table SS8.1) and Human Mortality Database (2006).

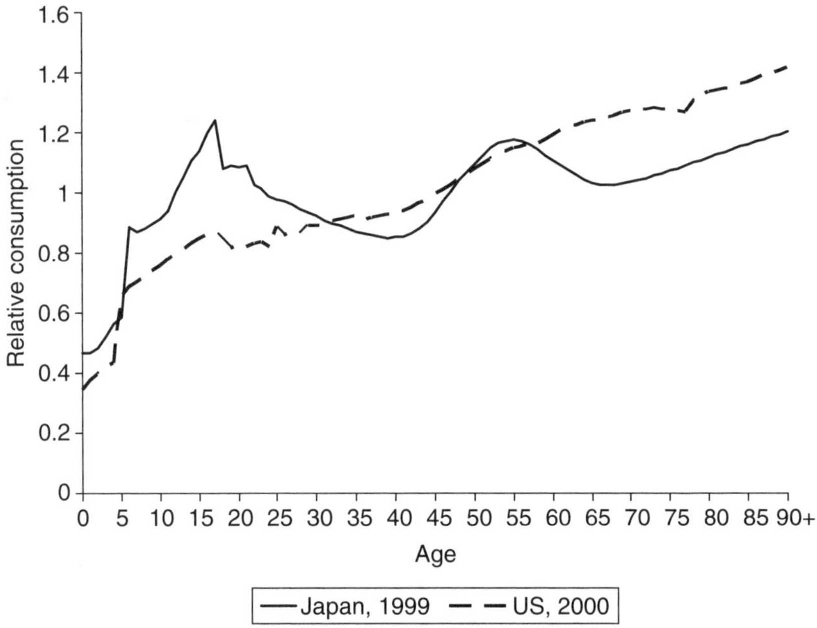

Notes: Consumption profiles are defined relative to the average for ages 20–64 in each country.

Source: National Transfer Accounts Database (2006).

Figure 5.5 Consumption profiles for Japan and the United States

Table 5.2 Current fertility, consumption-maximizing fertility and potential change in steady-state consumption: Japan and the United States, recent mortality and retirement profiles

Country	Current TFR	Consumption-maximizing TFR	Potential change in $\bar{a}$
Japan	1.35	2.50	9.92%
United States	2.03	2.79	2.78%

Source: Authors' calculations.

consumption rises almost uniformly with age, whereas in Japan it is more variable over the life course.[14] Relative to the Japan, consumption in the US is also shifted from the young to the elderly. Based on a consumption profile, the consumption support ratio is calculated as

$$a(t) = \frac{L(t)}{\Sigma_{s=1}^{2}\Sigma_{x=0}^{99} c_x A_x^s(t)}.$$

To determine the equilibrium age structure associated with recent lifecycle mortality, we use life tables for the year 2000 from the Human Mortality Database (2006). Fertility profiles are based on age-specific fertility rates (ASFRs). For Japan these were obtained from the National Institute of Population and Social Security Research (2003, table 4.6), and for the US they were constructed from birth data from the National Center for Health Statistics (2003) and population estimates from the US Census Bureau (2006). These ASFRs define a current total fertility rate for each country, which is reported in the first column of Table 5.2. To consider alternative fertility scenarios for a country, we scale the ASFRs proportionately at each age to obtain the desired total fertility rate. Given this fertility rate, F, and an initial population distribution, we apply the cohort-component female-dominant method using sex-specific life tables, scaled ASFRs, and an assumed sex ratio at birth of 1.05 males per female.[15] We project the population using this method until the consumption support ratio converges to its steady-state value, $\bar{a}(F)$.[16] The consumption-maximizing total fertility rate, F^m, is obtained by iterating this procedure using a grid search over successively smaller intervals of fertility rates.

As is evident from Table 5.2, the consumption-maximizing fertility rates are substantially higher than current rates of fertility in both Japan and the US, as well as higher than the replacement rate. There are sizable potential equilibrium gains in the level of consumption support ratio. Compared with the equilibrium value of a associated with current fertility, $\bar{a}(F^m)$ is approximately 2.8 percent higher in the United States. And Japan, where current fertility is far below replacement, could achieve an equilibrium consumption support ratio that is 9.9 percent higher. Comparing the consumption-maximizing fertility rates of the two countries, it may seem surprising that F^m is lower in Japan, despite higher life expectancy after retirement. This result is likely driven by the lifecycle consumption profile in Japan, which makes youth dependency more costly than in the United States.

Alternative Mortality and Retirement Scenarios

We next consider the impact of changing mortality profiles and retirement ages on the consumption-maximizing rate of fertility. Doing so allows us to isolate these separate channels of influence and resolve the theoretical ambiguity regarding the effect of the retirement age on the consumption-maximizing fertility rate.

As we have already noted, life expectancy among the elderly has been increasing in the developed world and is expected to continue to do so in the future. Although reductions in mortality are concentrated among the elderly, there are also smaller declines in mortality at all ages. Our empirical procedure is able to incorporate realistically these shifts in mortality over the whole lifecycle by using historical and projected life tables for the US and Japan. We focus on the implied mortality profiles for four years: 1980, 2000, 2020 and 2040.[17]

We define the retirement age as the average of the statutory age of retirement in a country and the effective retirement age, the latter being equivalent to the average age of exit from the labor force. The official retirement age in Japan has remained constant at 60 years since 1980. The effective age at retirement, however, has been substantially higher, at nearly 70 years for men and 66 years for women.[18] Unlike many other highly developed countries, Japan has not seen a strong secular decline in the effective retirement age. In the United States the statutory retirement age is undergoing a phased increase from 65 to 67, a process that began in 2003. Between 1980 and 2002, during which time the official retirement age was unchanged at 65, the effective age at retirement declined substantially, from 66.3 to 62.9 years for women, and from 66.4 to 65.0 years for men.[19] Thus trends in future elderly dependency due to changing retirement ages are unclear for both countries. To account for a change in either direction, our counterfactual retirement ages span an interval of three years on either side of the current sex-specific average retirement ages for each country.

Tables 5.3 and 5.4 show the results of our empirical calculations for Japan and the United States associated with combinations of the mortality profiles

Table 5.3 Consumption-maximizing fertility and potential gain in steady-state consumption: Japan, alternative mortality and retirement profiles

A: Consumption-maximizing TFR

Mortality profile	Average retirement age[a]				
	60.8	62.3	63.8	65.3	66.8
1980	2.38	2.27	2.16	2.05	1.94
2000	2.72	2.61	2.50	2.39	2.29
2020	2.84	2.73	2.62	2.52	2.42
2040	2.92	2.81	2.71	2.60	2.50

B: Potential gain in steady-state consumption relative to current TFR (%)

Mortality profile	Average retirement age[a]				
	60.8	62.3	63.8	65.3	66.8
1980	7.5	6.1	4.8	3.7	2.7
2000	13.5	11.7	9.9	8.3	6.9
2020	16.3	14.2	12.3	10.6	8.9
2040	18.2	16.1	14.1	12.2	10.4

Note:
[a] The average retirement ages correspond to gender-specific retirement ages that preserve the male–female gap observed in Table 5.1.

Source: Authors' calculations.

and retirement ages described above. Reading down the columns of Panel A of each table, we see that F^m rises as mortality rates fall. In all instances the consumption-maximizing fertility rate is higher than the current TFR in each country. As seen in Panel B of the two tables, given a retirement age, the potential equilibrium consumption gains from moving to a consumption-maximizing fertility rate become progressively larger in successive time periods. Since the largest recent and future reductions in mortality are concentrated among the elderly, these results are consistent with the theoretical model presented above. The potential gains in consumption are more pronounced in Japan, where the 1980 mortality profile implies a potential increase in a of only 4.8 percent; under the 2040 mortality profile a almost triples, rising to 14.1 percent.

Reading across the rows of Tables 5.3 and 5.4, we see that increases in the retirement age in the range we consider are always associated with declines in the consumption-maximizing fertility rate. This implies that marginal demographic cost of the elderly falls very rapidly, relative to the

Table 5.4 Consumption-maximizing fertility and potential gain in steady-state consumption: United States, alternative mortality and retirement profiles

A: Consumption-maximizing TFR

Mortality profile	Average retirement age[a]				
	60.8	62.3	63.8	65.3	66.8
1980	2.85	2.74	2.63	2.52	2.42
2000	3.01	2.90	2.79	2.68	2.58
2020	3.08	2.97	2.87	2.76	2.65
2040	3.19	3.08	2.98	2.87	2.77

B: Potential gain in steady-state consumption relative to current TFR (%)

Mortality profile	Average retirement age[a]				
	60.8	62.3	63.8	65.3	66.8
1980	3.1	2.4	1.7	1.2	0.8
2000	4.5	3.6	2.8	2.1	1.5
2020	5.2	4.2	3.3	2.6	1.9
2040	6.4	5.3	4.3	3.4	2.7

Note:
[a] The average retirement ages correspond to gender-specific retirement ages that preserve the male–female gap observed in Table 5.1.

Source: Authors' calculations.

marginal decrease in youth dependency directly induced by the longer work span. The consumption-maximizing response, then, is to induce an older population distribution through a lower fertility rate. These results accord with the common-sense view that increasing the retirement age can be used as a policy tool to offset the negative aggregate consumption effects of increases in elderly life expectancy. For example, between 2000 and 2040, the gender-weighted life expectancy at age 64 is expected to rise in Japan and the United States by approximately 2.6 and 1.9 years, respectively. Additional calculations imply that, given current fertility rates, the deleterious effect that this has on the equilibrium consumption support ratio can be offset by an increase in the retirement age of slightly under 2.3 years in Japan and 1.8 years in the United States.

Consumption-maximizing fertility rates of the future will clearly depend on the movement of retirement ages. If policy attempts in the United States are not successful in reversing the downward trend in the average age of labor force exit, then this trend will amplify the increase in F^m that arises due to mortality-based aging, as well as the decrease in the equilibrium consumption support ratio. Successful policies may mitigate these effects, although their net effect on lifecycle welfare will depend on the value of consumption relative to leisure. Even so, for plausible increases in the retirement age, F^m remains substantially above actual total fertility rates in Japan and the US.[20] In the following section we discuss policy interventions directed at raising the fertility rate toward the consumption-maximizing rate.

THE FEEDBACK FROM POPULATION AGING TO LOW FERTILITY

Our analysis in this chapter has treated declines in fertility, which are the driving force behind population aging, as exogenous. In this section we examine causation running in the other direction: from aging to fertility. The low level of fertility in most of the world's richest countries has been intensively studied, and yet is still not well understood. Kohler, Billari and Ortega (2002) provide a fairly comprehensive review of this phenomenon, particularly the rapid decline in total fertility rates in Southern Europe. Explanations range from the economic (rising female wages, human capital investment, labor market frictions) to the social (gender roles) to the institutional (state-sponsored childcare and tax relief). The study of the dramatic, unexpected and, to many, 'unnatural' decline in fertility below replacement has practically become a subfield of demography. We do not propose to explain completely why fertility is so low in this chapter, nor to speculate on whether all of the forces that have conspired to push fertility so low will continue to operate in the future. Instead, we examine two specific questions: first, whether population aging has contributed to the low fertility that we have so far observed in rich countries and, second, whether population aging may significantly reduce fertility in the future.

The mechanism we discuss bears similarities to the Easterlin (1987) hypothesis. Easterlin argued that members of crowded generations, suffering from low income during their early working careers, would make up for the gap between their earnings and the lifestyle that they had experienced in their parents' households (their 'consumption aspirations') by cutting back on the number of children they produced. The proposed explanations for the effect of aging on fertility replace the generational-crowding effect with a reduction in income due to the burden of old-age dependency.[21]

The notion that population aging has already contributed to low fertility is most strongly propounded by Drucker (1997), who writes (p. 7):

> The developed world is in the process of committing collective national suicide. Its citizens are not producing enough babies to reproduce themselves, and the cause is quite clear. Its younger people are no longer able to bear the increasing burden of supporting a growing population of older, nonworking people. They can only offset that rising burden by cutting back at the other end of the dependence spectrum, which means having fewer or no children.

Despite the rhetorical attractiveness of the idea, we find this explanation to be dubious.[22] Population aging cannot be the only cause of low fertility, since without low fertility there would be little aging to begin with. But to argue that population aging was even part of the explanation for the low fertility that Drucker was writing about would require an enormous degree of foresight on the part of parents. In most low-fertility countries, the total fertility rate hit extreme lows well before any adverse economic consequences of aging were visible. For example, although the TFR has fallen more or less steadily in Japan, from 2.14 in 1975 to 1.25 in 2005, most of this decline occurred before 1995, at which point economic dependency was at its *lowest* (Ogawa and Matsukura, 2005). Potential parents who did not have children at that time because of population aging would have been reacting to an adverse economic environment that they and their children would not be facing for at least 15 years.

The second hypothesis – that when the crunch from population aging arrives, it will further reduce fertility – strikes us as far more reasonable. The effect of aging on disposable income of working-age adults could well be large enough, in order to maintain their consumption, for those adults to cut back on childrearing. The effects of aging on the income of working-age adults will come through several channels. The most obvious channel is the dependency effect that we have highlighted in this chapter. The rise in the overall dependency burden is not a complete measure of the economic costs of population aging, however. The means by which society transfers resources to dependent groups can also exacerbate the burden.

In wealthy countries much of the support for the dependent elderly comes through public transfers. In Germany, for example, transfers net of taxes and inclusive of public health expenditures make up 65 percent of the income of people aged 65 and older (Burtless, 2006). Similarly, transfers to the elderly have become one of the most important functions of governments. In 2005, roughly a third of US federal outlays were transfers or spending directed at the 12 percent of the population aged 65 and over. Thus the coming rise in old-age dependency will have a much larger proportional effect on government budgets than it will on the resource constraint of societies as a whole. Funding government transfers to an increasing number of dependent elderly will require significant increases in taxes, with the associated distortions. The lag with which governments are reacting to the coming 'fiscal storm' will only exacerbate the magnitude of these necessary adjustments when they are finally made (Kotlikoff, Smetters and Walliser, 2001). This delay also shifts the financing burden to a later date, leading to concerns regarding intergenerational equity.[23] Intergenerational tension may be exacerbated by the fact that it is the elderly and near-elderly who will be in electoral power at the time when the burden of transferring resources to them grows. This makes it more likely that it will be working-age adults who bear the brunt of the required adjustment (Bohn, 2005).

In a companion paper (Hock and Weil, 2006) we explore the dynamics of the age-structure model presented in this chapter as extended to describe an economy with public transfers and endogenous fertility decisions on the part of workers. In this setup the consumption-maximizing fertility rate is that which minimizes the tax rate and is also the fertility rate that would be chosen by a social planner whose objective is to maximize the equilibrium utility of workers. We show that the privately chosen rate of fertility is always lower than the socially optimal rate because of the intergenerational externalities involved in a pay-as-you-go (PAYGO) system. We also consider how rising old-age dependency feeds back to low fertility. In response to an exogenous shock to the burden of old-age dependency (for example, a decrease in old-age mortality), working-age adults will adjust in part by lowering their fertility, which is at odds with the social planner's optimal response. As the demographic structure adjusts, this lower fertility will produce a further episode of aging and even lower fertility. There is thus a 'multiplier' effect of exogenous shocks on the fertility level. Cerda (2005) constructs a similar model with endogenous fertility and a PAYGO social security system in which low fertility feeds back, via the demographic structure, to produce ever rising payroll tax rates. Eventually social security becomes unsustainable.

In addition to these channels that run through disposable income, there may be other ways in which aging could lower the fertility rate. To the extent that children internalize as an ideal the family size that they observed growing up, a small generation (that is, the product of low-fertility parents) will, *ceteris paribus*, have lower fertility than the one that came before. In this regard it is particularly striking that the cohorts currently experiencing low fertility in countries such as Spain and Italy were themselves products of high-fertility parents, and current explanations for this rapid decline rely on other factors.[24] Even so, it is becoming apparent that 'ideal' family sizes are beginning to decline in low-fertility countries, if not at the same pace as realized fertility (Goldstein, Lutz and Testa, 2003; Heiland, Prskawetz and Sanderson, 2005).

Finally, it should be noted that our analysis has not considered the possibility that, in response to aging, governments may intervene in other domains. We assume a closed population in our discussion, and therefore do not address the effects of migration and migration policy. Nonetheless, the consensus seems to be that 'replacement migration' is not a sustainable strategy to offset population aging. The United Nations reports that, by 2050, low-fertility countries following such a strategy would have migrant populations constituting well over a majority of the total population (UN Population Division, 2000). It seems rather unlikely for this type of policy to be politically feasible. We concentrate instead on governmental intervention geared toward influencing the fertility rate. In this sense, population aging could have a positive effect on fertility by finally getting governments to do something to encourage people to have more children.

Although explicitly pronatal policies are sometimes politically contentious, pronatal motives generally underpin such family policies as state-regulated parental leave and daycare.[25] Child subsidies, in particular, provide a theoretically attractive mechanism for inducing the socially optimal fertility rate, with the magnitude determined by the child's expected lifetime contribution to the pension system (van Groezen, Leers and Meijdam, 2003).[26] In practice the long-term track record of pro-family policies in slowing or reversing fertility decline is mixed. Child subsidies do seem to affect the timing of births within cohorts; but, while recent evidence (Lalive and Zweimüller, 2005) suggests an effect on cohort completed fertility, this has yet to be firmly established (Grant et al., 2004). More importantly, as made clear by Figure 5.4 above, any government intervention that raised the fertility rate would lead to a period of increased dependency before the level of dependency fell.[27] It is hard to imagine that, in the midst of a fiscal crisis induced by high old-age dependency, a government would undertake to raise the dependency burden still further for a period of several decades. Thus it not very plausible that population aging would actually call forth substantial pronatalist policies.

SUMMARY AND CONCLUSION

Among the different ways that the population age structure affects the economy are capital accumulation (via both saving and investment demand), labor force productivity, intrafamily resource flows, levels of taxes and transfers, and the political equilibrium. In this chapter we have focused on a single, direct relationship between the age structure and the economy: specifically, the impact of youth and old-age dependency on consumption, holding constant the level of output per worker.

We began by introducing a new continuous-time, overlapping-generations model of population age structure and dependency. The model represents a useful alternative to existing OG models, which either feature unreasonably long time periods or are too complicated to be solved analytically. We used our model to analyze the relationship between fertility, mortality, the length of working life, and economic dependency, both in steady states and along transition paths. We also considered how changes in the other lifecycle parameters affect the consumption-maximizing level of fertility.

We then used a richer demographic model to conduct a quantitative examination of the level of fertility that maximizes consumption for a stable population. We used data on the age profile of consumption in Japan and the United States, along with data on mortality, average retirement ages and the age pattern of fertility. Our finding was that, in both countries, fertility is currently well below the level that maximizes consumption in the steady state. For example, in Japan, steady-state consumption with optimal fertility would be approximately 10 percent higher than steady-state consumption with current fertility. Forecasted declines in old-age mortality will raise both the consumption-maximizing rate of fertility and the potential steady-state gains from higher actual fertility rates.

Finally, we discussed the possible impact of population aging on fertility over the next several decades. While it is far from clear that the burden of old-age dependency has driven the recent declines in fertility in the developed world, the coming wave of population aging is far greater than anything previously experienced. It seems reasonable that such a large rise in economic dependency will, *ceteris paribus*, reduce fertility further. Moreover, not only are governments' ability to raise fertility limited, but also, given that higher fertility increases economic dependency for several decades before the consumption gains are realized, governments are unlikely to try. In ongoing work we are extending our continuous-time overlapping-generations model to allow for feedback from population age structure, via dependency, to the fertility rate.

NOTES

1. This effect is the 'second demographic dividend' discussed in Mason and Lee in this volume.
2. Gertler (1999) extends Blanchard's model in a fashion similar to ours but allows for only two age groups (working age and retired). Grafenhofer et al. (2005) present a model of probabilistic aging in which there are eight age groups, ranging from ages 20–29 to ages

85–89, which the authors use to assess quantitatively the effects of population aging on savings, consumption and the tax rate.

3. In our model we ignore childhood and early-adult mortality, assuming that death occurs only among the retired. The basic equations (5.1)–(5.3) could easily be adapted to incorporate these other forms of mortality. Analysis of this model would parallel that presented here, with qualitatively similar results.
4. Bloom et al. (2001) provide a useful summary of the literature on potential increases in capital due to population aging, while Cutler et al. (1990) and Mason and Lee (this volume) attempt to assess empirically how this might affect consumption. However, their estimates do not account for the increase in average depreciation rates that might arise owing to population aging in a vintage capital model (Blanchet, 1989). For an analysis of the potential effects of the age structure on productivity, see Feyrer (2007).
5. The decline in economic dependency early in the transition follows from the phase diagram. While o is still close to the $Z_o(y)$ locus, y is very far from its steady state and declining more rapidly. Our assertion of a turning point makes intuitive sense and can be established on the basis of numerical simulations of the model using realistic parameter values for highly developed nations.
6. This result also follows directly from the first- and second-order conditions to a consumption-maximizing problem in this framework.
7. These numbers represent simple, rather than gender-weighted, averages of sex-specific life expectancies at age 65. The data on period life expectancies come from Bell and Miller (2005). Other research (e.g. Lee and Carter, 1992) has led to even larger predicted gains in life expectancy, although Olshansky et al. (2005) indicate that this trend may actually be reversed in the United States because of rising obesity rates.
8. See, e.g., Munnell, Hatch and Lee (2004).
9. The comparative statics of the locus of stable populations, $Z_o(y)$, provide the basis for these results on potential equilibrium gains in the consumption–support ratio.
10. As youth dependency is reduced, the marginal rate of demographic substitution increases until it is once again equated with the ratio of relative consumption needs.
11. Here we switch from the gross reproduction rate (G in our theoretical model) to the more commonly used TFR.
12. We use life expectancies from the year 2000, interpolating between the one-year ages available from the Human Mortality Database (2006) when the average retirement age is fractional.
13. We are grateful to Ronald Lee, Andrew Mason, and Naohiro Ogawa for the use of these data. More information on the national accounts system can be found in Mason et al. (2005) and Lee, Lee and Mason (2006).
14. The first 'hump' in the graph of the Japanese consumption profile is driven by higher public expenditures on youth and a hump in the private consumption profile, whereas the second is attributable solely to private consumption.
15. Initial population distributions are based on population estimates in the Human Mortality Database (2006).
16. We define convergence as an annual change of less than 0.000001 percent.
17. The 1980 and 2000 life tables for both countries are taken from the Human Mortality Database (2006). Projected life tables for the US are from Bell and Miller (2005) and were provided to us for Japan by the National Institute of Population and Social Security Research, Tokyo (personal communication).
18. Data on the effective retirement age are from OECD (2004, table SS8.2).
19. Most of this decline for men came before 1995, at which time the downward trend in the male effective retirement age was reversed.
20. For example, even an increase in the retirement age of six years yields a consumption-maximizing TFR of 2.3 in Japan and 2.56 in the US.
21. Lutz , Skirbekk and Testa (2005) refer to this sort of phenomenon as a 'low fertility trap'. The authors also make the point that there is a mechanical aspect to such traps: once the age structure of the population has changed to the point where the number of women in their childbearing years is small relative to the number of older women, then standard

demographic momentum assures that, even if the TFR reverses its decline, it will take a very long time for the age structure of the population to revert to it usual shape.
22. The limited empirical work that has been done along these lines appears to be discordant. Boldrin, De Nardi and Jones (2005) demonstrate a partial correlation between the share of the population over the age of 65 and the TFR in a panel regression study of eight European nations. Their estimated coefficients imply a predicted decline of 0.3 in the TFR, which was over a quarter of the average actual reduction in the fertility in the sample. Kögel (2006), however, finds no cross-sectional correlation between pension spending and fertility when controlling for childcare utilization and female unemployment rates.
23. See, for example, the chapter by Ross Guest in this volume.
24. Sevilla-Sanz and de Laat (2006) and Berman, Iannaccone and Ragusa (2006) provide interesting analyses of the changing roles of gender norms and religiosity, respectively.
25. For further discussion and a more explicit and innovative approach, see the chapter by de la Croix and Gosseries in this volume.
26. Fenge and Meier (2005) show that under certain assumptions this is equivalent to a social security system in which retirees' pensions are tied to their previous fertility.
27. The introduction of child subsidies is lifecycle Pareto-improving in the model of van Groezen, Leers and Meijdam (2003) because child subsidies are financed through lump-sum taxes concentrated on the fecund. Under more realistic tax structures, however, the older nonfecund working population would bear some of the brunt of taxation, leading to a 'gap' generation with reduced consumption.

REFERENCES

Auerbach, Alan J. and Laurence J. Kotlikoff (1987), *Dynamic Fiscal Policy*, Cambridge: Cambridge University Press.

Bell, Felicitie C. and Michael L. Miller (2005), *Life Tables for the United States Social Security Area, 1900–2010*, Actuarial Study No. 120, Washington, DC: Office of the Chief Actuary, Social Security Administration.

Berman, Eli, Laurence R. Iannaccone and Giuseppe Ragusa (2006), 'From empty pews to empty cradles: fertility decline among European Catholics', manuscript, Department of Economics, University of California, San Diego.

Blanchard, Olivier A. (1985), 'Debt, deficits, and infinite horizons', *Journal of Political Economy*, **93**(2), 223–47.

Blanchet, Didier (1989), 'Age structure and capital dilution effects in neo-classical growth models', *Journal of Population Economics*, **1**(3), 183–94.

Bloom, David E., David Canning and Jaypee Sevilla (2001), 'Economic growth and the demographic transition', Working Paper No. 8685, National Bureau of Economic Research, Cambridge, Massachusetts.

Bohn, Henning (2005), 'Will Social Security and Medicare remain viable?', in Robin Brooks and Assaf Razin (eds), *Social Security Reform: Financial and Political Issues in International Perspective*, Cambridge: Cambridge University Press, pp. 44–72.

Boldrin, Michele, Mariachristina De Nardi and Larry E. Jones (2005), 'Fertility and Social Security', manuscript, Department of Economics, University of Minnesota Minneapolis.

Burtless, Gary (2006), 'Cross-national evidence on the burden of age-related public transfers and health benefits', Working Paper No. 2006-6, Center for Retirement Research, Boston College.

Cerda, Rodrigo (2005), 'On social security financial crises', *Journal of Population Economics*, **18**(3), 509–17.

Cutler, David M., James M. Poterba, Louise M. Sheiner, Lawrence H. Summers and George A. Akerlof (1990), 'An aging society: opportunity or challenge?', *Brookings Papers on Economic Activity*, (1), 1–73.

Drucker, Peter F. (1997), 'The future that has already happened', *Harvard Business Review*, **75**(5), 20–24.

Easterlin, Richard A. (1987), *Birth and Fortune: The Impact of Numbers on Personal Welfare*, 2nd edn, Chicago: University of Chicago Press.

Fenge, Robert and Volker Meier (2005), 'Pensions and fertility incentives', *Canadian Journal of Economics*, **38**(1), 28–48.

Feyrer, James (2007), 'Demographics and productivity', *Review of Economics and Statistics*, in press.

Gertler, Mark (1999), 'Government debt and social security in a life-cycle economy', *Carnegie–Rochester Conference Series on Public Policy*, **50**, 61–110.

Goldstein, Joshua R., Wolfgang Lutz and Maria-Rita Testa (2003), 'The emergence of sub-replacement family size ideals in Europe', *Population Research and Policy Review*, **22**(5–6), 479–96.

Grafenhofer, Dominik, Christian Jaag, Christian Keuschnigg and Mirela Keuschnigg (2005), 'Probabilistic aging', manuscript, University of St. Gallen.

Grant, Jonathan, Stijn Hoorens, Suja Sivadasan, Mirjam van het Loo, Julie DaVanzo, Lauren Hale, Shawna Gibson and William Butz (2004), *Low Fertility and Population Ageing Causes, Consequences, and Policy Options*, Leiden, Cambridge and Berlin: RAND Europe.

Heiland, Frank, Alexia Prskawetz and Warren C. Sanderson (2005), 'Do the more-educated prefer smaller families?', Working Paper No. 03/2005, Vienna Institute of Demography of the Austrian Academy of Sciences, Vienna, Austria.

Hock, Heinrich and David N. Weil (2006), 'The dynamics of the age structure, dependency and consumption', Working Paper No. 12140, National Bureau of Economic Research, Cambridge, Massachusetts.

Human Mortality Database (2006), University of California, Berkeley, US, and Max Plank Institute for Demographic Research, Rostock, Germany: http://www.mortality.org/.

Japan, National Institute of Population and Social Security Research (2003), *Population Statistics for Japan 2003*, Tokyo: available online at http://www.ipss.go.jp/p-info/e/psj2003/ PSJ2003.pdf.

Kögel, Tomas (2006), 'Argumente und Evidenz Gegen eine Koppelung der Rente an die Kinderzahl', manuscript, Department of Economics, Loughborough University.

Kohler, Hans-Peter, Francesco C. Billari and Jose Antonio Ortega (2002), 'The emergence of lowest-low fertility in Europe during the 1990s', *Population and Development Review*, **28**(4), 641–80.

Kotlikoff, Laurence, Kent Smetters and Jan Walliser (2001), 'Finding a way out of America's demographic dilemma', Working Paper No. 8258, National Bureau of Economic Research, Cambridge, Massachusetts.

Lalive, Rafael and Josef Zweimüller (2005), 'Does parental leave affect fertility and return-to-work? Evidence from a "true natural experiment" ', Discussion Paper No. 1613, Institute for the Study of Labor, Bonn, Germany.

Lee, Ronald and Lawrence R. Carter (1992), 'Modeling and forecasting U.S. mortality', *Journal of the American Statistical Association*, **87**(419), 659–71.

Lee Ronald D., Sang-Hyop Lee and Andrew Mason (2006), 'Charting the economic lifecycle', Working Paper No. 12379, National Bureau of Economic Research, Cambridge, Massachusetts.

Lutz, Wolfgang, Vegard Skirbekk and Maria Rita Testa (2005), 'The low fertility trap hypothesis: Forces that may lead to further postponement and fewer births in Europe', European Demographic Research Papers No. 4, Vienna Institute of Demography of the Austrian Academy of Sciences, Vienna.

Mason, Andrew, Ronald Lee, An-Chi Tung, Mun-Sim Li and Tim Miller (2005), 'Population aging and intergenerational transfers: Introducing age into national accounts', paper presented at the 2005 Population Association of America Annual Meeting, 31 March–2 April, Philadelphia.

Munnell, Alicia H., Robert E. Hatch and James G. Lee (2004), 'Why is life expectancy so low in the United States?', Issues in Brief, No. 21, Boston College, Center for Retirement Research, Boston, Massachusetts.

National Transfer Accounts Database (2006), Population and Health Studies Program, East-West Center, Honolulu, US and Center for the Economics and Demography of Aging, University of California, Berkeley, US: http://www.schemearts.com/proj/nta/web/.

OECD (Organisation for Economic Co-operation and Development) (2004), *Society at a Glance: OECD Social Indicators – 2005 Edition*, Paris.

Ogawa, Naohiro and Rikiya Matsukura (2005), 'The role of older persons' changing health and wealth in an aging society: The case of Japan', United Nations Expert Group Meeting on Social and Economic Implications of Changing Population Age Structures, 31 August–2 September, Mexico City.

Olshansky, S. Jay, Douglas J. Passaro, Ronald C. Hershow, Jennifer Layden, Bruce A. Carnes, Jacob Brody, Leonard Hayflick, Robert N. Butler, David B. Allison and David S. Ludwig (2005), 'A potential decline in life expectancy in the United States in the 21st century', *New England Journal of Medicine*, **352**(11), 1138–45.

Prskawetz, Alexia and Thomas Fent (2004), 'Workforce ageing and economic productivity: the role of supply and demand of labour: an application to Austria', manuscript, Vienna Institute of Demography, Austrian Academy of Sciences, Vienna.

Sevilla-Sanz, Almudena and Joost J. de Laat (2006), 'Working women, men's home time and lowest-low fertility', Working Paper No. 2006-23, Institute for Social & Economic Research, University of Essex, Colchester, UK.

UN (United Nations) Population Division (2000), *Replacement Migration: Is it a Solution to Declining and Ageing Populations?*, Geneva and New York: Department of Economic and Social Affairs.

US (United States) Census Bureau (2006), *Population Estimates*, Washington, DC: Population Division, Census Bureau, available online at http://www.census.gov/popest/estimates.php.

US (United States), National Center for Health Statistics (2003), *Vital Statistics of the United States, 2001, Vol. I, Natality*, Washington, DC: Government Printing Office.

van Groezen, Bas, Theo Leers and Lex Meijdam (2003), 'Social security and endogenous fertility: pensions and child allowances as Siamese twins', *Journal of Public Economics*, **87**(2), 233–51.

Weil, David N. (1999), 'Population growth, dependency, and consumption', *American Economic Review*, **89**(2), 251–5.

6. Transfers, capital and consumption over the demographic transition

Andrew Mason and Ronald Lee[1]

Economic development and demographic transition are linked in complicated and reciprocal ways. Economic development leads to declines in fertility and mortality, whereas changes in population size, growth rate and age distribution influence the pace of economic growth. It is this second causal direction that we will consider here: how the transition shapes development.

Recent studies suggest that many countries benefit from changes in age structure that raise the support ratio and concentrate the population in the working ages (Bloom and Williamson, 1998; Lee, Mason and Miller, 2000; Bloom and Canning, 2001; Lee, Mason and Miller, 2001; Mason, 2001; Bloom, Canning and Sevilla, 2002; Lee, Mason and Miller, 2003; Mason and Lee, 2004; Mason, 2005). Such gains appear to be transitory, however, because in later phases of the demographic transition, low fertility and rising life expectancy lead to population aging and a decline in the support ratio. The inceptions of fertility decline and of population aging bound the 'window of opportunity' during which conditions for sustained economic growth may – or may not – be realized.

As a general proposition, transitory gains can be transformed into sustainable gains by creating human or physical capital. The emphasis here is on physical capital and the proposition advanced is that the demographic transition leads to large increases in the demand for wealth relative to income or labor. The potential result, which we call the 'second demographic dividend', may lead to a period of more rapid economic growth and a permanently higher level of per capita income and consumption.

The societal demand for wealth arises in part because the population grows older and in part because people may save more at younger ages. Because the elderly in any population typically hold the most wealth, an increase in their share in the population leads to an increase in average wealth holdings. In addition the decline in the number of surviving children and the rise in longevity lead working-age people to save more, which also increases the accumulation of wealth. Policy and institutional context influence the extent to which these potential gains from the second demographic dividend are realized. In particular, heavy reliance on either public PAYGO pension programs or familial transfers to provide financial support for the elderly undermines the effects of the demographic transition on capital accumulation.

In other work we have explored these processes by simulating a model of lifecycle savings applied to Taiwan and the United States over the course of their demographic transitions. The present study extends this earlier work in two important ways. First, we make use of detailed and comprehensive estimates of the economic lifecycle (Lee, Lee and Mason, 2006) and the economic support system (Mason et al., forthcoming) that were not previously available. Second, in response to the many questions raised about the lifecycle saving hypothesis, we take a different approach to modeling consumer behavior. The lifecycle saving hypothesis tells us that, as individuals consume and save at each age, they are governed by the wish to smooth consumption over the lifecycle and are constrained by their lifetime earnings. The model used here acknowledges the pervasive nature of public and familial transfers and, in our view, is more realistic in many contexts. Consumption and age profiles are governed by tastes and perceptions about 'needs', but constrained by general standards of living. Consumption by the elderly depends less on what they earned during their working years and more on what their children and current generations of taxpayers are earning.

The structure of our chapter is as follows. First, we describe the key data on which our calculations are based, including estimated age profiles. Second, we present the theoretical model. Third, we use simulation analysis to track consumption, assets and other macroeconomic variables over a demographic transition. We then consider the sensitivity of the results to alternative parameters, discuss limitations and state our conclusions.

ECONOMIC LIFECYCLES: A COMPARATIVE PERSPECTIVE

Two fundamental aspects of the economic lifecycle are crucial to our purpose. First, how does economic dependency vary with age? The broad answer to this question is well-known: children and the elderly produce much less than they consume whereas prime-age adults produce much more. Little, however, is known about details, which are essential to understanding more about the timing and magnitude of macroeconomic effects of changes in age structure. Second, how do societies shift resources from the working ages to the dependent ages? One possibility is that prime-age adults transfer resources to children and to the elderly through public programs or through private institutions – the family in particular. The second possibility, relevant mostly to old-age support, is lifecycle saving. Prime-age adults accumulate assets. In old age they disaccumulate the assets and rely on the income generated by those assets. The mechanism by which assets are shifted across age groups is important because it determines whether population aging leads to the accumulation of assets or to the expansion of public and private transfer programs.

Estimates of the economic lifecycle for the United States in 2000 and Taiwan in 1977 are presented in Figure 6.1, panels A and B. The labor–income profiles incorporate and summarize, for men and women combined, labor force participation, hours worked, wages, and all of the factors that influence these variables. They are cross-sectional profiles and hence reflect the varied experiences of each of the age groups represented in the respective profiles. Despite the many ways in which Taiwan in 1977 differed from the United States in 2000, the labor–income profiles are strikingly similar. There are some discernible differences, however. The US labor–income profile rises somewhat more slowly with age and begins to decline at a somewhat later age than in Taiwan.

The consumption profiles shown in Figure 6.1 consist of both public and private consumption. Public consumption in the United States favors children, via spending on education, and the elderly, via spending on health care. Private consumption in the US rises steadily with age until around age 60 and then declines. Public and private consumption combined are highly favorable to the elderly, however. We estimate that average consumption by a 90-year-old was more than US$40 000 in 2000 as compared with only US$25 000 by a young adult. The difference between them is essentially a consequence of health care spending.

The situation in Taiwan in 1977 was very different. Consumption clearly favored young adults, with total consumption declining from about NT$40 000 per year for young adults to around NT$30 000 per year for those 90 or older. Public education programs were important in Taiwan in 1977, but public spending on health care was not.

The key difference between the two cases, then, occurs at the older ages. In the US, per capita consumption of those aged 58 and older exceeded per capita labor income. In Taiwan the crossover age was 62. In relative terms the gap between consumption and production at older ages is much larger in the US than in Taiwan. In contrast the dependency profiles at young ages appear to be quite similar in the two countries. The crossover ages are the same (26 years of age in both countries) and the magnitudes of the gap between consumption and production relative to labor income appear to be similar.

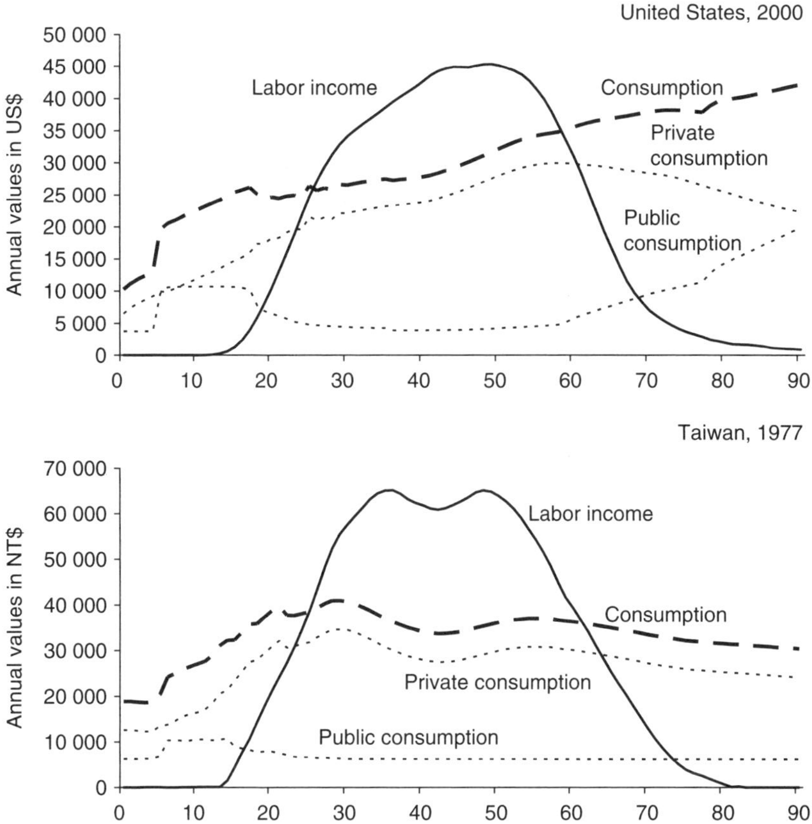

Source: Lee, Lee and Mason (2006, figure no. 1).

Figure 6.1 Consumption and labor–income age profiles for the United States, 2000, and Taiwan, 1977

The United States and Taiwan also differ in the way resources are shifted to the elderly. In the US, about 55 percent of consumption by the elderly is funded by income from their ownership of assets. Public transfer accounts for 37 percent and *inter vivos* familial transfers only 7 percent of consumption by the elderly (Figure 6.2). In Taiwan, asset-based reallocations are less important, representing about 35 percent of consumption by the elderly. Transfers are more important, with public transfers equal to 26 percent and familial transfers equal to 40 percent of consumption by the elderly. In both economies, public and familial transfers combined rival or exceed the importance of assets (Mason et al., forthcoming). Clearly, a focus on

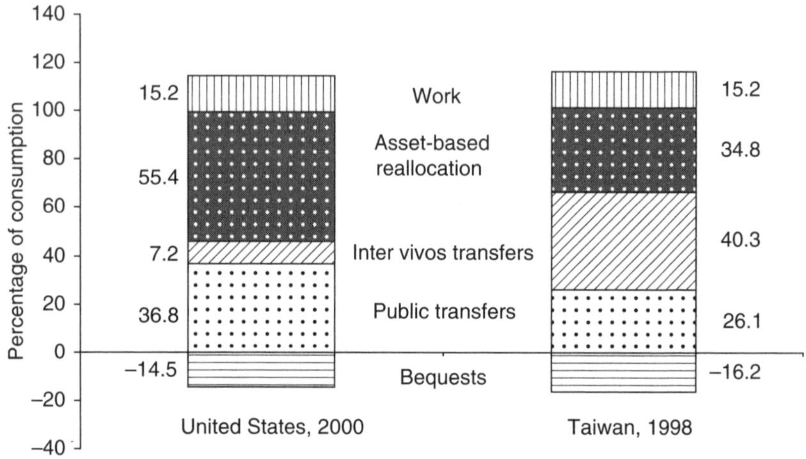

Source: Mason et al. (forthcoming, figure 8).

Figure 6.2 How the elderly finance consumption in the United States and Taiwan (ages 65+)

lifecycle saving and asset accumulation alone, or on transfers alone, would miss much of the story.

THEORY

Recent studies of the economic growth effects of population have focused on per capita income. Our own work has emphasized two effects of age structure on per capita income, for which we have coined the terms 'first' and 'second dividend'. The first dividend arises because the effective number of producers is growing faster than the effective number of consumers. Other things being equal, income per equivalent consumer rises. The underlying demographic cause is a decline in fertility and the share of children in the population. The second dividend arises to the extent that longer life and changes in age structure lead to more rapid accumulation of assets and, in a closed economy, to capital deepening. The second dividend is not a free lunch, however, because current generations must reduce their consumption in order to increase their wealth and achieve higher consumption in future periods.

These ideas can be more comprehensively addressed by considering how changes in age structure influence per capita consumption rather than per capita income. The following identity must hold for consumption per effective consumer:

$$\frac{C(t)}{N(t)} = c(t)\frac{Y(t)}{L(t)}\frac{L(t)}{N(t)}, \tag{6.1}$$

where $C(t)$ and $Y(t)$ are total consumption and labor income, respectively, and $c(t)$ is the ratio of consumption to labor income. $N(t)$ and $L(t)$ are the effective number of consumers and producers, respectively:

$$N(t) = \sum_{a=0}^{\bar{\omega}} \phi(a)P(a, t),$$

$$L(t) = \sum_{a=0}^{\omega} \gamma(a)P(a, t), \tag{6.2}$$

where $P(a, t)$ is the population aged a at time t, $\phi(a)$ and $\gamma(a)$ are age-specific, time-invariant vectors of coefficients measuring age variation in consumption and productivity, respectively.

The effect of current age structure on current consumption, the first dividend, is captured in equation (6.1) by the economic support ratio (L/N), the number of effective producers per effective consumer. Suppose the consumption ratio $c(t)$ and labor productivity $Y(t)/L(t)$ were unaffected by demography.[2] Per capita consumption would vary directly with the support ratio. An increase in the support ratio, which occurs during the demographic transition, would lead to higher consumption. Later, when population aging depresses the support ratio, consumption would decline. That would be the end of the story.

The story is quite different and much more complex if the consumption ratio $c(t)$ declines, as we will argue here, as the support ratio rises. Current per capita consumption would rise by less than the support ratio; but saving rates would increase, assets held by future generations would rise, and, if assets were domestically invested, labor productivity and wages would increase. If assets were invested abroad, then national income would rise. Domestic labor productivity and wages would be unaffected, but foreign labor productivity and wages would rise. But whether assets were invested domestically or abroad, higher levels of consumption could be sustained in the future. In this response rests the possibility for a second demographic dividend, which we explore in this chapter.

Assets, Lifecycle Wealth and Child Costs

Wealth is defined broadly as a net claim on future income. Individuals can consume more in the future than they produce only if they hold wealth. Wealth can take two broad forms, however. One form is *assets*, such as private savings, funded pensions, or a home. The second form is *transfer wealth*, consisting of the present value of net transfers received through familial support systems and through public programs, for example PAYGO pensions and publicly provided health care. Either assets or transfer wealth can be used to fund future expenditures in excess of future labor income. From the perspective of the individual, they are equivalent.[3] From the perspective of the macroeconomy, however, transfer wealth and assets are not equivalent. Accumulating more assets means that higher levels of aggregate consumption can be sustained in the future. Thus the effect on growth of changes in the demand for wealth is closely tied to whether that wealth is created by expanding transfer programs or accumulating assets. In this analysis we assume this to be a matter of exogenously determined policy.

The aggregate demand for wealth depends on the future trajectories of consumption and production. Our strategy is to assume that the cross-sectional age profiles of consumption and earnings estimated for a particular country in a particular year retain their shapes in the future, while their levels shift upward over time. The labor income profile is assumed to shift at some exogenously given rate due to technological progress.[4] The rate at which the consumption profile shifts is endogenous and depends on technological progress, population age structure, the shapes of the consumption and production profiles, and public policy.

If the profiles of consumption and production retain their shapes while population aging increases the numbers of elderly relative to workers, then the proportion of income shifted to the elderly by workers will have to increase. If this increased shifting is accomplished by increased saving by workers and dissaving by the elderly, then more capital per worker will be generated. If the increased shifting is accomplished by increased transfers to the elderly, there will be no increase in capital per worker. Here we will assume that the mix of saving and transfers used for shifting income to the elderly remains the same over time.

Our assumption that the cross-sectional shape of the consumption age profile is unchanging is fundamental and novel, and this requires some interpretation. In a strict lifecycle savings model, the age profile of consumption would be constant in steady state, but not otherwise. Instead it would depend on the relative economic fortunes of each generation. For example, the young in Taiwan who may earn six times as much as their parents did at a comparable age [$6 = \exp(30*.06)$] would consume correspondingly more at each age over their lifecycle. But this is not what we see, and not what would emerge under a system of familial co-residence and income sharing. In fact the cross-sectional age profiles of consumption in the US and Taiwan have been fairly stable in shape over the period from 1980 to 2000 for which we have calculated them. This is what we would expect if individuals in families are altruistically linked. Differences emerging from different earnings histories would be offset by both familial and public-sector transfers. This is our working hypothesis for the calculations reported below in this chapter.

The key idea is that variation in consumption across generations at any point in time is a product of preferences or altruism that expresses itself through the host of transfer programs (public and private) that permeate all modern societies. In the lifecycle model the consumption of the elderly depends on their tastes and their lifetime earnings. In this model the consumption of the elderly depends on general standards of living, the needs of the elderly, and social and familial preferences about the consumption of the elderly as compared with that of prime-age adults and children. In a lifecycle saving model, individuals save at the cost of their current consumption in order to consume more themselves in the future. In our approach, individuals save to raise the future consumption of all those to whom they are altruistically linked.

Given the trajectory of labor income, the lifecycle wealth of adults can be readily calculated for any consumption trajectory. The lifecycle wealth of adults can be decomposed into two components. One component is called 'child wealth', which is the present value of the net costs of supporting children in the future and will be negative. The second component, 'pension wealth', is the wealth used to fund consumption at older ages. Pension wealth consists of assets and pension-transfer wealth.

We do not know to what extent the future consumption needs of an aging population will be met by unfunded transfer systems versus funded systems or private saving. This will depend on how policies and institutions develop over coming decades.

For our simulations we will assume that the ratio of assets to pension-transfer wealth will remain constant.[5] Thus for any exogenous transfer policy and for any endogenous consumption trajectory we can compute a trajectory of assets. Which consumption trajectory is feasible depends on characteristics of the macroeconomy, such as the rate of return to assets.

Before turning more formally to the methods we use, a few comments are in order. First, the age boundaries assumed for dependency ratios, such as 20 and 65, are obviously arbitrary. Our calculations are based on the actual age profiles of labor earnings by age. Second, in any society it is the elderly who have the highest ownership of assets, following a lifetime of accumulation. Holding the age profile of capital, or equivalently saving rates, constant, and multiplying it times the changes in age distribution over the demographic transition would clearly imply rising capital to income ratios. We might call this a pure compositional effect. In our analysis, however, we do not hold the age profile of wealth constant. Rather, the demand for wealth by age will depend on fertility and mortality. Couples with fewer children assign a greater share of their lifecycle earnings to their own consumption, and therefore have a greater demand for wealth to provide for higher consumption in retirement. People who expect to live longer have a greater demand for wealth to finance their longer period of postwork consumption. These changes associated with the demographic transition and changes in age structure are also reflected in our analysis.

Assets $A(t)$

The approach to modeling assets can be motivated by considering a simpler case in which the lives of prime-age adults were divided into two distinct phases. During the first phase adults would raise their children. All labor income in excess of personal consumption would be devoted to childrearing. During the second phase adults would accumulate pension wealth: assets and transfer wealth needed to fund their retirement. Aggregate pension wealth at any point in time would be equal to the wealth held by adults, including the elderly, who had completed their childrearing (Mason, 2005).

A more realistic approach recognizes that supporting children and providing for retirement overlap. Adults at all ages hold at least some pension wealth and adults at all ages make transfers to children. Aggregate pension wealth depends on the pension wealth held by all age groups. This, in turn, depends on the total lifecycle wealth held by all adults and the capitalized obligation to support children.

Aggregate lifecycle wealth is the wealth that adults must hold, as a group, in year t to achieve a given path of consumption and labor income over the remainder of their collective existence. $W(t)$, the lifecycle wealth of all adults in year t, is equal to the present value of the consumption less the present value of the labor income of those adults over the remainder of their lives. Let $PV[\,]$ be the present value operator. Then,

$$W(a, t) = PV[C(a, t)] - PV[Y(a, t)], \qquad (6.3)$$

where $C(a, t)$ and $Y(a, t)$ are vectors of current and future consumption and current and future labor income, respectively, for the cohort of age a in year t. Summing $W(a, t)$ across all adult ages in year t yields aggregate lifecycle wealth, $W(t)$.

Lifecycle wealth comes in three forms: assets (A), transfer wealth associated with childrearing (T_k) and pension transfer wealth (T_p), that is,

$$W(t) = A(t) + T_k(t) + T_P(t). \qquad (6.4)$$

Transfer wealth associated with childrearing is the present value of the current and future costs of childrearing and hence is negative. Pension wealth is defined as $W_p(t) = A(t) + T_p(t)$, that is, assets plus pension-transfer wealth. Assets by assumption can be held only by adults.

The relative size of pension-transfer wealth is captured by $\tau(t) = T_p(t)/W_p(t)$ and the relative size of child-transfer wealth by $\tau_k(t) = T_k(t)/W(t)$. Substituting into equation (6.4) and rearranging terms gives the total assets of adults and, because only adults hold assets, aggregate assets in year t:

$$A(t) = [1 - \tau(t)][1 - \tau_k(t)]W(t). \tag{6.5}$$

Total assets depend on three factors: pension-transfer policy (both public and private), the cost of children, both public and private, and the lifecycle wealth required to support adult consumption. Transfer policy is exogenous, whereas the cost of children and lifecycle wealth are both endogenous.

Labor Income and Consumption: *Y*(*t*) and *C*(*t*)

Lifecycle wealth and child wealth depend on the trajectory of labor income and consumption. Labor income at each age depends on the effective number of producers belonging to that age group and the general level of wages, which shifts over time as a result of technological change. We assume that the rate of technological change is constant and exogenous.[6] Thus labor income of year t adults in period $t+x$ is:

$$\begin{aligned} Y(a, t+x) &= \bar{y}(t)G_y(x)L(a, t+x) \\ G_y(x) &= (1+g_y)^x, \end{aligned} \tag{6.6}$$

where $\bar{y}(t)$ is the labor income index for the current year t, g_y is the annual rate of growth in that index due to technological change, $G_y(x)$ measures the effect of technological change over an interval of x years, and $L(a, t+x)$ is the number of year t adults alive in year $t+x$ measured as equivalent producers.

By assumption the shape of the per capita cross-sectional profile of consumption is fixed and incorporated into the equivalent number of consumers. Consumption at each age grows at the same rate g_c, but that rate varies from year to year. Hence,

$$\begin{aligned} C(a, t+x) &= \bar{c}(t)G_c(t, x)N(a, t+x) \\ G_c(t, x) &= \prod_{z=0}^{x-1} [1 + g_c(t+z)], \end{aligned} \tag{6.7}$$

where $C(a, t+x)$ is the total consumption of year t adults in year $t+x$, $\bar{c}(t)$ is the consumption index that determines the level of the consumption profile in year t, $G_c(t, x)$ is the proportional increase in the consumption index between years t and $t+x$, $N(a, t+x)$ is the number of year t adults alive in year $t+x$ measured as equivalent consumers, and $g_c(t+z)$ is the rate of growth of the consumption index between period $t+z$ and $t+z+1$. The consumption trajectory, defined by the initial consumption index and the vector of consumption growth rates, is endogenous.

Lifecycle Wealth: *W*(*t*)

These general rules can be applied to year t adults to determine their labor income and consumption over their remaining adult years and hence their lifecycle wealth in year t. Let $NTOT(t, x)$ denote the number of effective consumers in year $t+x$ who were adults in year t. Similarly, $LTOT(t, x)$ denotes the number of effective producers in year $t+x$ who were adults in year t:

$$NTOT(t, x) = \sum_{a=a_0(t)+x}^{\omega} N(a, t+x)$$

$$LTOT(t, x) = \sum_{a=a_0(t)+x}^{\omega} L(a, t+x). \tag{6.8}$$

In a closed population NTOT and LTOT would depend only on survival rates, but in an open population they will include migrants who were adults in year t.

The labor income of year t adults at age $a \geq a_0(t) + x$ in year $t+x$ is:

$$Y(a, t+x) = \bar{y}(t+x)L(a, t+x), \tag{6.9}$$

and consumption by year t adults in year $t+x$ is:

$$C(a, t+x) = \bar{c}(t+x)N(a, t+x). \tag{6.10}$$

The present value in year t of the current and future lifetime consumption of all year t adults is given by:[7]

$$PVC(t) = \bar{c}(t)\sum_{x=0}^{\omega - a_0(t)} D(x)G_c(x, t)NTOT(t, x), \tag{6.11}$$

and the present value in year t of the current and future lifetime production of all year t adults is given by:

$$PVY(t) = \bar{y}(t) \sum_{x=0}^{\omega - a_0(t)} D(x) G_y(x) LTOT(t, x), \tag{6.12}$$

where $D(x)$ is the discount factor $(1 + i)^{-x-1}$. The lifecycle wealth of all year t adults in year t is:

$$W(t) = \bar{c}(t) \sum_{x=0}^{\omega - a_0(t)} D(x) G_c(x, t) NTOT(t, x) - \bar{y}(t) \sum_{x=0}^{\omega - a_0(t)} D(x) G_y(x) LTOT(t, \text{x}). \tag{6.13}$$

Child-transfer Wealth: $T^k(t)$

The final variable that determines assets in equation (6.5) is child-transfer wealth, which measures the costs to year t adults of providing resources consumed by children. If adults spend more on children in the current and future periods, then child-transfer wealth is a larger negative value. Or, as represented in equation (6.5), the ratio of child-transfer wealth to adult-transfer wealth is a larger negative value.

What determines child-transfer wealth? In part it depends on the difference between what children consume and what they produce in current and future periods. Production and consumption are determined in the same manner for children as for adults. The shape of the age profiles of production and consumption ($\gamma(a)$ and $\phi(a)$) are held constant for all ages, including those of children. The shifts of the profiles over time are governed by the shifts in the production and consumption indexes discussed above.

The cost of children to year t adults also depends on their share of the costs of children in future periods. By assumption all of the *current* costs of children are born exclusively by year t adults; that is, children do not support children. Year t adults are responsible only for a portion of the cost of children in subsequent years because some portion of the costs of children is shifted to persons who become adults after year t.

The share of child costs borne by year t adults depends on a host of factors, including the extent to which child costs are borne by families as opposed to taxpayers, the system of taxation that is used to finance public transfers to children, and the extent to which parents, grandparents and other family members finance familial transfers to children. The model distinguishes two ways in which child costs are financed: familial transfers and public transfers. Adult parents are assumed to bear the cost of familial transfers. Public transfers are financed through a proportional tax on labor income. The relative mix of these two mechanisms is an exogenously determined policy variable.

Child-transfer wealth is equal to:

$$T_k(t) = \bar{y}(t) \sum_{x=0}^{\omega - a_0(t)} D(x)G_y(x)KLTOT(t, x)$$
$$- \bar{c}(t) \sum_{x=0}^{\omega - a_0(t)} D(x)G_c(t, x)KNTOT(t, x), \qquad (6.14)$$

where $KLTOT(t, x)$ and $KNTOT(t, x)$ are the effective numbers of child producers and consumers, respectively, in year $t+x$ for which year t adults are financially responsible. A detailed description of the methods involved in calculating these variables is provided in the appendix.

Lifecycle Pension Wealth: $W_p(t)$

Pension wealth is equal to lifecycle wealth less child-transfer wealth. Combining the results from equations (6.13) and (6.14) and rearranging terms yields:

$$W_p(t) = \bar{c}(t) \sum_{x=0}^{\omega - a_0(t)} D(x)G_c(t, x)[NTOT(t, x) + KNTOT(t, x)]$$
$$- \bar{y}(t) \sum_{x=0}^{\omega - a_0(t)} D(x)G_y(x)[LTOT(t, x) + KLTOT(t, x)]. \qquad (6.15)$$

Lifecycle pension wealth is the discounted present value of current and future consumption by year t adults and their dependent children less the present value of current and future production by year t adults and their dependent children. Recall that assets in year t are equal to $[1 - \tau(t)]\ W_p(t)$. Thus equation (6.15) gives pension wealth and assets in each year conditional on the consumption trajectory as determined by $\bar{c}(t)$ and $G_c(t, x)$.

SOLVING FOR THE CONSUMPTION TRAJECTORY

The relationship between the trajectory of consumption and lifecycle pension wealth and assets is apparent from inspecting equation (6.15). If the consumption trajectory is higher, because either $\bar{c}(t)$ or an element in the vector of growth rates $G_c(t, x)$ is higher, lifecycle pension wealth in the current period and current assets must be higher. If, however, aggregate consumption is higher, saving must be lower, and the trajectory of assets must be lower. The feasible consumption trajectory is the one for which lifecycle accounting and the macroeconomic accounting lead to the same assets in all periods.

The solution will depend on whether the economy is open or closed. Here we assume that the economy is open and hence the rate of return to capital, r, is exogenous. Thus the aggregate flow constraint is governed by:[8]

$$A(t+1) = (1+r)A(t) + Y(t) - C(t). \tag{6.16}$$

Two methods are available for solving the model. We have used both methods, and they produce results that are equivalent in all important respects. One approach uses numerical search to find a solution using forward recursion. A second approach, which we will use for the results in this chapter, finds an exact closed-form solution based on backward recursion. In it we assume that the population achieves stability and the model reaches steady state at some point in the distant future, t^*.[9] Under those conditions the consumption index will grow at the same rate as labor productivity. We can solve directly for the consumption index and assets in year t^* and all years thereafter. Next we solve for consumption in year $t^* - 1$, given consumption in all subsequent periods, equation (6.16), and the lifecycle model that governs the demand for assets by consumers. We work backward to the present or historical periods.

SIMULATING THE DEMOGRAPHIC TRANSITION IN A SMALL OPEN ECONOMY

To fully appreciate the influences of population on the economy one must take a long view. The demographic transition and its accompanying changes in age structure occur over a period of several centuries. No country has yet completed the demographic transition, and historical records that predate the transition are available only in a few instances. The strategy we employ here is to use population estimates from 1950 to 2000 and UN projections to 2300 to capture nearly the entire demographic transition for a single country, Niger, selected because in 2000 it had the highest total fertility rate (TFR) of any country in the world, 7.9 births per woman.[10]

Niger's demographic transition follows the classic pattern. In 1950–55, life expectancy at birth for both sexes combined was only 36.2 years. It increased gradually to 44.3 years for 2000–05. More rapid increases are anticipated in the future, with life expectancy reaching 61.4 years in 2045–50 and eventually reaching almost 90 in 2300.

The TFR rose slightly from 7.7 births per woman in 1950–55 to peak at 8.2 births per woman during the period 1975–90. The medium scenario employed here assumes that the TFR will decline gradually to reach 3.6 births per woman in 2045–50 and replacement level, at just over two births per woman, in 2080 and thereafter.

Age structure is fundamental to our analysis, and the trends in three broad groups – the working ages (20–64), children (0–19) and the elderly (65+) – are charted in Figure 6.3. The early part of the demographic transition in Niger is dominated by the large and rising share of the child population. The percentage under the age of 20 reached 60 percent of the population in 2000, rising from 54 percent in 1950. The increase in the share of children was a consequence, in part, of the rise in the TFR, but mostly a consequence of improvements in child survival. The infant mortality rate dropped from 198 deaths per 1000 births in 1950–55 to 153 deaths per 1000 births in 2000–05. The percentage of the population in the working ages, 20–64, declined from 43.4 percent in 1950 to only 38.4 percent in 2000.

The twenty-first century is dominated by the rise in the working-age population and the decline in the child population. Between 2000 and 2090 the percentage of the population in the working ages increases from 38.4 percent to 61.6 percent, while the percentage in the child ages drops from 60 percent in 2000 to 28 percent in 2090. The twenty-second century is dominated by the rise in the elderly population and the decline in the working-age population. From the peak reached in 2090, the percentage of the population in the working ages drops to 50.0 percent in 2200. Over the same period the percentage of the population aged 65 and older rises from 10.3 percent to 27.9 percent. Changes after 2200 (not shown) are very slow, with

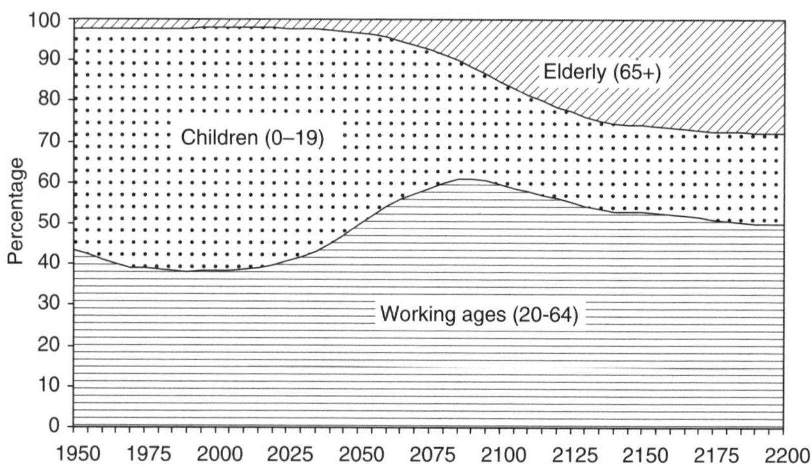

Figure 6.3 Age distribution of Niger's population, 1950–2200

the percentage in the old ages rising to about 30 percent. An important point to note is that this is a classic demographic transition in which fertility declines to replacement level. Although many countries have fertility rates well below replacement, the TFR is not projected to drop below two births per woman in Niger, even temporarily.

The simulation results rely on Niger's demography, but other important model parameters are not based, even loosely, on Niger. For the baseline simulation we use the age profiles of production and consumption for Taiwan in 1977 (Figure 6.1). The scaling of the profiles is arbitrary because there is no natural unit for measuring equivalent consumers and producers. We have scaled the production profile so that, when applied to the global population for 2000, it produces the world GDP in US$2000 (World Bank, 2005). We have scaled the consumption ratio so that the support ratio for the world in 2000 was one equivalent producer per equivalent consumer.

We assume that two-thirds of child costs are met through familial transfers and one-third through public transfers, figures consistent with the experience both in Taiwan and in the US. Assets are held constant at 65 percent and pension transfer wealth at 35 percent of pension wealth, a figure similar to that for the US in 2000. For the discount rate we use a risk-free rate of return of 3 percent. For the depreciation rate we use 3 percent (Mankiw, Romer and Weil, 1992, 414) and for the international real rate of return on assets we use 6 percent (Barro and Sala-i-Martin, 1995, 124), declining linearly to a steady-state rate of interest of 4.42 percent in 2300.[11] We assume that productivity growth is 1.5 percent per year. The sensitivity of the results to variation of key parameters is discussed below.

An important assumption is that the economy is small and open. Hence the accumulation of assets at the country level has no effect on wages or interest rates. These are determined in international markets. Global aging will influence interest rates and wage rates in ways that we intend to explore more in future research. The effects on consumption will be substantially greater when the influences of capital on labor income are incorporated into the model.

BASELINE SIMULATION

Key features of the demographic transition and its implications for consumption are captured in Figure 6.4. Early in the demographic transition the support ratio declined to a low level in 2000 because high fertility and declining infant mortality produced a population with many young dependants. The support ratio does not begin to rise until around 2020, but then it rises steeply, by about 50 percent, during the next 70 years. During this

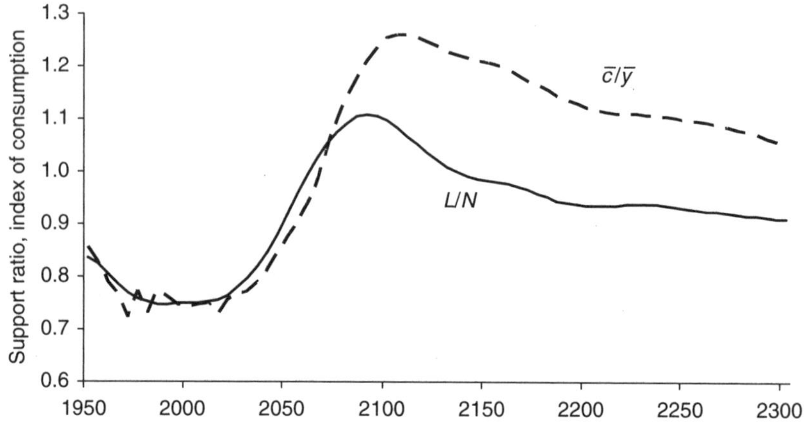

Figure 6.4 *The support ratio (*L/N*) and the index of consumption ($\bar{c}/\bar{y}$): Niger population, 1950–2300, Taiwan economic lifecycle*

phase, the first dividend phase, the direct effect of an increase in the support ratio, shown in equation (6.1), is to increase consumption per equivalent consumer by 50 percent.

The transitory nature of the first dividend is quite clear. The support ratio drops from its peak in 2090, at first rapidly and then more gradually. At the end of the transition the support ratio is well below the peak, about 10 percent above the 1950 support ratio. The first dividend has turned negative and is adversely influencing per capita consumption during this phase of the demographic transition.

In the absence of the second demographic dividend, the consumption index ($\bar{c}/\bar{y}$) would track the support ratio exactly. The index measures the extent to which consumption per equivalent consumer rises relative to productivity changes induced by technological innovation. Consumption deviates from the support ratio because consumers vary the shares of their income that they devote to consumption and saving, and, as a result, assets and asset income vary.

Early in the transition the consumption index fluctuates, but between 1950 and 2000 it declines by about the same amount as the support ratio. From 2010 to 2070, the consumption index is lower than the support ratio by roughly 5 percentage points. After 2010, the consumption index is growing at more or less the same rate as the support ratio. Just as the first dividend is coming to an end, the effects of the second dividend become apparent. Even though the support ratio begins to decline, consumption continues to increase relative to labor productivity. Consumption does

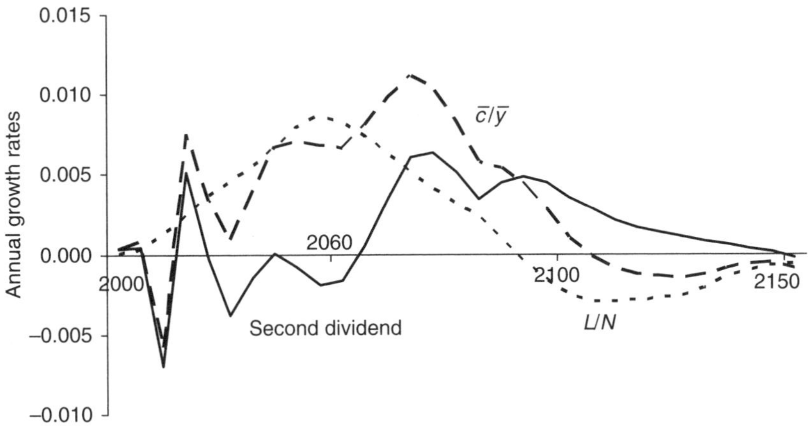

Figure 6.5 Dividend variables (annual rates of growth): Niger population, 2000–2150, Taiwan economic lifecycle

begin to fall early in the twenty-second century, but it remains above the support ratio peak for more than 150 years. In steady state the consumption peak is about 18 percent above the level produced by the first dividend alone. The reason that higher consumption can be sustained is that consumers have accumulated more assets. By doing so, they have converted a transitory dividend into a permanent one.

The annual growth effects of the dividends are modest but important (Figure 6.5). The peak rate of growth for the support ratio is 0.9 percent per year in 2045–50. Between 2030 and 2065 the support ratio increases by 0.5 percent per year or more. The consumption index grows at an annual rate peaking at about 1.1 percent per year for 2065–70 and exceeding 0.5 percent per year between 2030 and 2090. During this 60-year period the only other source of economic growth is technological progress of 1.5 percent per year. Hence the two demographic dividends combined contribute 25 percent or more of the economic growth experienced.

The second demographic dividend in a small open economy is the rate of growth of C/Y, the rate of growth of consumption relative to labor income. This is the difference between the rate of growth of the consumption index and the rate of growth of the support ratio. The second dividend is usually a small negative value between 2000 and 2055. Consumption is depressed by roughly 0.1 percent per year during the 55-year period. The first dividend turns positive in 2055 and remains positive until 2155. Between 2060 and 2105 the second dividend averages between 0.4 percent and 0.5 percent per annum.

Next we turn to the wealth effects of the demographic transition (Figure 6.6). A key point is that the demand for pension wealth is very weak in the early stages of the demographic transition, for several reasons. First, most adults are young and they have not yet accumulated much pension wealth, irrespective of their expectations about retirement. Second, those who are currently working, particularly those who have been working sufficiently long to have accumulated pension wealth, have little incentive to do so because they anticipate a relatively short period of retirement. Third, the costs of childrearing are very high. Because Niger's population is dominated by such a large number of children, and its support ratio is correspondingly low, consumption during retirement is low. Moreover the support ratio will continue to be low for decades. Hence anticipated consumption during retirement is low. This leads to an even lower demand for retirement wealth. Pension wealth is barely discernible only in 2020 and later.[12]

Of particular importance in the early part of the demographic transition is the decline in fertility and its implications for child costs. The wealth calculations emphasized here are the present values of future childrearing costs to year *t* adults. Between 1950 and 2025, the childrearing debt is very high, equal to six to seven times annual labor income. The childrearing debt declines for two reasons. First, fertility drops more rapidly than child mortality and hence the surviving number of children declines. That this is occurring is evident in the age-distribution graph shown above (Figure 6.3). Second, the age distribution of adults begins to shift toward older ages so that adults, as a group, have completed a larger portion of their childrearing.

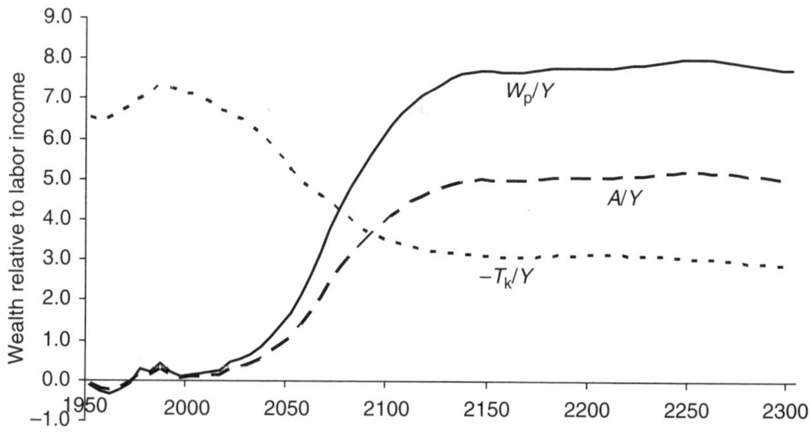

Figure 6.6 Components of wealth: Niger population, 1950–2300, Taiwan economic lifecycle

There is a countervailing effect, however, because consumption per child rises relative to labor income as the number of children declines. The process is largely completed after 100 years. At that point childrearing debt stabilizes at about three times annual labor income.

Pension wealth and assets rise very substantially over the transition. In 2000, there is a negligible demand for pension wealth, as explained above. By 2150, pension wealth has reached nearly eight times annual labor income and assets have reached nearly five times annual labor income, as compared with a value of about four times for the US today.

The impact of this enormous increase in assets is muted in the simulation results presented here because the economy is small and open. The effect of a fourfold increase in the ratio of capital to labor income, experienced between 2050 and 2100, for example, would be to double output per worker, given a standard Cobb–Douglas production function. This would produce an effect on consumption substantially higher in a closed economy. Of course, even if the world consists entirely of open economies, the rise of assets will produce increases in wages and output.

The final baseline results we present are for the aggregate consumption rate. Consumption as a fraction of labor income and consumption as a fraction of net national income ($Y+rA$) are charted in Figure 6.7. Consumption as a fraction of labor income is of interest because of the key role it plays in equation (6.1). Consumption rises about 30 percent relative to labor income between 2055–60 and 2150–55. This is the cumulative effect of the second dividend.

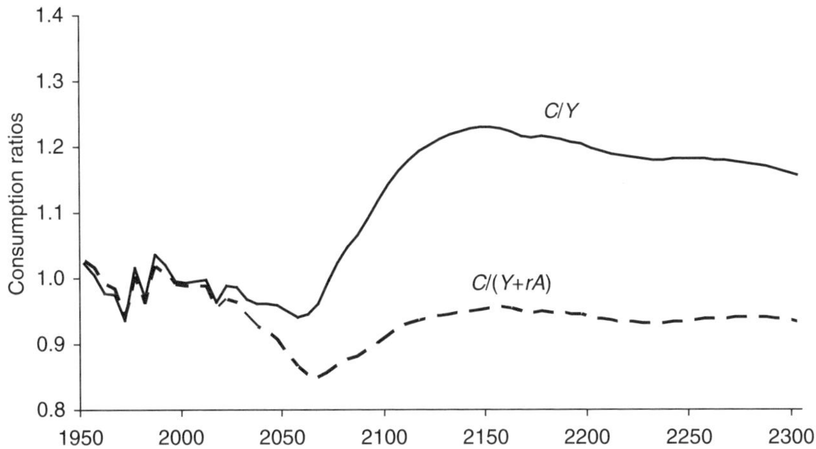

Figure 6.7 Consumption ratio: Niger population, 1950–2300, Taiwan economic lifecycle

The ratio of consumption to national income is of interest because its complement is saving as a fraction of national income. We see clear evidence of the saving boom often attributed to demographic effects in the literature: the saving rate rises from close to zero at the beginning of the simulation to peak at about 15 percent of national income. Thereafter the saving rate declines to a steady-state rate of about 6 percent of national income.

IS IT MORTALITY OR FERTILITY DECLINE?

The demographic transition is driven by changes in both fertility and mortality. Which plays the more important role in the demographic dividends? We explore this issue by considering demographic transitions that vary substantially from those projected for Niger. Two alternative scenarios are considered. In the first the declines in the age-specific fertility rates are delayed for 50 years and then follow the path of the baseline scenario shifted rightward by 50 years. All other parameters are held equal to their baseline values. The second scenario is similar in construction, except that the declines in age-specific death rates, rather than the declines in fertility rates, are delayed for 50 years.[13]

The effects of a delay in fertility decline are substantial, whereas the effects of a delay in mortality decline are modest. Figure 6.8 presents the support ratio and the consumption index for the three scenarios. The delay in fertility decline leads to further deterioration in the support ratio because constant fertility combined with a decline in infant and child mortality is leading to an increase in the number of surviving children and a substantially higher childrearing burden. The support ratio eventually recovers and reaches nearly the same height as the baseline scenario, but decades later. The delayed fertility decline depresses consumption over an extended period. Consumption does not recover to the value for 2000 until near the end of the century. Eventually consumption rises and stabilizes at the same steady-state value as in the baseline scenario.

The effects of delayed mortality decline are very different, in part because the effects of a decline in death rates at young ages are so different from the effects of a decline in death rates at older ages. When the decline in infant and child mortality is delayed, the number of surviving children declines relative to the baseline and hence the support ratio is higher and the costs of childrearing are lower. This leads to an immediate boost in consumption as compared with the baseline. Later in the simulation the support ratio is higher in the delayed-mortality scenario because higher death rates at older ages reduce the relative size of the old-age population. As compared with the baseline scenario, then, the cumulative effects of the first dividend on

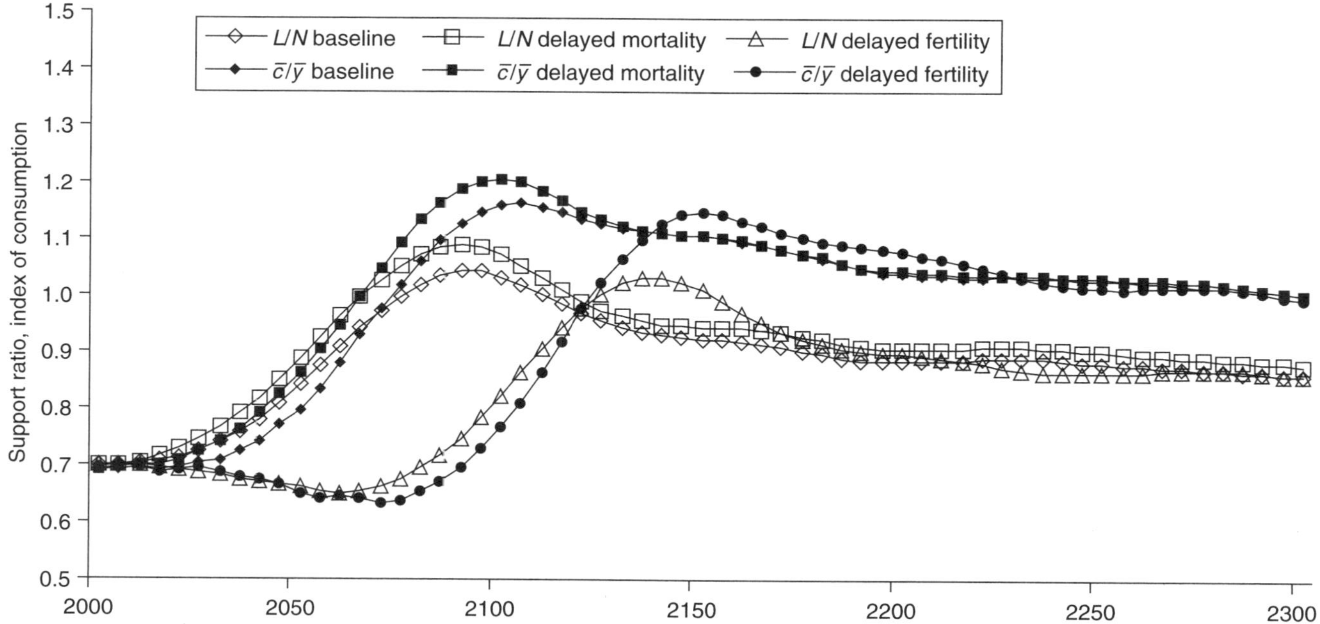

Figure 6.8 *The support ratio (L/N) and the index of consumption ($\bar{c}/\bar{y}$): alternative population scenarios, 2000–2300, Taiwan economic lifecycle*

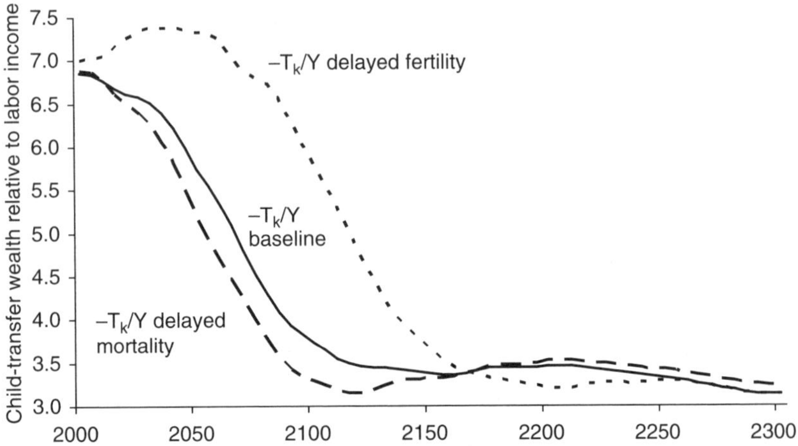

Figure 6.9 Child-transfer wealth relative to labor income ($-T_k/Y$): alternative population scenarios, 2000–2300, Taiwan economic lifecycle

consumption are consistently greater when mortality decline is delayed. This does not translate, however, into permanently higher consumption. The reason, as shown below, is that higher adult death rates under the delayed mortality-decline scenario lead to lower capital accumulation and a smaller second dividend.

As discussed above, an immediate and important impact of delayed fertility decline is to increase the number and cost of children, whereas the impact of delayed mortality decline is to reduce the number and cost of children (Figure 6.9). The capitalized value of the lifetime costs of childrearing declines from about seven times annual labor income in 2000 to about three times annual labor income in 2100 for both the baseline and the delayed mortality-decline scenarios. Child costs are reduced when mortality decline is delayed, but the differences are small. For the delayed fertility-decline scenario, child costs rise gradually during the first half of the twenty-first century and begin to decline only at mid-century. They remain above those of the other scenarios until well into the twenty-second century.

As compared with the baseline scenario, assets are reduced by a small amount in the delayed mortality-decline scenario (Figure 6.10). The costs of children are lower in the delayed mortality-decline scenario, which would lead to higher consumption at older ages and greater accumulation of assets. This is more than offset, however, by the reduced number of years lived at older ages. Under the delayed fertility-decline scenario, asset accumulation is very substantially depressed.

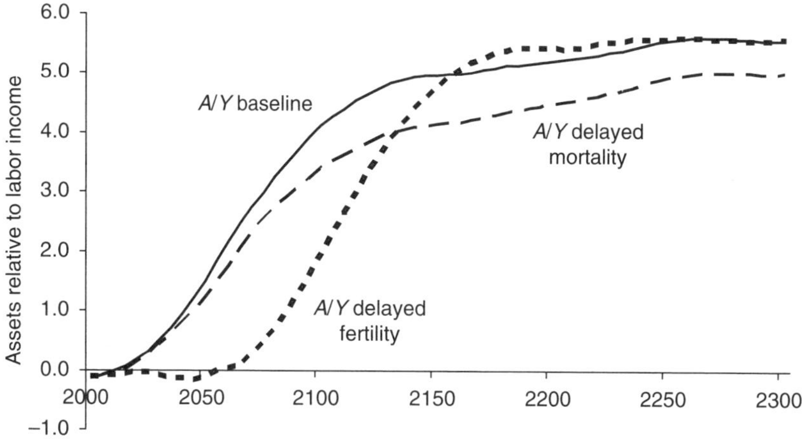

Figure 6.10 *Assets relative to labor income (A/Y): alternative population scenarios, 2000–2300, Taiwan economic lifecycle*

SENSITIVITY TO OTHER MODEL PARAMETERS

We conducted a series of additional sensitivity tests, and the results are presented in Tables 6.1 and 6.2. Three alternative simulations are carried out. The first uses the US age profiles of consumption and production (Figure 6.1) rather than the Taiwan profiles. The second considers the implications of relying more heavily on transfer wealth rather than assets to support old-age consumption by increasing the share of transfer wealth in pension wealth to 0.65 from 0.35. The third simulation considers the implications of shifting the costs of childrearing from parents to taxpayers by reducing the share of familial transfers to children from 0.67 to 0.33.

The US lifecycle differs from the Taiwan lifecycle in that consumption by children is lower and consumption by the elderly is higher relative to consumption by prime-age adults. Part of the high consumption at older ages is offset by higher production at older ages in the US. The differences in the economic lifecycle are summarized by the support ratios compared in Table 6.1. When the population age structure is young, in 1950 or 1990, for example, the support ratio based on the US age profiles of consumption and production are slightly more favorable (2.5 percent higher in 1950). When the population age structure is old (in 2090 or 2300, for example) the US support ratio based on the US age profiles is unfavorable. This is particularly the case toward the end of the demographic transition. In 2300, the US-based support ratio is 11 percent below the Taiwan-based support ratio.

Table 6.1 Effects of parameters on simulated values

Variable	Baseline	US lifecycle	$\tau = 0.65$	$\tau_f = 0.33$
First dividend period	1990–2090	1990–2085	1990–2090	1990–2090
Year second dividend ends	2015	2100	2095	2105
L/N, 1950	0.8352	0.8552	0.8352	0.8352
L/N, 1990	0.7465	0.7605	0.7465	0.7465
L/N, 2090 (2085 for US lifecycle)	1.1091	1.0904	1.1091	1.1091
L/N, 2300	0.9098	0.8130	0.9098	0.9098
$\bar{c}/\bar{y}$, 1950	0.8544	0.8816	0.8360	0.8453
$\bar{c}/\bar{y}$, 1990	0.7616	0.7753	0.7489	0.7566
$\bar{c}/\bar{y}$, maximum	1.2608	1.3010	1.1609	1.2230
$\bar{c}/\bar{y}$, 2300	1.0516	0.9159	0.9663	1.0595
L/N, annual growth (%), 1st div. period	0.40%	0.36%	0.40%	0.40%
$\bar{c}/\bar{y}$, annual growth (%), 1st div. period	0.46%	0.46%	0.44%	0.48%

Notes: First dividend period begins when L/N reaches a minimum and ends when L/N reaches a maximum. Second dividend ends when $\bar{c}/\bar{y}$, reaches its maximum value. Unless otherwise indicated, simulation is based on the following assumptions: Taiwan 1977 lifecycle profiles; annual labor productivity growth of 1.5 percent per year; family share of transfers to children of 0.67; a discount rate of 3 percent per year; an interest declining from 6 percent for 1950–2000 to a steady-state value of 4.3 percent for the Taiwan lifecycle and 3.51 percent for the US lifecycle; transfer wealth as a share of total pension wealth of 0.35; medium scenario of the UN Population Projections.

During the dividend phases the US age profiles are advantageous; the consumption index is higher from the beginning of the simulation through the first dividend period. The US-based consumption index reaches a higher maximum. As the dividend phases end, however, the relatively high level of old-age consumption in the US turns into a disadvantage. US-based assets are always higher than Taiwan-based assets, but part of that advantage is lost because interest rates are substantially lower (Table 6.2).[14] Greater assets are insufficient to overcome the adverse effect of a low US-based support ratio and lower rates of return to capital. Whether or not this would be true in a closed economy is a question that remains to be answered.

The implications of an increased reliance on transfers to support old-age consumption are substantial. During the first dividend period, growth of the consumption index in the baseline economy and the high-transfer economy are similar. The cost of relying more heavily on transfers comes

Table 6.2 Effects of parameters on simulated values of wealth relative to labor income and the consumption ratio

Variable	Baseline	US lifecycle	$\tau = 0.65$	$\tau_f = 0.33$
Child wealth, max	7.3611	7.8487	7.2455	7.5909
Child wealth, min	2.8959	2.2453	2.5422	3.1756
Pension wealth, max	8.0175	10.8529	5.7337	8.4977
Assets, max	5.2114	7.0544	2.0068	5.5235
$C/(Y+rA)$ max	1.0282	1.0012	1.0025	0.9967
$C/(Y+rA)$ min	0.8488	0.7515	0.9404	0.8413

Note: All assets values expressed relative to total labor income. See notes for Table 6.1.

when sustaining the second dividend, and it is substantial. Consumption at the peak (the end of the second dividend period) is almost 10 percent lower in the high-transfer economy, a disadvantage that persists in perpetuity. The reason, of course, is that the asset accumulation in the high-transfer economy has been much lower (Table 6.2). Note that the effect is more than proportional to the increase in the share of transfer wealth. Because consumption is reduced at older ages, the amount of pension wealth that is accumulated is also reduced and hence the adverse effect on assets is more than proportional.

The final sensitivity test considers the effect of an increase in the taxpayers' share of child costs. Instead of one-third, taxpayers are paying two-thirds of the cost of children. A rise in the burden on taxpayers increases the child costs for year t adults because taxpayers are on average older than parents. Thus year t adults will pay a higher portion of the future costs of children. The effect is quite modest even though the assumed change is quite extreme. Because we assume that taxes are levied on wages only, it may be that the average age of taxpayers is not much greater than the average age of parents. Given a different tax system, the effects could be larger.

QUALIFICATIONS AND FURTHER RESEARCH

The results presented here are promising, but much remains to be done. First, there are features of the theoretical model that require further development. The most obvious and important is to relax the small, open-economy feature of the model. Another is to relax the assumption that the cross-sectional consumption profile is fixed. We could, for example, explore the implications of a quantity–quality tradeoff for child expenditures or the implications of political economy models that might influence the consumption of the elderly. A second area requiring more work is empirical. Comparing results from the US and Taiwan shows that variation in the economic lifecycle across countries is important, and hence there is a need for more estimates of the economic lifecycle and more analysis of how it varies and why. Of equal importance is improving estimates and analysis of transfers. Again, we have estimates for Taiwan and the US that can be employed here, but we know very little about transfer policy in the comprehensive sense of the term used here. In particular, estimates of familial transfers are not widely available. Finally, the model does not incorporate the effects of capital accumulation on wages. Aging is a global phenomenon, and hence to the extent that capital accumulation increases worldwide, as implied by our model, wages will increase on a global scale. This may prove to be the most important implication of population aging for economic growth.

CONCLUSIONS

Over the coming decades we will find ourselves in uncharted waters. The share of the elderly population will reach unprecedented levels and not just in the industrialized world. Many low- and middle-income countries are also far along in their demographic transitions. Even if adults begin to delay retirement, it is virtually certain that the number of retirees will rise relative to the number of workers, in most countries and in the world as a whole.

If labor were the only factor of production, the first-order effects of population aging would be easily assessed. Per capita income and per capita consumption would vary directly with the economic support ratio. An increase in the number of retirees would add to the number to be supported but not to the number producing nor the amount produced. Thus per capita consumption would decline in direct proportion to the decline in the support ratio. The favorable effects of changing age structure that occur early in the demographic transition would be undone as young dependants are replaced by old ones.

Retirees do not, however, rely exclusively on the labor of others (through public and familial transfer systems). Retirees depend on pension funds, personal savings, homes acquired during their working years, and other assets to finance some part of their retirement. How much is a matter of some dispute and varies widely from place to place, but estimates we present show that assets are an important source of support for the elderly in Taiwan and especially in the United States. Thus the lifecycle demand for assets, the size of the capital stock, and total production increase as populations age. The size of the pie increases with aging, but the important question is by how much.

This chapter answers the question using a new conceptual approach. Our model acknowledges the close ties and pervasive links across generations. Consumption at each age is not governed by an individualistic lifetime budget constraint as in the lifecycle model. Rather, consumption is governed by altruism and constrained by total production.

The simulation results indicate that fertility decline, increased longevity, and the accompanying changes in age structure have potentially large effects on the demand for assets. Early in the demographic transition the demand for assets is near zero. By the time that the fertility transition has been completed in the baseline simulation, assets relative to labor income exceeds 3. For this to happen, however, requires a commitment to asset accumulation over transfer systems in the provision of old-age support. Perhaps the most important feature of the simulations to note is that the foundation for the second demographic dividend occurs early in the demographic transition. Long before fertility rates are low and life expectancy is high, a larger share of output is being committed to the accumulating assets. The first dividend eases the pain of forgoing consumption. Some of the resources previously devoted to supporting large numbers of children can be devoted to capital accumulation. In this way the demographic dividends provide an opportunity for sustaining permanently higher standards of living into the future.

The opportunities are significant, but they are not certain. They depend on public and familial transfer policy. If the response to population aging were exclusively to expand public transfer programs and to increase the burden on adult children of providing support to their parents, then we will merely be dividing a fixed pie among varying numbers of consumers.

APPENDIX

Child-transfer Costs

The cost of all children age z in year $t+x$ is:

$$
\begin{aligned}
COST(z, t+x) &= Y(z, t+x) - C(z, t+x) \\
&= \bar{y}(t)G_y(x)L(z, t+x) - \bar{c}(t)G_c(t, x)N(z, t+x) \\
&\quad z < a_0(t+x).
\end{aligned}
\tag{6.17}
$$

A fraction of the cost of children of age z in year $t+x$ is financed through transfers by year t adults; the remainder is financed through transfers by persons who were children or not yet born in year t. Let $TAX_k(z, t, x)$ be the share of child costs paid by year t adults. Then, child-transfer wealth in year t for year t adults is:

$$
T_k(t) = \sum_{x=0}^{\omega - a_0(t)} D(x) \sum_{z=0}^{a_0(t+x)-1} TAX_k(z, t, x)COST(z, t+x). \tag{6.18}
$$

Substituting for $COST$ from equation (6.17) yields:

$$
\begin{aligned}
T_k(t) &= \bar{y}(t) \sum_{x=0}^{\omega - a_0(t)} D(x)G_y(x)KLTOT(t, x) \\
&\quad - \bar{c}(t) \sum_{x=0}^{\omega - a_0(t)} D(x)G_c(t, x)KNTOT(t, x) \\
KLTOT(t, x) &= \sum_{z=0}^{a_0(t+x)-1} TAX_k(z, t, x)L(z, t+x) \\
KNTOT(t, x) &= \sum_{z=0}^{a_0(t+x)-1} TAX_k(z, t, x)N(z, t+x),
\end{aligned}
\tag{6.19}
$$

where $KLTOT(t, x)$ is the total number of children in year $t+x$ dependent on year t adults measured in equivalent production units and in year $t+x$ and where $KNTOT(t, x)$ is the total number of children in year $t+x$ dependent on year t adults measured in equivalent consumption units.

Tax Burden of Year *t* Adults

The share of year t adults depends on whether child costs are financed through public or private (familial) transfer programs. We assume that the shares of public and private transfers are constant and exogenous; that is, they are a matter of public policy. Let the familial share be τ^f and the public share be $1-\tau^f$. Then the share of cost paid by year t adults is a weighted sum of the taxes paid through a familial transfer system and the taxes paid through a public transfer system; i.e.,

$$TAX_k(z, t, x) = \tau^f TAX_k^f(z, t, x) + (1-\tau^f) TAX_k^g(z, t, x), \quad (6.20)$$

where $TAX_k^f(z, t, x)$ is the share of child costs paid by year t adults under a familial transfer system and $TAX_k^g(z, t, x)$ is the share of child costs paid by year t adults under a public transfer system.

We assume that all public transfers to children are financed by a proportional tax on the labor income of adults. Thus the share of public transfers borne by year t adults in year $t+x$ is:

$$TAX_k^g(z, t, x) = \sum_{a=a_0(t)+x}^{\omega} Y(a, t+x)/Y_A(t+x), \quad (6.21)$$

where $Y_A(t+x) = \Sigma_{a=a_0(t+x)}^{\omega} Y(a, t+x)$ is the total labor income of all in year $t+x$.

The tax share of year t adults in year $t+x$ is their share of labor income in year $t+x$. Note that the public tax share is independent of the age of the child, z. Henceforth we drop the z argument.

We assume that familial transfers are determined by parentage. If we let $F(z, t, x)$ equal the proportion of those aged z with parents (mothers) age $a_0(t)+x$ or older in year $t+x$, then

$$TAX_k^f(z, t, x) = F(z, t, x), \quad (6.22)$$

where F is calculated using the distribution of births to women:

$$F(z, t, x) = \frac{\sum_{a=a_0(t)+x-z}^{AGEM} B(a, t+x-z)}{\sum_{a=a_0(t+x-z)}^{AGEM} B(a, t+x-z)} \quad \text{for } x > z$$
$$= 1 \text{ for } x \leq z \quad (6.23)$$

and $B(a, t+x-z)$ is births to adult women aged a in year $t+x-z$.[15] Children who are x years or older are all the offspring of year t adults (mothers) and hence F has a value of 1. The value of F declines to zero as

x increases. (Note that F can be represented as a function of t and $x-z$. It is not really three-dimensional.)

We can substitute the terms defined in equations (6.21)–(6.23) into equation (6.20), and the share of year t adults is:

$$TAX_k(z, t, x) = \tau^f F(z, t, x) + (1 - \tau^f) \sum_{a=a_0(t)+x}^{\omega} Y(a, t+x)/Y_A(t+x). \tag{6.24}$$

Substituting into equation (6.19) yields child-transfer wealth for year t adults. Note that the tax shares devoted to childrearing are determined exogenously by population age structure, fertility and the age profile of earnings – all exogenous factors. Thus, in the determination of child-transfer costs, the only endogenous variables are the vector of the consumption index and the age at which individuals become adults.

Steady-state Results

The trajectory of assets must satisfy the macroeconomic flow constraint:

$$(1+r)A(t) + Y(t) - C(t) = A(t+1). \tag{6.25}$$

In steady state, assets grow at the same rate as total labor income, g_Y. Substituting $(1+g_Y)A(t)$ for $A(t+1)$, substituting for income and consumption, and rearranging terms, we find that assets in steady state must satisfy:

$$A(t^*) = \frac{1}{r-g_Y}[\,\bar{c}(t^*)N(t^*) - \bar{y}(t^*)L(t^*)]. \tag{6.26}$$

From the analysis of the lifecycle can be seen that the relationship between assets and lifecycle pension wealth is governed by an exogenously specified pension transfer policy:

$$A(t^*) = [1 - \tau(t^*)]\,W_P(t^*), \tag{6.27}$$

where $W_p(t)$ is given in equation (6.15). Combining the macro and lifecycle conditions, and noting that the growth rate of the consumption index must equal the growth rate of the production index in steady state, we conclude that the consumption index in steady state must satisfy:

$$\frac{1}{r-g_Y}[\bar{c}(t^*)N(t^*) - \bar{y}(t^*)L(t^*)] = [1 - \tau(t^*)]\,W_p(t^*). \tag{6.28}$$

Rearranging terms yields:

$$\frac{\bar{c}(t^*)}{\bar{y}(t^*)} = \frac{L(t^*)}{N(t^*)}\{1 + (r - g_Y)[1 - \tau(t^*)]w_p(t^*)\}, \tag{6.29}$$

where $w_p(t^*)$ is the ratio of lifecycle pension wealth to current labor income.

Equation (6.29) tells us the level of consumption that can be sustained in steady state given any level of labor productivity. Age structure determines the steady-state consumption ratio through two multiplicative factors: the economic support ratio and a second factor that captures the influence of age structure on lifecycle pension wealth and, hence, assets.

Backward Recursion

The backward-recursion solution computes the consumption index and hence all other variables in period $t-1$ conditional on the values in period t. The steady-state values are known. Hence we can begin in period t^*, solve for period t^*-1, and recursively solve for all periods t.

From lifecycle accounting, assets in period $t-1$ depend on pension policy and lifecycle wealth in year $t-1$. From equations (6.15) and (6.27):

$$\begin{aligned} A(t-1) = \bar{c}(t-1)(1-\tau) &\sum_{x=0}^{\omega - a_0(t-1)} D(x)G_c[t-1, x)(NTOT(t-1, x) \\ &+ KNTOT(t-1, x)] - \bar{y}(t-1)(1-\tau) \sum_{x=0}^{\omega - a_0(t-1)} D(x)G_y(x) \\ &\times [LTOT(t-1, x) + KLTOT(t-1, x)]. \end{aligned} \tag{6.30}$$

Pension policy may vary with year, but here we drop t to simplify notation. The right-hand-side variables include consumption in year $t-1$, consumption in year t and subsequent years, and labor income terms in year $t-1$ and later. Only the consumption terms in year $t-1$ are unknown and must be solved for. These are distinguished in:

$$\begin{aligned} A(t-1) = \bar{c}(t-1)&(1-\tau)N(t-1)D(0) \\ &+ (1-\tau) \sum_{x=1}^{\omega - a_0(t-1)} D(x)\bar{c}(t-1+x)[NTOT(t-1, x) \\ &+ KNTOT(t-1, x)] - \bar{y}(t-1)(1-\tau) \sum_{x=0}^{\omega - a_0(t-1)} D(x)G_y(x) \\ &\times [LTOT(t-1, x) + KLTOT(t-1, x)]. \end{aligned} \tag{6.31}$$

From macro accounting, we know that:

$$A(t-1) = \frac{A(t) + \bar{c}(t-1)N(t-1) - \bar{y}(t-1)L(t-1)}{1+r}. \tag{6.32}$$

This gives us two equations in two unknowns, assets and the consumption index in period $t-1$. Substituting for $A(t-1)$ yields:

$$\begin{aligned}
&\bar{c}(t-1)(1-\tau)N(t-1)D(0) + (1-\tau)\sum_{x=1}^{\omega - a_0(t-1)} D(x)\bar{c}(t-1+x) \\
&\quad [NTOT(t-1,x) + KNTOT(t-1,x)] \\
&\quad - \bar{y}(t-1)(1-\tau)\sum_{x=0}^{\omega - a_0(t-1)} D(x)G_y(x)[LTOT(t-1,x) \\
&\quad + KLTOT(t-1,x)] \\
&\quad = \frac{A(t) + \bar{c}(t-1)N(t-1) - \bar{y}(t-1)L(t-1)}{1+r}.
\end{aligned} \tag{6.33}$$

Multiplying both sides by $1+r$ and rearranging terms yields:

$$\begin{aligned}
&\bar{c}(t-1)N(t-1)[(1-\tau)(1+r)D(0) - 1] \\
&\quad = A(t) - (1+r)(1-\tau)\sum_{x=1}^{\omega - a_0(t-1)} D(x)\bar{c}(t-1+x) \\
&\qquad [NTOT(t-1,x) + KNTOT(t-1,x)] \\
&\qquad + \bar{y}(t-1)(1+r)(1-\tau)\sum_{x=0}^{\omega - a_0(t-1)} D(x)G_y(x)[LTOT(t-1,x) \\
&\qquad + KLTOT(t-1,x)] - \bar{y}(t-1)L(t-1).
\end{aligned} \tag{6.34}$$

Further algebra gives the consumption index for $t-1$:

$$\bar{c}(t-1) = \left(\frac{\begin{array}{l} A(t) - (1+r)(1-\tau)\displaystyle\sum_{x=1}^{\omega - a_0(t-1)} D(x)\bar{c}(t-1+x) \\ {[NTOT(t-1,x) + KNTOT(t-1,x)]} + \bar{y}(t-1) \\ \left\{ \begin{array}{l} (1+r)(1-\tau)\displaystyle\sum_{x=0}^{\omega - a_0(t-1)} D(x)G_y(x) \\ (LTOT[(t-1,x) + KNTOT(t-1,x)] - L(t-1) \end{array} \right\} \end{array}}{N(t-1)[(1-\tau)(1+r)D(0) - 1]} \right) \quad 6.35)$$

Assets in period $t-1$ can be calculated using either equation (6.31) or equation (6.32).

NOTES

1. Research for this chapter was funded by two grants from the National Institutes of Health, NIA R01-AG025488 and NIA R37-AG025247. Diana Wongkaren, Turro Wongkaren, Pablo Lattes, Timothy Miller and Gretchen Donehower provided excellent assistance with the computations.
2. In a closed economy a decline in labor force growth would lead to capital deepening and an increase in output per worker. This would not be the case, however, in a small open economy.
3. We abstract from uncertainty about whether future income streams are realized.
4. This analysis is confined to a small, open economy. Hence capital per worker is exogenously determined by international capital markets.
5. In 2000, approximately 35 percent of US pension wealth was transfer wealth and about 65 percent was assets.
6. In the current analysis we do not consider any feedbacks from capital deepening to wages. Hence the model considered here is appropriate for a small open economy in which the rate of return on investment is determined by international capital markets and the shift in the wage profile is determined by exogenous technological change.
7. We assume that income and consumption accrue at the end of the period.
8. We assume that assets are measured at the beginning of the period and that consumption and income accrue at the end of the period.
9. We assume that steady state is achieved in 2300, the last year for which long-range population projections are available. Simulated values for 2000 to 2150 are nearly identical when we assume steady state is reached in 2200.
10. Estimates and projections covering the 1950–2050 period are based on UN Population Division (2005). Projections from 2050 to 2300 are based on UN Population Division (2004). Long-range projections for most individual countries are unpublished but were provided to us by the Population Division. The long-range projections have been adjusted to eliminate a discontinuity in 2050 between the short-term and long-range projections.
11. We calculate the steady-state international rate of return using the same set of assumptions for the global economy and the global population distribution in 2300, weighted to reflect current differences in per capita income between the developing and developed countries. In the global calculations, however, the rate of return is endogenous. Details are available from us.
12. The small negative values for pension wealth in the earliest years are an artifact of the simulation methodology. The capital value of transfers to older children, those aged 25–29, are included in pension wealth rather than in child wealth.
13. These calculations were made by constructing a population projection model that closely mimics UN projections.
14. We determine the global economy and thus international interest rates using the same economic lifecycle as used for the Niger simulation. The results would be different if, for example, the Taiwan lifecycle were used to represent the global economic lifecycle.
15. We assume that children do not support children. All familial costs are shared among adult parents.

REFERENCES

Barro, Robert J. and Xavier Sala-i-Martin (1995), *Economic Growth*, New York, London and Montreal: McGraw-Hill.

Bloom, David E. and David Canning (2001), 'Cumulative causality, economic growth, and the demographic transition', in N. Birdsall, A.C. Kelley and

S.W. Sinding (eds), *Population Matters: Demographic Change, Economic Growth, and Poverty in the Developing World*, Oxford: Oxford University Press, pp. 165–200.

Bloom, David E. and Jeffrey G. Williamson (1998), 'Demographic transitions and economic miracles in emerging Asia', *World Bank Economic Review*, **12**(3), 419–56.

Bloom, David E., David Canning and Jaypee Sevilla (2002), *The Demographic Dividend: A New Perspective on the Economic Consequences of Population Change*, Santa Monica, California: RAND.

Lee, Ronald D., Sang-Hyop Lee and Andrew Mason (2006), 'Charting the economic lifecycle', NBER Working Paper 12379, National Bureau of Economic Research, Cambridge, Massachusetts.

Lee, Ronald, Andrew Mason and Tim Miller (2000), 'Life cycle saving and the demographic transition in East Asia', *Population and Development Review*, **26**(Supplement).

Lee, Ronald, Andrew Mason and Tim Miller (2001), 'Saving, wealth, and the demographic transition in East Asia', in A. Mason (ed.), *Population Change and Economic Development in East Asia: Challenges Met, Opportunities Seized*, Stanford, California: Stanford University Press, pp. 155–84.

Lee, Ronald, Andrew Mason and Tim Miller (2003), 'From transfers to individual responsibility: implications for savings and capital accumulation in Taiwan and the United States', *Scandinavian Journal of Economics*, **105**(3), 339–57.

Lee, Ronald D., Andrew Mason and Tim Miller (2001), 'Saving, wealth, and population', in N. Birdsall, A.C. Kelley and S.W. Sinding (eds), *Population Matters: Demographic Change, Economic Growth, and Poverty in the Developing World*, Oxford: Oxford University Press, pp. 137–64.

Mankiw, Gregory, David Romer and David Weil (1992), 'A contribution to the empirics of economic growth', *Quarterly Journal of Economics*, **107**(2), 407–37.

Mason, Andrew (2001), *Population Change and Economic Development in East Asia: Challenges Met, Opportunities Seized*, Stanford: Stanford University Press.

Mason, Andrew (2005), 'Demographic transition and demographic dividends in developed and developing countries', paper presented at United Nations Expert Group Meeting on Social and Economic Implications of Changing Population Age Structures, Mexico City.

Mason, Andrew and Ronald Lee (2004), 'Reform and support systems for the elderly in developing countries: capturing the second demographic dividend', paper presented at the International Seminar on the Demographic Window and Healthy Aging: Socioeconomic Challenges and Opportunities, China Centre for Economic Research, Peking University, Beijing.

Mason, Andrew, Ronald Lee, An-Chi Tung, Mun Sim Lai and Tim Miller (forthcoming), 'Population aging and intergenerational transfers: introducing age into national accounts', in D. Wise (ed.), *Developments in the Economics of Aging*, Chicago: National Bureau of Economic Research and University of Chicago Press.

UNPD (United Nations Population Division) (2004), *World Population to 2300*, New York: United Nations.

UNPD (2005), *World Population Prospects: The 2004 Revision*, New York: United Nations.

World Bank (2005), *World Development Indicators 2005*, New York: World Bank.

7. Effects of age structure on investment, saving and trade

Thomas Lindh and Bo Malmberg[1]

In their 1994 article, 'Capital flows to the New World as an intergenerational transfer', Allan Taylor and Jeffrey Williamson suggested that capital exports from old Europe could be seen as an intergenerational transfer to demographically younger nations overseas. Capital flows became a means by which gaps in the dependency rates could be bridged. The current aging of industrialized countries is therefore expected to change capital-flow patterns. There are, however, many ways in which age structure may affect saving, investment and trade patterns. A prediction of future capital flows is hard to base on empirics, since the extent of aging that lies before us has never been observed in history. In this chapter we focus on patterns in OECD countries to judge whether the sample shows any new trends different from those observed by, for example, Higgins and Williamson (1997) for East Asia and Higgins (1998) using a world sample.

During the first half of the twenty-first century a rapid expansion of the working-age population in the developing world will accompany an increase in the old-age population in the industrialized world. In the coming decades there will thus be room for new global intergenerational transfers in the form of international capital flows from the aging economies to the emerging ones. To what extent will this possibility be realized? One way to cast light on this question is to analyze how shifting age structures in the recent past have affected capital flows.

Before we present our approach it is of value to discuss the reasons why shifts in age distribution should have an effect on capital flows. It is well known that changes in age structure can affect national savings rates. The basic reason is that children and old people tend to consume more than they produce, whereas the per capita production of working-age adults tends to exceed what they need for their own personal consumption. Changes in age structure may affect the demand for investment too, but such age effects need not have the same profile as the age effects on savings. If the profiles of age effects on saving and investment are different, this implies that shifts in age structure will generate movements in the current account, effectively changing the net capital flows across countries.

Movements in the current account may also be due to changes in exports or in imports that are not necessarily due to changes in age structure. Trade is an alternative channel to equilibrate changing factor endowments due to variations in the population age structure. With perfect markets, this coordination between saving and investment decisions on the one hand and export and import volumes on the other can be reached without friction through relative-price adjustments. When an individual decides not to consume a part of earned income, this generates a surplus of goods on the market. The surplus can be used by someone else for investment purposes and then there will be no current-account effect as investment is financed by domestic savings. In the next step, however, the production generated by this investment can be exported and thus through the trade channel generate a surplus in the current account. Another possibility arises if some individuals decide to reduce their labor supply but keep up their consumption by using some of their accumulated savings. This creates excess demand on the market. If investment demand falls as much as saving does, this will equilibrate the market. But if investment demand does not decline, then imports may increase to close the gap and there will be a negative effect on the current account.

Although oversimplified, the reasoning above indicates that in order to analyze the effects of population aging on capital flows it is not enough to study the demographic effects on aggregate savings and take investment as exogenous. Other effects are also important, quite diverse and potentially sensitive to policy choices (Bean, 2004, gives a succinct statement). In this chapter we focus our empirical investigation on the investment rate. There are three reasons for doing so. First, it is the investment rate and not the savings rate that determines the national capital stock. Second, if age effects on investment differ from age effects on saving, then current accounts and international capital flows will also change. Although these points have been noted in the literature, the role of investment has generally been taken to be passive: that is, unlike saving, not reacting directly to the changes in age distribution. Third, different components of investment demand are not affected in the same way by aging. For example, housing investment is sensitive mainly to changes in the young age groups who are in the process of family formation and in the very old age groups who leave their dwellings, thus creating vacancies in the housing stock.

The conclusion we reach is that the aging of the post-World War II baby-boom generations can generate a cyclical movement up to 30 years long in the current account. The current account will improve as the baby boomers enter upper-middle age and then deteriorate rapidly when they start to move into early post-retirement. As they age even more, however, there are indications that the current account will stabilize and even become positive.

This forecast is driven by profiles in the age effects we identify for national savings and investment rates. The age profile for national savings peaks in upper-middle age, then becomes strongly negative for young retirees and finally bounces back toward zero for older retirees. The age profile for gross investment, in contrast, is at a low point for older retirees and for family-aged adults, those 30–40 years old. The investment effect is weakly positive for young adults (15–29 years old), is positive for middle-aged adults (50–64 years old) and surprisingly attains a maximum for the young retiree group (ages 65 to 74).

Breaking down the age effects by investment components gives a better understanding of this pattern. The relatively positive effect of young adults on investment is related to their positive effect on housing investment. Similarly a strong negative effect on housing investment of the 75+ age group explains why this age group has a negative effect on aggregate investment. For business fixed investment there is a strong positive relation to the 50–64 age group, whereas the positive effect of the 65–74 age group on investment can be traced back to their strong positive relation to inventory investment.

The age patterns of investment components that we find can, with one exception, be given relatively convincing explanations. The exception is the relation between young retirees and inventory investment. One approach to understanding this phenomenon is to consider the effects of age-induced shifts in savings and fixed-investment demand on trading patterns. If the demand for fixed investments declines and the savings rate stays constant, this leads to a reduction in imports and thus an improvement in the trade balance. Similarly, if a demographic shift leads to a lower savings rate but fixed investment stays constant, this may have an adverse effect on the balance of trade. Regressing the trade balance on age-share variables confirms that there are such correlations. Moreover, in the OECD data, a deteriorating trade balance is associated with increasing inventory investments, as if growing import volumes would require more stockpiling than an increase in exports. Thus it is possible that the positive effect of the 65–74 age group on inventory investment is connected to the adverse trade-balance effect of that age group.

Our results in particular differ from those presented earlier by Higgins (1998) with respect to the young retirees. That they do so indicates that the analysis of demographic effects on macroeconomic phenomena must consider seriously the impact that evolving financial institutions and changing lifecycle patterns of economic behavior may have on the empirical correlations that we can observe in the data.

Nevertheless, this explanation does not reverse the negative aging effects on the current account. It only points to a trade mechanism becoming more important in aging populations than an intergenerational-transfer effect as the instrumental channel for the negative aging effect on the current account. The reason may have to do with policy-dependent monetary policies affecting exchange rates and terms of trade or perhaps another factor we have ignored here. Migration is another way to equilibrate demographic imbalances that would affect relative wage relations and production decisions. So far we are unable to disentangle these complex relations but document the correlations behind the net current-account effects that aging has had in the OECD countries.

The disposition we follow below is first to present empirical evidence for cohort-size effects on the investment rate and differences in its components. Savings effects and the consequences for future OECD current accounts then follow. To illustrate differences in results for non-OECD countries, we report results from a World Bank country panel. Finally we explore the trade-balance connection before summarizing our findings and suggest further research to unveil the mechanisms behind them.

DATA SAMPLES

In all estimations we use cross-country panel data. This serves to alleviate problems with multicollinearity in time series and omitted unobservable variables. Panel data offer a possibility to control for country-specific effects due to cultural, geographical and institutional differences, as well as time-specific effects due to variations in the world business cycle.

A potential problem with panel data is parameter and model heterogeneity in the cross-country dimension. If age effects differ between cross-sectional units, biased or unstable parameter estimates may be the result. This problem is considerably alleviated when one uses a set of countries that are broadly similar in their institutional setup and economic history. The price to be paid for doing this is less demographic variation in the cross-section. We focus on an OECD-only sample that should suffer less from heterogeneity problems.[2] As a precaution we control our main OECD results using a broader world sample.

The OECD sample encompasses 20 of the OECD countries: Australia, Austria, Belgium, Canada, Denmark, Finland, France, Germany (BRD), Ireland, Italy, Japan, the Netherlands, New Zealand, Norway, Portugal, Spain, Sweden, Switzerland, the United Kingdom and the United States.[3] Turkey, Mexico, Hungary, South Korea and the Czech Republic were excluded beforehand owing to a lack of data for sufficiently long time periods. Greece, Iceland and Luxembourg were excluded after some experimentation because, as we had expected, they showed clear signs of being outliers as compared with the rest of the sample. Both Greece and Iceland have experienced episodes of extreme inflation, which make their data, especially on saving, unreliable (Loayza et al., 2000), whereas Luxembourg's economy is tightly interwoven with the economies of its much larger neighbors.

In most cases we use a full set of annual observations from 1960 to 1994. Economic data are taken from the OECD (1997) Statistical Compendium, mainly the National Accounts database. Disaggregated investment data are from the database OECD *Economic Outlook* with fewer observations (see below). Annual demographic data are from UN Population Division (1994) starting in 1950. West Germany is an exception: the UN data refer to the population sum for East and West Germany, and therefore we obtained age-structure data for West Germany from *Statistisches Bundesamt* (1952–96) through personal communication and used them for the estimations. For the projections in Figure 6.4, however, we had to use demographic forecasts for united Germany.

Since the age data refer to 31 December in each given year, we have lagged them one step to ensure that they refer to the initial age structure of the year to which annual economic variables refer. To balance lagged variables with current values we restrict the sample to the years 1961–94; our estimation sample therefore adds up to a total of 680 annual observations, decreasing to 660 observations when we use growth rates. Because of some missing data in *Economic Outlook* we have only 540 observations in the samples used for housing investment and private business investment. Portugal and the Netherlands are excluded from this sample, and the data start in 1965.

The broader world country sample was downloaded from the World Saving Data Base at the World Bank. A detailed description of the base is available in Loayza et al. (1998). The main advantage of this database, besides its comprehensiveness, is that data have been thoroughly checked for consistency and quality. The same data definitions have been used as above, but there is a difference between the real-growth estimates in the two samples: the original OECD data are PPP estimates whereas the World Bank data are fix-price estimates that have been rebased to 1987. There are also minor differences in the definitions of national-account concepts, since the OECD data are harmonized, and there is some variation in the time period for which data are available. As Attanasio, Picci and Scorcu (2000) use the same data set, we use a similar sampling criterion whereby the number of countries is traded off against time series long enough to generate a data set comprising 52 countries[4] for which data are available for at least 30 years for both national savings and gross investment. A sufficiently long period for the time series is crucial to identifying age effects. In one case (Haiti) we imputed the mean of values in 1965 and 1967 for national savings in 1966 to fill a lacuna. Otherwise the data are all contiguous from some year in the 1960s up to some year in the 1990s.

INVESTMENT AND THE AGE STRUCTURE

Not much attention has been paid in the literature to the connection between gross investment in the economy and demographic variables. Mostly it is assumed that they are linked via lifecycle saving in a closed economy, where investment is constrained by household saving. The lifecycle mechanism would typically predict that a general increase in savings is associated with an increase in saving for retirement by the middle-aged population, and perforce in a closed economy that will also raise investment.

Many researchers have questioned the lifecycle model, finding that saving continues even in old age, perhaps from bequest motives. Social insurance systems weaken the incentives for lifecycle saving through PAYGO systems for pensions and health care. An alternative channel between population and saving is, however, improved life expectancy, which raises the probability of survival into a dependent old age. Some recent papers on this connection are those by Bloom, Canning and Graham (2003), Zhang and Zhang (2005) and Sheshinski (2006). Zhang and Zhang evaluate the role of life expectancy empirically, using gross investment shares as a proxy for savings. Note that the increased incentive to save, then, will be associated with increases in the older age groups rather than in the middle-aged ones. At least that is the case in OECD countries, where life expectancy is now increasing in age intervals well above conventional retirement ages.

Several studies of current-account responses to demographic imbalances are also relevant. Williamson (2001) surveys some results. In this context it is natural to focus on the differences in demographic effects on investment and saving. Indeed Higgins (1998) finds in a world sample that the young are associated with negative current accounts; that is, investment is more positively related to this group than savings, and vice versa. The finding confirms Higgins and Williamson's (1997) results based on East Asian data. Their explanation essentially relies on a capital-dilution argument and a lifecycle saving model.

The capital-dilution argument in its simplest form is based on a Leontieff or Cobb–Douglas production function with homogeneous labor. Since these technologies entail capital–labor complementarity, increased investment is directly associated with an increased rate of inflow in the labor force, that is, mainly with increases in the share of young adults. In a small open economy where factor prices are not affected, this is a rather straightforward argument. Taking into account factor-price responses and cohort-size effects on wages (with limited substitution of labor vintages) makes it no longer so straightforward. If we allow price and exchange-rate responses in the model, an influx of abundant labor should lower the relative price of labor. Unless technologies really have complementarity between young labor and capital, these price responses would cause substitution for capital. With a high enough elasticity of substitution, investment demand might even fall.

However, from the productivity literature it is well known that complementarity exists between capital and skill (Griliches, 1969). Thus the capital-dilution argument should be more relevant in more-developed economies, where workers are more educated and also generally older when joining the labor force, than in less-developed ones. Increased life expectancy, especially in early stages, also works to decrease the outflow from the work force due to premature death and ill-health (Boucekkine, de la Croix and Licandro, 2003), thus underscoring a potential capital-dilution argument from another angle. But in this case the effects of capital–skill complementarity would tend to be associated with increases in the shares of mature and elderly workers.

Assessment of this hypothesis is complicated since aggregate investment consists of many components. One important component is residential investment, where demographically induced increases in demand are more likely to derive from the consumption side than from the production side of the economy. It is possible that an increase in the young work force is associated with young people moving out of the family home and thus causing housing demand to increase. It is by no means certain, however, and there is considerable variation over countries in the mean age of leaving the parental home. One important reason for this variation is the huge variation in financial-market integration and in the availability of credit for young people (Chiuri and Jappelli, 2003), even within the developed world. If young people are forced to save for a long time to acquire their own home, any positive demographic effect on residential investment will tend to be associated with more mature age groups unless domestic saving by itself boosts domestic investment. This may be the case for closed economies but is unlikely for open ones. Insufficient financial development thus exerts a strong moderating influence on the positive demand effect from young age groups, and final effects will depend also on links to external balances.

It therefore seems plausible to assume that some heterogeneity exists in the investment response to demographic shocks, depending on the level of economic and financial development. Previous empirical work (for example, Higgins, 1998) has assumed homogeneity in these responses. Our focus on OECD serves to evaluate the validity of this global homogeneity assumption since it is crucial for evaluating how aging will affect future capital flows. In financially integrated economies with an educated work force (and incidentally also higher life expectancy and more capital-intensive production) investment demand may well respond differently than in less developed economies to a given change in the age structure.

EMPIRICS OF INVESTMENT AND POPULATION

We use annual data instead of five- or ten-year averages. For country panels the common practice of taking averages over longer time periods to avoid business-cycle noise is dubious and may yield spurious results (see Attanasio, Picci and Scorcu, 2000). Attanasio and his colleagues also report that the panel estimation bias arising in dynamic models when using OLS is so small that the trade-off with precision by using less robust GMM estimators generally favors the OLS estimates. We concur with that assessment and report only least-squares estimates.

In our empirical work the age distribution is approximated by a sum of age-group shares in the population:

$$\tilde{\Phi}_t = \sum_{a=(0-14)}^{(75+)} n_{at}, \; a = (0\text{–}14), (15\text{–}29), (30\text{–}49), (50\text{–}64), (65\text{–}74), (75+).$$

We use six broad age groups with different economic behaviors and resources: children, young adults, family adults, the middle-aged, young retirees and old retirees. Although the exact delimitations are somewhat arbitrary and may vary over countries and time, the lifecycle phases they proxy for differ fundamentally both in social status and in economic resources, as well as needs and behavior.

An alternative approach would be to impose a polynomial restriction on the age-share coefficients, like Higgins (1998). The lesser variation in age structure in OECD as compared with the wide cross-sectional variation in a world sample creates estimation problems when doing so. In effect we get collinearity problems affecting the precision of the estimates, making us prefer the representation above. The age patterns are nevertheless similar to those reported below (results are available upon request).

We control for country-specific and time-specific omitted variables. In the panel-data literature it is generally asserted that if you wish to draw conclusions only about the sample at hand (and not about a more general population) fixed effects are the appropriate model to use, whereas random effects should be preferred in the converse case. In our case, using fixed country effects would thus be correct since we are interested in the age effects on savings in the OECD countries and how they may differ from those in more extended samples. In the time dimension, however, our interest goes beyond the sample period, and therefore a random-effects specification is more appropriate. But random-effects estimates are more sensitive to misspecification (Kiviet, 1995), and so it is prudent also to consider fixed time effects.

COHORT-SIZE EFFECTS ON INVESTMENT

In Table 7.1 we report coefficient estimates under the assumption of fixed country effects (first three columns) and alternatively fixed time and random time effects (in the last three columns).[5]

In the second column of the respective set we include the lag of GDP growth and the lag of the relative price of investment as controls.[6] In the third column we also include a lag of the dependent variable, since serial correlation is evident in the residuals. This could indicate omitted variables or other misspecifications, but experimenting with other controls such as interest rates, trade variables and government consumption had no substantial effect on the age coefficients. By including lags of the investment rate we control for persistent effects, and thus the parameter estimates decrease. A distributed lag model implies that the lag should reduce parameter estimates with about a factor of three. For most coefficients this is approximately the case, allowing for confidence intervals.

The fit of the random-effects regressions increases more than the difference in degrees of freedom can explain. The statistical significance of the age variables also becomes more secure. The theoretically preferred specification with random effects seems empirically preferable.[7]

The growth effect is strong and with the expected positive sign. The relative price of investment, however, has an ambiguous or positive sign. There is thus reason to suspect that endogeneity with regard to the investment-price variable may be a problem. Instead of catching movements along the investment-demand curve we may actually be observing shifts in investment demand that confound the estimates. The age-coefficient patterns in Figure 7.1 nevertheless show a stable bimodal pattern, with young adults relatively more positive than family adults, who have a consistent negative sign.

The strong positive effects from young retirees are very robust, with p-values ranging from 0.001 to 0.08 over different specifications. In this respect our estimates differ from those of Higgins (1998), who finds no such

Table 7.1 Gross investment rates: 20 OECD countries, 1961–94

	Fixed country effects					
Dependent variable:	Fixed time effects			Random time effects		
Gross investment rates	(1)	(2)	(3)	(1)	(2)	(3)
Growth		**0.513**	**0.252**		**0.527**	**0.272**
		(9.19)	(6.17)		(10.7)	(7.05)
Relative price of investment		0.036	$1.1 \cdot 10^{-4}$		0.030	$1.7 \cdot 10^{-3}$
		(1.90)	(0.01)		(1.55)	(0.14)
Lagged investment rate			**0.639**			**0.629**
			(17.5)			(16.7)
Age share 15–29	0.216	0.092	0.048	0.133	0.082	0.012
	(1.83)	(0.91)	(0.85)	(1.36)	(0.99)	(0.24)
Age share 30–49	**−0.303**	−0.240	−0.047	**−0.395**	**−0.330**	−0.116
	(2.01)	(1.74)	(0.72)	(3.09)	(2.74)	(1.86)
Age share 50–64	0.117	**0.298**	**0.181**	0.079	0.234	**0.151**
	(0.83)	(2.17)	(2.72)	(0.62)	(1.88)	(2.41)
Age share 65–74	**0.655**	**0.664**	0.213	**0.536**	**0.755**	0.215
	(2.43)	(2.96)	(1.71)	(2.11)	(3.78)	(1.89)
Age share 75+	**−1.491**	**−1.302**	−0.253	**−1.795**	**−1.392**	**−0.434**
	(3.10)	(2.99)	(1.23)	(6.51)	(6.21)	(3.11)
Adjusted R^2	0.10	0.26	0.58	0.19	0.40	0.62
$\chi^2(5)$ test of age var:	38.0	41.8	19.6	70.2	72.3	29.4
p-value	0.000	0.000	0.002	0.000	0.000	0.000

Notes: Based on 680 usable observations when only age-group shares are used as independent variables, and on 660 usable observations when lagged growth is included. In this and the subsequent tables, heteroskedasticity and autocorrelation-consistent standard errors are estimated by the Newey–West estimator allowing for three lags; thus a Wald test is used for joint significance of the age-share coefficients. The adjusted coefficient of determination refers to the fit to demeaned data, corrected for degrees of freedom lost by this operation. Bold coefficients indicate significance at the 5 percent level; absolute t-values are shown in parentheses.

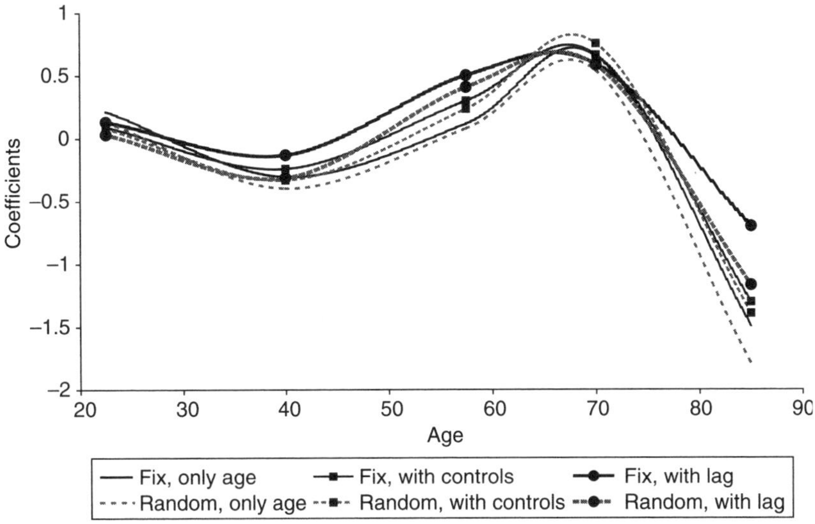

Notes: The mid-points of the age intervals are used to plot the coefficient values. The coefficients from the lag models have been multiplied with 1/(1-lag coefficient) in order to be comparable with the other coefficients.

Figure 7.1 Estimated age coefficients for gross investment rates in Table 7.1, illustrated by a smoothed curve

effects. To further investigate this result and try to identify plausible reasons for it we examine how different components of investment correlate with the age structure.

AGE EFFECTS ON INVESTMENT COMPONENTS

To explore which channel the age effects might work through, we ran the same regression equations as for gross investment but using components of aggregate investment as dependent variables. The results for the full specification with country-specific fixed effects and random time-specific effects are reported in Table 7.2 for private business gross fixed investment, housing investment, changes in inventory stocks and gross fixed investment.

Private business fixed investment is significantly boosted only by the middle-aged, 50–64 years; all the other age groups have insignificant positive coefficients. This age group, then, has effects on investment that are consistent with a lifecycle saving channel and may also be due to a

Table 7.2 Investment components: private business and housing investment, 18 countries, 1965–94

Dep. variables: *Investment rates*	Private business gross fixed inv. (1)	Housing investment (2)	Δ Inventory stocks (3)	Gross fixed investment (4)
No. of observations	540	540	627	660
Growth	**0.180**	**0.050**	0.048	**0.225**
	(8.80)	(4.49)	(1.41)	(9.82)
Relative price of investment	**−0.028**	**−0.013**	0.008	**−0.042**
	(2.97)	(3.50)	(0.90)	(4.48)
Lagged investment rate	**0.768**	**0.813**	**0.575**	**0.793**
	(15.7)	(34.6)	(8.21)	(23.1)
Age share 15–29	0.036	**0.044**	−0.019	0.046
	(1.10)	(2.80)	(0.64)	(1.48)
Age share 30–49	0.021	0.021	**−0.116**	−0.018
	(0.44)	(0.78)	(2.57)	(0.42)
Age share 50–64	**0.160**	0.044	−0.094	**0.193**
	(3.30)	(1.48)	(1.81)	(4.60)
Age share 65–74	0.013	−0.011	**0.259**	0.023
	(0.19)	(0.27)	(2.50)	(0.31)
Age share 75+	0.083	**−0.161**	0.153	−0.137
	(1.11)	(3.02)	(1.55)	(1.34)
Adjusted R^2	0.72	0.79	0.40	0.81
$\chi^2(5)$ test of age var:	24.0	20.4	13.1	26.0
p-value	0.000	0.001	0.022	0.000

Notes: Portugal and Netherlands are excluded for lack of data. Fixed investment is used for the basic 20-country sample; inventory stocks exclude Germany from the basic sample to achieve a balanced panel. Bold: significance at the 5 percent level; absolute t-values are shown in parentheses.

capital–skill–experience complementarity, but there is no clear evidence for any capital-dilution effect of the younger age groups.

Two age groups have significant effects on housing investment: young adults (positive) and old retirees (negative). This result is consistent with a housing-demand channel. In Lindh and Malmberg (2006) we further investigated this pattern, using Swedish time series, and found it to have strong predictive value.

For the fixed-investment component (excluding only changes in inventory stocks) in column 4, the only individually significant coefficient is the middle-aged group, but the group of age variables is still jointly significant. The coefficient pattern is consistent with a combination of the fixed private business investment and housing investment, while the positive young retiree effect and the negative mature adult effect on gross investment shown in Table 7.1 vanish when changes in inventory stocks are excluded. In column 3 it is verified that these effects on gross investment really derive from correlation with the changes in inventory stocks.

The hypothesis alluded to above, that increased experience and skill require complementary investment to maintain optimal capital intensity, may be far-fetched. But middle-aged people also transfer wealth accumulation from real assets to financial assets (see, for instance, Skinner, 1989), conceivably making it easier or at least cheaper for domestic firms to finance investment. Previous work on aggregate-growth connections to population lends some support to the experience hypothesis, though. In previous studies (Malmberg, 1994; Lindh and Malmberg, 1999) we found this positive productivity effect from the middle-aged, and Feyrer (2004) argues that it may have to do with the supply of experienced managers.

The equation with change in inventory stocks as the dependent variable somewhat surprisingly estimates that family adults have a negative effect whereas young retirees have a positive effect. The fit of this regression is not as good as for the other investment components, but the age variables are still jointly significant at the 5 percent level so that there is some correlation.

Note that the relative price of investment in Table 7.2 has significant negative effects on all investment components, as expected, except on the changes in inventory stocks. This strengthens the suspicion that there is an endogeneity problem with the relative price of investment with regard to gross investment and points to adjustments of inventory stocks as a potential feedback mechanism. It is, however, hard to come up with any plausible direct mechanism connecting population to changes in inventories that has any previous empirical support. Therefore we abstain from speculation here but later show that there is a trade connection (see section entitled 'Trade balances and the inventory puzzle' below).

There are definitely distinct age effects on different components. This makes it unlikely that domestic saving constrains investment as a whole. But lack of financial integration could nevertheless hypothetically cause different links to different components, for example by confining saving for residential purposes to the housing market. Our next step therefore is to examine the savings pattern.

SAVINGS, AGE STRUCTURE AND THE CURRENT ACCOUNT

Empirical analysis of cross-country aggregate savings data started with Leff (1969); Modigliani (1975) provides an early summary. Leff's results were criticized in the 1970s, but more recent research finds robust age effects on aggregate saving rates.[8] In spite of this, leading economists have questioned the importance of demographic change in explaining shifts in the saving rate. Three main arguments have been advanced.

1. In panel data the variation in age-specific saving rates over time is greater than the variation in the saving rate across age groups (Bosworth, Burtless and Sabelhaus, 1991; Poterba, 1994).
2. Using given age-specific saving rates over the lifecycle, movements in the population shares of different age groups are too small to account for observed movements in the saving rate (Bosworth, Burtless and Sabelhaus, 1991).
3. The age effects on saving rates estimated on aggregate data explain only a small part of the variation in the saving rate (Bosworth, 1993).

The first two arguments only refute a bare-bones lifecycle model, in which the behavior of each age group can be considered fixed and there are no other age-structure effects on the economy. Taking account of general equilibrium feedbacks, these arguments become less than persuasive. However, the results below show that the third argument is to some extent true. Age structure does not explain any large part of the short-run variation in saving rates, although it does explain substantially more of the trend (see Figure 7.2).

When interpreting the results one should bear in mind that consumption smoothing by households is only one venue for age-distribution effects on national saving rates. Since national saving rates are computed as a residual from investment and current accounts, the savings measure is also a result of firms' decisions regarding retained profits taken directly in connection with an investment decision. Public saving, whether it is the result of direct political decisions or is caused by automatic responses to demographic change in revenue or expenditure systems, is another important, although often unintentional, component of the national saving rate.

The estimated age effects, shown in Table 7.3, are somewhat unstable; and in the random time-effects case, joint significance for the age variables is secured only with controls but without the lagged dependent variable. The more robust fixed-effects estimates exhibit joint significance, however. The fixed-effects estimates attribute positive effects to all working-age groups while the random-effects estimates have a positive significant effect only for the middle-aged. In the fixed-time-effects specification the 75+ group also exhibits significant positive effects.

There are signs of misspecification in the savings estimates; for example, the increase in the long-run coefficient of the young retirees in the lag estimate may indicate this. Since our main focus in this chapter is on the

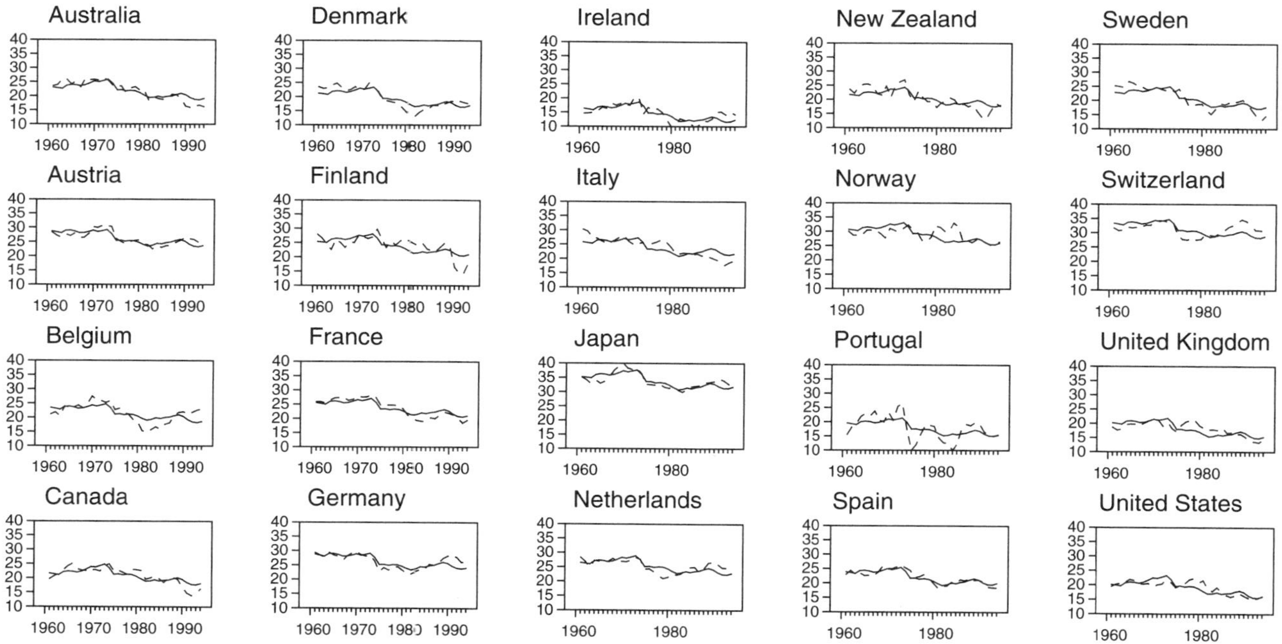

Figure 7.2 *Gross national saving rates when fixed country effects and random time effects are subtracted (dashed curves) compared with the pure age-share model estimate in column 4 of Table 7.3*

Table 7.3 National savings rates: 20 OECD countries, 1961–94

	Fixed country effects					
Dependent variable:	Fixed time effects			Random time effects		
National saving rates	(1)	(2)	(3)	(1)	(2)	(3)
Growth		**0.337**	0.036		**0.356**	0.043
		(6.27)	(0.97)		(6.40)	(1.15)
Relative price of investment		0.005	0.012		0.004	0.011
		(0.27)	(1.14)		(0.18)	(1.00)
Age group 15 to 29	**0.310**	**0.252**	0.085	0.198	0.140	0.005
	(2.94)	(2.54)	(1.63)	(1.88)	(1.43)	(0.12)
Age group 30 to 49	0.222	0.245	**0.128**	0.097	0.111	0.042
	(1.69)	(1.95)	(2.12)	(0.74)	(0.89)	(0.76)
Age group 50 to 64	**0.356**	**0.454**	**0.161**	**0.303**	**0.396**	**0.121**
	(2.96)	(3.79)	(2.75)	(2.48)	(3.27)	(2.12)
Age group 65 to 74	−0.074	−0.045	−0.114	−0.181	−0.134	−0.191
	(0.26)	(0.18)	(1.08)	(0.61)	(0.51)	(1.79)
Age group 75 and above	0.587	**0.709**	**0.365**	0.131	0.261	0.066
	(1.72)	(2.39)	(2.35)	(0.38)	(0.88)	(0.52)
Lagged saving rate			0.740			0.759
			(23.9)			(25.1)
Adjusted R^2	0.04	0.14	0.59	0.02	0.13	0.61
$\chi^2(5)$ test of age var:	15.2	21.2	12.9	9.08	13.2	8.17
p-value	0.009	0.001	0.024	0.106	0.022	0.147

Note: Based on 680 observations, 660 when growth is included. Bold: significance at the 5 percent level; absolute t-values are shown in parentheses.

investment equations, we keep to the same specification nevertheless in order to facilitate comparisons.[9] The positive but nonsignificant point estimate for old retirees is not a robust feature, although as remarked above it could be construed as an effect of increased longevity.

THE IMPACT OF AGE STRUCTURE ON THE CURRENT ACCOUNT

In Figure 7.3 we compare the investment coefficients with the corresponding random-effects estimates for saving. From this figure it is evident that demographic effects on the current account will appear in the OECD countries because of the differences in saving and investment profiles of age effects from the old population. According to our estimates, young retirees, in contrast to middle-aged adults, have a positive effect on investment but a negative effect on savings. This implies a negative current-account effect when a large cohort moves into retirement. Older retirees, on the other hand, have a strong negative effect on investment rates but a more neutral

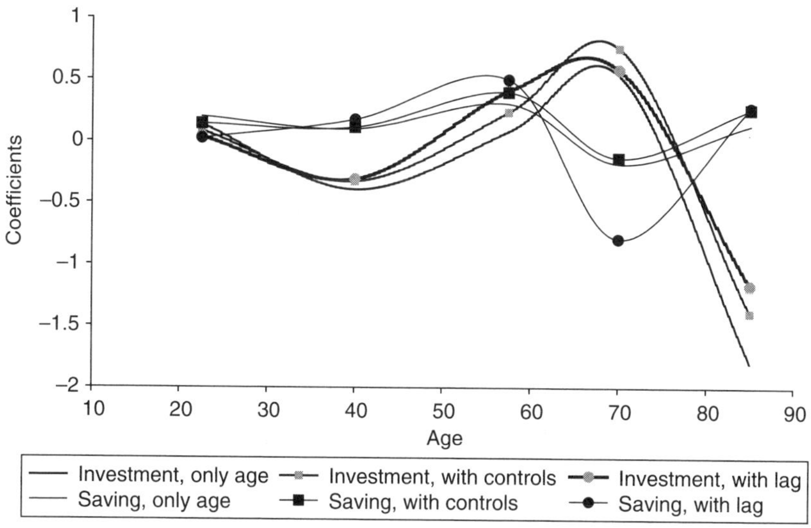

Note: As in Figure 7.1, it is the long-run coefficients for the lag models that are illustrated. The difference in coefficient estimates illustrates the corresponding current-account coefficients.

Figure 7.3 Age pattern of savings coefficients in Table 7.3 compared with age pattern of investment coefficients in Table 7.1, using random time-effects estimates

or maybe even positive effect on savings. This implies that the negative current-account effect peters out as large cohorts move from the early to the later part of retirement. Thus shifts in the age composition of the retired population appear as the main demographic feature for predicting future current accounts.

It is among the elderly that we find the really significant age effects on the current account. A positive effect on the current account of the older retirees may perhaps seem a bit counterintuitive. Theoretically, however, capital decumulation is a mechanism for mitigating negative effects on consumption (Aaron, Bosworth and Burtless, 1989). This idea receives some empirical support from our finding of a strong disinvestment effect from the 75+ age group. But, as is apparent from the housing-investment equation, the negative effect on this component is the more likely candidate. Nor can one exclude the possibility that the 75+ age group causes a demand shift toward nontradables rather than toward imports. There may also be a positive effect from the 30–49 age group, although significant differences hold only for some specifications.

The fixed- and random-time effects estimates for the current account essentially only repeat the information already presented in Tables 7.1 and 7.3, since the dependent variable is the difference between saving and investment. These estimates are therefore not presented, but the coefficients can be inferred from the differences in Figure 7.3. The age pattern that emerges is that family adults and the oldest may have positive effects on the current account whereas young retirees have a strong negative effect. The middle-aged group, which boosts both savings and investment, has a neutral effect on the current account. In contrast, Higgins (1998), using a world sample, finds much more substantial negative effects from young adults and positive effects from middle-aged people on the current account.

The total effect of the age distribution on the current account is not directly implied by the coefficients, since the growth of one age share is always accompanied by decreases in other age shares. We have to take the movement in the whole distribution into account.

Figure 7.4 graphs the implied impact of the age distribution on average OECD current accounts. To make the forecasts comparable, we have shifted them by the respective mean of each time series. Predicting random or fixed time effects is an arbitrary exercise, and so the forecasted variation is conditional on time effects (as well as country effects) being deducted. To make actual data comparable we have deducted the average of the mean of both forecasts over 1985–2003, the last two years being forecasts from OECD Main Economic Indicators (OECD, 1997), as downloaded in June 2002. Thus no significance should be attached to levels but only to the direction of change.

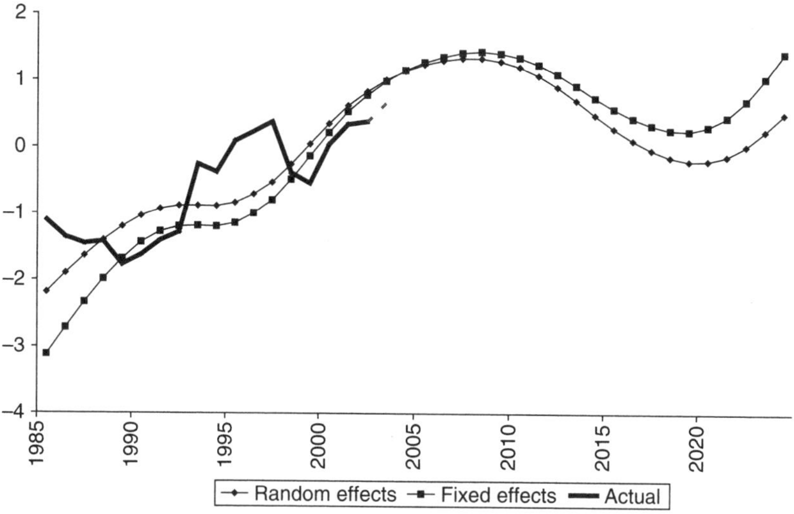

Note: The data have been normalized around the means of the predicted series. Therefore significance should not be attached to levels, but rather to the direction of change.

Figure 7.4 Average effect on current accounts of age-structure changes in the OECD countries (column 1, Table 7.4) compared with actual data and forecasts for 1999–2003

The span of variation of a little less than 3 percent over the period 1995–2025 in the effects that age structure will have on future current accounts is of a comparable order to that forecasted on a world scale in Higgins's (1998) estimates.[10]

Thus we would expect that the average OECD country for the moment is experiencing a current-account surplus or at least diminishing deficits. Disregarding business-cycle variations, that is also what we see, even in the out-of-sample period beyond 1994. The positive trend in the current account will reverse around 2005 owing to the large post-World War II cohorts starting to retire. Effective retirement age varies widely over the sample, but somewhere around 60 should be an approximate average. The downward trend continues up to a few years after 2015, when the age cycle turns again.

TRADE BALANCES AND THE INVENTORY PUZZLE

One feature in our empirical findings reported above stands out as a rather curious puzzle. Why would an increase in the young retirees' share of the population be associated with increasing inventory stocks?

As our explorations above reveal, this link is the main reason why gross investment tends to be higher than savings when the number of young retirees increases. Since that implies a negative current-account effect, it is the basic reason why our OECD estimates differ from the world sample estimates obtained by Higgins by implying current-account deficits in the first stages of the aging process.

In Table 7.4 we explore whether a regression of the trade balance on the age shares also turns up this peculiar finding. The fixed-effects model has trouble identifying any significant age effects in this case, but as we move to the random-effects specification a pattern appears in which mature adults improve the trade balance and young retirees worsen it. Comparing this pattern with the current-account effects implied by savings and investment regressions, we find that the most conspicuous difference is that the positive old-retiree effect is missing in this case. Since the only difference between the current account and the trade balance is the net foreign-factor income, our tentative conclusion is that these age groups are associated with factor incomes from abroad either by remittances from children or, more likely perhaps, from capital income abroad.

The puzzling young-retiree effect in contrast seems tied to changing export and import patterns. Indeed we can confirm that the change in inventory stocks is significantly correlated to deteriorating trade balances. In particular the growth of imports increases with the change in inventory stocks while exports improve.

OECD AND NON-OECD PATTERNS

To make sure that the patterns we find in the OECD data are indeed different from those found in world samples, we use a database described in detail in Loayza, Lopez, Schmidt-Hebbel and Servén (1998). To avoid using observations with too short time series, we include in our analysis only countries with at least 30 annual observations of both national saving and gross investment. This sample encompasses 1696 investment observations and 1653 savings observations. We have subdivided the countries into the 20 OECD countries we use above and 33 others that consist mainly of non-OECD countries but include, for example, Greece and Iceland.

Credit restrictions should be more important outside the OECD core countries, thus implying more saving (less borrowing) for the young. Investment effects from the young could, however, be higher there since work life is generally started earlier, necessitating investment to maintain capital intensity.

The estimation results confirm statistically significant differences between

Table 7.4 Trade balance/GDP: 20 OECD countries, 1960–94

	Fixed country effects					
Dependent variable:	Fixed time effects			Random time effects		
Trade balance/GDP	(1)	(2)	(3)	(1)	(2)	(3)
Growth		**−0.204**	**−0.172**		**−0.195**	**−0.186**
		(3.33)	(4.64)		(4.28)	(5.12)
Relative price of investment		−0.006	**0.030**		−0.017	**0.030**
		(0.23)	(2.64)		(0.65)	(2.65)
Age group 15–29	−0.075	−0.029	−0.020	0.100	0.104	0.031
	(0.60)	(0.21)	(0.38)	(0.72)	(0.74)	(0.70)
Age group 30–49	0.170	0.150	0.038	**0.479**	0.464	**0.144**
	(0.90)	(0.73)	(0.53)	(2.16)	(1.97)	(2.23)
Age group 50–64	−0.304	−0.384	−0.124	−0.165	−0.229	−0.073
	(1.66)	(1.93)	(1.88)	(1.25)	(1.58)	(1.36)
Age group 65–74	−0.535	−0.580	**−0.246**	−0.514	**−0.708**	**−0.276**
	(1.53)	(1.55)	(2.02)	(1.91)	(2.47)	(2.47)
Age group 75+	−0.441	−0.485	−0.257	0.421	0.259	0.001
	(0.50)	(0.54)	(0.97)	(1.42)	(0.81)	(0.01)
Lagged trade balance			**0.800**			**0.801**
			(20.6)			(18.0)
Adjusted R^2	0.03	0.06	0.64	0.10	0.13	0.65
$\chi^2(5)$ test of age var:	10.4	12.1	12.0	25.7	18.6	15.0
p-value	0.065	0.003	0.035	0.000	0.002	0.001

Note: Based on 680 observations, 660 when growth is included. Bold: significance at the 5 percent level; absolute t-values are shown in parentheses.

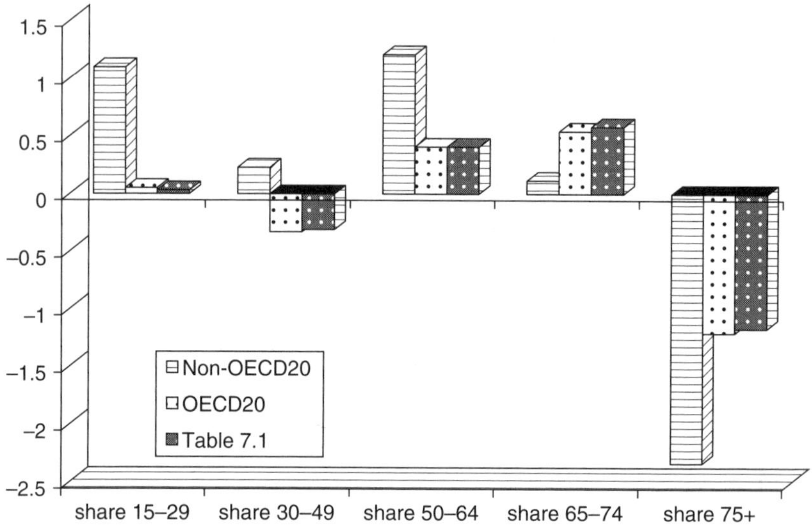

Note: The computed long-run coefficients are displayed. The world data sample is divided into OECD20 and the rest. For comparison the long-run OECD estimates in Table 7.1 are also shown.

Figure 7.5 Comparison of investment age-coefficient estimates of the full specification, including lags

the samples. Since we use unbalanced panels, which cannot be made directly comparable to previous tables, these results are not reported in detail but are available from us upon request. Figure 7.5 compares the coefficients for the age groups in the two groups of countries and with the estimates in Table 7.1. The OECD20 estimates are nearly identical for the investment equation.

The national saving-rate pattern shown in Figure 7.6 for OECD20 is not identical to that in Table 7.3, but except for the negative effect from old retirees it is not too far off. This confirms the earlier suspicion that the savings estimates for the oldest group are unstable. The overall pattern in OECD20 is not statistically significant either. The non-OECD20 sample exhibits significant age patterns, however, and as expected much stronger positive savings effects from young and family adults with a savings maximum for family adults rather than the middle-aged as in OECD20.

Overall the patterns for non-OECD20 are clearly similar to those found by Higgins (1998) in his world sample using aggregation over more than a decade. There are differences, though, some of which may be attributed to the difference between our methodologies but may be due also to collinearity problems in the non-OECD20 sample.[11]

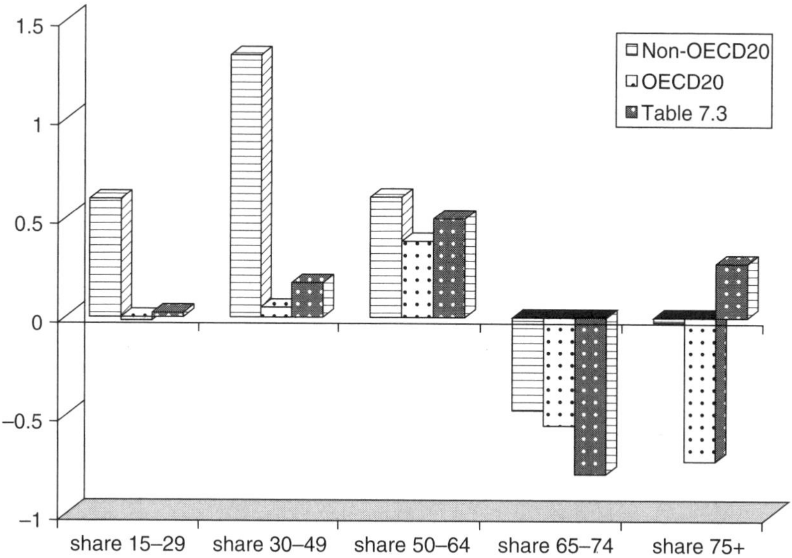

Note: The computed long-run coefficients are displayed. The world data sample is divided into OECD20 and the rest. For comparison the long-run OECD estimates in Table 7.3 are also shown.

Figure 7.6 Comparison of savings age-coefficient estimates of the full specification, including lags

SUMMARY AND CONCLUSIONS

We find a statistically significant relation between age structure on the one hand and investment and saving on the other. This result corroborates previous findings. Disaggregating investment into components and regressing age shares on them, we find support for at least three different mechanisms through which age structure influences investment. One is housing investment, which is stimulated by large 15–29 age groups and depressed by large 75+ age groups. Another mechanism is that 50–64-year-olds stimulate business investment. This result may be explained in at least three different ways: (1) high productivity in experienced labor that is complementary to capital, (2) high domestic savings stimulating investment in general, and (3) portfolio shifts from real to financial assets. The third mechanism we find is that family adults, those aged 30 to 49, are associated with depleting inventory stocks whereas young retirees, those aged 65 to 74, are associated with accumulating inventories. This is a more puzzling connection, but the channel seems to run in this case through trade patterns in which young retirees stimulate imports while mature adults stimulate exports. For some reason changes in the trade balance correlate negatively with changes in inventory stocks.

We suspect that both accounting conventions and changes in real exchange rates and terms of trade may be behind the connection between inventories and trade. On the one hand, accounting conventions require that changes in inventories be accounted for only when an actual change in volume occurs, whereas changes in the prices of goods are required to be accounted for as capital gains or losses. On the other hand, import values include freight and other transport charges whereas exports are valued free on board. This makes it rather complicated to figure out how exchange-rate fluctuations interact with actual inventory changes. At least we could not get it straight within this project and were forced to leave the issue for further research.

Other results, for example those reported by Bruér (2004), indicate that real exchange rates also correlate with age structure in a predictable way, although the connection between exchange rates and the current account seems to differ across countries. This difference could be due to whether or not dissaving of pension claims occurs through public transfers, which in general would not affect real investment. Such dissaving would typically hold for countries with extensive PAYGO social security systems. Alternatively, dissaving through private channels or funded systems could entail some real disinvestment, with rather different implications. Herbertsson and Zoega (1999) discuss these issues further, showing that taxes have a strong tendency to be lower when the working-age population is relatively larger.

Our conjecture is that an aging population shifts domestic demand first toward imports and then toward nontradables. Depending on social security institutions and monetary policies, this tendency may spill over in different ways on price mechanisms; but in the end it shows up in the current account and investment, which are the real variables since national saving rates are only residuals.

According to our empirical findings, increasing population shares of young retirees will cause current-account and trade-balance deficits while later this effect will be reversed as retirees age further. It will be of considerable interest for policymakers in developed countries that are rapidly aging to clarify these connections in order to avoid misconstrued policies. For example the temporary current-account deterioration that we predict should not necessarily be taken as an external balance problem. It may just be smoothing the path for the age transition we are facing; and combating it with restrictive monetary policies may be totally misconceived, causing more problems than it solves. We have to admit, though, that neither we nor, it seems, macroeconomists in general really understand the mechanisms at work here. For that reason more research is urgently needed.

The puzzle posed by Feldstein and Horioka (1980) may be relevant to our results. The inexplicably high correlation between investment and domestic saving has generated many empirical and theoretical studies because it has been interpreted to imply a lack of capital mobility that is at odds with the integration of international capital markets. In an early assessment of the evidence Frankel, Dooley and Mathieson (1986) pointed out that the correlation seemed to be higher in industrialized countries and higher after 1973 than before. But we would expect industrialized countries to have better-integrated financial markets, and so this observation is puzzling.

Our results indicate that the explanation of the FH puzzle is not likely to be that national savings constrain investment rates. If that were the case, different investment components would react similarly to age-structure-induced changes in savings. We show that this is not the case in OECD countries. The cause is thus likely to be found in some other variable, presumably in the price system, coordinating investment and domestic saving.

In the OECD sample at hand we can verify a high savings–investment correlation (around 0.78) both in short-run annual data and between the country means of the variables. Purging the data for age effects actually strengthens the FH correlation between country means to 0.82 but decreases it to 0.72 in annual data. The correlation is much higher in the OECD than it is in the rest of the world (0.54 with country means, strengthened to 0.56 when data are purged of the estimated age effects). Thus movements in age structure seem to have some role in desynchronizing investment and saving rates. It is a minor role, however.

The distinct effects on investment in OECD countries are associated mainly with the inventory stock channel. Increases in the group of young retirees are associated with increasing inventory stocks. Projecting our estimates into the future leads to a forecast that OECD countries will on average have had improving current-account balances up to approximately the present, but that the tide will turn and a demographically induced deterioration of the current accounts in OECD will take place. Of course, this could be prevented by stabilization policies, but only at a cost, for example slower growth.

Further research on these issues is needed. Clarification of the impact of age structure on these variables will also contribute to long-term forecasting since age structure is one of the very few explanatory variables that we can project for several years ahead and still be rather confident that the uncertainty is manageably small.

NOTES

1. We greatly appreciate useful comments from seminar and conference participants at the Stockholm School of Economics, Uppsala University; ECARES Seminar, Université Libre de Bruxelles; the Workshop for Age Effects on the Macroeconomy, in Stockholm; the Workshop on Demographic-Macroeconomic Modelling, Rostock. We are also grateful for ideas that emerged in several discussions with Jan Häggström and Mats Kinnwall. Research funding from the Bank of Sweden Tercentenary Foundation and Handelsbanken Marketing is gratefully acknowledged.
2. Pesaran, Smith and Im (1996) discuss panel data with moderate time and cross-sectional dimensions and a lagged dependent variable, finding that the standard fixed-effects model may be subject to considerable estimation bias if there is parameter heterogeneity among countries. Attanasio, Picci and Scorcu (2000) claim that in practice this seems to be a minor problem, in particular if the more robust LS estimators are used. One remedy would be to estimate time-series models for each country and then take the mean of the parameters as an estimate of the average effect. This mean-group estimator assumes, however, that the coefficients of the variables vary randomly across countries (see Swamy, 1970). But in our case one may well suspect that the variation is systematic and dependent on other variables. One way to take account of systematic variation in coefficients across countries is explored in Higgins (1998), who interacts growth variables with the age groups, a specification based on Fry and Mason (1982) and Mason (1987) and often referred to as the variable-rate-of-growth model. A case might also be made that a comprehensive social security system acts as a substitute for saving. As a proxy, government consumption can be interacted with age structure. We did experiment to derive age profiles of interaction specifications of the savings equation calculated by using the country mean growth rate and mean government consumption in the sample. The profiles were consistent with the patterns reported in this chapter, although the relative size of the coefficients was highly sensitive to the interaction variables. We therefore abstain from presenting the results.
3. The disaggregated investment data from *Economic Outlook* were trimmed; Portugal had data only for total fixed investment, and the data on private investment in the Netherlands for 1960–68 did not subdivide private investment into business and housing investment. Several countries were missing data for the first years in the 1960s. We have checked to be sure that our data conform to the convention that total investment less government investment equals private investment, which in turn equals the sum of business and housing investment. In two cases (the first decades for Italy and Canada) we made corrections. In two other cases we used this convention to generate missing private investment data (the whole series for the United States and the 1960s for the Netherlands). The 1991 and forward data for unified Germany seem to have been simply added to the older West German series, but attempts to correct for this had only minor impact, and so we abstained from making a correction in this case.
4. The countries in the sample are Australia, Austria, Belgium, Bolivia, Brazil, Burkina Faso, Canada, Chile, China, Côte d'Ivoire, Costa Rica, Denmark, Ecuador, Egypt, Finland, France, Greece, Guatemala, Honduras, Haiti, India, Ireland, Iceland, Israel, Italy, Japan, Luxembourg, Morocco, Mexico, Malaysia, Netherlands, New Zealand, Norway, Panama, Philippines, Portugal, Paraguay, Singapore, Salvador, South Africa, South Korea, Spain, Sweden, Switzerland, Thailand, Trinidad & Tobago, Tunisia, Taiwan, United Kingdom, United States, Uruguay and West Germany.
5. We implemented the estimation by subtracting time and country means from all variables. In the case of random time effects the cross-section mean was weighted by variance components derived from the fixed-effects estimate. The standard errors of the OLS estimations were corrected to be robust to heteroskedasticity and autocorrelation (see Newey and West, 1987). The residuals of our regressions show evidence of fat tails, but estimates of minimum absolute deviations, which are less sensitive to outliers (Huber, 1973), had little effect on the age-group coefficients.

6. The choice of controls is based on Higgins (1998). Both control and age variables have been lagged one step. The age variables are point estimates referring to 31 December of the current year. We use the lags of the controls to ameliorate problems with contemporaneous correlation between the residual error and the explanatory variables because we were unable to find valid instruments. This is not crucial to the results but contributes to a more robust specification in spite of losing 20 observations.
7. As is well known, dynamic panel estimates are biased (Nerlove, 1971; Nickell, 1981). This particular bias is inversely proportional to the number of time-series observations, 34 in this case. This in itself hardly causes much concern, but it does prevent using a Hausman test to choose between the specifications since both estimators are inconsistent under the null hypothesis. However, the coefficient estimates are close enough for judgment to favor the more efficient random-effects estimator.
8. Loayza et al. (2000) find a negative effect from old-age dependency ratios in a comprehensive cross-country panel.
9. Aggregating the two oldest age groups makes the patterns more stable. Including interaction terms of growth and age structure also helps (see Fry and Mason, 1982).
10. Table 7 in that article predicts a positive age effect on the current account in both the OECD and the rest of the world up to 2010 of around 3.2 percentage points.
11. Checking for collinearity problems, we found that the highest variance inflation factor for the age variables in the OECD20 sample is 4.22, whereas the three largest variance inflation factors in the non-OECD20 sample are between 11.4 and 24.6. Variance inflation factors are the diagonal elements of the inverted covariance matrix. If these elements are big, they indicate that this matrix is close to singular and may yield misleading coefficient estimates. As a rule of thumb, values above 10 are considered problematic.

REFERENCES

Aaron, H., B. Bosworth and G. Burtless (1989), *Can America Afford to Grow Old? Paying for Social Security*, Washington, DC: Brookings Institution.

Attanasio, O.P., L. Picci and A.E. Scorcu (2000), 'Saving, growth, and investment: a macroeconomic analysis using a panel of countries', *Review of Economics and Statistics*, **82**(2), 182–211.

Bean, Charles (2004), 'Global demographic change: some implications for central banks', speech given at Federal Reserve Bank Kansas City Annual Symposium, Jackson Hole, Wyoming.

Bloom, David E., David Canning and Bryan Graham (2003), 'Longevity and life cycle savings', *Scandinavian Journal of Economics*, **105**, 319–38.

Bosworth, B., G. Burtless and J. Sabelhaus (1991), 'The decline in saving: evidence from household surveys', *Brookings Papers on Economic Activity*, **1991**(1), 183–241.

Bosworth, B.J. (1993), *Saving and Investment in a Global Economy*, Washington, DC: Brookings Institution.

Boucekkine, Raouf, David de la Croix and Omar Licandro (2003), 'Early mortality declines at the dawn of modern growth', *Scandinavian Journal of Economics*, **105**(3), 401–18.

Bruér, Mattias (2004), 'Empirical studies in demography and macroeconomics', PhD dissertation, Department of Economics, Uppsala University.

Chiuri, M.C. and T. Jappelli (2003), 'Financial market imperfections and home ownership: a comparative study', *European Economic Review*, **47**, 857–75.

Feldstein, M.S. and C.Y. Horioka (1980), 'Domestic saving and international capital flows', *Economic Journal*, **90**(358), 314–29.

Feyrer, James (2004), 'Demographics and productivity', Dartmouth College Working Paper, Dartmouth, New Hampshire.
Frankel, J.G., M.P. Dooley and D.J. Mathieson (1986), 'International capital mobility in developing countries vs industrial countries: what do saving–investment correlations tell?', Working Paper 2043, National Bureau of Economic Research, Cambridge, Massachusetts.
Fry, M.J. and A. Mason (1982), 'The variable rate-of-growth effect in the life-cycle saving model', *Economic Inquiry*, **20**, 426–42.
Griliches, Z. (1969), 'Capital–skill complementarity', *Review of Economics and Statistics*, **51**, 465–8.
Herbertsson, Tryggvi Thor and Gylfi Zoega (1999), 'Trade surpluses and life-cycle saving behaviour', *Economics Letters*, **65**, 227–37.
Higgins, Matthew (1998), 'Demography, national savings, and international capital flows', *International Economic Review*, **39**(2), 343–69.
Higgins, Matthew and Jeffrey G. Williamson (1997), 'Age structure dynamics in Asia and dependence on foreign capital', *Population and Development Review*, **23**, 261–93.
Huber, P. (1973), 'Robust regression: asymptotics, conjectures and Monte Carlo', *Annals of Statistics*, **1**, 55–82.
Kiviet, J.F. (1995), 'On bias, inconsistency, and efficiency of various estimators in dynamic panel data models', *Journal of Econometrics*, **68**, 53–78.
Leff, N.H. (1969), 'Dependency rates and saving rates', *American Economic Review*, **59**, 886–96.
Lindh, Thomas and Bo Malmberg (1999), 'Age structure effects and growth in the OECD, 1950–90', *Journal of Population Economics*, **12**(3), 431–49.
Lindh, Thomas and Bo Malmberg (2006), 'Demography and housing demand – what can we learn from residential construction data?', *Journal of Population Economics*, Online May 2006, 1–19.
Loayza, N., K. Schmidt-Hebbel and L. Servén (2000), 'What drives private saving across the world?', *Review of Economics and Statistics*, **82**(2), 165–81.
Loayza, N., H. López, K. Schmidt-Hebbel and L. Servén (1998), 'The world saving database', manuscript, World Bank, Washington, DC.
Malmberg, Bo (1994), 'Age structure effects on economic growth: Swedish evidence', *Scandinavian Economic History Review*, **42**(3), 279–95.
Mason, A. (1987), 'National saving rates and population growth: a new model and new evidence', in D.G. Johnson and R.D. Lee (eds), *Population Growth and Economic Development: Issues and Evidence*, Madison, Wisconsin: University of Wisconsin Press, ch. 13.
Modigliani, Franco (1975), 'The life cycle hypothesis of saving twenty years later', in M. Parkin and A.R. Nobay (eds), *Contemporary Issues in Economics*, Manchester: Manchester University Press, pp. 2–36.
Nerlove, Marc (1971), 'Further evidence on the estimation of dynamic economic relations from a time series of cross sections', *Econometrica*, **39**(2), 359–82.
Newey, W.K. and K.D. West (1987), 'A simple, positive semi-definite, heteroskedasticity and autocorrelation consistent covariance matrix', *Econometrica*, **55**(3), 703–8.
Nickell, Stephen (1981), 'Biases in dynamic models with fixed effects', *Econometrica*, **49(**6), 1417–26.
OECD (Organisation for Economic Co-operation and Development) (1997), *Statistical Compendium*, **97**(1), Paris: OECD Publications.

Pesaran, H., R. Smith, and K.S. Im (1996), 'Dynamic linear models for heterogenous panels', in L. Mátyás and P. Sevestre (eds), *The Econometrics of Panel Data: A Handbook of the Theory with Applications*, 2d rev. edn, Dordrecht: Kluwer Academic Publishers, ch. 8.

Poterba, J.M. (1994), 'Public policies and household saving', NBER Working Paper No 6774, University of Chicago Press for National Bureau of Economic Research, Cambridge, Massachusetts.

Sheshinski, Eytan (2006), 'Note on longevity and aggregate savings', *Scandinavian Journal of Economics*, **108**(2), 353–6.

Skinner, J. (1989), 'Housing wealth and aggregate saving', *Regional Science and Urban Economics*, **19**(2), 305–24.

Swamy, P. (1970), 'Efficient inference in a random coefficient regression model', *Econometrica*, **38**, 311–23.

Taylor, Allan M. and Jeffrey G. Williamson (1994), 'Capital flows to the New World as an intergenerational transfer', *Journal of Political Economy*, **102**, 348–71.

UN (United Nations) Population Division (1994), *Global Estimates and Projections of Population by Sex and Age: The 1994 Revision*, New York.

Williamson, J.G. (2001), 'Demographic shocks and global factor flows', Federal Reserve Bank of Boston Conference Series, no. 46, 247–65.

Zhang, Jie and Junsen Zhang (2005), 'The effect of life expectancy on fertility, saving, schooling and economic growth: theory and evidence', *Scandinavian Journal of Economics*, **107**(1), 45–66.

8. Population aging and health care spending in Japan: public- and private-sector responses

Naohiro Ogawa, Andrew Mason, Maliki, Rikiya Matsukura and Kazuro Nemoto[1]

In many industrialized countries life expectancy at birth is rapidly approaching 80 years. Since the early 1980s Japan's life expectancy at birth has been at the highest level in the world. Despite their high health status, however, the Japanese people pay relatively little for medical care by international standards (Campbell and Ikegami, 1998; Jeong and Hurst, 2001; Imai, 2002). In 2002, for example, Japan's total medical spending as a share of GDP was 7.9 percent, below the OECD average of 8.6 percent.

Since establishing universal medical insurance coverage in 1961, the Japanese government has adopted numerous policy measures and programs to contain the costs of medical care. The majority of the policy and program changes have been made since the early 1980s, when the formidable problems of population aging facing Japan in the twenty-first century began to attract the attention of policymakers. Given that Japan's population aging is the most advanced of all the industrialized countries and is projected to increase for the next few decades (Ogawa, 2005), it is highly likely that the country's medical insurance plans will be further modified in the years ahead.

Although a considerable amount of empirical work has been undertaken to quantify the effects of population aging on the costs of medical care in Japan (Ogawa, 2003; Ogawa et al., 2003; Cabinet Office, 2005), none of the empirical studies has dealt separately with rising public and private medical costs. In this chapter we employ a new methodological approach to examine how, and to what extent, the public and private sectors have been affected by the government's policy and program changes in response to Japan's unprecedented population aging.

For this purpose we shall first discuss the key health care policies and programs that have effectively kept Japan's spending on medical care at a relatively low level in the postwar period. Then, using microlevel data derived from four rounds of the National Survey on Family Income and Expenditure, and drawing upon the newly developed framework of the National Transfer Accounts (NTA) system, we shall estimate the changing age profile of intergenerational transfers of both private and public health care resources over the period from 1989 to 2004. Finally, we shall relate our previous discussion of past policy developments to the computed results.

In the next section we briefly review the two crucial factors influencing Japan's medical expenditures over the past few decades: the country's demographic transformations and its economic growth performance. Then, in the following section, we briefly describe Japan's medical insurance plans and discuss some of the basic features of those plans. Next we present an analysis of Japan's deteriorating demographic capacity for family support and the abrupt value shifts related to the provision of in-home care by adult children for their elderly relatives; and we follow this analysis with a discussion of our data sources and several methodological issues. The two subsequent sections examine our estimated results based on the age profiles of private and public health expenditures and present an analysis of the net flow of private and public health spending. In the final section we summarize our principal findings and discuss their policy implications.

Although the chapter focuses on Japan and its medical-policy responses to population aging, its situation is relevant to other developed societies, which also must cope with mushrooming medical costs. Japan's medical and health policy responses to its rapid population aging are also likely to serve as a useful model to an increasing number of developing countries, particularly in Asia, that are undergoing rapid demographic transformation and in the process of establishing their own medical-insurance schemes. Despite its rapid economic development, Japan has retained some of its traditional cultural values, and for that reason the Japanese medical care model may be of interest to policymakers in the developing region who wish to combine the best of traditional and modern approaches to providing health care services to the elderly.

RECENT DEMOGRAPHIC DEVELOPMENTS AND ECONOMIC GROWTH IN JAPAN

Immediately after its short-lived baby-boom period (1947–49), Japan experienced a dramatic fertility decline (Retherford and Ogawa, 2006). Between 1947 and 1957, the total fertility rate (TFR) declined by more than 50 percent, from 4.54 to 2.04 births per woman. Subsequently there were only minor fluctuations around replacement-level fertility until the first oil crisis in 1973. Thereafter the TFR started to fall again and in 2005 reached 1.26 births per woman, which was an all-time low in postwar Japan.

Although Japan's recent very low fertility has attracted a great deal of attention domestically and internationally (Retherford and Ogawa, 2006), much less attention has been paid to the unprecedented rapidity of its mortality transition. Between 1947 and 2005, life expectancy at birth in Japan rose from 50.1 to 78.5 years for men and from 54.0 to 85.5 years for women. Thus male life expectancy became the fourth highest in the world, after that of Hong Kong, Iceland and Switzerland; and female life expectancy became the world's highest. Moreover, between 1947 and 2005, Japanese life expectancy at age 65 grew from 10.2 to 18.1 years for men and from 12.2 to 23.2 years for women, indicating a marked increase in the retirement period and in the joint survival to older ages of both husbands and wives.

Figure 8.1 plots the data on the average age of the 50 oldest Japanese men and women to die in each year over the period from 1950 to 2004. For both sexes the average age at death among the 50 oldest persons rose substantially in Japan over the second half of the twentieth century. Moreover, the

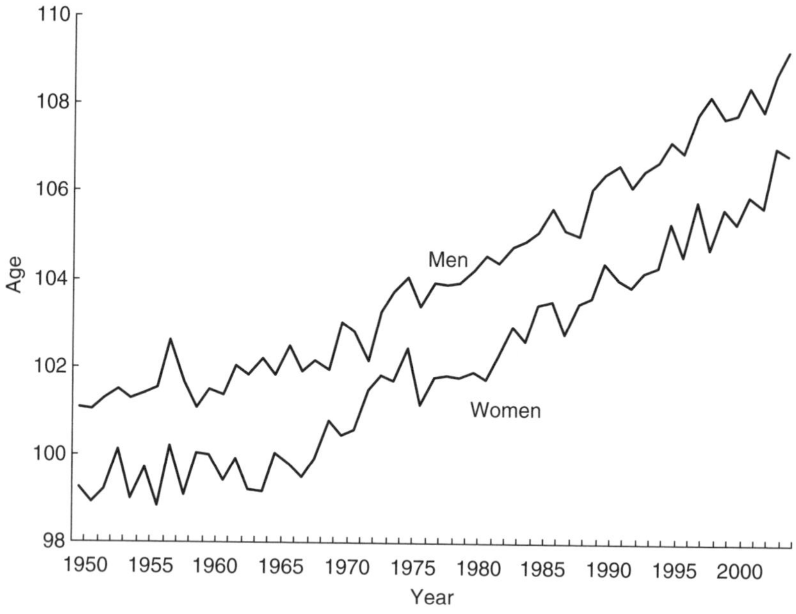

Source: Ministry of Health, Labor and Welfare, *Vital Statistics* (various years).

Figure 8.1 Average age at death among the 50 oldest persons, by sex: Japan, 1950–2004

plotted average age trends indicate that the tempo of life prolongation has increased considerably for both sexes since 1973, when Japan's medical programs were substantially upgraded to include free medical services for persons aged 70 and over (Ogawa, 2005).

Because of these dramatic improvements in longevity, the age distribution of the Japanese population has also been changing significantly over the past several decades. The relative size of the young population has declined, while the relative size of the elderly population has increased. In 1984, the elderly (those aged 65 and over) accounted for only 10 percent of the population, less than in other industrialized countries. Despite this delayed onset of population aging, in 2005 Japan became the first country in which the aged comprised more than 20 percent of the population. In contrast, in 2005, the proportion of those in the 0–14 age group was 13.7 percent, the lowest in the world at that time. These demographic developments imply that fewer children will be available to provide familial support and pay taxes when they mature, and the deficit will strain the public support system in the years to come. Policy responses to these population changes will influence the Japanese economy, intergenerational equity and social welfare for decades.

Japan's changes in age composition since World War II have occurred in parallel with spectacular economic growth. At the close of the war the Japanese economy was severely damaged, but by the end of the 1950s its productive capacity had recovered to the prewar level. During the 1960s, Japan's real GDP grew at a phenomenal rate of about 11 percent per annum. After the first oil crisis in 1973, however, its economic growth performance became much less impressive. The average annual growth rate of real GDP was 4.2 percent in the 1980s.

Following the Plaza Accord in 1985, Japan entered a bubble economy, but the investment boom ended abruptly in the early 1990s and a number of leading banks and other financial institutions declared bankruptcy. Government tax revenues dropped dramatically and government debts accumulated at an unprecedented rate, reaching US$8.3 trillion in 2005, or approximately 1.5 times the country's GDP for that year (Ministry of Finance, 2006). Japan's current government debt is by far the worst among the industrialized nations. Moreover, its international competitiveness has deteriorated. In the early 1990s, the Japanese economy was ranked first in international competitiveness, but by 2006 it was ranked seventeenth (IMD, 2006). In addition, the household savings rate has been on a downward trend in recent years. In 2000, it was 9.8 percent, but by 2004 it had declined to 2.8 percent (Cabinet Office, 2006).

Unfortunately the Japanese government implemented a series of inappropriate macroeconomic policies to rectify these unfavorable economic conditions. It took the government several years to realize that drastic economic-restructuring policies were needed to make the economy more competitive in international markets. Because of the government's delayed policy responses, some economists call the 1990s 'Japan's lost decade' (Yoshikawa, 2001). Since 2002, however, the Japanese economy has been slowly improving, thus recording the longest postwar boom.

THE GOVERNMENT MEDICAL PROGRAM

The government instituted both a universal pension scheme and a medical program in 1961. Since then Japan's Social Security system has grown remarkably. It encompasses not only those two components but also the Long-term Care Insurance Scheme (implemented in 2000) and other smaller programs such as the Employment Insurance Scheme.

As shown in Figure 8.2, the share in GDP of Social Security expenditures accounted for by the two main components has changed substantially over time. In 1970, pension benefits paid out corresponded to 0.65 percent of GDP, whereas the medical benefits paid out amounted to 2.79 percent of GDP. By 2003 the expenditures for pension benefits had increased to 8.20 percent of GDP and the medical benefits had increased to 6.52 percent. The major shift toward pension benefits has occurred

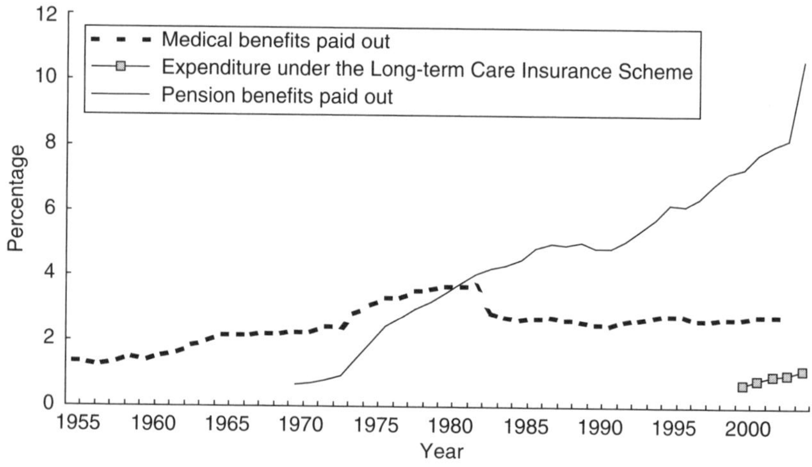

Source: Health and Welfare Statistics Association (2006).

Figure 8.2 Patterns of growth of expenditures for selected Social Security components relative to GDP: Japan, 1960–2003

mainly because of population aging and the maturation of the pension system. In addition, major policy and program changes have been made in the medical plans to rein in snowballing health costs, as we shall discuss below.

Unlike the United States, where market forces are favored in the development and allocation of health resources, Japan has a health care system that is highly regulated by the government, combining a mainly private provision of services with mandatory health insurance (Imai, 2002). Because Japan's health insurance plans are occupation-specific, most enrolment is automatic, and there is little choice of coverage for either consumers or insurers. Five major health insurance plans are currently in operation. The association-managed Health Insurance Plan (AHIP), the government-managed Health Insurance Plan (GHIP), and the National Health Insurance Plan (NHIP) are the three largest; together they cover 87 percent of the population. Employees of large-scale enterprises are enrolled in the AHIP, and employees of small or medium-sized businesses are enrolled in the GHIP. Persons not covered by other plans are enrolled in the NHIP. Members of the NHIP tend to be older than those in the other plans, primarily because a large proportion of NHIP members are self-employed small-business owners and farmers.

Under all of these plans, service providers (hospitals and clinics) are paid directly by insurers (the third-payer system). Nearly all prices are strictly controlled by a fee schedule, and fees for various medical services are set out in the schedule. Any extra charges (or 'balancing billing') are prohibited. The fee schedule, which is revised every two years, is determined through negotiations between insurers and the providers. As is generally the case in Europe and elsewhere, the process of setting fees is highly political. Nevertheless the priority placed on fairness and political 'balance' among constituents helps to contain costs and to ensure access to health care in Japan (Campbell and Ikegami, 1998).

As a result of the policy emphasis on egalitarianism, quality tends to be sacrificed as Japanese physicians increase their caseloads to maintain their income. This emphasis can be seen as a side-effect of the spending-control mechanism that operates through price fixing by the government. Thus the practice of giving 'gifts' to physicians in exchange for high-quality medical services is widespread. According to one estimate for the year 1990 (ibid., 5), the total amount of such monetary gifts roughly corresponds to 0.1 percent of GDP. Dissatisfactions with the system that are often voiced by patients include a long waiting time, short consultation time, insufficient explanation by doctors and lack of medical information for the patient (Imai, 2002). Although evidence is rather limited, it is generally believed that the percentage of patients who are satisfied with their health care system is lower in Japan than in North America or Western Europe (Mckinsey Global Institute, 2000).

In 2005, the medical plan premium was 8.2 percent of a worker's earnings for both the AHIP and the GHIP (Health and Welfare Statistics Association, 2006). The cost of the premium is split between employee and employer, and the government provides small subsidies to cover administrative and management costs. In the case of the NHIP, the amount collected from each household varies, depending on the household's annual income and assets. In addition the government provides the GHIP and NHIP with subsidies from the regular General Account budget, and the amount of the subsidies is calculated as a fixed percentage of outlays as stipulated by law. In the case of the AHIP, the government subsidizes part of its administrative costs.

Since the establishment of universal health coverage in 1961, many revisions have been made to the government medical plans (Table 8.1). The country's extraordinary economic growth performance during the 1960s led to the provision of free medical care services for persons aged 70 and over beginning in early 1973. As a result of slower economic growth triggered by the first oil crisis in late 1973, however, the provision of free medical care services for the elderly was abolished in 1983 and elderly patients were required to make nominal contributions. Initially, the amount of the contribution was 400 yen (approximately US$2, based upon the 1983 exchange rate) per month for outpatients and 300 yen per day for inpatients. Since then the contributions have been raised periodically, as indicated in Table 8.1.

Younger patients too were required to share the increasing medical costs. In 1984, a 10 percent co-payment was introduced into the health insurance plans. The amount of the co-payment was raised to 20 percent in 1997 and to 30 percent in 2003. Starting in 2002, elderly patients were required to make a 10 percent co-payment, and in October 2006 the co-payment for the elderly was raised to either 20 percent or 30 percent, depending upon their annual income.

In 1983, another major change was introduced into the Japanese medical care system. The Health Service System for the Elderly, a new account specifically for persons aged 70 and over, was established. Because of the NHIP's lower premium rates and older age composition, its financial foundation was weaker than that of the other four plans and required heavy government subsidies from its inception. To ease NHIP's financial difficulties, the four other medical plans for employees have been required to make contributions to the NHIP since 1984, compensating for differences in age composition between the plans. As shown in Figure 8.3, since 1984 the costs of the Health Service System for the Elderly have been

Table 8.1 Evolution of Japan's medical care system, 1961–2006

Year	Policy or program development
1961	Universal coverage of medical services established
1973	Free medical care services provided to those aged 70 and over
1981	Contribution to the cost sharing of medical expenses increased; Policy of fee exemption for high-cost medical services introduced
1983	Free medical services for those aged 70 and over abolished, and elderly patients required to make monthly contributions of 400 yen (equivalent to US$2 based on the 1983 exchange rate) per month for outpatient care and 300 yen per day for inpatient care; Law on Health Service System for the Elderly (those aged 70 and over) established
1984	10% co-payment for non-elderly introduced
1986	Elderly contributions increased: for outpatients, from 400 to 800 yen per month; for inpatients, from 300 to 400 yen per day
1987	Law on the Health Services Facilities of the Elderly enforced
1990	10-year Gold Plan implemented
1993	Elderly contributions increased: for outpatients, from 900 to 1000 yen per month; for inpatients, from 600 to 700 yen per day
1995	Elderly outpatients' contributions increased from 1000 yen to 1010 yen per month
1996	Elderly contributions increased: for outpatients, from 1010 to 1020 yen per month; for inpatients, from 700 to 710 yen per day
1997	Co-payment for non elderly raised from 10% to 20% Elderly contributions increased: for outpatients, from 1020 yen per month to 500 yen per visit; for inpatients, from 710 to 1000 yen per day
1998	Elderly inpatients' contributions increased to 1100 yen per day
1999	Elderly contributions increased: for outpatients, from 500 to 530 yen per visit; for inpatients, from 1100 to 1200 yen per day
2000	Long-term Care Insurance made effective; Contributions for the elderly abolished and payment limits set (3000 yen per month for outpatients, 37 200 yen per month for inpatients)
2002	10% co-payment required of elderly patients; 20% co-payment required of those with higher income
2003	Co-payment for non-elderly increased from 20% to 30% Diagnosis Procedure Combination introduced at 82 specially designated hospitals
2006	Co-payment for elderly increased from 10% to 20%

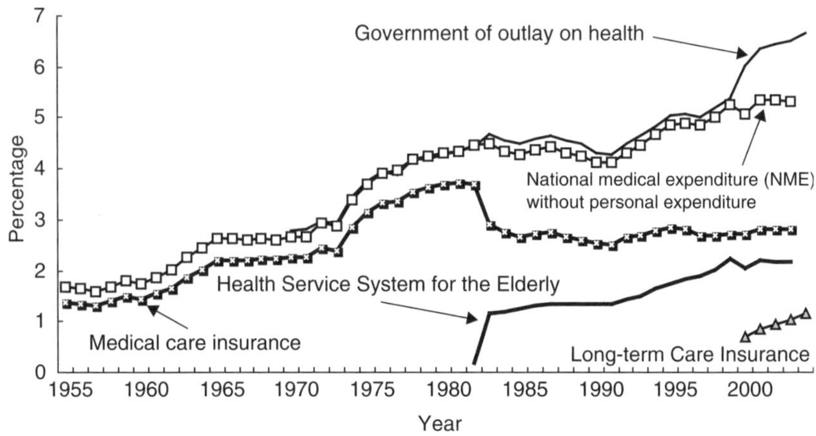

Source: Health and Welfare Statistics Association (2006).

Figure 8.3 Growth of medical costs for selected components of the health system relative to GDP: Japan, 1960–2003

growing rapidly. Hence the patterns of cost growth for the components of the medical care system have varied considerably ever since, although the total medical costs (in nominal terms) have been rising continuously throughout the period under review.

As a consequence of the establishment of this special account for the elderly under the NHIP, the financial situation of the AHIP, which has the youngest age composition, has deteriorated rapidly. Various proposals to integrate the five plans into one unified plan are currently under discussion.

A few points of interest emerge from the data from four countries plotted in Figure 8.4. Japan's ratio of the total health expenditure to GDP has been at a relatively low level by international standards, particularly compared with other industrialized countries. As can be seen from Figure 8.4, the pattern of growth of Japan's health care spending relative to its GDP changed substantially, beginning in the early 1980s. From 1960 to 1980, it increased from 3 to 7 percent. Over the subsequent period, 1980–2002, it grew only marginally, from 7 to 8 percent. A primary factor contributing to this slowing of the growth trend of health costs has been tighter control by the government over an increase in the price index for the fee schedule.

The price index for the fee schedule of Japan's medical services rose rapidly in the late 1960s and during the 1970s, but its growth slowed thereafter (Figure 8.5). More importantly, the fee schedule was adjusted downward by 1.3 percent in 2002, for the first time in the history of Japan's health insurance system. In 2006, it was further lowered by 1.36 percent.

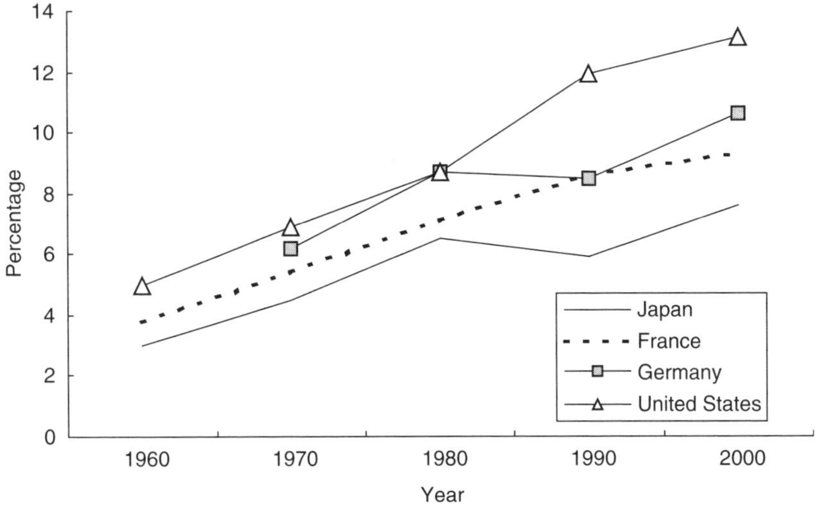

Source: OECD (2006).

Figure 8.4 Growth of total health expenditure in relation to GDP: selected countries, 1960–2000

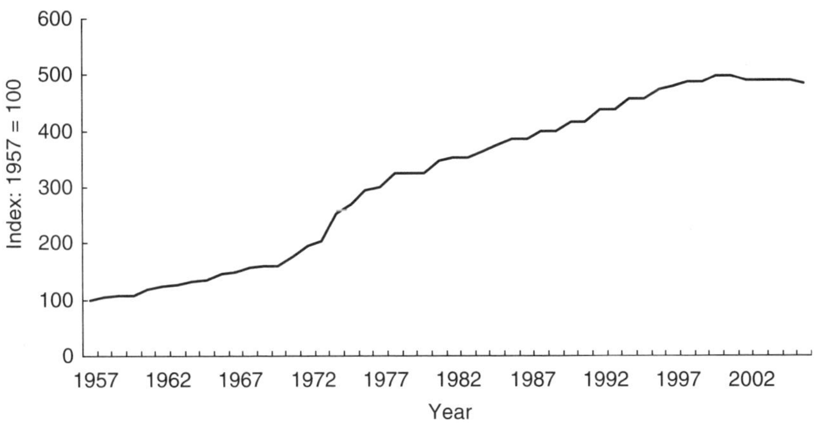

Source: Health and Welfare Statistics Association (2006).

Figure 8.5 Change in the unit price of medical services: Japan, 1957–2006

Despite the implementation of cost-containment measures through the adjustment of the fee schedule and co-payments, total expenditures on medical care have been rising (see Figure 8.3). Numerous factors are considered to be responsible. Among them are rapid population aging, remarkable medical technological progress and the changing pattern of Japan's morbidity and mortality (Campbell and Ikegami, 1998). Apart from these factors, improved availability of medical services has led to a rise in cost. In 1970, the government adopted a new policy for increasing the number of physicians through an expansion of the education program. Its goal was to raise the service ratio of physicians from 127 to 150 per 100 000 population by 1985. This target was achieved in 1983, and by 2002 the ratio exceeded 206 per 100 000, resulting in an excess supply of physicians.

As mentioned earlier, Japanese physicians tend to provide excessive medical services with a view to increasing their income, and this in turn leads to a rise in government medical expenditures. Primarily to put a brake on the escalating cost of health care, and partly to avoid possible unemployment among physicians, in 1995 the government reduced the number of students admitted to medical schools by 10 percent.

Another cause of rising medical costs, which is related to the supply side of health care services, has been the rapid increase in the number of hospital beds and their utilization. The number of hospital beds per 100 000 people rose from 735 in 1960 to 1331 in 1988 (Health and Welfare Statistics Association, 2006. In parallel with the fast growth in the number of hospital beds, the average length of stay in inpatient-care institutions became by far the longest among all the industrialized countries (Figure 8.6). Because inpatient services are substantially more costly than outpatient services, the cost related to hospitalization was a main cause of the rising total medical expenditure in Japan until the late 1980s.

Why did the Japanese people stay in hospitals for such long periods? One explanation lies in the phenomenon known as 'social hospitalization'. The Japanese people believe that a social stigma is attached to the word 'institution'. Psychologically the word 'hospital' is more acceptable to families caring for the elderly than the word 'institution'. The proportion of the elderly institutionalized has been strikingly lower than that for other industrialized nations (Campbell and Ikegami, 1998). The other explanation, which is more cogent, is that, because there was a severe shortage of long-term care facilities for the elderly, the overwhelming majority of older inpatients received medical care at general hospitals, substantially raising the average duration of hospitalization. For example, in 1985, the average length of hospitalization for those aged 65 and over was 87 days, as compared with 11 days for those aged 0–14 (Health and Welfare Statistics Association, 1988). To reduce the duration of hospitalization, the government made

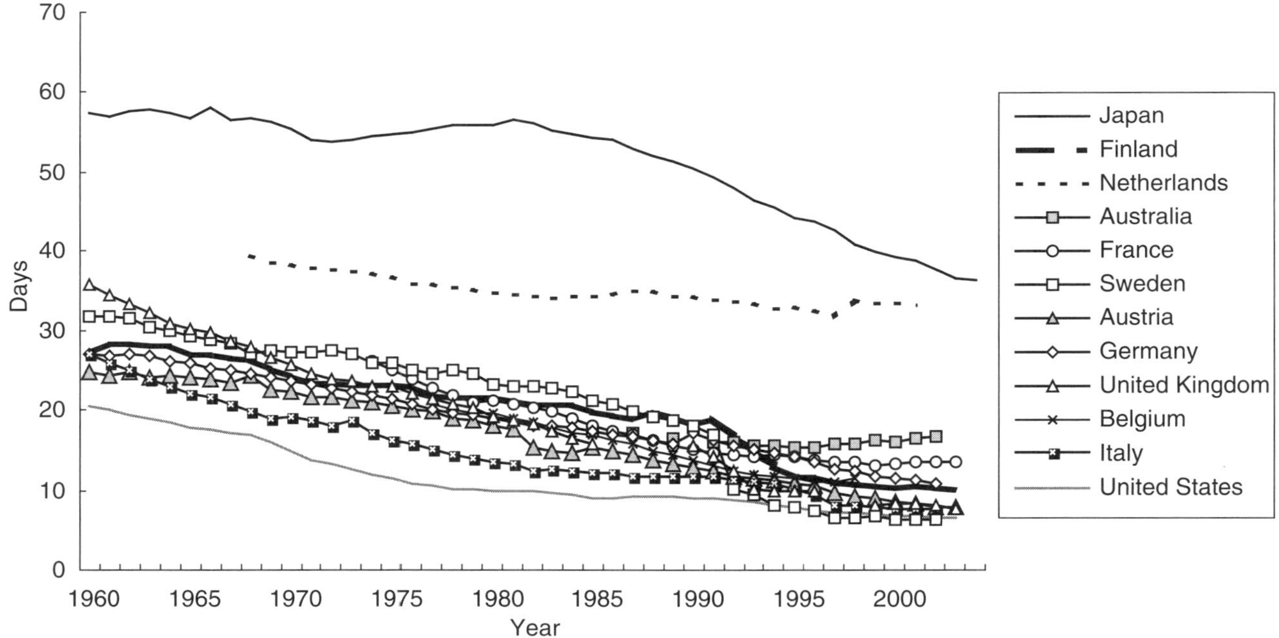

Source: OECD (2006).

Figure 8.6 Trends in average duration of hospital stays: Japan and selected industrialized countries, 1960–2004

numerous policy and program changes. One of them, approved in 1983, was to establish institutions for the long-term care for the elderly. In 1987, among the country's 9841 hospitals, only 8.5 percent of them specialized in providing long-term geriatric care; by 2004, that proportion had grown to 47.3 percent (Health and Welfare Statistics Association, 2006). The elderly who receive long-term geriatric care are required to pay considerably more than their counterparts who receive in-patient services at ordinary hospitals.

In addition, because institution-building is a slow process, and Japan's population aging was expected to accelerate during the next few decades, the government emphasized in its 1987 White Paper on Health and Welfare that responsibility for looking after elderly patients should be shifted from hospitals to family caregivers, who are usually middle-aged women. To facilitate this transfer process, the government increased its budgetary allocation for the social service programs for elderly patients through its ambitious ten-year project called 'the Gold Plan' for the period 1990–2000. Through this plan, central and local governments improved the number and quality of such social services as home-helpers, short-stay facilities, and day-care centers for the elderly.

In 2000, the government initiated the largest and most radical program of mandatory long-term care insurance in the world (Campbell and Ikegami, 2000). The primary objective of the Long-term Care Insurance Scheme is to improve the quality of care for the elderly by eliminating inefficiencies that have resulted from the intermixing of medical treatment and long-term care functions. The scheme collects obligatory insurance contributions from a broad sector of the population (all persons aged 40 and over). The benefits provided include such services as home visits by home-helpers, visits to day-care centers, and long-term stays in nursing homes for older persons who are bedridden or suffer from senile dementia. However, because the demand for such services increased much more quickly than had been anticipated, the sustainability of the scheme was threatened, and so the government adjusted downward the benefits for mild cases. The revised program for elderly people with less severe handicaps went into effect in April 2006. It provides such preventive services as training to increase strength, nutrition, and oral care (how to chew and so on).

As a consequence of these policy changes, the average hospital stay has been declining since the late 1980s (Figure 8.6). To reinforce this trend the government implemented a new cost-containment scheme, called the 'Diagnosis Procedure Combination', in 2003. Under this scheme the cost of hospitalization is calculated on the basis of the number of days of hospital stay, and the weights assigned to the cost per day decline as the number of days increases. Although its impact on inpatient costs is expected to be substantial in the long run, the scheme was applied in only 82 large hospitals when it started in 2003. Although the number of hospitals enrolled in the scheme has been gradually increasing over the past few years, it is still too early to assess its effect.

Using a long-term simulation model developed by the Nihon University Population Research Institute (the NUPRI model), we have projected the total medical expenditure measured in nominal terms over the period 2000–25. The simulated result shows that the total expenditure on medical care is expected to rise almost 1.9 times over the 25 years. As a percentage of GDP, it is projected to grow from 5.6 percent in 2000 to 6.6 percent in 2025.

DETERIORATING FAMILY SUPPORT AND NORMATIVE SHIFTS

In general, Japan's current demographic and economic characteristics are similar in many ways to those of other industrialized countries, but there are some important differences. Family organization is one example (Ogawa and Retherford, 1993, 1997). Unlike Western European countries, multigenerational households are still fairly common in Japan (Ogawa and Ermisch, 1996; Ogawa, Retherford and Matsukura, 2006). According to the 2001 round of the International Survey of Lifestyles and Attitudes of the Elderly (Cabinet Office, 2002), the proportion of persons aged 60 and over who were living alone in Japan was only 10 percent in that year (Figure 8.7). By contrast, corresponding figures were 36 percent for Germany, 40 percent for the United States and 42 percent for Sweden. Owing to rapid demographic shifts and changing lifestyles, however, the proportion of the elderly living alone in Japan has been steadily rising over the past two decades. Although the Japanese government often views the low level of one-person households among the elderly as a unique asset that can be tapped to offset the adverse effects of population aging on the sustainability of the Social Security system (Ministry of Health and Welfare, 1978), the validity of this view has become increasingly questionable as the process of population aging advances.

In addition, social values among the Japanese people have been changing rapidly over the past few decades. Some of the important value shifts are well captured in time-series data gathered in a series of nationwide surveys concerning fertility and family planning, which the Mainichi Newspapers have conducted every other year since 1950 (Population Problems Research Council, 2000). Since 1963, successive rounds of these surveys have included a question on the attitude of married women under

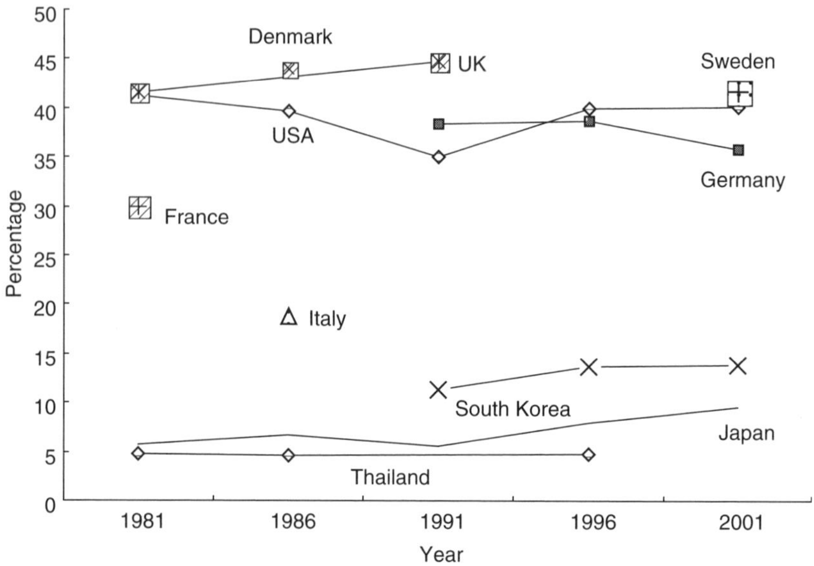

Source: Cabinet Office (2002).

Figure 8.7 Change in the proportion of those aged 60+ living alone: selected countries, 1981–2001

age 50 toward taking care of aged parents. The precoded response categories are (i) 'good custom', (ii) 'natural duty as children', (iii) 'unavoidable due to inadequacy of public support resources', and (iv) 'not a good custom'. The results, plotted in Figure 8.8, indicate that the proportion of respondents who believed that providing care for elderly parents was either a good custom or children's natural duty was, by and large, stable over the period from 1963 to 1986. Between 1986 and 1988, however, a dramatic decline occurred in this proportion, and the trend is still under way. The two years between 1986 and 1988 correspond to the period when the government shifted more of the burden of care for the elderly from the state to families. It is conceivable that the middle-aged women responded negatively to that change.

Despite these normative shifts on the part of potential caregivers, as the aging process advances, the number of elderly patients who need intensive nursing is expected to increase at an alarming rate. Using the NUPRI model, we estimated the number of those aged 65 and over who will be bedridden or suffer from senile dementia during the next 25 years, assuming that the age–sex-specific pattern of the incidence of these cases remains unchanged throughout the projected period. The number of bedridden

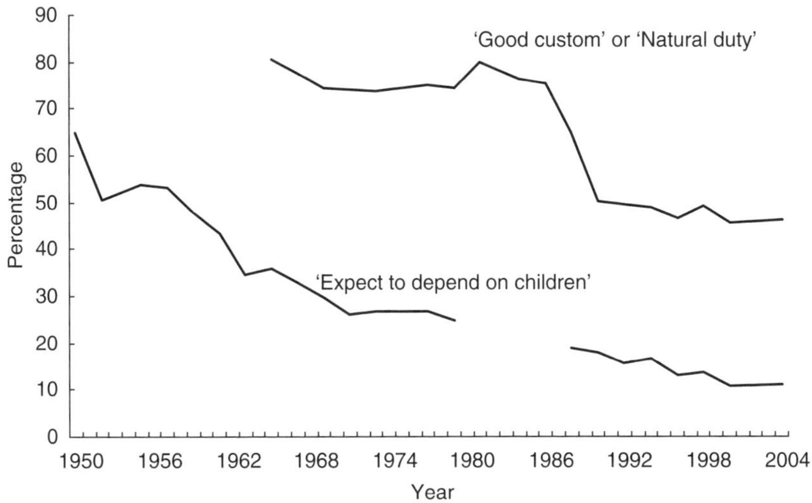

Sources: Mainichi Newspapers of Japan (2000, 2004).

Figure 8.8 Trends in norms and expectations about care for the elderly: Japan, 1950–2004

patients, either at home or at medical institutions, will grow 2.2 times, that is, from 1.25 million in 2000 to 2.70 million in 2025. The total number of senile dementia cases will increase 2.4 times, from 1.64 million to 3.99 million during the corresponding period.

Substantial proportions of these elderly patients have been and will be looked after at home by their adult children, particularly by middle-aged women who are not in the labor force. Bearing this family-support pattern in mind, we have projected the ratio of elderly patients at home to women at various ages outside the labor force. The estimated results are shown in Figure 8.9. As indicated, the ratio of the aged at home who are bedridden or suffer from senile dementia to women outside the labor force has grown over time. For instance, approximately one out of every seven women aged 40–49 assumed responsibility for taking care of one infirm elderly person at home in 2000, but almost half of the nonworking women of this age group are likely to provide in-home care for elderly patients in 2025.

These results indicate a dramatic rise in the burden placed upon middle-aged Japanese women providing in-home nursing for the infirm elderly. They are subject to revision, depending upon the future direction of the Social Security system, family policies and employment practices.

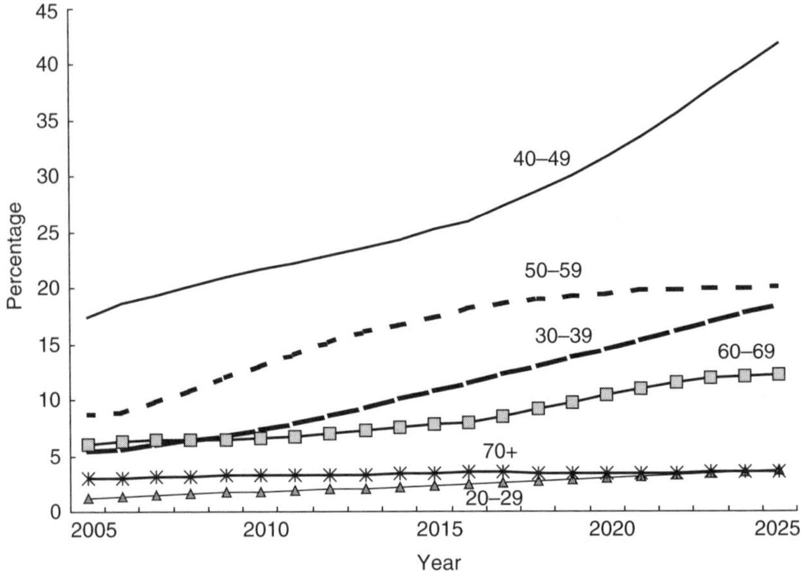

Source: Calculated by using the NUPRI long-term simulation model.

Figure 8.9 Projected ratio of the elderly suffering from senile dementia or bedridden to the nonworking adult female population at various ages: Japan, 2005–25

DATA SOURCES AND METHODOLOGY USED TO COMPUTE HEALTH EXPENDITURES

Although many factors affect health expenditures, age is one of the most important. It is closely related to the incidence of illness, and often illnesses that affect the elderly are the most serious and costly to treat. Thus in Japan, as in most other countries, the elderly consume a disproportionate share of health care services, and population aging will likely lead to an increase in the share of GDP devoted to health.

Although the elderly consume health care services, they do not necessarily bear the costs associated with providing those services. As explained above, a substantial portion of health care spending in Japan occurs through public health schemes that are heavily subsidized by taxpayers, and health insurance has provided especially attractive terms for the elderly, thus sheltering them from those costs. Some portions of health care costs are also borne by non-elderly Japanese through private transfers. The remainder of this chapter focuses on analyzing health-expenditure data for the years 1989, 1994, 1999 and 2004 with the aim of exploring how health care consumption and costs have varied by age and how they are likely to change over the next few decades.

The analysis presented here is part of a larger effort to understand how public and private consumption vary by age, how this leads to intergenerational transfers to the elderly and to children, how the methods used to effect intergenerational transfers are changing, and how these changes will interact with population aging to influence economic growth and intergenerational equity in Japan (Ogawa et al., 2006). This work is being done as part of a larger international effort to construct a system of National Transfer Accounts that measures the reallocations of resources across age groups in a manner consistent with National Income and Product Accounts (Mason et al., forthcoming). The health sector is an important component of this work because health consumption by the elderly (and the very young) is quite significant and because so much of health care spending is financed through transfers from one age group to another.

The methodological details involved in estimating National Transfer Accounts are available at the website for the National Transfer Accounts (NTA) Database, www.ntaccounts.org, and will not be repeated here. In addition, important methodological details that apply only to the analysis for Japan are presented at that site (in particular the supplementary material to the working paper on Japan health spending).

An important component of the analysis presented here comprises estimates of private and public consumption of health care services for individuals classified by single years of age for 1989, 1994, 1999 and 2004. To estimate age profiles of private consumption we draw heavily upon household data gathered in the four rounds of the National Survey on Family Income and Expenditure (NSFIE). Unfortunately, the NSFIE data on private health expenditure are available only for households and not for each household member. For that reason we are not able to calculate the medical expenditure for each individual in a straightforward fashion.

To overcome this data limitation, we have employed the estimation methodology previously used by Mason et al. (forthcoming) to link the household's private health expenditure to the individual level. Regression techniques are employed to allocate the observed expenditure in each household to its members, yielding an estimate of health spending for individuals. The estimated values are used to estimate per capita spending on health care by single year of age. We have experimented with alternative specifications, and most have produced similar results. The final per capita age profiles have been adjusted proportionately to match aggregate control totals based on National Income and Product Accounts for Japan. A detailed discussion pertaining to this adjustment process is available at the NTA Database website, www.ntaccounts.org.

The Statistics Bureau of the Japanese government has been conducting the NSFIE at five-year intervals since 1959. One of the primary objectives of the survey is to shed light on the structure of household economies and the regional differences in family incomes and expenditures, principal durable goods owned, and assets and liabilities.

A comparable sampling framework was applied to the four rounds of the NSFIE, which we have used in the present study. For expository purposes we discuss the 2004 round, which is similar in all important respects to earlier rounds analyzed here. The sample size of the 2004 wave of the NSFIE was approximately 55 000 private households with two or more members and about 50 000 one-person households. The sampling ratio for one-person households was considerably greater than that for multi-person households. For each household type, the selection procedure was a stratified random sampling based on geographical locations. Because it is difficult to design the stratified random sampling procedure based upon geographical locations without creating some variability in sampling ratios over the regions, the NSFIE is subject to the regional variability of sampling ratios. For this reason, when microlevel data from the NSFIE are analyzed, each observation needs to be properly weighted. Private households with two or more members were surveyed for the period of three months from September through November 2004, and one-person households were surveyed for the period of two months from October through November 2004.

The age profile of public consumption of health services is estimated from administrative records on health care services provided directly by governmental units and from information about reimbursement of public health insurance programs detailed above. The value of services provided by private providers but reimbursed by public health insurance is counted as public health consumption in these accounts. The age-profile data are relatively complete and individual-specific rather than household-specific. Detailed sources are provided in the supplementary material on the NTA Database website.

National Transfer Accounts are constructed so as to be consistent with National Income and Product Accounts. Estimates based on the microlevel data derived from each round of the NSFIE need to be scaled up to the national level. To fulfill this task we have explored using two major data sources of private health expenditure: data from the *Annual Report on National Accounts* (2006) published by the Cabinet Office, and data from the Ministry of Health and Welfare (later renamed Ministry of Health, Labor and Welfare). These two data sources provide data on the aggregate household health expenditure on a time-series basis. Figure 8.10 compares the aggregate data from these two sources over the period 1980–2003. Because

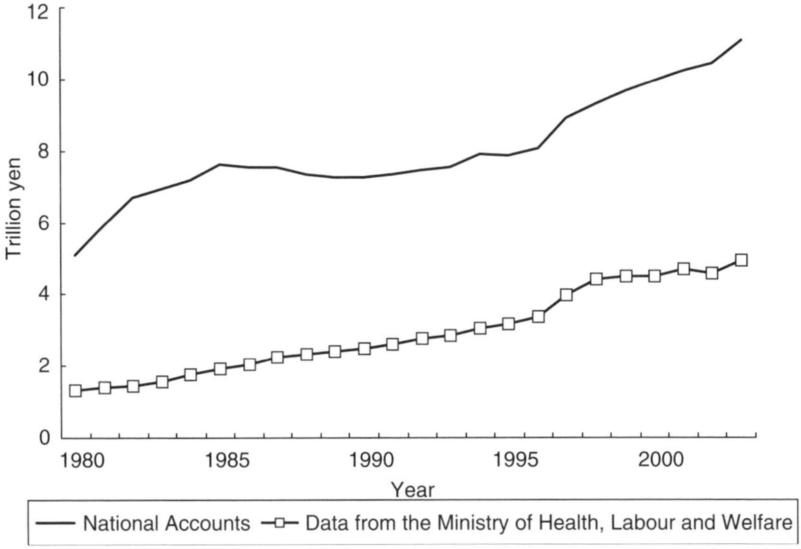

Sources: Cabinet Office (2006); Ministry of Health, Labor and Welfare, *National Medical Expenditures* (various years).

Figure 8.10 National private health expenditure in trillion yen: Japan, 1980–2003

the personal health-related expenditures reported in the national income accounts include all spending on health at the familial level, they cover the costs for medical treatments at medical institutions as well as costs for the purchase of nonprescription drugs. In contrast, the data on personal expenses gathered by the Ministry of Health, Labor and Welfare cover only the costs of medical treatments at medical institutions. This is due to the fact that the data compiled by the Ministry are generated from information on costs covered by patients. In view of these differences in the coverage of the two data sources, we have opted to use information from the National Accounts as macroeconomic control variables. Public consumption includes reimbursements from national health insurance programs.

ESTIMATED AGE PROFILES OF PRIVATE AND PUBLIC HEALTH EXPENDITURES

The age profiles of health spending in Japan are similar in broad respects to those found in other industrialized countries. Young children, particularly those 0–4 years old, are much more costly than older children.

Between the ages of 10 and 40, health spending is relatively steady and low. The amount of spending increases with age after age 40, rising to ever higher levels. In 2004, individuals in their 70s, for example, consumed 4.3 times as much health care on average as individuals in their 30s.

Given that health care is consumed much more by the elderly than by the young, it is virtually certain that health care spending will increase as Japan's population ages. The age profiles of spending, however, are changing and will continue to change in the future, responding to important features of Japan's health care system and health care policy. First, unlike the United States, where the prices of medical services are determined to a greater extent by the interplay of demand and supply, the Japanese government controls the prices of health care services. Second, Japan has national health insurance that covers virtually everyone whereas the US public system is primarily a system for the elderly. As is shown below, however, the role of the public sector varies considerably with age. Third, the Japanese government is heavily involved in controlling the supply of services, from determining how many health personnel will be trained to determining what kinds of services will be provided, and under what conditions.

Although the public health care system in Japan is nearly universal, the private sector is far from negligible. Private health care consumption as a percentage of total health care consumption has varied between 24 and 29 percent according to our calculations, but the relative importance of the private sector varies with age. For young children only, private consumption of health care represents more than half of total health care spending. For older children and non-elderly adults, private consumption varies between about 30 and 40 percent of total health care spending. As people age, the public sector becomes increasingly dominant, with public consumption accounting for 90 percent or more of total consumption for those aged 85 and older. Thus the age profiles of health expenditure are very different for private consumption and public consumption, and hence we estimate and discuss them separately. The profiles have been estimated for four years (1989, 1994, 1999 and 2004) and cover a period during which Japan has been trying to prepare for the rapid population aging that is coming. The estimated results are displayed in Figures 8.11 and 8.12.

As shown in Figure 8.11, private consumption of health care by young children is very high as compared with consumption by older children and younger adults. Private consumption begins to rise from about age 40 and reaches a peak at about age 65. Thereafter private consumption declines steadily up to age 80 and beyond, depending on the year of the survey. In every year analyzed, private spending on the health care of the elderly is less than private spending on the health care of young children, although

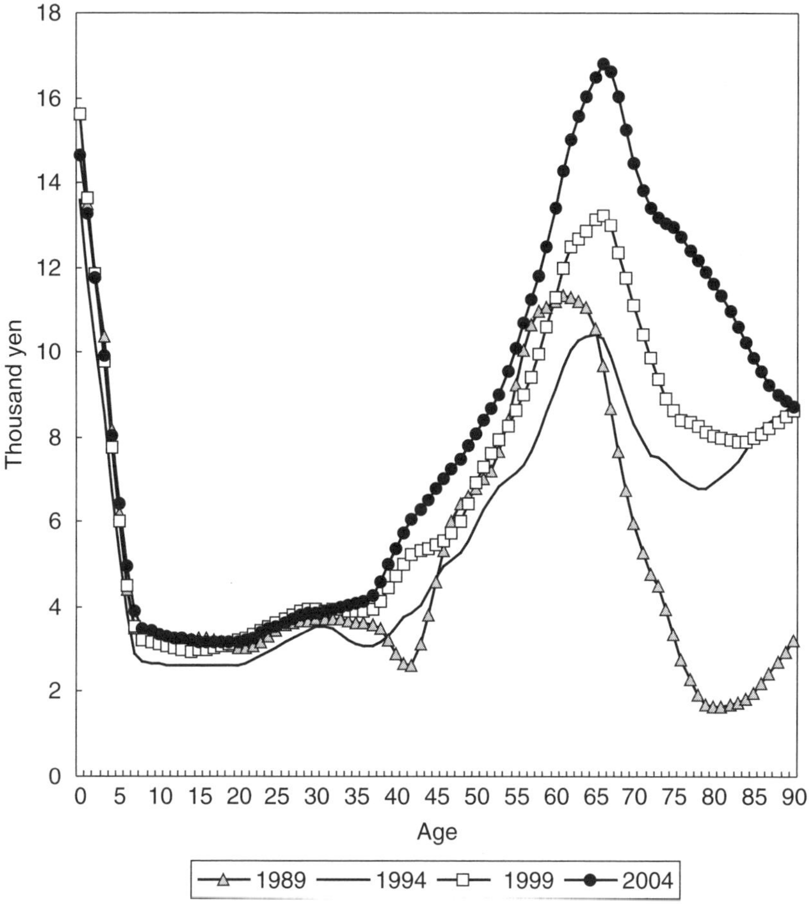

Figure 8.11 Monthly per capita private health spending, by age, estimated by the regression method, real value: Japan, selected years, 1989–2004 (base year = 2000)

total spending on the health care of the elderly is substantially greater. Again, medical services for the elderly are much more heavily subsidized than are medical services for their younger counterparts.

The trends in health care spending between 1989 and 2004 were very different, depending on age. For those under the age of 35, the period was one of remarkable stability. On average, real per capita spending increased by 0.2 percent per year during the 15-year period analyzed. There were some noticeable changes during the period, however. Per capita private spending declined considerably at younger ages between 1989 and 1994 and then recovered over the next ten years. These changes seem to be explained by the bursting of the bubble economy in the early 1990s and the slow economic recovery after the turn of the century.

The trend in private health care spending for the elderly is quite different, reflecting not only the price constraint imposed by public policy but also the many changes in the extent of subsidies outlined above. In real terms, per capita private health spending increased significantly between 1989 and 1994 and again between 1999 and 2004. During the 15-year period as a whole, the age profile for those aged 65 and older shifted upward at an annual real rate of 8.6 percent.

What explains these trends? As mentioned earlier, the government raised co-payments from 10 to 20 percent in 1997 and from 20 to 30 percent in 2003, and the impact of these changes can be observed from the response of those aged 40 and over. The changes were even more pronounced for the elderly. As shown in Table 8.1, the cost-sharing program for the elderly aged 70 and over had been repeatedly revised upward, and a 10 percent co-payment (and a 20 percent co-payment for those with higher income) was imposed upon elderly patients in 2002. Evidently these program and policy changes have had a very substantial impact on private health expenditure.

As compared with the private health expenditure, the age profile of public expenditure shows a very distinctive J-shape. Per capita public health spending is relatively low among children and younger adults, but then rises sharply with age, particularly among those who are 70 and older, as shown in Figure 8.12. Per capita public health expenditure increased significantly between 1989 and 1994, mainly because of the changes in the fee-schedule and also the introduction of the Gold Plan in the 1990s. Between 1994 and 1999, per capita public spending was relatively stable, especially at older ages. Although it is not obvious from the figure, per capita spending for many non-elderly adults and older children declined by as much as 15 to 20 percent during that period. The changes (and lack of change) during the period reflect the tight controls maintained on prices and increases in the share of costs borne by patients. The only group to experience a significant increase in per capita public health spending during the period was those aged 2 and under.

Further retrenchment occurred between 1999 and 2004. The declines in per capita public health expenditure were concentrated among the elderly. The introduction of the Long-term Care Insurance Scheme is the principal reason for this decline, as indicated in Figure 8.3. Figure 8.12 shows the Long-term Care Insurance expenditure in addition to the public health expenditure. As discussed earlier, the Long-term Care Insurance expenditure has been increasing since the scheme's inception in 2000 owing to its

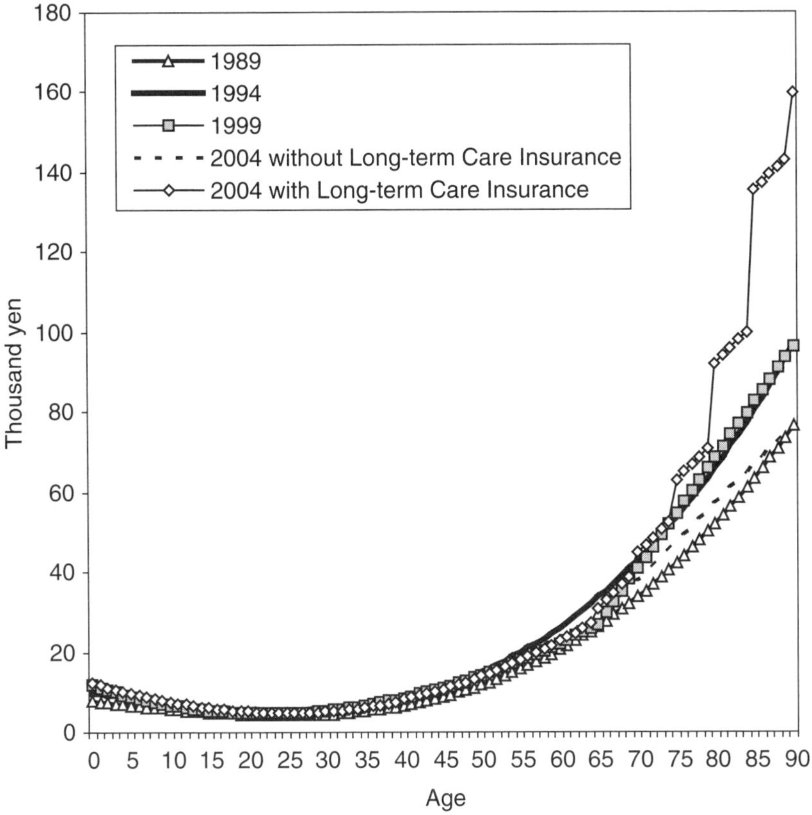

Figure 8.12 Change in monthly per capita health care expenditures, by age: Japan, selected years, 1989–2004

unexpectedly high demand among the elderly. With the Long-term Care Insurance expenditure added, the total health care benefits received by the elderly are much higher than those in 1999.

If we consider the 15-year period, and ignore long-term care, Japan has successfully maintained a cap on health spending. For adults in the 21–59 age group, the age profile increased by 0.9 percent per year during the period. For those in the 60 and older age group the age profile shifted upward by 0.5 percent per year during the period. General prices over the same period increased at an average rate of 0.63 percent per year. For the most part, then, per capita public spending on health did not increase. The only exception to this generalization is that, for children, public per capita spending increased moderately, at 2.8 percent per year.

WHO PAYS FOR HEALTH CARE NOW AND IN THE FUTURE?

To this point the analysis has been limited to estimating consumption of health services by age. For the most part, however, those who are paying for health care services are not the same as those who are receiving the services. As we have already noted, more than 80 percent of total expenditures on health care is funded by taxpayers. Moreover, some portion of private spending is borne by family members other than those receiving the services, mainly the adult children of the elderly. The purpose here is to assess the extent to which the costs of health care services are being shifted across age groups, primarily from children and the elderly to those in the working ages. Given the decline in the size of the workforce that Japan is experiencing, increases in health care costs will create fiscal problems to the extent that they are channeled through the public sector, and personal financial hardship to the extent that they are channeled through the private (familial) sector.

The estimates presented here are preliminary, and we anticipate that more refined estimates will become available as work on this topic continues. Again the analysis is based on methods developed as part of the broader effort to estimate National Transfer Accounts for Japan. The costs of public health care are borne by taxpayers. The age pattern of these costs depends on the system of taxation – that is, the resource being taxed, the variation in the resource by age and variation in tax rates by age. Japan's Social Security system, including public health insurance, is funded through taxes on labor income. We assume that the tax rate is independent of age. The age profile of labor income is estimated on the basis of the NSFIEs, as described above. The net flow of public spending is calculated as the value of public health care consumed by each age group less taxes paid by the corresponding age group to finance public health care consumption.

The same principles govern the calculation of private transfers, although the calculation methods are different. Private transfers reported here consist of only intrahousehold transfers. These we calculate at the household level using the NSFIE. Household members with personal income exceeding their consumption make transfers to members with consumption exceeding their personal income. We assume that health care transfers within the household are directly proportional to the share of health care in the total consumption of the individual receiving the transfer. In other words, within-family transfers are not aimed at particular needs, but health care transfers will be larger if, as is likely to be the case, large medical expenses lead to an increase in intrahousehold transfers. The magnitude of private health care transfers is understated because interhousehold transfers in response to health care needs are not included in the calculation. A more detailed description of the methodology is available at www.ntaccounts.org.

Figure 8.13 shows aggregate annual private and public consumption of health care by age in Japan for each of the four years analyzed and net private and public health care transfers by age for each year. Aggregate private spending and public spending are calculated by multiplying per capita flows by the population in each age group. Net aggregate public and private transfers for health are also reported. A positive net flow indicates that the age group, including the young and the old in this case, has net transfer inflows. A negative value, experienced by those in the working ages, indicates that the age group is experiencing a net transfer outflow.

The implications of population aging for aggregate health care consumption are starkly apparent if we compare 1989 (panel A) with 2004 (panel D). Health care consumption by the young and prime-age adults has changed little during this period as per capita health care costs have been kept in check and population size in many of these age groups has been relatively constant or declined. In contrast, health care consumption by the elderly has increased very substantially as a result primarily of an increase in their numbers. The relative importance of the public sector increases markedly with age. For the young and prime-age adults, public and private consumption are not greatly different, but for the elderly the public sector dominates. Changes in public policy have shifted some consumption from the public to the private health sector, but the public sector remains dominant for the elderly.

Who pays for health care? The answer to this question is found by examining both net health care transfers and net health care consumption. Private expenditures on health care are equal to the difference between private consumption and private net transfers. This is most easily illustrated for children, who consume health care but do not pay for it. Rather it is primarily their parents (and grandparents) and taxpayers who bear the cost. As can be seen in the figure, net private transfers equal private consumption for children. Net private health transfers to the elderly are substantial, and their relative importance varies with age. Those in their 60s and early 70s are paying more than half of the cost of their health care, but the remainder is being shifted to younger adults, most often to adult children with whom the elderly are co-residing. The extent to which the elderly are self-sufficient declines fairly substantially at older ages.

The private costs of health care are borne by prime-age adults. Net private transfers reach their (negative) peak for individuals who are in their 30s and early 40s. Many are parents bearing the health costs of their children. At these ages private transfers for health more than exceed private

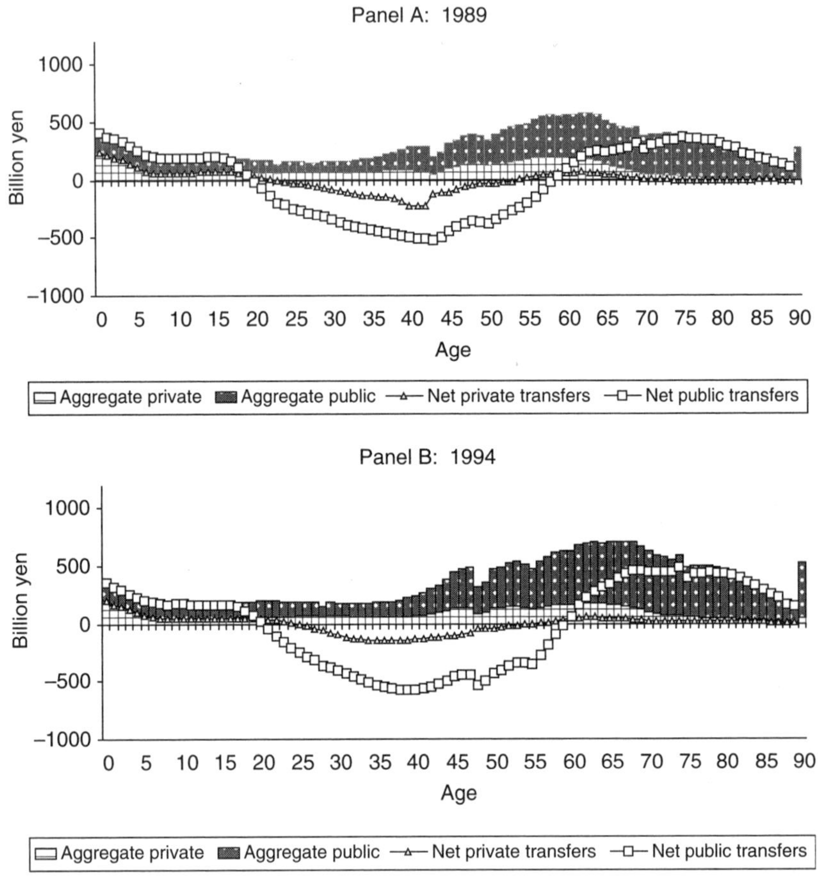

consumption of health. The combined private cost is greater for these age groups than for any others in the population.

The series in Figure 8.13 are stacked to show total consumption of health care and total net health-cost transfers. Children do not pay for any of their health care costs, but the elderly pay for a portion of their own. The share of the total cost borne by the elderly declines substantially with age, to a greater degree than in the case of private spending. By the time the elderly are in their 80s they are paying for only a small fraction of their health care costs. The remaining costs are shifted to prime-age adults.

Net public transfers and net total transfers reach their (negative) peak at a somewhat older age than net private transfers, because taxes to support health care are tied to labor income. As a consequence the largest share of health care costs is falling on older workers. This has been increasingly the

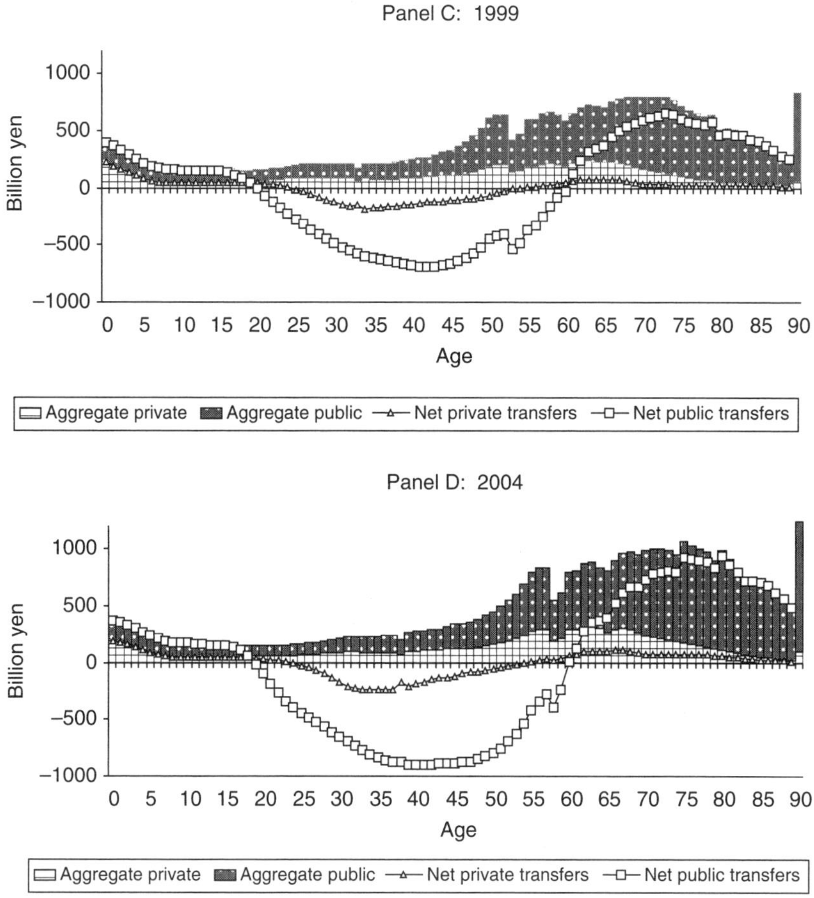

Figure 8.13 Annual health expenditures and net health transfers: Japan, selected years, 1989–2004

case as population aging has occurred. Although our focus here is on health care spending, the same trend is characteristic of other social security-type spending. In 2004, for example, the social security benefits to the elderly were approximately 70 percent of total benefits, while the children received approximately 4 percent (National Institute of Population and Social Security Research, 2006). Health care costs will prove to be increasingly burdensome as the number of elderly grows and the number of workers begins to decline. The extension of the retirement age may provide partial relief. This could eventually lengthen the negative net flow beyond 60 years of age. Nonetheless, much of the growth in population will be at older ages,

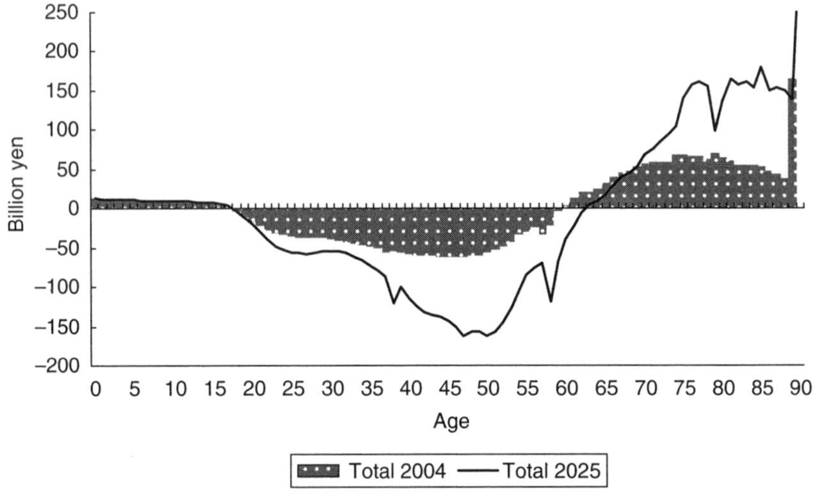

Figure 8.14 Monthly population-weighted net total health transfers: Japan, 2004 and 2005 (nominal value, in trillion yen)

when health care costs are high, and their costs will be borne entirely by older workers.

The effect of population aging on health spending was significant in 2004, as depicted in Figure 8.14. Using the profile for 2004, we have projected the net flow of health transfers to the elderly in 2025. The calculation shows that the net flow of health transfers to the elderly will almost double, while the net flow to prime-age adults will become an increasingly large deficit.

SUMMARY AND CONCLUSION

It is well known that Japan's medical care services are rather inexpensive by international standards, although the health status of the Japanese people is one of the best in the world (Campbell and Ikegami, 1998). Over the past few decades Japan's population has been aging at an unprecedented rate, and its proportion aged 65 and over is currently the highest in the world. To shed light on how the Japanese health care system has been coping with the formidable pressure of rapid population aging over the past two decades or so, we have analyzed, by heavily relying upon the framework of the National Transfer Accounts system, the change in the age profiles of both private and public health expenditures over the period from 1989 to 2004. In addition we have discussed these intertemporal shifts in private and public health expenditures by linking them to the changes in health care policies and programs implemented during the same time period.

One of our major findings is that the stringent fee schedule has lent itself to effectively keeping the country's total health spending under tight control. The other finding is that a series of age-based policies and programs, such as the introduction of the co-payment system and the cost-sharing scheme for the elderly, have been effective in keeping the total medical expenditure within a manageable range. The Long-term Care Insurance Scheme has also played a significant role in mitigating the effects of population aging on the country's total medical expenditure over the past few years.

Many uncertainties characterize the future prospects of Japan's health care delivery system, particularly given the further acceleration of population aging in the years ahead. It is anticipated that the number of Japanese aged 65 and over will increase from 27 million in 2005 to 37 million by 2025. Not only is the number of the elderly projected to increase, but also more advanced technological developments are anticipated in the medical field. Thus it is very likely that Japan's future medical care spending will continue to rise.

Although the Japanese health care system offers equitable access to the entire population at relatively low cost, it is conceivable that the government's huge deficits may lead to efforts to replace the public program with private health insurance. It is also possible that the balance-billing restriction may be removed with the passage of time.

To encourage higher fertility, a number of local governments have recently begun providing substantial subsidies to parents to cover the co-payment for medical care for children below age 15. In another policy change, in April 2006, the Japanese government drastically reduced the benefits available to the elderly through the Long-term Care Insurance Scheme, a move that is likely to mitigate the growth of the country's medical care expenditure. The impact of these changes on the total health care expenditure, both private and public, remains to be seen.

NOTE

1. Research for this chapter was funded by the US National Institutes of Health, NIA R01-AG025488.

REFERENCES

Cabinet Office (2002), *Report on the Fifth International Survey of Lifestyles and Attitudes of the Elderly*, Tokyo: Gyosei Printing Company.

Cabinet Office (2005), *Long-term Model for the Japanese Economy*, Tokyo: Cabinet Office Publishing.

Cabinet Office (2006), *Annual Report on National Accounts 2005*, Tokyo: Shumposya Shashin Insatsu Kabushikigaisya.

Campbell, John C. and Naoki Ikegami (1998), *The Art of Balance in Health Policy*, Cambridge: Cambridge University Press.

Campbell, John C. and Naoki Ikegami (2000), 'Long-term care insurance comes to Japan', *Health Affairs*, **19**(3), 19–39.

Health and Welfare Statistics Association (1988), *Kousei no Shihyou: Kokukumin Hukushi no Douko (Journal of Health and Welfare Statistics 35-12)*, Tokyo: Kousei Toukei Kyoukai (in Japanese).

Health and Welfare Statistics Association (2006), *Kousei no Shihyou: Hoken to Nenkin no Doukou (Journal of Health and Welfare Statistics 53-14)*, Tokyo: Kousei Toukei Kyoukai (in Japanese).

Imai, Yutaka (2002), 'Health care reform in Japan', OECD Economics Department Working Papers, No. 321, Organisation for Economic Co-operation and Development, Paris.

International Institute for Management Development (2006), *IMD World Competitiveness Yearbook*, Lausanne, Switzerland.

Jeong, Hyoung-Sun and Jeremy Hurst (2001), 'An assessment of the performance of the Japanese health care system', OECD Labour Market and Social Policy Occasional Papers, No. 56, Organisation for Economic Co-operation and Development, Paris.

Mainichi Newspapers of Japan (2000), *Summary of the Survey on Twenty-fifth National Survey on Family Planning*, Tokyo.

Mainichi Newspapers of Japan (2004), *Summary of the 2004 Round of the National Survey on Population, Families and Generations*, Tokyo.

Mason, Andrew, Ronald Lee, An-Chi Tung, Mun-Sim Lai and Tim Miller (forthcoming), 'Population aging and intergenerational transfers: Introducing age into national accounts', in David Wise (ed.), *Developments in the Economics of Aging*, Chicago: National Bureau of Economic Research and University of Chicago Press.

McKinsey Global Institute (2000), *Why the Japanese Economy is Not Growing: Micro Barriers to Productivity Growth*, Washington, DC: McKinsey & Company.

Ministry of Finance (2006), 'Report on the balance of government guaranteed bonds', available online at http://www.mof.go.jp/gbb/1806.html.

Ministry of Health and Welfare (1978), *White Paper on Health and Welfare*, Tokyo: Health and Welfare Statistics Association (in Japanese).

Ministry of Health, Labor and Welfare (various years), *National Medical Expenditures*, Tokyo.

Ministry of Health, Labor and Welfare (various years), *Vital Statistics*, Tokyo: Kousei Toukei Kyoukai.

National Institute of Population and Social Security Research (2006), 'Report on the social security benefits', available online at http://www.ipss.go.jp/ss-cost/j/kyuhuhi-h16.html.

OECD (Organisation for Economic Co-operation and Development) (2006), *OECD Health Data 2005*, Paris.

Ogawa, Naohiro (2003), 'Population aging and its impact on the socioeconomic system in Japan', *Aging in Japan 2003*, Tokyo: Japan Aging Research Center, pp. 123–50.

Ogawa, Naohiro (2005), 'Population aging and policy options for a sustainable future: the case of Japan', *Genus*, **61**(3–4), 369–410.

Ogawa, Naohiro and John F. Ermisch (1996), 'Family structure, home time demands, and the employment patterns of Japanese married women', *Journal of Labour Economics*, **14**(4), 677–702.

Ogawa, Naohiro and Robert D. Retherford (1993), 'The resumption of fertility decline in Japan: 1973–92', *Population and Development Review*, **19**(4), 703–41.

Ogawa, Naohiro and Robert D. Retherford (1997), 'Shifting costs of caring for the elderly back to families in Japan', *Population Development Review*, **23**(1), 59–94.

Ogawa, Naohiro, Robert D. Retherford and Rikiya Matsukura (2006), 'Demographics of the Japanese family: entering uncharted territory', in Marcus Rebick and Ayumi Takenaka (eds), *The Changing Definition of the Japanese Family in the 1990s*, New York and Abingdon: Routledge, pp. 19–38.

Ogawa, Naohiro, Makoto Kondo, Masao Tamura, Rikiya Matsukura, Tomoko Saito, Andrew Mason, Shripad Tuljapurkar and Nan Li (2003), 'Long-term perspectives for Japan: an analysis based on a macroeconomic–demographic–social security model with emphasis on human capital', Nihon University Population Research Institute, Tokyo.

Population Problems Research Council (2000), *The Population of Japan: An Overview of the 50 Postwar Years*, Tokyo: The Mainichi Shinbun.

Retherford, Robert D. and Naohiro Ogawa (2006), 'Japan's baby bust: causes, implications, and policy responses', in Fred R. Harris (ed.), *The Baby Bust: Who Will Do the Work? Who Will Pay the Taxes?*, Lanham, Maryland: Rowman & Littlefield, pp. 5–47.

Yoshikawa, Hiroshi (2001), *Japan's Lost Decade*, Tokyo: International House of Japan.

PART IV

Policy

9. Procreation, migration and tradable quotas

David de la Croix and Axel Gosseries[1]

Tradable quotas or permits as a rule aim at reducing negative externalities at the lowest possible cost.[2] They are especially suitable in contexts of imperfectly defined or hard-to-delimit (downward) property rights. Air pollution consisting of uniformly mixed pollutants (for example CO^2) provides a typical illustration. By the latter, we refer to pollutants such that the location (and sometimes the timing) of emissions does not affect the way the particles end up physically locating themselves in the atmosphere. For such uniformly mixed pollutants, a regulator concerned with reducing pollution levels can perfectly replace a command-and-control tool that imposes uniform targets on each of the polluting entities (typically a plant), with a scheme for trading quotas. Uniform mixing means that there are no risks of hot spots, that is, concentrations in given locations, which are potentially problematic if pollutants are prone to threshold effects. A tradable-quotas scheme thus consists of extending geographically the legal notion of 'source', shifting from a plant-based one to treating a whole area as a single source. In addition, such a scheme can also enlarge the temporal scope of the target by allowing for banking, that is, keeping pollution permits for use at a later period.

At the level of such enlarged spatio-temporal units, the pollution-reduction target can remain exactly the same in the aggregate as under a command-and-control regime. Yet, given the cost-reduction potential allowed for by the tradability of the pollution permits among pollution emitters, the pollution-reduction target can be set at an increasingly low level. For example, if a plant requires for its production a higher set of permits than the one initially received for the relevant period, it can buy additional permits on the market from other plants that have not fully used theirs. While not jeopardizing compliance with the global target of emission reduction, such flexibility granted to each plant, allowing it to better take into account differences in marginal abatement costs, has a clear cost-reduction effect.

Not only does the scheme allow one to take into account such inter-plant differences in marginal abatement costs, it simultaneously generates financial incentives for some plants to move below their own quotas and develop cleaner technologies. Such incentives will ease the pollution-reduction process by leaving more room for other plants to negotiate their transition in a globally more cost-effective way. In fact, regardless of its initial quota level, each polluter will have an interest in equalizing its marginal pollution-reduction cost with its gain from selling an extra permit. In short, tradable permits, by better taking into account differences in marginal reduction costs among the different emitters involved, allow for at least the same level of pollution reduction to be reached at a lesser cost, provided of course that a set of conditions is met, such as low transaction costs.[3] The command-and-control approach toward plants that produce emissions would certainly be stricter with firms, but it is ineffective when dealing with uniformly mixed pollutants. Moreover, it does not generate local incentives to move significantly below the pollution-abatement target.

Tradable permits can be compared with another key incentive-based mode of regulation: taxation. Whereas taxation focuses on price (the quantities emitted adapting accordingly), the tradable permits are focused on quantity (the prices of quotas adapting accordingly). Both allow in their own way taking into account differences in abatement costs among the polluters involved. As with taxation, while allowing for more efficient regulation, tradable-quotas schemes allow governments to take into consideration equity issues at three levels: first, in fixing the level of the global cap for the relevant region; second, in translating this cap into quotas and allocating them on the basis of an appropriate algorithm (when an auction is not relied upon); and, third, in setting restrictions (or not) on their tradability.[4] Without claiming that tradable quotas should be systematically preferred to other methods of regulation, we shall offer a preliminary account of what such proposals could entail in the field of population policy. One advantage of tradable quotas over taxes is that they require no information as to the responsiveness of households to incentives. The price of quotas will adjust to meet the objective, even if the relevant elasticities are small, yet there is no doubt that tradable quotas have their limitations. This is true whenever there are good reasons to be concerned with hot spots. It is also the case when the number of actors or the nature of the externality involved makes it difficult to administer quotas, when output restrictions are likely to lead to problematic effects at the input level, or when large price fluctuations occur.

Tradable-permits schemes have been widely implemented at the domestic level, especially in the United States, to deal with air pollution (see, for example, Ellerman et al., 2000, on the US Acid Rain Program); and it is now being put in place at the international level, as the Kyoto Protocol illustrates. Beyond the field of pollution control, such schemes have been implemented in the natural resources and agricultural domains to deal with either overexploitation (for example of fisheries or water reserves – see, for instance, Davidse, 1997) or overproduction (for example of milk or sugar beets – see, for instance, Cardwell, 1996). Interestingly, tradable quotas have also been proposed in a variety of other policy domains without being implemented, as far as we know. For example, in the field of inflation control, Lerner (1978) and Lerner and Colander (1980) designed a scheme allocating to firms tradable rights to increase wages not more than proportionally to the increase in general labor productivity. In employment policy, Salais (1994) proposed a scheme allocating to firms quotas limiting their right to 'workforce adjustment', aiming at reducing overdismissal and consequently the rate of unemployment.[5] In the public health field, Smith and Coast (1998) suggested a scheme of tradable permits of antimicrobial prescription to be allocated among general practitioners in order to address the problem of growing resistance to antimicrobials resulting from the overprescription of such drugs. Casella (1999) envisaged a scheme allocating to states tradable deficit permits in order to reach in a more cost-effective way the budget-deficit targets set at the European level.

This chapter is part of a wider project aiming at exploring such nonconventional applications of the mechanism, assessing both its promises and its limitations as precisely as possible. Here, insofar as population policy is concerned, we focus specifically on fertility and migration. Surprisingly, one of the first tradable-quotas proposals ever put forth was made in this field: Boulding's (1964) scheme of tradable procreation licenses to combat overpopulation. In contrast, in the area of migration, with the exception of imperfect forms of tradable-quotas schemes for dealing with asylum seekers and refugees (Schuck, 1997; Hathaway and Neve, 1997), we know of no tradable-quotas proposal.

In this chapter we shall thus proceed in two steps. In the area of fertility we shall first define the problem at issue and then draw upon Boulding's proposal, developing our own view on the matter. We shall describe our own proposal and spell out its likely effects. In the area of migration we shall again first specify the nature of the problem. Then we shall present two proposals, conjecturing some of the effects of one of them, comparing it more specifically with a Bhagwati tax.[6] As we go along we shall also keep an eye on parallels and differences between the schemes proposed in the fertility and migration fields.

Before proceeding, we should mention that our proposals may startle or shock some readers, for a variety of reasons. Let us mention just four of the possible objections and address each of them briefly. The first is that tradable-quotas proposals, insofar as they imply setting up markets, would be part of a hidden deregulation agenda. This does not need to be the case, once we consider both the fact that such proposals sometimes apply to areas that have not been regulated so far,[7] and the fact that the target-setting side of the scheme is as central as its market element, the latter being just a means of reaching the former in a more cost-effective way. The second objection is that, in the view of many, freedom of movement within a very large geographical area is a self-evident fundamental right. And many equally claim that the right to procreate should remain unrestricted. There is much to discuss about such an objection to tradable quotas on the grounds of their violating fundamental rights, but the discussion would probably revolve around two central issues. One reason for regarding a right as limited simply has to do with the fact that the interests it protects may be extended so broadly that those interests are not regarded as fundamental anymore.[8] Examples are having a very large number of children or claiming the right to visit any country in the world without restrictions. Another reason to limit the scope of rights, even when we remain within their core scope, is their possible conflict with the exercise of the very same right by others or with other rights. Moreover, other things than fundamental rights may also matter (such as equal opportunity for welfare). To be sure, at some level, a case can even be made for a fundamental right to pollute, since even our most basic survival activities necessarily entail emissions of pollutants such as CO^2. This does not mean that our right to pollute should have no limits, even if we argue that it constitutes a fundamental right.

The third and fourth sources of worries relate specifically to the two areas to which we propose to apply the idea of tradable quotas. One can be referred to as the 'people-as-pollution' objection. In the case of pollution permits, many people object to the very idea of allowing firms to make money out of what they may regard as an unconditionally bad behavior, that is, polluting. Conversely, many would object to regarding immigrants or newborns, both clearly persons worthy of moral respect, through the prism of negative externalities. As we shall see below, defining a level at which migration and procreation may be regarded as undesirable from the perspective of an impartial social planner is not an easy task. Even the notion that immigrants are costly to their host countries is challenged to a large extent by the available evidence. Still, targets for socially justifiable fertility rates or migration levels can make sense, whatever the difficulties involved in deciding what they should be. And if they do, they do not need to imply that human beings should be treated as particles of pollutants. Such targets would just mean that individuals' very existence (in the case of procreation) or their movements from one country to another (in the case of migration) have effects on others that should be given due consideration, out of the same basic respect for persons.

There is a final objection to tradable quotas that could be termed the 'people-as-commodities' one, which focuses on the tradability of quotas itself and what it means. Does it necessarily imply that people as such should be treated as mere tradable goods? The answer is, not more than when we pay a worker a wage for her labor, or when we ask someone for a price of a house, or when we grant subsidies to parents who decide to reproduce more than others.[9]

These are just a few of the possible objections to the proposals we discuss below. Boulding (1964) anticipated such reactions, admitting that his own proposal would be seen as 'far fetched', and to us it is an interesting sociological question why people may have such a reaction. One point is certain: the belief that such a proposal is 'unrealistic' is due in part to concerns of a normative nature that should be properly identified and considered. This means that what we are doing here is only – and necessarily – part of a larger picture.

FERTILITY

In this section we summarize in nonmathematical terms our main findings from an earlier study (de la Croix and Gosseries, 2006). For a more comprehensive and technical treatment, the reader is referred to that paper.

Under- and Overprocreation

In many countries the actual fertility rate is viewed as too high or too low. The perception of a gap between the actual rate and a preferred one, given the local or general circumstances, is triggered by various possible concerns. Typically concerns about overprocreation are related to concerns about the Earth's carrying and feeding capacity. This environmentalist perspective is especially vivid when it comes to the planet's global population. Other concerns may lead to an assessment of underprocreation, usually at the local level.

They may have to do with the relative sizes of various coexisting birth cohorts, which threaten the financial viability of pension schemes or health care systems. This is especially likely in cases of declining fertility or when other demographic factors (such as increases in life expectancy) require higher fertility to preserve appropriate relative sizes among cohorts. Population aging is not the only reason for concern about the fertility rates of a given population. Differential fertility among ethnic groups (such as among Roman Catholics and Protestants in Northern Ireland, or among first-generation immigrants and natives in many European capitals), or among groups with different educational levels may feed some people's concerns as well.

In short, there are concerns about the environment and natural resources that focus mostly (but not only) on the current global absolute fertility rate. And there is a whole set of concerns about relative fertility rates (differences in fertility among birth cohorts, age groups, ethnic groups, educational groups and so on) often at a regional or local level. Yet not all such concerns are well-informed or legitimate. For example, some of the concerns about the relative fertility of coexisting ethnic groups are clearly fed by attachment to inherited privileges, if not by xenophobic motives, that should be dealt with before we even consider regarding differential fertility rates as a legitimate source of concern.

There is also a philosophical problem that makes it especially difficult to set a meaningful target for an 'optimal' population size or composition. This problem, which Parfit (1984) called the 'repugnant conclusion', is absent when we decide to reduce or increase fertility rates strictly out of concern for already existing people. But excluding the people to come from any moral concern in this respect seems problematic. In contrast, if we are concerned about defining an optimal population, not merely with reference to already existing people, but also taking into account the welfare of the additional people who might exist as a result of our demographic choices, things become extremely tricky. Under a veil of ignorance, for example, it is unclear whether a 'representative individual' would prefer to take the risk of not coming to existence unless her life were to have a minimal quality.

To put it differently, it makes sense to consider that an action can be bad only if it negatively affects at least one person. Following this 'person-affecting' intuition, and adding a requirement of impartiality to it, there seems to be no reason to look only at the effect on already existing people (hence excluding future people) when asking whether a population size should be seen as optimal. If this is true, then the problem is that what we should decide and the beings with reference to whom we should make our decision could be mutually dependent.

In other words, should I take into consideration the well-being of Paul in deciding whether I should bring Paul into existence, even if I am sure that Paul would lead a minimally decent life and also knowing that, if Paul were not conceived, he could not possibly be harmed? We shall not attempt to answer this question here. The point is simply that defining a proper fertility rate with reference to an optimal population target, taking the well-being of future people into consideration, is not an easy task and may even be an impossible one.[10] In contrast, in the migration case that will be dealt with below, such a philosophical problem does not necessarily occur since it makes sense to assess migration targets merely with reference to how *existing* individuals are likely to fare as a result. Fixing the population of reference (those already alive as well as future people), the well-being of which should be our focus in deciding about procreation, is thus especially difficult. It is fundamentally more challenging than deciding about the population of reference (for example, all our contemporaries) when it comes to deciding about the desirability of a given migration pattern. This does not mean that defining a migration target will be devoid of other problems.

That said, different means can be envisaged for reaching desired fertility rates. And, while taking seriously the tradable-quotas proposal, we do not endorse the narrow view that this tool should be adopted as the exclusive one at all levels to deal with overpopulation, underprocreation, or both. To name but a few alternatives, in the case of underprocreation, we have seen, especially after World War II (and sometimes before) the introduction of generous family benefits, partly justified on pronatalist grounds. Extensive paid or unpaid parental leave, the public provision of day care and the availability of parent-friendly workplaces are also effective means for increasing fertility rates. In the case of overprocreation, information campaigns, free contraceptives, the improvement of women's education and access to the labor market (thus raising the age at which women have their first child) are common strategies.

Two remarks are in order here. First, it is clear that fertility is the only acceptable demographic variable that policymakers can influence when dealing with global overpopulation. Causing mortality to rise is morally unacceptable and relying upon migration is useless. In the case of underpopulation at the local level, all three demographic variables can be influenced: increasing fertility, reducing mortality and, for some of the problems listed above, increasing immigration. Second, in the case of overpopulation, as the means to reduce fertility become more coercive, serious concerns arise as to their effectiveness and fairness. Fairness in this case can be understood to refer to parents or to prospective parents, given the possibly unfair restriction of their interest in having children (with the qualifications mentioned above[11]) and to children, since any significant sanctions on parents who violate strict rules are likely to affect their dependent children, who did not choose to be born. One way of addressing these concerns could be to combine a tradable-quotas scheme at the international level with noncoercive, yet effective, measures at the domestic level.

Taking Boulding Seriously

Let us now move to Boulding's original proposal, advanced out of concern about overpopulation. He stated it as follows:

> I have only one positive suggestion to make, a proposal which now seems so far-fetched that I find it creates only amusement when I propose it. I think in all

seriousness, however, that a system of marketable licenses to have children is the only one which will combine the minimum of social control necessary to the solution to this problem with a maximum of individual liberty and ethical choice. Each girl on approaching maturity would be presented with a certificate which will entitle its owner to have, say, 2.2 children, or whatever number would ensure a reproductive rate of one. The unit of these certificates might be the 'deci-child,' and accumulation of ten of these units by purchase, inheritance, or gift would permit a woman in maturity to have one legal child. We would then set up a market in these units in which the rich and the philoprogenitive would purchase them from the poor, the nuns, the maiden aunts, and so on. The men perhaps could be left out of these arrangements, as it is only the fertility of women which is strictly relevant to population control. However, it may be found socially desirable to have them in the plan, in which case all children both male and female would receive, say, eleven or twelve deci-child certificates at birth or at maturity, and a woman could then accumulate these through marriage.

This plan would have the traditional advantage of developing a long-run tendency toward equality in income, for the rich would have many children and become poor and the poor would have few children and become rich. The price of the certificate would of course reflect the general desire in a society to have children. Where the desire is very high the price would be bid up; where it was low the price would also be low. Perhaps the ideal situation would be found when the price was naturally zero, in which case those who wanted children would have them without extra cost. If the price were very high the system would probably have to be supplemented by some sort of grants to enable the deserving but impecunious to have children, while cutting off the desires of the less deserving through taxation. The sheer unfamiliarity of a scheme of this kind makes it seem absurd at the moment. The fact that it seems absurd, however, is merely a reflection of the total unwillingness of mankind to face up to what is perhaps its most serious long-run problem. (Boulding, 1964, 135–6)

Heer (1975) and Daly (1991, 1993) discuss Boulding's proposal. Tobin (1970) makes a similar one.[12] Without discussing in detail each of the features of his proposal,[13] we wish to stress two significant ones. First, licenses would be allocated in principle to women only. While Boulding envisages making them accessible to men as well, through an initial allocation, purchase, inheritance or gift, he does not envisage the possibility that the state or another entity, such as an NGO, combating overpopulation, would be entitled to purchase them (see Heer, 1975 for a discussion of this point). Second, as to the distribution of the licenses, Boulding conjectures which categories of people would buy them and from whom (the rich from the poor but also from the philoprogenitive – among whom the poor may be overrepresented – and from nuns and maiden aunts); what its effects on inequalities of income would be (it would reduce them in the long run, possibly because the poor would sell some of their licenses to the rich and hence have fewer children themselves, the average income within the coming generations rising accordingly); and what should be done if license prices were to rise too much ('grants to enable the deserving but impecunious to have children').

We propose to modify and generalize Boulding's proposal. We first describe the model economy in which we are operating. It is populated by households differentiated by their productivity. Highly productive households (highly skilled workers) receive a higher wage income than the less productive (low-skilled) workers.[14] Households have the same preferences for consumption, number of children and education of their children. They have to decide how to spend their labor income by determining how much to consume for themselves, how many children to rear, and how much education to provide for each of them. Apart from education costs, the only cost related to childrearing is an opportunity cost: the more children they have, the more time they must spend rearing them instead of working in the labor market.[15] For highly skilled persons the opportunity cost of having children is relatively high compared with the cost of education. For low-skilled parents, the opposite holds. As a consequence, it will be optimal for highly skilled parents to have fewer children but to invest more in their children's education. This differential fertility pattern is in line with what is found in the data, both within countries and across countries if one considers national income levels. Differences in educational level have consequences for social mobility. Better-educated children have a greater probability of becoming highly skilled parents in the future than do less-educated ones, and this probability allows us to address issues of intergenerational equity.

Against this background, our twofold proposal can be summarized as follows. We envisage here a domestic form of the proposal. A government would set for each birth cohort a fertility objective of v children per person. This fertility objective would be pursued through the (possibly joint) operation of permits to procreate ('allowances') and permits not to procreate ('exemptions'). Coupling the two instruments (allowances for dealing with overprocreation and exemptions for dealing with underprocreation) gives room for more systematization of our theoretical exploration. In practice, their simultaneous operation in a given jurisdiction would allow the regulator to reach the fertility objective strictly (neither less nor more).[16]

We now detail the implementation sequence of procreation entitlements, considering first the sequence for allowances, which are designed to prevent fertility from being above the target. At her majority, every woman receives for nothing (not through an auction) v procreation permits, each of them corresponding to the right to give birth to one child. Each time she gives birth to a child, she must cede one procreation allowance back to the procreation agency. Procreation rights can be sold and purchased at any time at a market price. Next we consider the sequence for exemptions, which are designed to prevent fertility from remaining below the target. Each time a woman gives birth to a child, and as soon as her fertility becomes larger than the target v, she will receive free of charge from the procreation agency one exemption right per additional child. At the standard menopausal age, each woman who has fewer biological children than the target must give the procreation agency exemptions for the difference between the target and observed fertility, which she will have purchased on the procreation-exemptions market. Parents with more children than the target can sell on the market the unused exemptions. For example, if v were set at 1.1 child per parent, a couple would dispose of 2.2 permits to procreate. Imagine that they decide to have only one child. At that child's birth they will cede to the state one allowance. At the end of the mother's reproductive age span they will have had to buy 1.2 exemptions on the market. In contrast, if they end up having three children, they will have had to buy on the market 0.8 extra allowances. But they will also have received from the procreation agency 0.8 tradable exemptions.

Three Effects

Our concern is with the twofold impact of introducing such a scheme, that is, on the parents' income and on the educational level of their children. Exploring the model allows us to identify three key effects that we shall briefly discuss below. To emphasize the two first effects on income inequalities, we start with the plainest case of fixed, rather than tradable, quotas allocated on an equality per capita basis. A third effect will then become apparent as we take into consideration the tradable nature of allowances and exemptions.[17]

The first effect we single out can be called the 'differential-productivity effect'. In describing it we restrict ourselves to a case in which we aim at combating overpopulation and assume for a moment that low-income and high-income people have the same fertility level (we call this a 'uniform-fertility world'). We now introduce a population target lower than the business-as-usual fertility level. Such a target is translated in turn through equal per capita nontradable allowances. The fertility level of our two classes of people, that is, the skilled (high-income) and the unskilled (low-income), will be reduced to the same extent. This means that both the skilled and the unskilled will increase their income as a result of the increased working time made available through the reduction of their fertility. However, although both are reducing their fertility and increasing as a result the time they spend working to the same extent, the hourly wages of the skilled are greater than those of the unskilled. This means that, in such a world of uniform fertility, the introduction of a fixed-quota scheme on a per capita basis will actually increase income inequalities between the unskilled and the skilled. The incomes of the skilled will increase relatively more than those of the unskilled.

Let us now relax the 'uniform-fertility' assumption and shift to a more realistic world in which unskilled people tend to have more children than skilled people. This will allow us to consider a second type of effect, the 'initial differential-fertility effect'. Given the assumption that quotas are allocated on a per capita basis and that they are fixed, imposing our global population target will require that skilled and unskilled people adopt the same fertility level. Since, in the business-as-usual case, skilled people have fewer children than unskilled people, the unskilled people will have to reduce their fertility more than skilled ones. Doing so in turn means that the unskilled will increase their working time more than the skilled people. Hence, if this were the only effect at work, introducing a fixed and equal per capita quota regime in a context of differential fertility would tend to reduce income inequalities.

In short, if a fixed and equal per capita quota regime were introduced, the effect of differential productivity on relative income is such that income inequalities could be expected to increase, whereas the effect of differential initial fertility on relative income would tend to reduce income inequalities between the two groups. Since the two effects point in opposite directions, which of them is likely to dominate? Given our account of the background economy, the initial differential fertility will be the key variable. If it is large, the differential-fertility effect could well dominate the differential-productivity effect, rendering our nontradable-quotas scheme redistributive. One parameter affecting the initial discrepancy between the fertility of the rich and that of the poor is the elasticity of educational outcomes in response to investment in education. If this elasticity is large, that is, if educational outcomes tend to react significantly enough to marginal increases in educational investments, the incentive for the highly skilled parents to educate their children is strong, causing them to choose a small number of children.

A third effect on income inequalities arises from the introduction of tradability. Let us imagine that we move from fixed quotas, allocated on an equal per capita basis, to a scheme allowing for the tradability of such quotas. To determine the effect of this change on inequality, it is first necessary to identify the sign of the procreation price. The procreation price is the market value of procreation entitlements. A negative price implies that fertility is encouraged, that is, exemptions have a positive value while allowances have no value. A positive price implies that fertility is discouraged: exemptions have no value whereas allowances are costly. Depending on the price of the allowances and of the exemptions, this effect will tend either to reduce income inequalities or to increase them, owing to the interplay of tradability with differential fertility and differential productivity. More precisely, there are actually three relevant scenarios in this respect.

First, if the procreation price is negative, fertility is encouraged, which means that the unskilled will tend to have more children than the fertility target and the skilled will tend to have fewer. In such a case tradability will lead to rich-to-poor cash transfers, the unskilled selling their exemptions to skilled people.

Second, when the procreation price is positive and large, the cost of having children becomes very significant. And this cost as a fraction of income is larger for the poor than for the rich, given the productivity differential. This leads to a situation in which skilled people actually have more children than the population target and unskilled people have fewer. The former will thus buy allowances from the latter, leading to significant rich-to-poor cash transfers.

Third, there is an intermediate scenario in which the price of allowances is both positive and small. In such a case the productivity differential is not sufficient to make the low price of allowances attractive enough for the unskilled to change their business-as-usual fertility level. Given the business-as-usual fertility differential, they will buy allowances from skilled people, and this in turn will lead to poor-to-rich cash transfers, hence to an increase in income inequalities. Is this third scenario of practical importance? Yes, because, in the case of reform aiming at reducing population, the need for political feasibility will require the fertility target to be set at a level not much lower than the actual average fertility rate. In such a case, the price of allowances is unlikely to be high. This means that, if we consider the tradability effect alone, a population control policy will tend, in practice, to be anti-redistributive. However, knowing whether this is the case once we consider the three effects examined here is a different matter.

So far we have considered three possible effects on income of introducing a scheme for tradable procreation allowances and exemptions. A full empirical and normative assessment of the effects of such a scheme would of course require much more than that. One would need to find out which of the three effects dominates in actual circumstances. One would have to determine as well the extent to which the overall impact on income inequalities is actually relevant to analyzing the scheme's impact on welfare inequalities of skilled and unskilled people. Moreover, one would have to look at the interplay between the scheme's overall impact on income differentials and its impact on educational achievements of the next generation. One situation that may occur is that, with a pronatalist policy, tradability may reduce income inequalities within the generation of parents but worsen the average educational level of their children; and this in turn could increase the income inequalities between the two generations. Finally, a crucial variation in the scheme would consist of setting quotas for countries rather than for individuals. This would possibly permit the implementation of effective domestic policies that would not be quota-based (for example, raising the educational level of women in poor countries) and simultaneously a tradable-quotas scheme at the interstate level, with the hope of achieving the best of both worlds.

MIGRATION

Under- and Overmigration

We now briefly explore the tradable-quotas idea as a tool for migration policy. As in the case of procreation, it is crucial to understand, among all the possible goals, which one the proposed scheme would be pursuing here. First, one may want to reach a certain level of migration out of concern for protecting the environment and natural resources. Both the frequency of migratory moves and the dispersion of residences and firms they may lead to can be environmentally unfriendly. Second, migrations may raise concerns of a cultural nature.[18] Admittedly, they sometimes reduce cultural and linguistic heterogeneity: for example, when driven by family-grouping motives or when members of Diasporas move back to their motherland. Yet in many cases the perception is that migration increases local cultural and linguistic heterogeneity, requiring the accommodation of very different practices, the coexistence (compossibility) of which cannot be guaranteed a priori.

Without prejudging the importance and (absence of) legitimacy of such environmental and cultural sources of concern about migration, we focus here on the impact of emigration on the wealth of the countries of origin. Migration targets may be set with the aim of maximizing aggregate global wealth or with the view of reducing inequalities of wealth between poorer countries of migrants' origin and richer countries of their destination. To be sure, there may be an economic case for concentrating certain activities involving skilled workers in some areas of the globe (see, for example, Fujita and Thisse, 2002). Doing so could increase aggregate global wealth. In the absence of a global fiscal jurisdiction, however, the usual tax-and-transfers channel is not available for translating such an increase in global wealth into redistributive transfers. Moreover, if we were concerned about equalizing wages only, *ceteris paribus* there could be a case for fully open borders, which would go against the idea of tradable quotas since the latter presupposes a target. Yet there could be other reasons not to opt for fully open borders, for example the loss of human capital-generated positive externalities and concerns for the viability of fragile democracies or of advanced social security systems. If some of these reasons for restricting free movement are legitimate, tradable quotas may be part of the second-best set of options that could serve the purpose of reducing global inequalities through the engineering of each of the scheme's three components (target, allocation of quotas and tradability).

In the case of procreation, one of the options is to have a joint policy addressing both local underprocreation and global overprocreation. In the case of migration the problem is not that local and global policies operate in opposition. Rather, it is that we must deal with two sides of the same coin simultaneously: that is, the possible undermigration of unskilled workers and the risk of overmigration of skilled workers beyond the point at which brain drain would worsen the situation in the poor country of origin. To put it differently, although the introduction of a scheme of tradable procreation quotas would definitely affect the educational level of the next generation, that effect does not need to be its very goal (rather than a mere side-effect). In contrast, in the migration case, achieving a certain global distribution of skilled and unskilled people would be regarded as the scheme's central goal. Moreover, in the case of procreation, we are concerned about achieving both a global cap on population size and the distribution of the corresponding quotas among countries. In the migration case, while environmentalists or others may want to impose a global cap on the amount of international migration for a given period, we limit ourselves here to focusing on net movements of skilled and unskilled people between poor and rich countries.

More precisely, we start by conjecturing that the current level of migration by unskilled workers is lower than what is good for the countries of origin.[19] As to the levels of migration of skilled workers, it could at some point exceed a level of brain drain viewed as desirable from the point of view of reducing global inequalities. The proposed scheme, or set of measures, would aim at allowing the productivity-enhancing concentration of highly skilled people while limiting it out of concern for the need to retain a certain proportion of skilled workers in their countries of origin – a concern for having a ratio of skilled to unskilled workers similar to the concern for preserving a certain ratio of working to nonworking people through a tradable procreation quotas scheme. Whereas countries experiencing aging are mostly concerned about the shrinking proportion of workers in relation to children or pensioners, countries experiencing massive emigration tend to be concerned about the shrinking proportion of skilled workers. Before describing the actual proposals, we note that they can be coupled with other measures, such as an increase in official development aid or the relaxation of trade barriers.

Proposal 1: tradable emigration permits among skilled individuals

The traditional view is that brain drain is a threat to the country of origin because it deprives it of its most talented citizens. Yet a recent literature argues that, up to a certain level, brain drain is actually beneficial to the country of origin. At least three mechanisms underlie such a beneficial effect. First, remittances sent back to the country of origin by working emigrants constitute a nonnegligible transfer (Faini, 2006; Cinar and Docquier, 2004). Second, a real chance of emigrating may have a positive influence on schooling decisions by households, among which some will stay at home: people may be willing to improve their skills in the expectation of earning a better income abroad (Beine, Docquier and Rapoport, 2003). Third, besides affecting the decision of whether or not to invest in higher education, enhanced opportunities for skilled people to work abroad may also affect the types of skills in which they invest. Mariani (2006) argues, for example, that increased chances of skilled migration raise the expected profits from investing in skills valued abroad and simultaneously decrease rents from rent-seeking activities. Given such effects, it is possible, at least in theory, to identify an emigration rate that maximizes some wealth, income or welfare objective for the poor country. Calculating this figure would require not just identifying the factors that would maximize human capital production at home, but also taking into account such things as remittances and positive Diaspora externalities. It may well be that brain drain is detrimental to the wealth of the poor country of origin only once a high threshold has been crossed (Beine, Docquier and Rapoport, 2003). We call such a threshold a 'fair brain-drain threshold'. Whereas the nondetrimental level of brain drain may be within the range of 15 to 20 percent, on average, of the native skilled labor force, the maximizing target may possibly range from 5 to 10 percent. Beyond this level, brain drain is likely to start having adverse effects on the country of origin. Below it, the net social return of the emigration of skilled workers remains positive in the generally poor country of origin, while not being as high as it could be.

So, each country of emigration would have to specify a domestic cap on annual or quinquennial skilled emigration. Once this 'fair brain-drain' cap has been identified, our first proposal consists in setting up at the domestic level, that is in the country of origin, a scheme of tradable emigration rights among skilled individuals only. Whether citizens belong to the skilled category could be decided by reference to their educational level or an equivalent recognition of skills. The cap would be stated in terms of the number of skilled people allowed to work abroad over a given period. The total number of skilled people in the population would be divided by the number of people allowed to emigrate. This fraction would yield the quota that each skilled citizen would be granted for a given period. For example, if the number of skilled people in the population were 1000 (we assume counterfactually that this figure is exogenous) and only 100 of them were allowed to leave the country, each skilled person would be granted a tradable emigration permit having a value of 0.1. Someone wishing to emigrate would thus have to buy nine extra permits to be entitled to work abroad. There would be a market for such permits.

Unskilled people would not be subject to this scheme, emigration being thus freer in their case, at least on the exit side. Among the important design issues, one would have to decide whether the permits for skilled workers were to be for permanent or temporary emigration, a possible variation that does not obtain in the procreation case, for obvious moral reasons.

How does this proposal for tradable emigration permits compare with a Bhagwati tax? The latter typically consists of an income tax levied by the country of residence on a skilled immigrant, the proceeds of which are sent back to the immigrant's country of origin (Bhagwati and Partington, 1976; Bhagwati and Hamada, 1982). It is thus an income tax that applies abroad to a country's nationals who emigrate, and therefore belongs to the 'global', citizenship-based model of income tax as opposed to the 'schedular', or residence-based model.[20] What makes it special is that it is aimed specifically at skilled workers, pursuing the specific purpose of addressing the problem of brain drain. Tradable emigration quotas would differ in several respects. First, under our proposal, the tax money would not need to be collected abroad. Hence a quota would not be vulnerable to income-tax paradise problems. Admittedly, however, a fiscal substitute for our tradable emigration permits proposal could take the form of an exit tax, to be collected by the country of origin before the emigrant crossed the border.[21] It would be difficult, however, to make an exit tax sensitive to the emigrant's expected income in the host country. This point connects with a second difference between our proposal and the Bhagwati tax. In the tax case the amount paid by each emigrant fluctuates with the income received in the host country. Under our proposal the market price for permits would rise with the income level abroad (as a general equilibrium effect), but the amount paid to emigrate would not be so closely connected to a worker's actual income in the host country as in the case of a progressive Bhagwati tax. Third, with our proposal the level of emigration would not be sensitive to fluctuations of expected return from emigration, but the price of permits would be. Fourth, in principle – at least if the emigration quotas were subject to a free-of-charge initial allocation rather than to an auction – the money paid would go into the pockets of only skilled people, rather than into the general budget of the state, which would then decide about its use.

Our proposal also differs in at least two ways from Becker's proposal of an entrance fee in potential countries of immigration (Becker, 2005).[22] First, as in the tax case, the fee mechanism is price-focused rather than quantity-focused. Second, the fee, given its supposed uniformity, is unlikely to translate the different national emigration optima obtaining in the countries of origin. In other words, the fee will be the same regardless of the country of origin and regardless of the fact that one country of origin would already have reached its optimal emigration target, or 'fair brain-drain target', whereas another would not.

What are the likely effects of our emigration-permits proposal? Let us compare them with the well-documented effects of a Bhagwati tax. In doing so we first concentrate on the proposal's effect on income inequalities in the country of origin. As we have said, one specific feature of the permits proposal is that the permits would be allocated to skilled workers only, as if, in the case of a tax, the proceeds were distributed to skilled people only.[23] Hence, because of this allocation to skilled workers only, tradable permits are likely to increase income inequalities between skilled and unskilled workers, in contrast with a world of free movement. That is not the case with a Bhagwati tax, unless the proceeds are distributed in an anti-redistributive manner (which we exclude here). This is true at least if we leave aside general-equilibrium effects on the wage differential via the local labor market (see, for example, Bhagwati and Hamada, 1974).

A second type of effect is the one on incentives to invest in higher education. Let us suppose that the taste for migration differs among the population. When it comes to deciding whether or not to invest in higher education, those with little taste for migration (home-loving people) are likely to stay home anyway, whatever policy is put in place (free movement, Bhagwati tax or tradable emigration permits). In their case, the Bhagwati tax will not affect their incentive to educate themselves. This is so because the tax affects only foreign income and the proceeds are distributed independently of the skill level of recipients. In the case of permits, they would accrue only to skilled workers. That being so, they would raise the skill premium at home, generating an incentive to acquire an education. The situation is reversed when we shift from the home-loving to those having a strong taste for migration (or a low mobility cost). If we abandoned free movement, the skilled persons going abroad would see a reduction in their income prospects, regardless of whether we are dealing with permits or with a Bhagwati tax. For those persons, both systems reduce the incentive to pursue an education.

These are just two effects of the proposed scheme. Many more should be looked at, including the effects on social mobility in the country of origin, the difference it makes if higher education is publicly funded or not, and the effect on incentives to education resulting from the fact that, in our model, unskilled people are freer to move than skilled ones. Moreover, an assessment of the overall effect of the proposal on income inequalities would be needed. This would require an assessment of the interplay between the reduction of international income inequalities pursued by the target on emigration set by the country of origin, and the likely increase in domestic income inequalities generated by the proposal. The effect on education should also be assessed through its consequences on international income inequalities.

Proposal 2: tradable reception duties among host countries for unskilled immigrants

The emigration of unskilled, as opposed to skilled, migrants may also have a beneficial effect on poor countries of origin (World Bank, 2005, 64–6). Above and beyond the benefits from remittances, the mere fact of reducing the supply of unskilled labor locally raises the wages of those who stay. Moreover, in the case of temporary emigration, a skill-upgrade effect may result when workers are confronted with different work practices abroad. This skill upgrade will benefit productivity back home once the emigrants return to resume working at home. In many cases, however, potential host countries are reluctant to accept large numbers of unskilled migrants.

One way of increasing access by unskilled workers from poor countries to jobs in rich ones is analogous to the process that Hathaway and Neve (1997) and Schuck (1997) propose for dealing with asylum-seekers. For a given regional area (such as the European Union) the current amount of immigration by unskilled workers would be assessed. This assessment would serve as a baseline aggregate immigration level. The introduction of a scheme involving tradable reception duties could achieve a threefold goal. First, to the extent that unskilled workers are seen as a burden for the host countries (which is admittedly very disputable), the initial allocation of such quotas could be done in such a way as to distribute the 'burden' more fairly than is currently done.[24] Possible allocation criteria would include population size, GDP per capita and the territorial size of the receiving country. Second, one could move away from the baseline and set the number of unskilled immigrants allowed to enter progressively higher, up to a level at which immigration would become detrimental to the country or countries of origin or undesirable for other reasons. Here again a tradable-quotas scheme can serve the goal of increasing immigration rather than restricting it. Third, the tradability of such quotas would allow fairer burden sharing among receiving countries while introducing some flexibility into the system, and would tend to reduce the aggregate costs (if any) of accepting a certain number of unskilled workers. There would be an international market in which some countries would pay other countries to welcome more unskilled workers than their quotas in exchange for money. In the case of asylum-seekers, such a scheme, limited to receiving countries, could be said to be incomplete because quotas would be allocated to states not directly responsible for the creation of refugees. They would thus need to be 'percentage quotas' since the number of people seeking asylum or qualifying as refugees could not be determined beforehand by the prospective host countries, the criteria used to determine which people qualify as refugees being defined independently. In contrast, with our proposal there is no such problem of incompleteness since the goal is not primarily to make sure that as few people as possible remain unskilled and since the receiving countries could freely decide on the aggregate level of unskilled immigrants that would be fair for them to accept.

CONCLUSION

Throughout this chapter we have emphasized the many differences between issues of procreation and migration. And we have stressed the fact that tradable-quotas schemes have limitations, like any other policy mechanism. Yet we believe that the properties of such schemes, including the distributive ones, should be investigated by social scientists, even in unusual applications such as moderating fertility and optimizing brain-drain policies. At this stage it would be premature to draw general conclusions as to the desirability of setting up such schemes. Several points deserve emphasis, however.

Tradable procreation quotas should be considered first. An international rather than a domestic regime, coupled with effective but noncoercive domestic measures, such as raising women's educational level as well as their access to the labor market, may be politically the most promising avenue for tradable quotas in that area. We have focused here on three effects. The initial differential-fertility effect and the productivity-differential effect have opposite signs. Moreover, the tradability effect, if political constraints are taken seriously, is likely to be anti-redistributive. Its relative weight, however, is not totally clear. These three effects on income inequalities need to be carefully studied in connection with their effects on educational levels.

When we consider the case of tradable emigration quotas, we see again that a great deal of complexity is involved. We find significant differences between it and a Bhagwati tax at various levels. The possibility exists that the scheme for tradable emigration quotas will end up having significant strengths when compared with the Bhagwati tax proposal. In our future research we plan to address the issues raised by tradable emigration rights and tradable reception duties within the framework of general equilibrium models.

NOTES

1. We warmly thank Gustaf Arrhenius, Thierry Bréchet, Alexandra Casella, Frédéric Docquier, Gregory Ponthière, Edoardo Traversa and Yannick Vanderborght for comments on earlier drafts of this chapter.
2. On the difference between efficiency and cost-effectiveness, see Smith and Coast (1998, 221).
3. For detailed information on tradable pollution permits, see Dales (1968), Montgomery (1972) and Tietenberg (2001). For an introductory piece, see Ellerman (2005).
4. For a discussion of fairness issues in the context of climate change, see Gosseries (2006).
5. For a different scheme in the employment field, see Hamminga (1995).
6. A Bhagwati tax is a tax by a developing country on the income of emigrants residing in developed countries. This idea was proposed by economist Jagdish Bhagwati as a method for a developing country to recover its investment in the human capital of citizens who, after receiving educational subsidies, migrate to developed countries in order to earn higher incomes.
7. See Ellerman (2005, 129) on *de novo* regulation.
8. On the right to procreate, see, e.g., Statman (2003).
9. For an interesting treatment of the commodification debate, see Sandel (1998).
10. For a philosophical treatment of this matter, see Arrhenius (2000a, 2000b). For economic discussions see Nerlove, Razin and Sadka (1989); Blackorby, Bossert and Donaldson (1995); Golosov and Tertilt (2006); Michel and Wigniolle (2007).
11. See Sen (1996).
12. LaFollette (1980) proposed licensing parenthood out of concern for making sure that people would be able to meet the high demands of parental responsibility. His proposal leads to a restriction on the freedom to procreate, with two significant differences from our proposal. On the one hand, it would go against the proposal's very spirit to make such licenses tradable. On the other hand, once the license is granted under LaFollette's scheme, there is no limit to the number of children one would be entitled to have.
13. For such a discussion, see de la Croix and Gosseries (2006).
14. For the purposes of this discussion we use the words 'skilled' and 'highly skilled' as synonyms, and 'unskilled' and 'low-skilled' as synonyms as well.
15. Allowing for low-skilled nannies would mitigate this effect but could not remove it entirely.
16. We do not discuss in detail here how to deal with such questions as how child mortality should be taken into account, whether the model can address the possibility of divorce, whether it will too strongly disadvantage single parents, whether it might encourage fathers not to recognize their paternity so as not to have to cede their allowances, whether cohort-specific population targets allow for less flexibility than period-based targets, what to do about women able to have children beyond the normal childbearing period, and so on.
17. Here we leave aside a fourth possible effect that occurs in the case of a grandfathered allocation (that is, based on the procreation level as reached in a given base year), rather than made initially on an equal per capita basis. Such an allocation is plausible in the case of an interstate scheme. Compared with the pollution-control case, the initial differential fertility rate is such that the grandfathering effect, taken alone, would be more redistributive than an equal per capita allocation: contrary to the pollution case, in which richer people generally lead more energy-intensive lives. See de la Croix and Gosseries (2006) for further discussion of this effect.

18. Such a cultural concern, beyond the ethnic one, is present in the procreation debate too. One aspect of the concern about an aging population is that a society with a higher proportion of old people will have different values from those of a younger society, likely as a result of both age and cohort effects. What is at stake in this case is not too great a cultural diversity, but rather the reverse risk of cultural domination by a specific age group or birth cohort. See, for example, Hinrichs (2002).
19. For the view that it also turns out to be lower than what is good for host countries, see Pritchett (2006).
20. On the distinction between global and schedular models of income taxation, see Bhagwati (1982).
21. For an example of exit tax, see Colombo (1998).
22. See Becker's blog, 'Sell the Right to Immigrate', http://www.becker-posner-blog.com/archives/2005/02/sell_the_right.html.
23. We concentrate on the proceeds-distribution side only insofar as the effects on income inequalities are concerned, leaving aside the levying dimension.
24. Drinkwater et al. (2003) describe in detail the conditions under which the immigration of unskilled labor is actually beneficial to host countries.

REFERENCES

Arrhenius, Gustaf (2000a), 'Future generations. A challenge for moral theory', PhD thesis, Uppsala University.

Arrhenius, Gustaf (2000b), 'An impossibility theorem for welfarist axiologies', *Economics and Philosophy*, **16**, 247–66.

Becker, Gary (2005), 'Sell the right to immigrate', http://www.becker-posner-blog.com/archives/2005/02/sell_the_right.html.

Beine, Michel, Frédéric Docquier and Hillel Rapoport (2003), 'Brain drain and LDC's growth: winners and losers', Discussion Paper, Institute for the Study of Labor (IZA), Bonn.

Bhagwati, Jagdish (1982), 'Introduction', *Journal of Public Economics*, **18**, 285–9.

Bhagwati, Jagdish N. and Koichi Hamada (1974), 'The brain drain, international integration of markets for professionals and unemployment: a theoretical analysis', *Journal of Development Economics*, **1**, 19–24.

Bhagwati, Jagdish N. and Koichi Hamada (1982), 'Tax policy in the presence of emigration', *Journal of Public Economics*, **18**, 291–317.

Bhagwati, Jagdish and Martin Partington (1976), *Taxing the Brain Drain: A Proposal*, vol. 1, Amsterdam: North Holland.

Blackorby, C., W. Bossert and D. Donaldson (1995), 'Intertemporal population ethics: critical-level utilitarian principles', *Econometrica*, **63**(6), 1303–20.

Boulding, K. (1964), *The Meaning of the Twentieth Century*, New York: Harper and Row.

Cardwell, M. (1996), *Milk Quotas*, Oxford: Clarendon Press.

Casella, Alexandra (1999), 'Tradable deficit permits: efficient implementation of the stability pact', *Economic Policy*, **29**, 323–47.

Cinar, Dilek and Frédéric Docquier (2004), 'Brain drain and remittances: implications for the source country', *Brussels Economic Review*, **47**(1), 103–18.

Colombo, John D. (1998), 'A proposal for an exit tax on nonprofit conversion transactions', *Journal of Corporation Law*, **23**, 779–802.

Dales, J.H. (1968), *Pollution, Property and Prices. An Essay on Policy-Making in Economics*, Toronto: Toronto University Press.

Daly, Herman (1991), *Steady-State Economics*, 2nd edn, Washington, DC: Island Press.
Daly, Herman (1993), 'The steady-state economy: toward a political economy of biophysical equilibrium and moral growth', in Herman Daly and K. Townsend (eds), *Valuing the Earth: Economics, Ecology, Ethics*, Cambridge and London: MIT Press, pp. 325–63.
Davidse, W. (ed.) (1997), *Property Rights in Fishing*, The Hague: Agricultural Economics Research Institute (LEI-DLO).
De la Croix, David and Axel Gosseries (2006), 'Population policy through tradable procreation entitlements', Discussion Paper 2006/81, CORE, Louvain-la-Neuve.
Drinkwater, Stephen, Paul Levine, Emanuela Lotti and Joseph Pearlman (2003), 'The economic impact of migration: a survey', Discussion Paper 8, Flowenla (HWWA), Hamburg.
Ellerman, A. Denny (2005), 'Note on tradeable permits', *Environmental and Resource Economics*, **31**, 123–31.
Ellerman, D., P. Joskow, R. Schmalensee, J.-P. Montero and E. Bailey (2000), *Markets for Clean Air: The U.S. Acid Rain Program*, Cambridge: Cambridge University Press.
Faini, Riccardo (2006), 'Remittances and the brain drain', Discussion Paper no. 5720, CEPR, London.
Fujita, Masahisa and Jacques-François Thisse (2002), *Economics of Agglomeration*, Cambridge: Cambridge University Press.
Golosov, Jones and Michele Tertilt (2006), 'Efficiency with endogenous population growth', *Econometrica*, in press.
Gosseries, Axel (2006), 'Cosmopolitan luck egalitarianism and climate change', *Canadian Journal of Philosophy Supplementary Volume Series*, in press.
Hamminga, B. (1995), 'Demoralizing the labour market: could jobs be like cars and concerts?', *Journal of Political Philosophy*, **3**(1), 23–35.
Hathaway, James and A. Neve (1997), 'Making international refugee law relevant again: a proposal for a collectivized and solution-oriented protection', *Harvard Human Rights Journal*, **10**, 115–212.
Heer, D. (1975), 'Marketable licenses for babies: Boulding's proposal revisited', *Social Biology*, **22**(1), 1–16.
Hinrichs, Karl (2002), 'Do the old exploit the young? Is enfranchising children a good idea?', *European Journal of Sociology*, **43**(1), 35–58.
LaFollette, H. (1980), 'Licensing parents', *Philosophy and Public Affairs*, **9**(winter), 182–97.
Lerner, A. (1978), 'The market as a cure to stagflation', University of California, Berkeley, 8 June, seminar paper.
Lerner, Abba and David C. Colander (1980), *MAP: A Market Anti-Inflation Plan*, New York: Harcourt Brace Jovanovich.
Mariani, Fabio (2006), 'Migration as an antidote to rent-seeking', mimeo, EUREQUA, University of Paris 1.
Michel, Philippe and Bertrand Wigniolle (2007), 'On efficient child making', *Economic Theory*, **31**(2), 307–26.
Montgomery, W.D. (1972), 'Markets in licenses and efficient pollution control programs', *Journal of Economic Theory*, **5**(3), 395–418.
Nerlove, M., A. Razin and E. Sadka (1989), 'Socially optimal population size and individual choice', in K. Zimmermann (ed.), *Economic Theory of Optimal Population*, pp. 19–38.

Parfit, Derek (1984), *Reasons and Persons*, Oxford: Clarendon Press.
Pritchett Lant (2006), *Let Their People Come: Breaking the Gridlock on Global Labor Mobility*, Washington, DC: Center for Global Development.
Salais, R. (1994), 'Politiques d'emploi et normes sociales: Esquisse d'une analogie avec les politiques de l'environnement', mimeo, Groupement de recherches Institutions, Emploi et Politique Economique, Paris.
Sandel, M. (1998), 'What money can't buy: the moral limits of markets', *The Tanner Lectures on Human Values*, Salt Lake City: University of Utah, pp. 87–122.
Schuck, Peter (1997), 'Refugee burden-sharing: a modest proposal', *Yale Journal of International Law*, **22**(2), 243–97.
Sen, Amartya (1996), 'Fertility and coercion', *University of Chicago Law Review*, **63**(3), 1035–61.
Smith, Richard and Joanna Coast (1998), 'Controlling antimicrobial resistance: a proposed transferable permit market', *Health Policy*, **43**, 219–32.
Statman, Daniel (2003), 'The right to parenthood: an argument for a narrow interpretation', *Ethical Perspectives*, **10**, 224–35.
Tietenberg, Tom (ed.) (2001), *Emissions Trading Programs*, vol. I, *Implementation and Evolution*; vol. II, *Theory and Design*, Aldershot, Lancaster: Ashgate Publishing.
Tobin, James (1970), 'On limiting the domain of inequality', *Journal of Law and Economics*, **13**(2), 263–77.
World Bank (2005), *Global Economic Prospects 2006: Economic Implications of Remittances and Migration*, Washington, DC.

10. Australia's Future Fund: a social welfare analysis

Ross Guest

This chapter evaluates Australia's Future Fund from a social welfare perspective. The Fund is a vehicle for tax smoothing whereby the federal government plans to run budget surpluses that will be deposited into a fund to be managed by an independent board of directors. The accumulation phase of the Fund will continue until at least 2020, after which funds can be withdrawn for the specific purpose of meeting the federal government's superannuation liabilities. Creation of the Future Fund is motivated by the desire to smooth out the fiscal costs of population aging, one such cost being the government's superannuation liabilities. The economic rationale for this, although not explicitly articulated by the government, appears to be twofold: an efficiency argument based on minimizing the deadweight losses from taxation, and an intergenerational equity argument by which it is considered equitable to reduce the taxation burden on future young generations that would otherwise be associated with the fiscal costs of funding the retirement incomes and health expenditures of an older population.

The chapter begins with a discussion of the anticipated operation of the Future Fund and the way in which it shifts the taxation burden of population aging between generations: current generations bear a greater tax burden, and future generations a lesser burden, than they would under continuously balanced budgets. Simulations are then reported of the efficiency and equity effects of the Fund based on an overlapping-generations Computable General Equilibrium (CGE) model. Although the simulations are stylized, they serve to illustrate how tax smoothing brings unambiguous efficiency gains but has implications for intergenerational equity that are less clear-cut because it tends to create generations of winners and losers. These efficiency and intergenerational equity effects are weighed here by means of a social welfare function. The conclusion is that tax smoothing of the order implied by the Fund yields net gains in social welfare that range from 0.15 to 0.55 percent in equivalent annual increases in GDP, which implies gains of between $60 and $220 per year per person, given a population of 20 million and a GDP of $800 billion. Positive net gains such as these provide support for tax smoothing. Other considerations that the simulations do not capture, however, make the policy of tax smoothing via the Future Fund more controversial than these simulation results suggest.

There have been other studies of the macroeconomic implications of tax smoothing in the context of population aging. In a seminal study of the macroeconomics of population aging for the United States, Cutler et al. (1990) found trivially small gains from tax smoothing of the costs of aging. Floden (2003) has argued that the findings of Cutler and his associates apply to the US only because tax rates there are relatively low. He found the efficiency gains to be nontrivial for a number of other OECD countries that have higher tax burdens. Both of these studies applied infinitely lived dynasty models and were therefore unable to say anything about intergenerational equity. Oksanen (2003), in a study for the European Commission, was concerned with intergenerational fairness of tax smoothing in response to population aging; but he applied a simple partial equilibrium analysis. He concluded in favor of partial smoothing on intergenerational equity grounds. Davis and Fabling (2002) estimated the efficiency gains of smoothing the costs of aging in New Zealand. They found gains a little larger than those found by Cutler and his associates but smaller than those found by Floden. Theirs was also a partial analysis based on a calibrated deadweight loss function. The innovation in the present study is that it uses a multisector, overlapping-generations CGE model to trace explicitly the effects of tax smoothing on each age cohort and attempts to weigh both efficiency and equity effects by using a social welfare function. A more technical explanation of the simulation model that is applied here can be found in Guest (2006), which discusses the equity and efficiency effects of tax smoothing in Australia, but without the detailed discussion of the Future Fund.

The analysis requires an overlapping-generations model, which allows us to identify winners and losers from tax smoothing. The fact that some generations lose from tax smoothing and others win implies the need for some method of evaluating the gains against the losses in social welfare. The social welfare function employed here uses alternative value judgments regarding the choice of a discount rate in valuing the utility of future generations on the basis of time, and society's degree of aversion to inequality between generations at a given point in time.

The idea that governments should smooth the tax burden over time was first advanced by Barro (1979). He showed that, in a deterministic setting, a constant tax rate over time would minimize the distortions in behavior arising from taxation. In doing so he assumed that the distortions would increase more than proportionally to increases in the tax rate, a finding that had already been established analytically by Harberger (1964), cited in

Browning (1987). An important distortion, or deadweight loss, arises from the substitution of leisure for income in response to taxation on labor. Moreover, taxes on income from capital distort consumption between time periods, favoring consumption today relative to consumption tomorrow (Lucas, 1990). A policy of tax smoothing would reduce the magnitude of these distortions and thereby boost economic welfare for any given intergenerational income distribution.

The chapter proceeds as follows. First, I describe the motivation for, and operation of, the Future Fund in some detail. Second, I analyze in general terms the relationship between economic dependency, the Fund balance and the tax rate. Third, I outline some intergenerational equity implications that I then quantify by using simulations in the subsequent section. Next, I explain how social welfare judgments can be made using the simulation model. I then apply empirical data and discuss the results. The concluding section offers a brief discussion of further policy implications and political economy issues associated with the Future Fund.

RATIONALE FOR AND OPERATIONAL DETAILS OF THE FUTURE FUND

The Australian government has been reducing its net indebtedness since the late 1990s and is projecting a positive and rising net asset position from 2006 onward (Figure 10.1). This has been, and will continue to be, achieved through budget surpluses. In September 2004, the federal treasurer announced that a Future Fund would be established, into which budget surpluses would be deposited.

The establishment of the Fund is motivated by several factors (see Australian Government, 2005, Statement 7). The primary motive is the

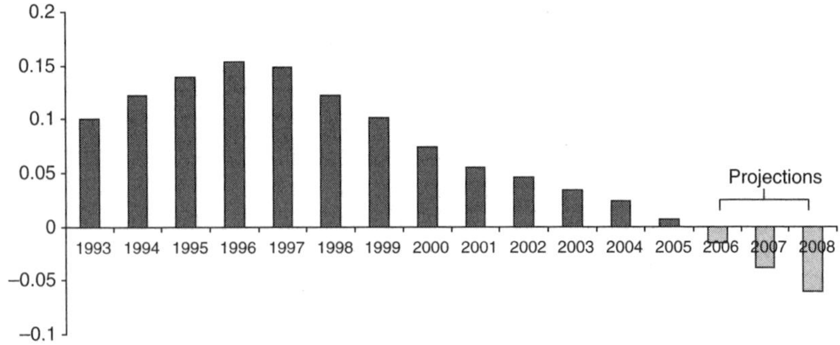

Figure 10.1 Net Commonwealth government debt to GDP, 1993–2008

desire to fund fully the Australian government's superannuation liabilities, quoted at 'around $91 billion' in the 2005–06 Budget Papers. This is consistent with the broader aim of spreading the fiscal costs of population aging over time, as evidenced in its 2005–06 Budget Papers, Statement 7: '[the Future Fund] will reduce calls on the budget in the future, at a time when significant intergenerational pressures are expected to emerge'. These 'pressures' are the spending implications of an aging population. They consist mainly of health and care expenditures for the aged, and pensions, which are expected to account for an increase in government spending of about 6 percent of GDP between 2005 and 2045 (Productivity Commission, 2005). In addition, an aim of the Fund is to maintain a liquid market in Commonwealth Government Securities (CGS) even though the government has no need to issue new debt to fund recurrent expenditure. The government plans to issue about $5 billion of CGS each year, which will be deposited into the Fund.

In March 2006, the Future Fund Act received royal assent in the Commonwealth Parliament. The act covers matters concerning the operation, governance and investment mandate of the Fund. The Fund will be managed by an independent board of guardians who will report to the treasurer and the minister for finance and administration. The board will be advised by a Future Fund management agency, and the funds will be invested in a diversified portfolio of financial assets in accordance with a broad investment mandate issued by the treasurer and the minister for finance and administration. The investment mandate (Treasurer, 2005) directs that the board:

- Adopt a long-term benchmark of an average return of at least 4.5 to 5.5 per cent real per annum but recognises that the Fund may have returns lower than this while the Board develops and implements its investment strategy;
- Determine an acceptable but not excessive level of risk for the Fund;
- Establish an internal limit on holdings of any listed company in order to ensure that it does not trigger the takeover provisions under the *Corporations Act 2001* or hold a stake of more than 20 per cent in any foreign publicly listed company;
- Only acquire a direct equity holding in Telstra if shares are transferred to the Fund by the Government or gifted to the Fund with the approval of the Government;
- Act in a manner that minimises the potential to cause any abnormal change in the volatility or efficient operation of Australian financial markets or adversely affect the Government's reputation in these markets; and

- Have regard to international best practice for institutional investment in determining its approach to corporate governance principles.

The main issue that has been raised regarding this investment mandate is that the legislation does not explicitly protect the board from pressure from politicians or special interest groups in the community to invest funds in particular sectors such as infrastructure and 'socially responsible' sectors, however those may be defined. The lack of such protection is a potential problem, because if taxpayers' resources are to be allocated to politically favored sectors, this would be more transparently achieved through direct budgetary allocations than indirectly through the Future Fund.

Comparable schemes have been adopted in other countries (Nielson and Webb, 2005), the closest example being the New Zealand Superannuation Fund. Like the Future Fund, the Superannuation Fund was established specifically to fund future government superannuation payments, although in New Zealand, unlike Australia, government-funded superannuation is a universal entitlement akin to a pension: that is, it is paid to all citizens over 65 years of age. In Ireland, the National Pensions Reserve Fund is designed to meet a somewhat wider range of fiscal costs associated with population aging and, unlike the case of Australia's Future Fund, the government is required to contribute a specified percentage of GNP toward the fund. In France and Norway, the distinguishing feature of their schemes is that the investment mandate requires that investments meet certain guidelines regarding what is considered to be ethical and socially responsible. Moreover, the scheme in Norway is not restricted to addressing the fiscal costs of population aging. It is also designed to cushion the effects of the 'Dutch disease', whereby a boom in oil export revenue would tend to cause a contraction in other sectors of the economy via a rising real exchange rate.

The Future Fund is in a sense narrower than these other schemes because its funds are precommitted to meeting only superannuation payments to Australian public servants. Almost all of these superannuation payments are made on a pay-as-you-go basis (Nielson and Webb, 2005). But tying the funds to a specific purpose such as this is artificial in the sense that prefunding one particular item of spending frees consolidated revenue to meet other spending commitments. Hence by targeting the government's superannuation liabilities that are a function of the population age structure, the Future Fund is effectively a way of meeting the wider fiscal costs of population aging.

Indeed all such schemes are essentially mechanisms for prefunding anticipated fiscal costs. Prefunding enables the burden of these costs to be smoothed out over time. In this sense they share similar economic effects with private superannuation (or retirement income) schemes. All prefunding schemes, private or public, imply consumption smoothing, by which is meant reductions in current consumption in order to boost future consumption.

It is worth noting that consumption smoothing can be achieved by alternative mechanisms. Instead of using current taxation revenue to create a financial asset fund such as a future fund, the government could allocate the revenue to creating physical assets such as public infrastructure: ports, roads, telecommunications, universities, hospitals, aged care facilities and so on. Both physical assets and financial assets effectively provide revenue streams that alleviate the call on future revenue. Some commentators have gone further and argued that the interests of future generations would be better served by leaving the tax revenue in the hands of the private sector – that is, not raising the current tax burden in the first place – which would encourage private-sector investment in place of public-sector investment. I shall return to these and related issues briefly in the concluding section of the chapter.

ECONOMIC DEPENDENCY, THE FUTURE FUND BALANCE AND THE TAX RATE

In establishing the long-run relationship between the tax rate, economic dependency and the Future Fund balance, I assume for simplicity that the government commences its planning period with zero net liabilities, which is approximately true for the federal government of Australia in 2005. I further assume that all future surpluses are deposited into the Future Fund, as is the government's stated intention. The government faces the following dynamic budget constraint:

$$\left(\frac{F}{Y}\right)_j = \left(\frac{F}{Y}\right)_{j-1}\left(\frac{1+r}{1+x}\right)_j + \left(\frac{T}{Y}\right)_j - \left(\frac{G}{Y}\right)_j, \qquad (10.1)$$

where F is the balance in the Fund, Y is GDP, r is the real interest rate facing both the public and private sectors, x is the growth rate of GDP, G is government spending, and T is taxes, which are levied at a flat rate on both labor and capital income.

All government spending, G, is assumed to be age-related spending consisting of both consumption spending such as on health, aged care, caregivers and education, and transfer payments such as age pensions, family tax benefits, and unemployment allowances. To keep the algebra tractable I make some further stylized assumptions, which are relaxed in the simulation model without affecting the intuition highlighted in the algebraic results here. These further assumptions and notation are consistent with those in the chapter by Hock and Weil in this volume. I assume:

- three age groups: young (Y), working age (M) and old (O);
- A_Y, A_M and A_O are the number of people in each age group;
- age-related spending accrues to the old and the young but not to the working aged;
- spending on the old is a constant fraction, β, of the real wage, W;
- spending on the young is a constant fraction, πβ, of W;
- there is no income from capital or foreign assets, and hence all income is wage income, taxed at the flat rate, τ.

Given these assumptions, government spending, taxes and income are respectively

$$G_j = A_{Y,j}\pi\beta W_j(1-\tau_j) + A_{O,j}\beta W_j(1-\tau_j), \tag{10.2}$$

$$T_j = \tau_j W_j, \tag{10.3}$$

$$Y_j = A_{m,j} W_j. \tag{10.4}$$

Substituting (10.2), (10.3) and (10.4) into (10.1):

$$f_j = f_{j-1}\left(\frac{1+r}{1+x}\right)_j + \tau_j - y_j\pi\beta(1-\tau_j) - o_j\beta(1-\tau_j), \tag{10.5}$$

where $y_j = (A_Y/A_M)_j$ and $o_j = (A_O/A_M)_j$ are the youth and old-aged dependency ratios and $f_j = (F/Y)_j$.

I further assume that the government's objective is to achieve a stable long-run balance of the Future Fund (FF) as a proportion of GDP, which would be required for the economy to reach a steady state. In addition, a positive long-run balance in the FF is necessary to achieve tax smoothing where the tax rate is lower in the long run, but higher in the short run, than it would otherwise be. If instead the balance in the FF were allowed eventually to run down to zero, the tax rate would return to the balanced budget tax rate. I therefore solve (10.5) for the constant tax rate that would achieve the steady-state condition: $f_j = f_{j-1}$, which gives

$$\tau = \frac{\beta(y\pi + o) - f(r-x)/(1+x)}{1+\beta(y\pi + o)}, \tag{10.6}$$

where all variables f, r, x, r and o take their steady state values.

Equation (10.6) shows the long-run relationship between the constant tax rate, economic dependency and the balance in the Fund. For example, an increase in the old-age dependency ratio, o, implies a higher tax rate for a given long-run Fund balance (as a ratio to GDP). This is shown formally by:

$$\frac{d\tau}{do} = \frac{\beta(1 + f^*)}{1 + \Phi^2} > 0, \tag{10.7}$$

where $f^* = f(r - x) / (1 + x)$ and $\Phi = \beta\,(y\pi + o)$. An increase in the long-run old-age dependency ratio need not be financed by an increase in the long-run tax rate. It could instead be financed by building up a larger long-run Fund balance by imposing a higher tax burden on earlier generations, which would reduce the long-run tax rate. This can be seen in equation (10.6) as a higher value of o offset by a higher value of f. These relationships reflect the fact that some generation(s) must pay for higher old-age dependency. The Future Fund is the vehicle for shifting this burden between current and future generations. The more aggressively the burden is shifted to the present generation, the larger is the balance in the Future Fund.

INTERGENERATIONAL EQUITY

Compared with continuously balanced budgets, tax smoothing implies a higher tax rate for an initial period and a lower tax rate thereafter. This clearly affects the lifetime after-tax incomes of generations differently. This section sketches in intuitive terms some of the implications for intergenerational equity of the type of tax-smoothing exercise that is implied in the Future Fund. Numerical results of simulations are reported at the end of the chapter.

Consider the effects on four generations: the young, working age, old and a fourth generation – the unborn. Under tax smoothing the young pay higher taxes for an initial period but lower tax rates in the future compared with a balanced-budget scenario. The net effect on their lifetime (after-tax) income is an empirical question, depending on the degree of tax smoothing and also on a taxpayer's subjective rate of time preference. For example, with a greater degree of smoothing, tax rates are initially higher and for a longer period than with the balanced-budget tax rate. The rate of time preference is relevant because it determines a taxpayer's willingness to defer consumption when tax rates are high, by lending or reducing borrowing, and therefore to transfer taxable income to the future when tax rates are lower. The lower the rate of time preference, the more likely are young households to be better off with tax smoothing, because they will be more willing to transfer income to the future when the tax rate is lower.

Generations of working age will be worse off than young people because they pay the higher initial tax rate immediately and face a shorter period of their lives in which to receive the benefit of the lower subsequent tax rate. Indeed they may be retired or dead by the time the lower tax rate eventuates. The result is that middle-aged households are almost certainly worse off under tax smoothing than they would be under balanced budgets, irrespective of their rate of time preference.

Older people, who are assumed here to be retired at the time that the tax-smoothing policy is instituted, are relatively unaffected by the switch from a balanced-budget regime to a tax-smoothing regime. Because they are retired their incomes are lower and hence the higher initial tax rate has less impact than for working-age people. They will almost certainly be dead by the time the lower tax rate arrives. Hence they will be only marginally worse off under the tax regime.

The fourth generation referred to above, those yet unborn, are the generation most likely to be better off under tax smoothing because by the time they enter the work force the tax rate will be lower than it would have been had the balanced-budget regime been maintained. In addition, we can expect unborn generations to enjoy higher lifetime incomes due to technical progress than those generations currently alive. This comparison also applies, albeit to a lesser extent, to generations currently alive: the young can expect to enjoy higher lifetime incomes than the old.

The combined assumptions of ongoing technical progress and diminishing marginal utility explain why it is common to discount the utility of future generations in evaluating intertemporal social welfare. Koopmans (1960) provides an alternative strong defense of discounting the future, arguing that otherwise the consumption of generations near the present would have negligible weightings in social welfare if the time horizon were long enough. The future could swamp the present in social importance. This could justify crushing the present generation to yield an infinitely small increase in the utility of each future generation. For a comprehensive discussion of the issues on discounting and intergenerational equity, see Portney and Weyant (1999), in particular the chapter by Cline (chapter 13). Although there is much debate about the appropriate rate of discount – the so-called social discount rate – there is a consensus that it should be greater than zero in the context of technical progress. A generally acceptable range is 1.5 to 3 percent, on the basis that the rate at which marginal utility falls with increases in consumption (the elasticity of marginal utility) is around 1.5 percent and the long-run annual rate of labor–productivity growth is between 1 and 1.5 percent. Multiplying these together gives the annual reduction in marginal utility due to higher consumption generated by technical progress.

If we accept that a positive discount rate ought to apply to the utility of future generations, it provides a case for tilting the burden of population aging upward over time: that is, a rising average tax rate over time. But this conflicts with the efficiency case for pure tax smoothing in which the deadweight losses from taxation are minimized with a constant tax rate over time.[1] A socially optimal balance can in principle be struck between these potentially conflicting objectives by maximizing a social welfare function that consists of the utility of all current and future generations, whereby a 'social judge' determines the rate at which future utility is discounted. This is the aim of the simulation model discussed below.

THE SIMULATION MODEL

This section outlines the simulation model in nonmathematical terms.[2] The simulation model is an open-economy, OLG (overlapping-generations) model with four sectors: firms, households, government and an overseas sector. Firms produce a single good, and households consume that good and leisure. A period of time is five years and a new generation of householders is born during each period. Each household consists of one person who dies at age 90 with certainty, implying that there are 18 overlapping generations of householders alive at any time. The households supply labor between the ages of 15 and 70. Hence there are 11 generations of workers. The firms are owned by households and are not taxable entities; they are simply vehicles for combining labor and capital to produce output. Households pay the same single tax rate on income from both capital and labor. Future values of the demographic variables and the parameters are known with certainty, except for the tax-smoothing shock, which comes as a surprise, requiring households to adjust their plans accordingly.

All firms are identical and produce output of a single good according to a Cobb–Douglas production function. They employ capital up to the point at which the marginal product of capital is equal to the cost of capital. This determines the optimal capital-to-labor ratio, which in turn determines the real wage.

The real wage, after tax, in turn determines labor supply as a result of households maximizing utility from consuming goods (both public and private) and leisure. Public-consumption goods generate utility but, following the approach in Foertsch (2004), are separable from both private consumption and leisure. In fact all public consumption is exogenous. All households are identical. They determine consumption of goods and leisure at a point in time by usual condition for an optimum, which equates relative marginal utilities of the two goods to their relative price.

Households also have an intertemporal allocation problem, which they solve in the usual way by equating the marginal rate of substitution between consumption at time t and $t+1$ with the marginal rate of transformation between consumption between time t and $t+1$. This maximization is carried out subject to a lifetime budget constraint that is specified in such a way that households must bequeath 10 percent of their lifetime income to their offspring, who are assumed to be the generation born 30 years later. The figure of 10 percent is a realistic average percentage for Australia. It turns out to imply, roughly, that, if a couple earn average weekly earnings over their lifetime, they have two children, and they own an average-priced house when they die, they would bequeath a sum equal to the value of the house divided between the two children. The solution to the houshold's intertemporal optimization results in a smooth consumption path over time, relative to the path of income.

Government spending consists of the spending of all levels of government in Australia and is an exogenously given share of GDP. This share is set equal to 0.3 for the period up to 2002, after which it increases according to the increase in age-related spending of the Australian government, in Productivity Commission (2005, 307). All government spending other than transfer payments is assumed to be government consumption spending. For simplicity, total transfer payments paid by the government in a given year are allocated evenly across all householders alive in that year, rather than being allocated to certain generations. The categories of age-related government consumption spending are given in Productivity Commission (ibid.) and consist of health, aged care, caregivers and education; and the categories of government transfer payments are age and service pensions, family tax benefits, disability-support benefit, unemployment allowances and parenting payments. The resulting series for aggregate government spending to GDP, G/Y, is plotted in Figure 10.2 as the series labeled 'Balanced budget' because under balanced budgets G/Y would also equal T/Y. As Figure 10.2 indicates, age-related spending of the Australian government is projected to increase by 6 percent between 2003 and 2045 according to the Productivity Commission (ibid.).

The budget constraint facing the government is given by equation (10.1). The budget constraint facing the national economy is, being an open-economy model, that the excess of current investment over current saving equals the current increase in foreign liabilities.

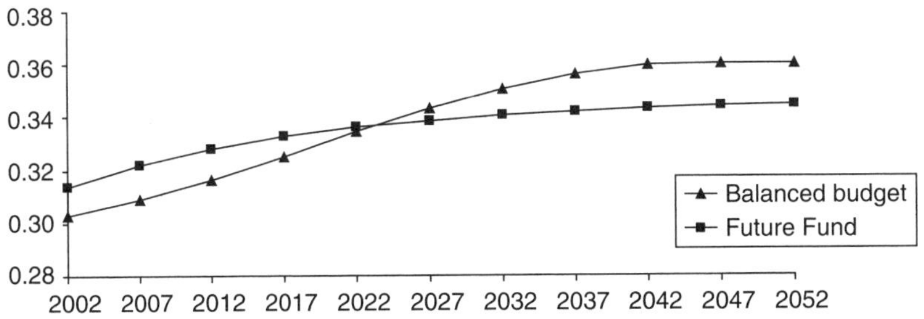

Figure 10.2 Fiscal pressure from population aging: projected path of tax to GDP ratio

SOCIAL VALUE JUDGMENTS

We want to weigh both efficiency and intergenerational equity effects of smoothing the fiscal costs associated with population aging. Evaluating intergenerational equity necessarily requires value judgments that can be made explicit by defining a social welfare function as a social evaluation of the consumption levels of different generations. Here it is assumed that the social judge evaluates only the consumption that occurs in the present and the future. This implies that there is no regard for past consumption even by cohorts still alive, on the grounds that past consumption cannot be influenced by current and future policy. The social welfare function applied here is

$$V = \sum_{k=-16}^{\overline{T}} \left[\sum_{i=\max\{1,2-k\}}^{18} N_{i,k+i-1} \frac{\Pi_{i,k}^{1-\beta_s}}{1-\beta} (1+\theta)^{1-(k+i)} \right], \qquad (10.8)$$

where k refers to the period in which a generation is born (recall that each time period is five years in length) and i refers to the age of the generation alive in period $k+i-1$. Hence $N_{i,k+i-1}$ refers to the population of age i born in period k. Consumption, Π_i, is an index of the consumption of both goods and leisure that is planned to take place by generation k in period $k+i-1$. The Π_i is weighted by $N_{i,k+i-1}$, which is the size of generation i in period $k+i-1$.[3] The term in the square bracket is the weighted discounted sum of the current and future consumption of householders born between periods k and $\overline{T}$ where $\overline{T}$ is an arbitrarily long time in the future. Hence the outer summation in equation (10.8) begins at $k = -16$, which is the generation of persons born in the period 1912–16 who are aged 86–90 in 2002–06. The social judge is not concerned with past consumption, even of cohorts still alive, because only current and future consumption can be affected by policy. Hence the inner summation begins at $i=1$ for householders born in period 1 or later, but $i=2-k$ for older householders. This implies, for example, that for householders born in period -16, the inner summation would begin at $i=18$ because they are in the last period of their lives in period 1.

The social judge discounts consumption through the parameters β and θ. The parameter θ is a social discount rate, which is the rate at which future consumption is discounted in deriving social welfare. The justification for discounting the future was discussed above in the section on intergenerational equity. The parameter β measures the social degree of aversion to variability in consumption at any given point in time. It is analogous to the rate of risk aversion in an individual's utility function. Essentially θ discounts for the time period in which consumption occurs whereas β discounts for the size of consumption on the basis of diminishing marginal utility.

EMPIRICAL APPLICATION

The aim of this section is to find the approximate magnitude of the effect of tax smoothing via the Future Fund on social welfare according to the model described above. This requires demographic projections and calibration of parameters in the model.

Data and Parameters

The demographic data consist of actual historical population levels and projected future population levels for each age group. These data are given in the following Australian Bureau of Statistics (ABS) catalogues: historic population, Catalogue 320109.1; projected population, Catalogue 3222.0; labor force participation rates by age, Catalogue 6291.0; and wage rates by age, Catalogue 6310.0 (ABS, 2005). The data source for government expenditure is Productivity Commission (2005) as described above.

Table 10.1 gives the parameter values. The value for labor-augmenting technical progress is the value used for the projections of fiscal pressure in Productivity Commission (2005, 95). The interest rate of 4 percent is a typical value of the world interest rate used in CGE simulations, and the assumption is that Australia is a small open economy. The household's rate of time preference is equal to the rate that would, if the tax rate were constant, ensure that consumption grew at the long-run rate of growth of output. The capital elasticity of output is calibrated in such a way that the initial capital-to-output ratio is equal to 3.0, the approximate actual value

Table 10.1 Base case parameter values and initial values

Labor-augmenting technical progress	0.0175
Interest rate	0.04
Household's rate of time preference	0.005
Capital elasticity of output	0.25
Initial capital to output ratio	3.0
Initial tax rate on all income	0.3
Foreign liabilities to GDP ratio, D/Y, in 2003	0.6
Elasticity of marginal utility with respect to consumption index	2.0
Elasticity of substitution between consumption and leisure	0.8
Bequest as a proportion of household's lifetime income	0.1

for Australia in 2002. The initial tax-to-GDP ratio is set equal to 0.3, the actual value for Australia in 2002. The ratio of foreign liabilities to GDP in 2002 is set equal to its actual value of 0.6 by calibration, in particular, by finding the required ratio of foreign liabilities to GDP in the period 1912–16, which is the period when household members aged 86–90 in 2002 were born. The values of the elasticity of marginal utility and of substitution between consumption goods and leisure are set equal to 2 and 0.8, respectively, which are common values used in related studies in the literature (see, for example, Foertsch, 2004).

There is no assumption that the economy is in a steady state prior to the tax-smoothing policy shock, nor that the economy converges to a steady state. Nevertheless, the properties of the OLG model lead to fairly well-behaved state variables. In particular, debt and the capital stock do not take extreme values at any point in the optimal path.

Simulation Results

Figure 10.2 plots two paths of the tax rate: the balanced budget case referred to above and a path denoted 'Future Fund', which is derived by partially smoothing the tax rate. The actual path that the tax rate will take under the Future Fund has not been determined as a matter of government policy. However, using recent budget surpluses of around 1 percent of GDP and the aim of fully funding the government's superannuation liabilities, the path in Figure 10.2 is a reasonable projection. The Future Fund scenario implies budget surpluses of around 1 percent of GDP for the next 20 years, after which the surpluses decline to zero by about 2040 (illustrated in Figure 10.3). The implication of the Future Fund scenario for government assets is shown in Figure 10.4. The stock of government assets stabilizes at around 35 percent of GDP by 2035.

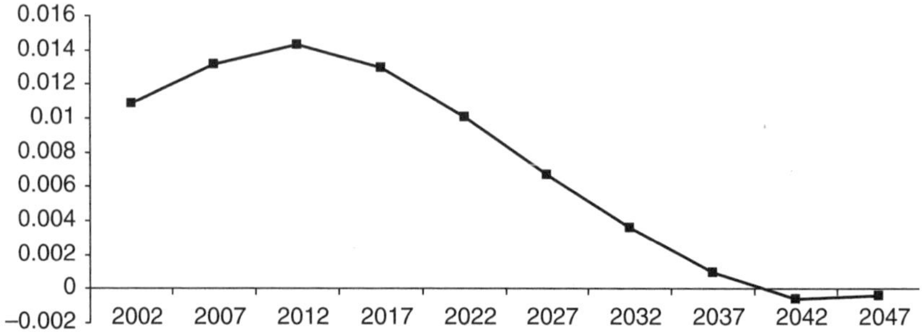

Figure 10.3 Budget surpluses (ratio to GDP)

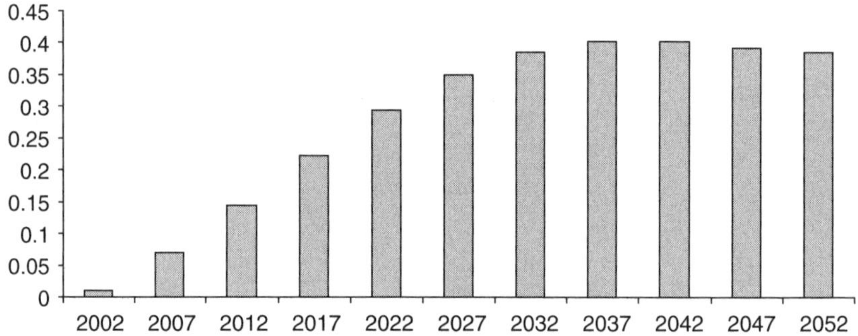

Figure 10.4 Net government assets (ratio to GDP)

Figure 10.5 shows the percentage change in lifetime income after tax as a result of the Future Fund, for each generation currently alive and future generations born up to the year 2052. Generations born from 1947 to 1977 will be worse off. The magnitudes are arguably not large, however, ranging from a 0.3 to a 0.8 percent reduction in lifetime income compared with balanced budgets. The latter number applies to the generation of Australians born between 1957 and 1961. They are the worst affected because they are now earning the highest incomes of their lifetimes and therefore pay relatively high taxes. They will continue to pay higher taxes for the remainder of their working lives than they would under balanced budgets because tax rates are higher under the Future Fund until 2022. Generations born around 1980 have lifetime incomes that are virtually unaffected by the Fund: the higher taxes paid initially are offset by lower taxes later on. Generations born after 1980 are increasingly better off under the Fund, with the greatest gains (around 2.3 percent) going to the generations born after 2022. These results are consistent with the discussion in intuitive

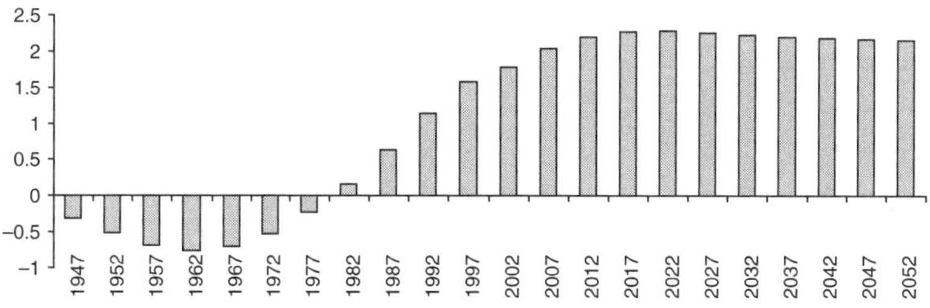

Figure 10.5 Percentage change in lifetime income after tax as a result of the Future Fund, for a representative household whose members were born in the years indicated

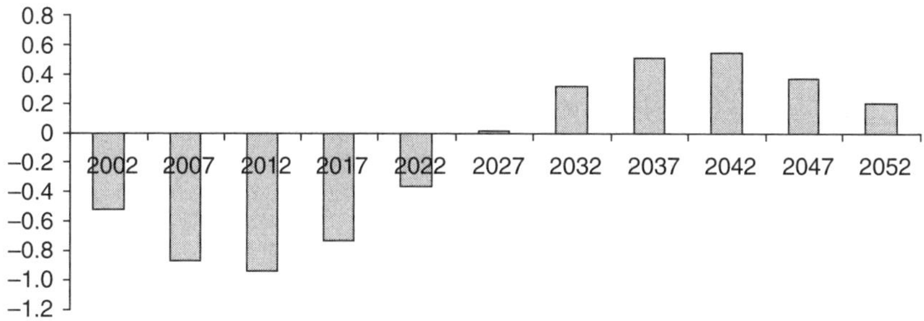

Figure 10.6 Percentage change in labor supply from tax smoothing

terms in the section on simulations, where it was predicted that middle-aged workers would be almost certainly worse off, unborn generations would be unambiguously better off, and young generations currently alive would or would not be worse off, depending on their rate of time preference.

The effect of tax smoothing on labor supply is shown in Figure 10.6. The most striking feature of this figure is that the initial decrease in labor supply, caused by higher tax rates at first, is much greater than the ultimate increase in labor supply caused by lower tax rates. This is because the tax-smoothing shock is unanticipated. When it occurs in 2002, all current generations of workers find that their lifetime plans are no longer appropriate and immediately adjust. The adjustment occurs through the negative substitution effect of higher taxes on their choice of leisure versus work, which causes a drop in labor supply. As time goes on, new generations of workers arrive at the same time as the gap between the smooth tax rate and the balanced budget rate narrows and eventually becomes negative. For these new

Table 10.2 Equivalent annual gain in GDP from the Future Fund

Parameters		Annual gains	
Social discount rate (θ_s) %	Aversion to inequality parameter (β_s)	%	\$* per capita
0.0	2.0	0.53	214
4.0	2.0	0.29	118
8.0	2.0	0.21	85
4.0	0.2	0.42	169
4.0	1.0	0.41	165
4.0	10.0	0.15	58

Note: * The $ p.a. per capita calculation is based on a GDP of $800 billion and a population of 20 million.

workers there is no policy shock that requires a sudden jump to a new path; they can spread out the effects over a longer time. This explains the subdued positive response of labor supply in the long run relative to the negative effect immediately after the shock, as shown in Figure 10.6.

Having identified the generations of winners and losers from tax smoothing, I turn now to the social welfare function defined in equation (10.8) to make a net social evaluation of the tax-smoothing effect of the Future Fund. The results are reported in Table 10.2 in terms of annual gains in GDP per annum. These were calculated by finding the annual increase in GDP, under continual balanced budgets, that generates the same value of social welfare as in the Future Fund scenario. The results are reported for a range of values of the two key parameters in the social welfare function: the social discount rate, θ, and the parameter measuring the social aversion to inequality in consumption, β. The values chosen for θ range from 0 to 8 percent; and the values chosen for β range from 0.2 to 10. The first point to note is that the gains are positive for all the parameter combinations. This indicates net social gains from the tax-smoothing effect of the Future Fund. The magnitudes of the annual gains range from 0.15 to 0.53 percent of GDP. They amount to $58 and $214, respectively, per annum per person, based on a GDP of $800 and a population of 20 million.

CONCLUSION

The simulations reported here suggest small welfare gains from the Future Fund. This conclusion must be qualified, however, by a number of considerations that are not captured by the simulation model. Some of them were mentioned at the outset of this chapter. One issue is the risk that the Fund will be raided for political purposes. The Future Fund Act provides some protection against this risk by restricting the spending of the Fund to the discharging of the government's superannuation liabilities. Nevertheless, there is no guarantee that the revenue stream from the assets will be used to lower taxes. It may simply be seen as a supplementary revenue stream that is available for new spending. In that case Australians would pay higher taxes in the short run but would never receive the payoff in lower future taxes. Another risk is that, in the likely event (assumed in the simulations in this chapter) that the balance in the Fund will outlast the government's superannuation liabilities, the revenue stream would at that point be available for other purposes. And of course there is always the possibility that current legislation restricting the uses of the funds could be amended.

Another consideration is the risk of political interference in the investments undertaken by the Fund. The investment mandate does not provide absolute protection from such interference, which can be even subliminal. One can easily imagine political pressure to invest in so-called 'socially responsible' firms or industries such as those involved in 'sustainable' technologies. The legislation itself would constrain the asset allocation of the Fund, such as the maximum allowable stake of 20 per cent in any foreign publicly listed company. Any such constraints, explicit or potential, may imply that the return on the Fund is less than that which could have been achieved if the Fund were left in the hands of the private sector.

This last point raises perhaps the strongest argument against the Future Fund. The consumption possibilities of future generations are maximized through the optimal saving of the current generation. Optimal saving depends on a trade-off between the returns from saving and the cost of saving in terms of the value of current consumption forgone. The issue is whether there is a sufficiently well-identified case of undersaving by the private sector to justify the government's boosting national saving through the Future Fund. If such a case cannot be made, then the welfare of future generations is maximized by leaving society's intertemporal consumption allocation to the private sector. But even if a case of undersaving by the private sector can be made, it may be better for the government to address this at its root cause, which may well be other government policies, in the taxation domain for example, than to compensate with another government policy intervention in the form of the Future Fund. Or it may be better for the government to create alternative assets other than the financial assets created through the Future Fund. This was mentioned above in the section of this chapter analyzing the relation between economic dependence, the Fund balance and the tax rate. For example, physical assets such as infrastructure, hospitals and so on are alternative ways of providing for the consumption needs of future generations.

It should also be noted that the simulation model applied here is subject to all of the usual criticisms of highly aggregated representative agent models. The outcomes should therefore be regarded as being subject to wide confidence bounds. Applying wide confidence bounds to the small simulated gains suggests that the welfare effects could in fact range from small negative effects to larger positive effects.

A final, albeit minor, consideration is the bureaucratic costs associated with the management of the Fund itself. All together, the risks associated with the Future Fund are sufficient to cast doubt on its merits from a social welfare perspective, notwithstanding the small positive effects from the simulations reported here.

NOTES

1. The argument for raising the tax burden gradually over time is supported, for the United States, by Elmendorf and Sheiner (2000), but not so much from an intergenerational-equity point of view. Rather, their point is that the optimal saving rate falls in response to aging. Therefore there is no need to increase government saving now by raising tax rates to prefund future fiscal costs such as Medicare and Medicaid. The government can achieve fiscal balance over time by slowly raising tax rates so that future fiscal costs can be met partly by future taxpayers. They argue that the cost of this policy in terms of the dead-weight losses that are created by varying tax rates is very small, according to empirical evidence in Cutler et al. (1990).
2. The technical detail is in Guest (2006) and is available upon request.
3. Larger generations are weighted more heavily in the social welfare function; otherwise individuals in larger generations are penalized simply because there are more people of the same age living at the same time.

REFERENCES

ABS (Australian Bureau of Statistics) (2005), 'Statistics by catalogue number', available on-line at http://www.abs.gov.au/AUSSTATS/.

Australian Government (2005), 'Budget 2005–06', A.G.P.S., Canberra, available on-line at http://www.budget.gov.au/2005-06/.

Barro, R. (1979), 'On the determination of public debt', *Journal of Political Economy*, **87**(5), 940–71.

Browning, E.K. (1987), 'On the marginal welfare cost of taxation', *The American Economic Review*, **77**(1), 11–23.

Cline, W.R. (1999), 'Discounting in the very long term', in P.R. Portney and J.P. Weyant (eds), *Discounting and Intergenerational Equity*, Washington, DC: Resources for the Future, pp. 131–40.

Cutler, D.M., J.M. Poterba, L.M. Sheiner, and L.H. Summers (1990), 'An aging society: opportunity or challenge?', Brookings Papers on Economic Activity, vol. 1, pp. 1–74, The Brookings Institution, Washington, DC.
Davis, N. and R. Fabling (2002), 'Population ageing and the efficiency of fiscal policy in New Zealand', New Zealand Treasury Working Paper 02/11, New Zealand Treasury, Wellington.
Elmendorf, D. and Sheiner, L. (2000), 'Should America save for its old age? Population aging, national saving, and fiscal policy', Federal Reserve Board Working Paper, 00-03, Washington, DC.
Floden, M. (2003), 'Public saving and public policy coordination in aging economies', *Scandinavian Journal of Economics*, **105**(3), 379–400.
Foertsch, T. (2004), 'Macroeconomic impacts of stylized tax cuts in an intertemporal computable general equilibrium model', Technical Paper Series, Congressional Budget Office, Washington, DC.
Guest, R. (2006), 'Smoothing the fiscal costs of population ageing in Australia: effects on intergenerational equity and social welfare', unpublished manuscript, Griffith Business School, Griffith University.
Harberger, A.C. (1964), 'Taxation, resource allocation, and welfare', in *The Role of Direct and Indirect Taxes in the Federal Revenue System*, NBER Other Conference Series, No. 3, University Microfilms, Ann Arbor, MI.
Koopmans, T.C. (1960), 'Stationary ordinal utility and impatience', *Econometrica*, **28**, 287–309.
Lucas, R.E. (1990), 'Supply-side economics: an analytical review', *Oxford Economic Papers*, **42**, 293–316.
Nielson, L. and R. Webb (2005), 'The Future Fund', Research Note no. 43, 2004-05, Parliament of Australia, Canberra.
Oksanen, H. (2003), *Population Ageing and Public Finance Targets*, European Commission Economic Papers, No. 193, December, European Commission, Brussels.
Portney, P.R. and J.P. Weyant (eds) (1999), *Discounting and Intergenerational Equity*, Washington, DC: Resources for the Future.
Productivity Commission (2005), *Economic Implications of an Ageing Australia*, Canberra: Commonwealth of Australia.
Treasurer (2005), Press release by the Treasurer and Minister for Finance and Administration, 5 May, Canberra.

11. Is Asia prepared for an aging population?

Peter S. Heller[1]

The challenges faced by industrial countries in the West and Japan with the prospective retirement of the 'baby boom' generation are well recognized. Generous and well-developed social insurance systems (for pensions and medical care) now confront the 'perfect demographic storm' arising from an unanticipated demographic transition to higher longevity and lower fertility rates.[2] Since the cost of these systems had been assumed to be financed by a growing working-age population, the sharp drop in fertility that has prevailed since the early 1960s has shrunk the size of the pool of workers available to support the cost of social transfers. Industrial governments thus face the unpleasant choice of either raising taxes and contribution rates or cutting back on the promises being made to future retirees in order to ensure fiscal sustainability. Even putting aside the issue of fiscal sustainability, these countries face the prospect of slower economic growth and the social and economic challenges posed by the large growth of the elderly and very elderly segments of their populations.

Asia too has experienced a similar demographic phenomenon. This has been particularly the case for its more developed countries – the Republic of Korea (hereafter referred to as Korea), Singapore, the Hong Kong Special Administrative Region of the People's Republic of China (hereafter referred to as Hong Kong SAR), Thailand and Malaysia – as well as rapidly growing China. Although lagging two decades or so behind the industrial countries, the sharp decline in fertility rates, sometimes resulting from deliberate policy initiatives as in China and Korea, and rising longevity rates will result in a rising elderly dependency ratio by 2020–30, largely offset by a declining youth dependency ratio. The obvious questions to be posed are how these aging Asian countries are positioned and what policy dilemmas their societies will face in addressing the challenges of an aging society. Specifically, how will their future economic growth rates respond to the aging of the work force and the ultimate slowing of its growth? Are their social insurance systems well adapted to confront the issues posed by a rising elderly dependency ratio and the types of medical-cost pressures associated with rising longevity, or are there significant lacunae in their social insurance policy frameworks? Will they face significant fiscal challenges akin to those in the industrial countries? Are there any Asia-specific challenges that arise from their 'position in the queue' as 'second-round' aging societies? Is there reason for concern about China's 'getting old before it gets rich?' This chapter considers these questions, focusing on China, Hong Kong SAR, India, Indonesia, Korea, Malaysia, the Philippines, Singapore and Thailand.

A PERSPECTIVE ON ASIA'S AGING PROCESS

A perspective on the preparedness of a country to address, in the future, the challenges of a relatively aged population requires consideration of both its present demographic structure and its economic policies. The former provides an insight into the likely pace of demographic change and the economic opportunities afforded by the transitional bulge in the size of the labor force. Consideration of the latter reveals whether current economic policies are supportive of a rapid pace of economic growth during the period before the elderly become a significant share of the population.

Demography

Writers on the 'demographic dividend' associated with the transition from high to low fertility and mortality rates have focused principally on two facets of the process (see, for example, Bloom and Canning, 2005). The first is the large pool of potentially employable labor of working age in the first phase of the process; the second is the potential for high savings rates by these workers, particularly as they move into their most productive working years and as the consumption-support needs of their young dependants lessen. Both facets provide an enormously important window of opportunity for rapid and buoyant economic growth through an enhanced labor force and high investment rates. The opportunities afforded by high savings rates relate to achieving both a higher aggregate per capita income level by the time the population becomes aged and the building up of a stock of assets, both real and financial (and internal and external), that can be drawn upon to help finance the consumption needs of an elderly population.

The flip side of the transition of course is the eventual subsequent movement of the population structure toward significantly higher elderly dependency ratios (and smaller youth dependency ratios) as the rate of growth of the working-age population falls and the share of the longer-lived retired population (defined by some arbitrary retirement age, usually 60 or 65) rises. For the industrial countries, it is around 2010 when the rapid

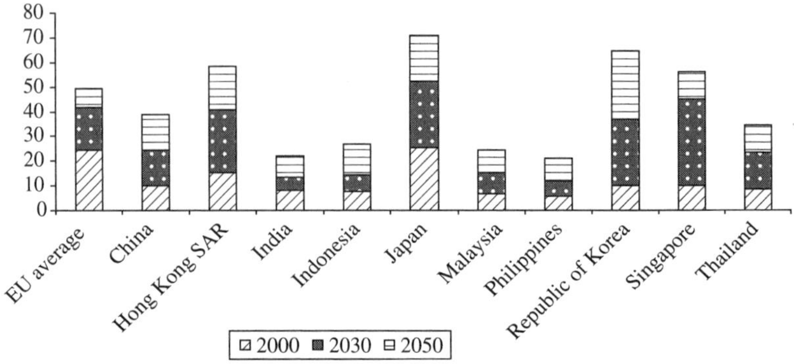

Notes: Data refer to projected shares of the population aged 65 and above relative to the population aged 15–64 under the assumption of medium levels of fertility rates. In this and the following figures, EU average refers to the simple average of data for the following six countries: Belgium, France, Germany, Italy, Netherlands and the United Kingdom.

Source: UN Population Division (2005).

Figure 11.1 Old-age dependency ratios in selected Asian countries: 2000, 2030 and 2050

shift toward a higher share of the elderly begins, and issues of old-age support begin to bite, increasing the pressures for lower savings rates and higher consumption rates.

Asian countries sit astride this demographic transition at various points (Figure 11.1). Some, such as Hong Kong SAR, Korea and Singapore, are much more advanced in the process, with the elderly dependency ratio converging to the levels currently observed in industrial countries as early as 2030 and further dramatic increases occurring in subsequent years. Korea, for example, has the fastest aging of any country in the world. Its rapid aging process is also illustrated by the speed at which the share of the very elderly (over age 80) in the population is rising; that share is projected to almost quadruple, rising to industrial-country levels by 2020 (Figure 11.2). China's and Thailand's demographic transitions follow, their demographic-dividend period lasting until about 2035–40 and both the elderly and very elderly shares rising quickly thereafter. Malaysia follows closely; its demographic-dividend period is expected to last slightly longer, up to 2045. India, Indonesia and the Philippines are next, with a high share of the elderly only beginning to emerge some time after 2050.

China's situation is unusual in several respects (Jackson and Howe, 2004). Its size obviously commands attention. The number of its elderly already dwarfs that of many industrial countries. But more importantly, the pace of aging in its urban centers (where about a third of the population

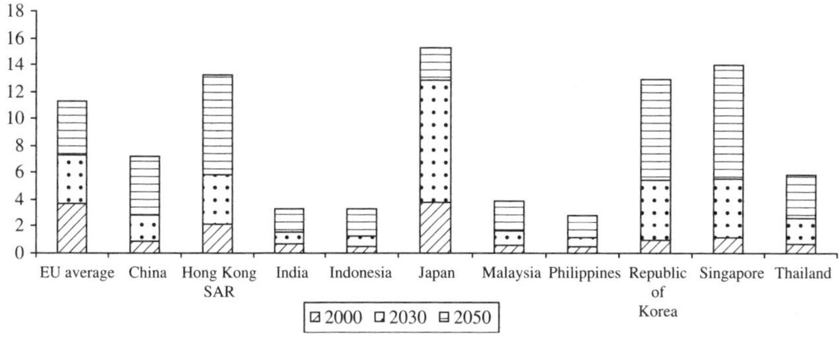

Note: Data refer to projected shares of the population aged 80 and above in the total population under the assumption of medium levels of fertility rates.

Source: UN Population Division (2005).

Figure 11.2 Very elderly dependency ratios in selected Asian countries: 2000, 2030 and 2050

lives) has been far greater than in the rural areas, reflecting both sustained lower fertility and higher longevity. Even with rural-to-urban migrants included as part of the urban population, the closing of the demographic-dividend period may occur much earlier in urban China – say during 2025–30 – than in rural China, when it is expected to occur around 2035–40. Many critical policy issues will rest on how these urban–rural differentials are addressed both across and within provinces, and at the family and policy levels.[3] These issues will be compounded by the rapid pace at which urbanization is occurring in China, where the share of the population in the urban areas is projected to rise from a third to more than half between 2006 and 2020 (Figure 11.3). The oft-mentioned gender gap (the shortage of women relative to men due to differences in the birth rates of boys and girls) will also be an important issue to be reckoned with in China. It will raise concerns not only over the scarcity of potential wives but also over the scarcity of potential caregivers for the elderly.

Asia's Economies

Asia's economies also illustrate the possibilities afforded by the demographic dividend. Certainly, Hong Kong SAR, Korea and Singapore richly took advantage of the potential of their demographic dividend by maximizing their labor utilization and achieving high national savings rates, as reflected in per capita incomes either at or approaching industrial-country levels (particularly if incomes are defined in terms of purchasing-power

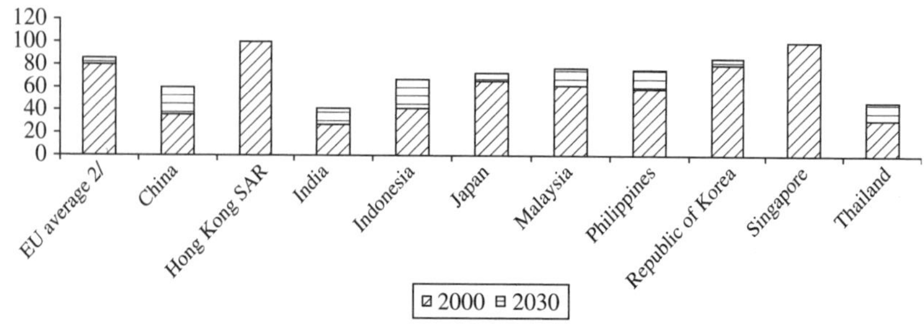

Note: Data refer to projected share of urban population in the total population under the assumption of medium levels of fertility rates.

Source: UN Population Division (2006).

Figure 11.3 Urbanization rate in selected Asian countries: 2000 and 2030

parity, or PPP). Malaysia and Thailand are well in the ranks of middle-income countries, particularly if per capita GDP is defined in PPP terms. They have pursued a development strategy built on exploiting their demographic dividend, with a resulting strong performance in economic growth. China, coming from much further behind economically and despite its extraordinarily rapid economic growth and high savings and investment rates, still faces many challenges if it is to create productive jobs for its large labor pool in the coming years. Despite its similarity to Malaysia and Thailand in its stage of demographic transition, it has an income level much closer to that of the Philippines, with dramatic differences between urban and rural areas, the latter areas being much on a par with Asia's low-income countries.

The Philippines, India and Indonesia are in the lower ranks of Asia's middle-income countries. They have relatively low incomes per capita, national savings rates at least 10 percent of GDP below the aforementioned Asian countries, and the potential for labor absorption from the rural sector and productive investments in human capital still to be fully exploited.

Will these countries be 'old before they are rich'? Korea and Singapore are already converging on per capita income levels among the upper-middle income country group. By the time their elderly dependency ratios begin to mount, their aggregate per capita income levels in GDP terms will be in the range experienced by many industrial countries today. Countries such as Indonesia, Malaysia and the Philippines can expect, at current growth rates, to see their per capita income levels rise to a third to two-thirds of current EU-6[4] levels by the time their elderly dependency ratios converge to current EU-6 levels (around mid-century). In PPP terms, these per capita income levels may prove closer to industrial-country levels.

Most analysts expect China to continue to see dramatic economic growth. If its per capita income continues to rise at the pace expected during 2006–10, per capita GDP could quadruple by 2022 and grow by a factor of eight by 2030, the year in which it matches today's European elderly dependency ratio. This would yield a per capita GDP level about 40 percent of that of the EU-6 countries today and an even higher level if measured in PPP terms. These results of course mask the fact that the sharp differentials in income levels within China between urban and rural areas are likely to persist, with the result that the income status of many of China's elderly will be far below what might be suggested by aggregate per capita income levels. In contrast, by the time India reaches today's elderly dependency ratio of the EU-6 countries (much later of course, say around 2050) its GDP per capita would still be less than 20 percent of today's EU-6 per capita income level, though again higher in PPP terms.

Thus, for most of these countries, the challenge of accommodating an aged population will consist only in part of increasing aggregate income. A greater challenge will be to improve the distribution of income across generations, increase the willingness of younger generations to support the elderly, and create political viability for the institutional mechanisms chosen to intermediate this intergenerational transfer.

Present Social Insurance Systems in Asia

Virtually all the Asian countries under discussion have wrestled with the issues involved in developing social insurance systems to manage the risks associated with retirement and medical care. The variety in the observed strategies principally reflects differences in national perspective and the specifics of each country's history and institutions. The appropriateness of these strategies in addressing the long-term demographic transition, including the prospects of an aging population, has probably been at most only a small factor in policy design.

Pension systems

Two approaches to pension systems stand out. The first is that of the central provident funds (CPF) of Singapore and Malaysia (and, to a limited extent, Thailand) and the recently established (in 2000) Mandatory Provident Fund of Hong Kong SAR (see Asher and Nandy, 2006b; Thillainathan, 2004). These systems essentially use a defined-contribution approach. They contrast with the various civil service and private employer-based defined-benefit schemes observed in Korea, Thailand, the

Philippines and India. The CPF approach involves prefunding particular, potentially large expenditure requirements before retirement (such as for housing, education and, in some cases, medical care) as well as people's income needs during retirement. It implies commensurately high national savings rates. The high mandatory savings rates (in the mid-30 percent range of wages up to a wage ceiling), coupled with reasonably effective investment strategies by the funds' financial managers for the significant accumulated assets in the funds, provide for a lump-sum payment at retirement, the eligible age of which ranges from 55 to 62.[5] The replacement rate that would be entailed by the purchase of an annuity with this lump sum is still not generous, however, ranging from 20 to 40 percent. Both systems entail the potential risk for households of using funds too early – albeit for legitimate needs before retirement – and for too limited a period after retirement. Because the funds can be drawn on before retirement, there is the risk that they will prove an inadequate retirement vehicle for many elderly. The threat applies to both partners of a couple, but the greatest threat is to widows who did not work outside the home.

For the defined-benefit schemes, coverage ranges from being largely universal, as in Korea (at least in principle) and increasingly the Philippines, to covering at most 30 percent of the labor force (parts or all of the formal modern sector and workers in the civil service) in the other countries. Replacement rates for covered workers vary. For covered workers in Thailand, they are at most 30 percent.[6] The deferred-benefit schemes are largely pay-as-you-go (PAYGO) in structure, with only the Korean scheme offering some prefunding. This makes these schemes heavily reliant on their capacity to raise contribution rates from workers in the event of future operational deficits, and as a result they are particularly vulnerable to an increase in the elderly dependency ratio. For example, Thailand's Old Age Pension Fund (OAPF) scheme is expected to exhaust its reserves by mid-century. Achieving universal coverage can prove difficult. Korea's scheme took approximately 15 years from the time in which the National Pension scheme was introduced to the point that mandatory subscription was required. Moreover, about 15 percent of subscribers are not contributing to the scheme as required.

Relative to the others, China's pension system is very much in a state of flux, reflecting the dramatic structural transformation of China's economy over the last 20 years (Asher et al., 2005; Pi, 2005; Trinh, 2006). In urban areas the government has begun to replace the fragmented pension system, for which state enterprises and the government have been responsible, with a three-pillar system involving a mandatory defined-benefit PAYGO scheme as the first pillar, a mandatorily funded defined-contribution scheme as the second pillar, and a voluntary savings scheme as the third pillar. The government is largely responsible for meeting pension liabilities to existing retirees and to those with vested rights.

The new schemes cover less than half the urban work force, however. Pooling rarely extends beyond the municipal level. Noncompliance is rife among employers, particularly in the private sector. The funds associated with the individual account system have been used by municipalities largely to finance pension payments to existing retirees. Indeed the urban pension system still appears to be underfunded. Optimistic estimates of the implicit 'legacy debt' associated with the previous urban pension system range from 50 to 150 percent of GDP and are even higher under more conservative assumptions. Moreover, recent examples of corruption in Shanghai in the management of the investments of pension-fund assets give rise to concern about the adequacy of even available financial assets to meet future pension liabilities.

In rural areas the commune pension system, which previously provided retirement benefits for its members, albeit at very low income levels under the premarket system, has fallen apart. It is being replaced, if at all, by minimal social safety net transfers.[7] In sum, less than a quarter of China's workers are covered by the new pension scheme. High individual savings rates by Chinese workers may reflect their recognition of the limitations of the still-evolving formal retirement and medical insurance schemes.

Medical care

Health-care systems are particularly difficult to categorize. Some countries, such as Malaysia, Hong Kong SAR and Indonesia, are heavily reliant on budget-financed systems, which offer universal access to care in principle; but the quality of services effectively available varies widely according to a household's income and place of residence (WHO, 2004; Pillay, 2005; Wagstaff, 2005). Even where facilities for care are available, in some countries (for example, in rural China) the cost of care that must be borne out of pocket limits effective access to quality health care. In some countries the private sector may also be a key provider. This may reflect the inadequacies of the public health care system, as in India, or it may be an intrinsic element in the design of the medical care system, as in Thailand. In other countries the private sector caters largely to a narrow segment of the population.

Korea, Thailand and the Philippines have adopted a social health insurance system, though only the former two offer relatively universal coverage (Jowett, 2005; Kim, 2005; Koh, 2005; Tangcharoensathien et al., 2005; Yang, 2005). Korea has also decided to introduce a scheme for long-term care as of 2008. Universality in coverage does not necessarily imply full access to all possible medical services or low co-payments. In Korea, effective co-payments are quite high and the range of medical services covered remains limited. Singapore relies on the private financing of medical care, either directly by the household on an out-of-pocket basis or from employer-financed insurance, though it has several public schemes that partly address the challenge of obtaining catastrophic care and medical care for the indigent (Asher and Nandy, 2006a).

Before the market reforms of the 1980s, China provided universal medical care, albeit at differing levels of quality for urban and rural areas and depending on the type of economic organization providing the care. This system collapsed in the 1980s with the introduction of the market economy, the breakdown of the rural communes, the growing importance of private enterprises, and the weakened state of many state-owned enterprises.[8] As with pensions, the cost, availability and system of financing of medical care now varies dramatically, both between and within the urban and rural sectors. Medical spending has risen rapidly in China in the last two decades, fueled almost entirely by uncontrolled, largely supply-induced spending in public and private urban-sector units involving the acquisition of high technologies and financed by the out-of-pocket spending of households. There is a network of public hospitals and clinics in both the urban and rural areas; but because government-financed allocations are tightly constrained, effective access to most medical services for much of the population is contingent on whether an individual can pay for diagnostic tests, drugs and many kinds of treatment.

In the urban areas a basic employee medical-insurance scheme has been introduced that involves a combination of a medical savings-account system, limited risk pooling and health insurance. But coverage is only gradually being extended to private-sector employees, most urban migrant workers are not covered, the benefits provided by the system are very limited, and there is costly cross-subsidization of many elderly retirees. In some urban areas the government is also experimenting with the concept that has been called the Community Health Service (CHS). The CHS relies on community-based clinics that are partially financed by the government and are staffed by nurse practitioners and family physicians. They are intended to provide primary care to all individuals, including migrants, who reside in the urban areas. This scheme still relies on individual co-payments for tests and drugs, and individuals must pay significant charges for much of the care provided by public hospitals.

In the rural sector, government medical units provide care, but most of the costs are borne by households. Social health insurance is largely absent for 90 percent of rural residents. A new rural cooperative medical scheme is now being developed and aggressively expanded, but it remains poorly funded, is likely to cover only an additional 20 percent of the rural population, and is still voluntary and thus subject to adverse selection pressures. It also still requires co-payments as high as 70 percent of the total medical bills on average; and it makes users pay 'up front', essentially disqualifying the poor from gaining access to care and benefits under the scheme. Moreover, the scheme focuses on catastrophic health events. Access to essential health care remains entirely dependent on out-of-pocket payments.

HOW WELL-POSITIONED ARE ASIAN COUNTRIES TO ADDRESS THE CHALLENGES OF AN AGING POPULATION?

There are two principal aspects to a country's strategy in dealing with the prospect of a significant aging of its population in the future. The first is macroeconomic and entails the pursuit of a policy of rapid economic growth. A rise in saving and investment rates early in the demographic transition can facilitate the achievement of a much higher per capita income level by the time the demographic structure shifts. It allows a country room to meet the consumption needs of the larger share of the retired population while still satisfying the standard-of-living aspirations of those of working age. The second is microeconomic, relating to the institutional mechanisms and incentives that govern how this higher income ends up being distributed between the working and retired portions of the population. Four broad strands of government policy bear on meeting the challenge of an aged population in the microeconomic sphere.

First, governments may influence or mandate individuals to provide for their old-age security by smoothing their consumption over their lifetime; governments may also seek to provide some kind of protection to limit the likelihood of elderly destitution. As is evident in the Asian case, they can do this by explicitly mandating savings or by providing incentives to save or to make family transfers.[9] The government can also introduce social insurance policies that entail an intergenerational pact providing for significant transfers from the working-age population to retired households. Policies that enhance the productivity of savings, particularly those that strengthen the functioning of the financial sector, are also critical elements of policy in this regard.

Second, government policies may seek to provide incentives to individuals and enable them to remain engaged in the labor force for a longer period as life expectancy increases. Promoting and facilitating a longer working life, by reducing the share of the elderly dependent population, correspondingly reduces the magnitude of the intergenerational transfer that is needed as a population ages.

Third, government policies in the sphere of health care can both increase the capacity of individuals to participate in the labor force during part of their elderly years and reduce the financial burden of medical care to be borne by the elderly during their retirement. They can achieve the latter objective by enabling the elderly to earn income to pay for medical and long-term care.

Fourth, government policies may seek to encourage a higher rate of fertility or increased immigration, essentially lessening the pace at which the elderly dependency ratio rises.

The Macroeconomic Strategy

Asian countries have had a 'double imperative' in considering their appropriate macroeconomic policy stance. Policies should be supportive of rapid economic growth. They should also recognize that, with an aging population, governments will eventually have to address the challenges associated with a substantial increase in the elderly dependency ratio (see Mason and Lee's chapter in this volume). The relative importance of each of these imperatives depends on both a country's proximity to the time when its elderly dependency ratio rises and the extent to which the country's per capita income level is converging to industrial-country levels.

The first imperative for growth underscores the importance of mobilizing resources for development both domestically and, especially for lower-income countries, externally. Such mobilization is usually associated with a deficit in the current account, reflecting investment in excess of savings. It also involves the productive employment of the large pool of potential workers in the working-age group. Such a policy should also be accompanied by policies that focus on domestic productivity growth, financial-sector reform and enhanced competitiveness.

The second imperative, which is also linked to the exploitation of the demographic dividend, involves taking advantage of the period when the size of dependent population groups is relatively small, affording the possibility of a high savings rate that can be used to realize higher economic growth through increased productivity and a high investment rate.

In macroeconomic terms, the double imperative implies that one would certainly want to see high investment rates, and possibly also a current-account deficit, in the early part of the demographic transition for these countries and that this should be reflected in high growth. As the countries move toward having a larger elderly dependency ratio and workers are increasingly in their higher earning years, saving for retirement becomes more important and it should be possible for the countries to run current-account surpluses. In effect, a high savings rate associated with the need to reduce the burden of fiscal debt and build up assets (at least in the private sector) – that is, prefunding – becomes a critical imperative. Recognizing the double imperative forces attention not only on growth but also on adopting a strategy for some prefunding of the burden of an aged population in the future.

In this light it is interesting to consider the sequencing of Asian countries' demographic transition in relation to the aging of the present industrial countries, and especially in relation to the aging of other Asian populations. The major industrial countries will soon enter a period when one might expect a shift in their macroeconomic balances toward a current-account deficit as their elderly reduce their savings rates or dissave. One might expect that their relative decumulation of assets, whether involving the sale of foreign or of domestic assets, would be matched by offsetting current-account surpluses in those countries that are still 15 to 20 years from the time when the demographic structure will shift to become more aged. As noted, this latter group of countries would most likely include Korea, Singapore, Thailand, Malaysia and, most importantly, China. Current-account surpluses in these latter countries would be the logical counterpart to current-account deficits in today's aging industrial countries. At a minimum the high savings and investment rates observed in these Asian countries would appear appropriate if the focus is on meeting the challenge of dealing with the future aging of their populations.

Other key Asian countries, notably India, Indonesia and the Philippines, are much further from the time when their demographic structure will include a substantial share of the elderly. For them, the growth imperative dominates the effect of the demographic dividend issue in terms of a higher domestic savings rate. It would thus be appropriate to see these countries run current-account deficits, reflecting the pressures for investment for growth. Given their lower income levels, the pressures are less for mobilizing savings to prefund a period, still far in the future, when their populations will be aged. Thus one might see the aforementioned earlier group of aging countries of Asia eventually financing investments in (or buying the investment assets of) not only the industrial West, as its population structure is more heavily weighted with elderly groups, but also the later-aging countries of Asia.

An interesting issue to speculate upon is whether this sequenced strategy for dealing with the aging of a population will continue to be applicable a few decades into the future, when the populations of the large countries of South and Southeast Asia themselves begin to approach the decade before they are aged. At that point in the future, suppose one observes these countries also ratcheting up their savings rates, including possibly accumulating external assets from both present industrial countries and those countries in early-aging Asia that have begun to be aged as well. The challenge that will confront the global macroeconomy then will be the relative buoyancy of the remaining younger-population countries in South Asia, the Middle East and Sub-Saharan Africa and the perceived profitability of investments in those regions.

Microeconomic Strategies

Only three of the countries under examination (Korea, Singapore and, perhaps, Malaysia) can be said to have social insurance systems that are sufficiently universal in coverage that their design features can be evaluated for robustness or adequacy in addressing the needs of a future aged population. The operative questions are whether these systems ensure that the replacement incomes of most households, in retirement, are adequate to meet the implied standard of living; whether they will prevent the destitution of the most vulnerable elderly; and whether the elderly will have access to a reasonable standard of medical and long-term care, given the limits that may pertain to accessing the most advanced possibilities of medical science (see Asher and Nandy, 2006a). Examining the strengths and weaknesses of the three systems from this perspective highlights the issues that the other Asian countries still need to address. Such an assessment reveals how far Asian countries are from a comprehensive policy framework to address the intergenerational challenges inherent in an aged population.

Korea

In principle, Korea's largely PAYGO pension and social health-insurance system should be the most responsive to the challenges of an aged population. Yet it has a key weakness mirroring that of many industrial countries, viz., that its pension promises, in terms of the replacement rate at the current age of eligibility for retirement, are too generous, implying a fiscally unsustainable position. Estimates suggest that Korea's pension fund will be exhausted by 2041, forcing painful policy choices between higher contribution rates, lower benefits or a postponement in the retirement age.

Korea's medical-care system does not overcommit the amount of generally available benefits it offers. The operative question is more whether it can sustain the greater financial pressures that may arise as the population ages, given that higher medical costs may occur years after the initial retirement age, when pension outlays need to be financed. Over time a larger share of the elderly will eventually give rise to demands for more care, in part because of the higher costs of dealing with chronic health conditions, and to demands for available sophisticated medical technologies. Yielding to these demands will progressively strain the finances of Korea's social health-insurance system, increasing the burden on taxpayers and forcing higher contribution rates. It will also probably result in larger out-of-pocket costs for retirees, lowering their effective income-replacement rate or forestalling access to needed medical services.[10]

The lesson of Korea for other Asian countries is not the inappropriateness of the basic social insurance approach. Rather, it is the importance of having a system design in which parameters (replacement rate, age at retirement, indexation provisions and so on) and policy controls (such as eligibility for specific medical services and co-payment rates) are set with considerations of financial sustainability in mind, and with due regard to the possibility of such downside risks as greater longevity or lower interest rates. The fact that many countries have not yet moved to a universal system can be seen as an opportunity in the sense that the design of a system can still take account of the implications of an aging population. But even this advantage is tempered by the fact that, for the limited share of workers currently covered under the existing social insurance systems in those countries, the underlying system design (policy parameters and the rest) may prove financially unsustainable if extended more broadly within the population. This implies the need for structural reforms of some key parameters of the social insurance systems.

Singapore and Malaysia

Singapore and Malaysia are similar to Korea in their use of a provident-fund approach for pensions, implying a defined-contribution system that is fully funded. Among the key challenges they face, as would other Asian countries considering such a defined-contribution strategy, is to ensure that their mandated savings rate is high enough to allow for a sufficient accumulation of assets by the time the population becomes aged so as to provide an adequate replacement income thereafter, and to ensure that the provisions of the system will not allow the funds to be withdrawn too early.[11] The two principal risks, almost all borne by households, are longevity risk, the possibility that the accumulated assets may prove insufficient to yield an adequate replacement rate over a longer life span; and market risk, lower-than-anticipated yields from investments during the accumulation phase prior to retirement, inadequate real returns on assets during retirement, or both.[12]

Other important issues concerning the operation of a defined-contribution system relate to the management and investment of the accumulated funds and the availability of a well-developed market in annuity products for the retired population. In small countries, international diversification of assets and hedging by the provident funds may be an appropriate strategy, particularly if domestic financial markets are underdeveloped. Diversification becomes attractive to the extent that the government maintains a conservative fiscal stance, such that the market for government securities is very thin. But international diversification carries risks. Singapore and Malaysia have opted largely for centrally managed investment portfolios, balancing domestic and now external investments. In both cases, while financial governance appears sound, some concerns have been expressed in varying degrees by critics, *inter alia*, on grounds of a lack of transparency and political interference in investment decisions. Moreover, the annuity market, particularly in Malaysia, appears to be underdeveloped. And, in common with similar systems, annuity purchase rates are very low, reflecting that the decision to purchase annuities is voluntary. Finally, like other countries that have adopted defined-contribution systems, neither country appears to have fully addressed the complex issue of what type of social safety net should be established to prevent elderly destitution and how it should be financed. This is an issue still to be tackled by most Asian countries with aging populations.

In the area of medical care, Singapore and Malaysia provide useful cautionary lessons for other Asian countries. Malaysia still has a largely budget-financed medical-care system, one that has been relatively effective. It is now considering a move to allow a greater role for private health insurance. The government system allows for greater control in determining the quality and quantity of available services and technology, the magnitude of remuneration of health care practitioners, the possibilities of quantity discounts from pharmaceutical suppliers, and the use of generic drugs. But budget-financed systems can also be subject to administrative challenges and political economy pressures in setting budgetary aggregates. In considering a greater role for private health insurance, the government in principle has scope to regulate the operation of the private system to ensure the operation of a global budget constraint that would limit overall spending on health care in the economy. But opening up the system to private insurance needs to be carefully controlled to limit pressures that push up costs and to address the sources of market failure in the health care sector. Indeed, Malaysia has already experienced significant brain drain from the public to the private sector, worsening the quality of care and creating cost pressures in the public health system. Care will also need to be taken to structure the insurance market to obtain a reasonably broad risk pool so as to avoid adverse-selection pressures that would prevent people in poorer health from obtaining coverage.

Singapore, in contrast, has a largely private system, where out-of-pocket spending dominates, and the key operative assumption is that supply restrictions and demand restraint by households, which are required to bear a significant proportion of costs, will limit the extent of cost inflation and demand pressure. By mandating savings for medical care, the government also forces individuals to prefund some of the cost of catastrophic incidents. But inflationary cost pressures in the health care sector are nevertheless emerging in Singapore. These have not been reflected in a rising medical expenditure share in GDP only because of Singapore's rapid economic growth. It remains to be seen whether Singapore's system can be robust to both the pressures of an aging population with slowing GDP growth and to the dynamic cost pressures associated with rapid technological change in the medical sector.

China

China's authorities are well aware of the challenges posed by an aging population and have sponsored a number of studies by eminent domestic and outside experts to explore potential policy strategies in the spheres of pensions and medical care. Some of these strategies are reflected in several experiments in selected cities and provinces, yet, for most of China's population, a coherent national strategy for addressing the challenges that will be faced once the population becomes aged remains to be put in place.

With regard to retirement income, although the central government has effected some limited intergovernmental fiscal redistribution across and within provinces, stark differentials remain between the rural and urban sectors, both within and across provinces. These would require major policy initiatives to narrow. The absence of any nationwide social insurance risk pool effectively implies that the differentials would also be manifest in the way in which retirement incomes are financed. So, while China is engaged in an effort to raise the level of its per capita income before its population becomes old, the way in which rural and urban GDP is respectively distributed as between the working-age and elderly populations remains largely segmented. Even provision for province-wide risk pooling would be an enormous start. Centralization from the county and municipal level up to the provincial level, particularly if supported by some equalization and back-up transfers from the center and complemented with provision for some cross-province portability of benefits, would be a desirable initiative.

Under the status quo, this means that the rural aged are essentially relying for their old-age support on their private savings, highly limited transfers from the state, and family support from children still in the rural sector or working as urban migrants. With only limited social pooling within the rural areas and a rising elderly dependency ratio, the prospects for significant government support appear limited unless derived from the central government, possibly in connection with some form of minimum-income guarantee or social safety-net scheme (see Yi et al., 2006).[13] While higher provincial or local taxes to mobilize revenues would of course be an option, this may prove infeasible on both political-economy and incentive grounds.

Although operating at a higher income level, China's urban areas confront perhaps even more difficult pressures. The worsening demographic balance is more acute in the urban areas, particularly for those who are urban residents as opposed to migrants. Current experiments with pre-funded defined-contribution schemes in fact have amounted to simply an intergenerational-transfer scheme akin to a PAYGO system, whereby the contributions, while notionally contributed by working-age individuals and saved, are used only partly to build up real assets. The bulk in fact finance payments to existing retirees previously employed in the civil service or state enterprises. This risk of using the funds for other than the defined-contribution accounts jeopardizes the viability and sustainability of the defined-contribution system. As already noted, concerns about governance in the investment of these funds is also emerging as a critical issue.

As the urban population ages and the elderly-dependency ratio worsens, the relevant policy alternatives are likely to require some mixture of larger contributions and higher tax rates for those formally working in the urban sector (that is, nonmigrants); a broadening of the coverage and contribution base of such schemes to include young urban migrant workers, thereby deferring somewhat the point at which the fiscal squeeze becomes more acute; greater subsidies by the central government to urban social security schemes, possibly involving the transfer of state assets to the system; less generous benefits (for example, greater reliance on price indexation, more realistic assumptions about life expectancy, more limited returns on available annuities for savings accumulations); an increased eligibility age for pensions, thus effectively delaying the retirement age; introducing a phased retirement; and strengthening the financial sector to enhance the productivity and return of savings, particularly if individual defined contributions are used to accumulate financial assets.[14] Of course even more ambitious would be a move to a social security system embodying national pooling.

In the area of medical care, China's government recognizes that an aged population will inevitably involve a greater demand. But the demand will be compounded by the heavier burden of chronic diseases that are associated with a rapidly urbanizing population. As already noted, while China is not short either of medical practitioners and professionals or of modern medical facilities in the urban areas, the present system of health financing substantially prices out many households in the rural sector and those outside the urban formal sector. The cost of most services and drugs must be paid out of pocket, and limited budget support forces rural medical units and urban public hospitals to derive much of their income from such sources. Private care is available but largely on an out-of-pocket basis to those who can afford it. Only those working in viable state enterprises, the government and some elements of the formal private sector can count on affordable access to medical care.

Formally the government does not face a challenge of fiscal sustainability arising from the higher costs of medical care associated with an aged population. That is only because its present explicit social health-insurance commitments are so limited. The challenge that will arise will be one of political economy – dealing with discontent from an aging, urbanized population whose increased demand for medical care is unaffordable to many. Potential problems in the future will be exacerbated by the current evolution of the Chinese medical-care system, in which all the income incentives of those in the medical sector are linked to the prescription of drugs and high-cost modern technologies. Without a mechanism for dealing with the excess supply of beds and health professionals in the urban areas, or for using a global budget constraint to set limits on pricing in the sector (as is done in Japan or Korea), inflationary pressures on medical costs will add to the already large burden of medical care associated with an aging population.

The current state of China's system for financing medical care also has important implications for the third strand of microeconomic policies, that related to enhancing the incentives for and capacity of individuals to participate longer in the work force as their life span increases. Much of China's population still resides and works in the rural sector and is engaged in blue-collar or agricultural work. In urban areas too many workers have blue-collar jobs, work long hours under difficult conditions and have only a limited capacity to pay for medical care in the event of illness or injury. Rising incomes (which lead to diets high in fat and increased obesity), the rapid pace of urbanization (associated with higher rates of hypertension) and the persistence of unhealthy cultural habits (particularly tobacco consumption) are also increasing the prospective burden and costliness of future illness, although ironically they may lessen the future pension burden by limiting improvements in life expectancy.

A further aggravating factor is widespread environmental pollution, affecting air and water quality. The State Environmental Protection Administration (SEPA) estimates that two-thirds of China's urban population live in cities with bad or very bad air quality, which is compounded by the frequency of acid rain. SEPA also estimates that '75% of the water in the country's seven most important river systems is of a quality unfit for human consumption' (Heymann, 2006, 8). The combination of the strains on health arising from the character of much of the work of the labor force, the effects of poor environmental conditions, and the present limited access to medical care by rural and informal urban-sector households may make it very difficult for such workers to participate actively in the labor force in their elderly years.[15]

The contrast with Western industrial countries is stark in this regard. In those countries, early retirement in the face of dramatic improvements in longevity largely reflects social norms and the prevailing generosity of social insurance systems, rather than a physical incapacity to work longer. As a solution to financially unsustainable social insurance systems, policies that create incentives for longer labor force participation (that is, delayed or phased-in retirement) and low unemployment rates would appear to be not only appropriate but also feasible. For China, with its rapid catching-up in income and urbanization, strengthened preventive health policies and improved access to medical care in the present may be a critical prerequisite for the country's future elderly to be able to function effectively in the labor force and to postpone the age of retirement. In effect, current weaknesses in health policies may narrow China's future policy options for financing its aging population.

FINAL OBSERVATIONS

The report card on Asia's preparedness for an aging population is decidedly mixed. Most Asian countries are pursuing policies supportive of rapid income growth that will enlarge the size of the income pie available for financing higher living standards at the time their populations become aged. Most have also pursued a policy of fiscal consolidation, reducing public debt and providing flexibility to absorb greater burdens of public spending in connection with their aging populations in the future and also providing fiscal space to deal with inevitable uncertainties in the pace of aging and its fiscal consequences. With the exception of China and perhaps Korea, most of the countries face only a limited level of implicit debt associated with existing social insurance obligations.

It is in the sphere of social insurance for pensions and health and of labor market policies where much effort is still needed to create a policy framework that can accommodate the challenges of an aging population. With the exception of Singapore, there is little evidence of policies to create incentives for a longer participation in the labor force.[16] Indeed, in China, the overwhelming priority to address widespread unemployment has led to pressures for early retirement, at age 55 for women and age 60 for men. Asian countries cannot be faulted too seriously for this neglect, since Western industrial countries themselves have moved only slowly to remove disincentives for a longer working life. Moreover, for the current elderly of Asia, postponing the retirement age may prove difficult because their health status may suffer from more arduous earlier working lives.

The policy imperative, however, should be to ensure that, as more comprehensive social insurance systems are in put into place, existing systems are reformed in some key policy provisions. These include a gradual deferral in the age of eligibility for retirement benefits; actuarial neutrality in linking benefit levels to the length of the prospective retirement period; adequate incorporation, in benefit calculations, of the prospective longevity of cohorts at the time of retirement; a move to payout methods that provide for income payouts rather than lump-sum payments; and restrictions on the use of funds before retirement. As noted for the case of China, addressing the current health-care challenges of increasing access to medical care and changing unhealthy behavior related to diet, tobacco consumption and exercise may be critical; and successful interventions could have a high payoff in future years by improving the quality and capacity of an aging labor force.

Most of the social insurance systems that have emerged in Asia have not been designed with the anticipation of an aged population, suggesting that these countries will face difficult issues of intergenerational burden sharing and complex ethical issues associated with medical care options for the elderly. The contrast between India and China is particularly striking. India's social insurance system is still minimal, both in its limited coverage of the population in any type of pension system and in the dominance of its private medical care system. Because its population is still in the early stages of aging, it has a much wider window of opportunity for policy decisions than does China. It can design a new system for social health and retirement insurance that takes account of the prospects of an aging population. China, in contrast, has far less time available to develop such a solution. Perhaps because of the collapse of its previous social insurance system and the government's acute awareness of the rapidity of the aging process, one can observe most clearly there the effort to grapple with the challenge of a rapidly aging population.

And yet China also illustrates how difficult this can be and the looming deficiencies that still need to be addressed. There and elsewhere in Asia social insurance systems will have to grapple with the design of a zero-pillar safety-net scheme to address the needs of the large number of the elderly who have resided in the urban informal sector or the rural sector, outside the coverage of formal social insurance schemes. Long-term care will also be a serious burden that is not on the radar screens of any Asian countries other than Singapore and Korea. With increasing longevity an important segment of the population may be subject to long periods of disability; and with shrinking family size and a large share of 'single' elderly households, the burden of these groups will need to be addressed.[17]

Finally, it is worth noting that other approaches may need to be part of the arsenal of policy choices to which Asian governments turn as they consider the combination of policies to address an aging population.[18] For example, China, faced with an inadequate pension system for rural households, may wish to consider allowing the transfer of ownership rights to rural land, endowing those households with additional assets to finance their retirement. In some rural areas the value of the land may be significant. Even for the many parts of China where rural land is of limited value, better ownership rights may facilitate consolidation of rural land plots, thereby raising returns to the labor remaining in the rural areas and fostering further rural-to-urban migration. Strengthening financial institutions and markets would allow greater productivity to be achieved on the savings accumulated by households for retirement. Encouragement of some emigration may allow a segment of the elderly population to be supported by remittances from family members. In the sphere of health care, coordinated policy actions across sectors, including education, urban planning and the environment, may be needed to promote healthful lifestyles and reduce the burden of chronic diseases.

NOTES

1. This chapter has benefited from the thoughtful comments of Hana Brixi, William Hsiao, Thomas Lindh, Andrew Mason, Anna Rappaport and the participants in the Conference on Population Aging, Intergenerational Transfers, and the Macroeconomy. The views expressed here are my own and do not necessarily represent those of the International Monetary Fund or IMF policy.
2. Private defined-benefit systems in the United States and the United Kingdom have been subject to a different type of 'perfect storm', namely, the combination of poor investment returns, low interest rates for valuing liabilities, and the demographic trends noted above.
3. The role of urban migrants will be particularly important, whether they are urban taxpayers (effectively facilitating some intergenerational transfers to urban elderly) or a source at least of remittances (if not of direct caregiving) to elderly relations still living in the rural areas.
4. The EU-6 countries comprise France, Germany, Italy, Poland, Spain and the United Kingdom.
5. The associated asset buildup in capital goods has been largely domestic but with some international diversification of asset holdings as well.
6. A mandatory provident fund exists for central-government employees, teachers and some state-enterprise employees. Although this adds some assets at retirement, the provisions force the withdrawal of a lump sum at retirement and do not encourage annuitization (Chaiyasoot, 2005).
7. Coverage of these transfers is very low. Since poor townships do not have the resources to finance them, the transfers are nearly nonexistent in those localities.
8. For a general discussion of health-sector issues in China, see Yip and Hsiao (2001); Tang (2003); Blumenthal and Hsiao (2005); UN Health Partners Group in China (2005); WHO (2005).

9. Mason and Lee, in their chapter in this volume, discuss the importance that family transfers have played in Taiwan in supporting elderly populations.
10. Thailand's system also does not appear well designed for long-term fiscal sustainability, despite the fact that it provides for a low replacement rate.
11. Already there is concern in Singapore about this challenge. News reports note that many elderly are participating in low-wage service-industry jobs to supplement their incomes, and that accumulations derived from the low salaries paid in the 1960s and 1970s are not sufficient to keep up with the cost of living. They also emphasize that housing prices have fallen by 30 percent since the mid-1990s, so that the value of retirees' accumulated assets has shrunk significantly (Burton, 2006).
12. Thailand's provident fund also at present encourages lump-sum payments at retirement, thereby placing all of the longevity and market risk on the backs of the retirees. One aspect of the market risk relates to the potential for housing prices to fall or soften in real terms. This has already proved to be a problem in Singapore. Some have speculated about the potential for an oversupply of housing if many people try to sell all at the same time.
13. It is possible that a zero pillar scheme may contribute to weakening the current gender preference for sons. If parents can expect income support from daughters, they may feel less need to depend on the traditional support of sons.
14. The Chinese financial sector needs much strengthening to facilitate the productive use of savings accumulated in defined-contribution accounts. At present it appears that defined contributions in municipalities piloting this type of approach are being used largely to finance current benefit payments to existing retirees, implying effectively a PAYGO system with implicit liabilities for the relevant government unit.
15. These issues are also relevant to India. The Community Environmental Monitors, an independent environmental and health agency in India, estimates the enormously high levels of toxic gases and chemicals in the atmosphere affecting Indians in both cities and villages (*New York Times*, 4 June 2006).
16. Singapore is seeking to provide incentives to employers to hire the elderly, including policies to reduce wages for workers above age 60.
17. Singapore has probably given the most thought to these issues (see Singapore, Committee on Ageing Issues, 2006).
18. Such issues are explored with considerable insight by Mohan (2004).

REFERENCES

Asher, M., N. Barr, P. Diamond, E. Lim and J. Mirrlees (2005), 'Social security reform in China: issues and options', unpublished study available at http://econ-www.mit.edu/faculty/download_pdf.php?id=1176.

Asher, Mukul G. and A. Nandy (2006a), 'Health financing in Singapore: a case for systemic reforms,' *International Social Security Review*, **59**(1), 75–92.

Asher, Mukul G. and A. Nandy (2006b), 'Social security policy in an era of globalization and competition: challenges for Southeast Asia', unpublished study available at http://econ-www.mit.edu/faculty/download_pdf.php?id=1176.

Bloom, D., and D. Canning (2005), 'Global demographic change: dimensions and economic significance', *Global Demographic Change: Economic Impacts and Policy Challenges*, Kansas City, Missouri: Federal Reserve Bank of Kansas City, pp. 10–56.

Blumenthal, D. and W. Hsiao (2005), 'Privatization and its discontents: the evolving Chinese health care system', *New England Journal of Medicine*, **353** (15 September), 1165–70.

Burton, John (2006), 'Straits under strain: why inequality is centre stage in Singapore's election', *Financial Times* 4 May, p. 11.

Chaiyasoot, N. (2005), 'Key policy issues in establishing national pension fund', Power Point presentation, July, available at http://www.oecd.org/dataoecd/57/7/34745398.pdf.

Heymann, Eric (2006), 'Environmental sector [of] China: from major building site to growth market', Deutsche Bank Research, 28 February, available at www.dbresearch.com/PROD/DBR_INTERNET_EN-ROD/PROD0000000000196788.pdf.

Jackson, R. and N. Howe (2004), *The Graying of the Middle Kingdom*, Washington, DC: Center for Strategic and International Studies.

Jowett, M. (2005), 'Implementing universal national health insurance: the case of the Philippines' (prepared for the World Bank Flagship Course, June 2005).

Kim, M.K. (2005), 'The Korean Health Insurance System: opportunities and challenges', paper presented at the annual conference of the International Social Security Association, http://www.issa.int/pdf/seoul05/kang.ppt

Koh, M.J. (2005), 'Overview of Korean Retirement Pension Plan', unpublished Power Point presentation, www.oecd.org/dataoecd/56/38/34723005.PDF.

Mohan, R. (2004), 'Fiscal challenges of population aging: the Asian experience', *Global Demographic Change: Economic Impacts and Policy Challenges, Symposium Proceedings*, Kansas City, Missouri: Federal Reserve Bank of Kansas City, pp. 299–368.

New York Times (2006), 'Indian air is highly polluted, study finds', 4 June, p. 14.

Pi, D. (2005), 'Developments in public old-age benefit schemes: China's Old-Age Social Insurance Scheme' (unpublished), http://www.issa.int/pdf/seoul05/2dehai.pdf.

Pillay, S. (2005), 'Can we afford to fall sick?', *Aliran Monthly*, **25**(4): http://www.aliran.com/oldsite/monthly/2005a/4e.html.

Singapore, Committee on Ageing Issues (2006), *Report on the Ageing Population*, available at www.mcys.gov.sg/successful_ageing/report/CAI_report.pdf.

Tang, Shenglan (2003), *Developing Urban Social Health Insurance in a Rapidly Changing Economy of China: Problems and Challenges*, available at http://www.shi-conference.de/downl/Session%202%20Abstract%20Dr%20Shenlan%20Tang.pdf.

Tangcharoensathien, Viroj, P. Prakongsai, W. Patcharanarumol and P. Jongudomsuk (2005), 'Universal coverage in Thailand: the respective roles of social health insurance and tax-based financing', PowerPoint presentation, December, available at http://www.shi-conference.de/downl/Session%204%20Abstract%20Dr%20Tangsaroensathien.pdf.

Thillainathan, R. (2004), 'Pension and financial market reforms and key issues on governance', unpublished paper, available at www.ier.hit-u.ac.jp/pie/Japanese/discussionpaper/dp 2003/dp197/text.pdf.

Trinh, T. (2006), *China's Pension System*, Frankfurt: Deutsch Bank Research, http://www.dbresearch.de/PROD/DBR_INTERNET_DE-PROD/PROD000000 00001960V25.pdf.

UN (United Nations) Health Partners Group in China (2005), *A Health Situation Assessment of the People's Republic of China*, http://www.wpro.who.int/NR/rdonlyres/0267DCE8-07AB-437A-8B01-03D474D922CD/0/hsa_en.pdf.

UN (United Nations) Population Division (2005), *World Population Prospects: The 2004 Revision Population Database*, New York: Department of Economic and Social Affairs of the United Nations Secretariat, available at http://esa.un.org/unpp/.

UN (2006), *World Urbanization Prospects: The 2005 Revision*, New York: Department of Economic and Social Affairs of the United Nations Secretariat.
Wagstaff, A. (2005), 'Health systems in East Asia: what can developing countries learn from Japan and the Asian Tigers?', World Bank Policy Research Working Paper No. 3790 (December), Washington, DC.
WHO (World Health Organization) (2004), *Regional Overview of Social Health Insurance in South-East Asia*, New Delhi: WHO, Regional Office for South-East Asia.
WHO (2005), 'Macroeconomics and health: China report', unpublished manuscript, Geneva.
Yang, B. (2005), 'National health insurance in South Korea: opportunities and challenges', paper presented at the International Symposium on Achievements and Challenges of National Health Systems, Taipei, Taiwan (March).
Yi, Z., Z. Wang, J. Leiwen and D. Gu (2006), 'Projection of family households and elderly living arrangement in the context of rapid population aging in China – a demographic window of opportunity until 2030 and serious challenge thereafter', unpublished manuscript, Center for Study of Aging and Human Development and Geriatric Division, Durham, NC.
Yip, W. and W. Hsiao (2001), 'Economic transition and urban health care in China: impacts and prospects', annex, unpublished manuscript, Harvard University, Cambridge, Massachusetts, available at http://www.eldis.ids.ac.uk/static/DOC18920.htm.

Index